FILM VOICES

THE **SUNY** SERIES
CULTURAL STUDIES IN CINEMA/VIDEO
WHEELER WINSTON DIXON | EDITOR

FILM VOICES

Interviews from *Post Script*

edited by

GERALD DUCHOVNAY

STATE UNIVERSITY OF NEW YORK PRESS

Published by
State University of New York Press, Albany

© 2004 State University of New York and *Post Script, Inc.*

All rights reserved

Printed in the United States of America

No part of this book may be used or reproduced in any manner whatsoever without written permission. No part of this book may be stored in a retrieval system or transmitted in any form or by any means including electronic, electrostatic, magnetic tape, mechanical, photocopying, recording, or otherwise without the prior permission in writing of the publisher.

For information, address State University of New York Press,
90 State Street, Suite 700, Albany, NY 12207

Production by Marilyn P. Semerad
Marketing by Anne M. Valentine

Library of Congress Cataloging-in-Publication Data

Duchovnay, Gerald, 1944–
  Film voices : interviews from Post Script / by Gerald Duchovnay.
    p. cm. — (SUNY series, cultural studies in cinema/video)
  Includes bibliographical references and index.
  ISBN 0-7914-6155-6 — ISBN 0-7914-6156-4 (pbk.)
    1. Motion pictures—Production and direction. 2. Motion picture producers and directors—United States—Interviews. 3. Motion picture producers and directors—Interviews. I. Title. II. Series.

PN1995.9.P7D76 2004
791.4302'3—dc22

2003066185

10 9 8 7 6 5 4 3 2 1

Dedicated to the Memory of

Arthur Stander
Charles Mazer
Robert E. Waxman

CONTENTS

List of Illustrations xi

Preface xiii

Acknowledgments xv

Introduction 1
GERALD DUCHOVNAY

PART I. HOLLYWOOD VOICES

CHAPTER ONE 17
Robert Altman
LEO BRAUDY AND ROBERT P. KOLKER

CHAPTER TWO 33
Francis Ford Coppola
RIC GENTRY

CHAPTER THREE 51
Sydney Pollack
LEO BRAUDY AND MARK CRISPIN MILLER

CHAPTER FOUR 63
Clint Eastwood
RIC GENTRY

CHAPTER FIVE 91
Oliver Stone
RIC GENTRY

PART II. INDEPENDENT VOICES

CHAPTER SIX 109
Barbara Hammer
GWENDOLYN AUDREY FOSTER

CHAPTER SEVEN 129
Robert Downey Sr.
WHEELER WINSTON DIXON

CHAPTER EIGHT 143
Don Bluth
GERALD DUCHOVNAY

CHAPTER NINE 153
Jamie Babbit
WHEELER WINSTON DIXON

PART III. INTERNATIONAL VOICES

CHAPTER TEN 169
Paul Verhoeven
CHRIS SHEA AND WADE JENNINGS

CHAPTER ELEVEN 195
Stephen Frears
LESTER D. FRIEDMAN AND SCOTT STEWART

CHAPTER TWELVE 215
Atom Egoyan
PETER HARCOURT

CHAPTER THIRTEEN 225
Louis Malle
RICHARD A. MACKSEY

PART IV. BEHIND—AND IN—THE SCENES

CHAPTER FOURTEEN 241
James Woods
RIC GENTRY

CHAPTER FIFTEEN 265
Dede Allen
RIC GENTRY

CHAPTER SIXTEEN 297
Vittorio Storaro
RIC GENTRY

CHAPTER SEVENTEEN 317
Horton Foote
GERALD C. WOOD

List of Contributors 329

Index 333

ILLUSTRATIONS

FIGURE 1.	Robert Altman on location.	18
FIGURE 2.	Francis Ford Coppola shooting *The Cotton Club*.	34
FIGURE 3.	Sydney Pollack working on *Havana*.	52
FIGURE 4.	Clint Eastwood directing *Midnight in the Garden of Good and Evil*.	64
FIGURE 5.	Oliver Stone during the shooting of *JFK*.	92
FIGURE 6.	Experimental filmmaker Barbara Hammer.	110
FIGURE 7.	Robert Downey Sr. on the set of *Putney Swope*.	130
FIGURE 8.	Don Bluth and staff working on *The Secret of NIMH*.	144
FIGURE 9.	Jame Babbit directing *But I'm A Cheerleader*.	154
FIGURE 10.	Paul Verhoeven on the set of *RoboCop*.	170
FIGURE 11.	Stephen Frears on the set of *Hero*.	196
FIGURE 12.	Atom Egoyan on the set of *Exotica*.	216
FIGURE 13.	Louis Malle working on *Pretty Baby*.	226

FIGURE 14. Actor James Woods.   242

FIGURE 15. Film editor Dede Allen.   266

FIGURE 16. Cinematographer Vittorio Storaro.   298

FIGURE 17. Horton Foote on location.   318

PREFACE

In 1978, about a dozen colleges and university instructors interested in film and fiction participated in a National Endowment for the Humanities Summer Seminar at The Johns Hopkins University. The seminar was directed by Leo Braudy (now of the University of Southern California) and focused on how character is presented in fiction and film.

As is the case with many of these NEH seminars, participants often bond because of similar interests and general compatibility. Near the end of the seminar, six or seven of the participants wanted to continue the dialogue established during our six weeks together. We agreed to start a newsletter to discuss ideas begun in the seminar and to open the newsletter to others who might be interested in participating in our discussions. (This, of course, was prior to e-mail and chat rooms.) We agreed that if we could sustain the newsletter for a year or two, we would then try to change the format from newsletter to journal. After about eighteen months and several issues of the newsletter, some of us decided to begin a journal. Those collaborating on this project consisted of Robert Ginsberg (Penn State, Delaware County), Wade Jennings (Ball State University), Judy Riggin (Northern Virginia Community College), the late T. J. (Ted) Ross (Fairleigh Dickinson University), Gerald Duchovnay (Jacksonville University, Florida), and Leo Braudy, who offered his good offices to assist us with establishing an editorial board. After several meetings, the group asked me if I would serve as the general editor. Without knowing what was involved, I agreed. The others said they would do what they could to raise funds and solicit editorial staff and submissions.

Since there were several other film journals at the time (and many more since), we thought an interdisciplinary journal, with articles that were accessible to scholars and the general reader, would be the approach we should take. The journal's name, *Post Script: Essays in Film and the Humanities*, hammered out in a hotel suite at a film conference in Tallahassee, Florida, in 1980, sought to capture our intent. With nominal support from Jacksonville University and some contributions by most of the members of the original editorial board, we secured enough funds and submissions to publish our first issue in November 1981.

Uncertain of the journal's reception and future funding, the editorial staff recommended that in addition to the articles, we should try to include substantive interviews and some book reviews. We knew that *Film Quarterly* had an issue devoted to book reviews, so we did not want to duplicate what they were doing. *Literature/Film Quarterly* focused on filmed adaptations, and numerous journals had interviews, but for the most part they were brief remarks connected to the director, actor, or cinematographer's latest film. Our goal was to try to go beyond the moment. By 1983 J. P. Telotte, one of the contributors to several of our early issues, joined the editorial board and suggested we consider adding an annual bibliography of film studies. This bibliography would list and annotate articles on film that appeared in English language publications that would be relatively accessible to most of our readers. The editorial staff agreed that this would be a useful resource for those who wanted a ready reference and who did not have access to the more substantive (and expensive) *Film/Literature Index* (State University of New York Press, Albany) or the *International Index to Film Periodicals* (Fédération Internationale des Archives du Film, Belgium).

After the first few years of testing the waters, *Post Script* established its format, which, except for a major design change when it moved from Jacksonville University to Texas A&M University-Commerce in 1990, has remained fairly consistent. Since 1981 we have published three issues a year. Those issues have included an annual bibliography, an occasional brief note on articles previously published, substantive essays on film acting, film as visual art and cinematic style, film history, aesthetics, film and technology, genre studies, and interdisciplinary studies, as well as book reviews and interviews. We have also devoted full issues to special topics—French cinema, Spanish cinema, film and philosophy, Shakespeare and film, Chinese cinema, Japanese cinema, Hong Kong cinema, autobiography and film, Gen-X film, Canadian cinema, Paul Verhoeven, the films of Kurosawa Akira, and literacy and film.

While we have not received (or published) as many interdisciplinary essays as we initially hoped for, our readers have frequently commented on the usefulness of the bibliography and especially the interviews. We have been asked on numerous occasions to collect and publish our interviews since they offer a window into the film-making process during the last twenty years. Those that are reprinted in this volume are representative of the diverse voices that have appeared since 1981 in *Post Script: Essays in Film and the Humanities*.

ACKNOWLEDGMENTS

This collection would not be possible without the assistance of those who agreed to be interviewed and the individuals who did the interviewing and submitted the material to us for our consideration. The name that appears most frequently in this anthology is Ric Gentry, a member of the *Post Script* staff and a filmmaker and freelance writer. To Ric and to the others whose contributions have graced our pages—Leo Braudy, Robert Kolker, Mark Crispin Miller, Gwendolyn Audrey Foster, Wheeler Winston Dixon, Chris Shea, Wade Jennings, Peter Harcourt, Richard A. Macksey, and Gerald Wood—I, as general editor of *Post Script*, extend a sincere thank-you. Without them, our subscribers in this country and abroad, and our institutional cosponsors (Texas A&M University-Commerce and Georgia Institute of Technology), this collection of interviews would not be possible. Jay Telotte, my coeditor of *Post Script* since 1985, has been supportive of this project from its inception and assisted in the selection of the interviews. I would also like to thank Vivian Freeman, Stacie Bockemehl, and especially Marscha Brown, who have assisted in preparing transcripts of these interviews.

Crystal Hurley, Dick Fulkerson, and Donna Dunbar-Odom have been most gracious in tending to some administrative details so that I could find time to complete this collection. For their assistance I am most thankful. A manuscript owes much to those who shepherd it through the press. Wheeler Winston Dixon, the series editor, and James Peltz, the acquisitions editor, offered enthusiasm and encouragement; special kudos to Marilyn P. Semerad (production manager) and Margaret Copeley (copyeditor) for their editorial assistance.

Most of all I must thank my family for their continued support, and especially to Brian, Bram, and Aviva for their encouragement and love.

All the interviews in this book first appeared in *Post Script: Essays in Film and the Humanities (PS)*. The editor of this volume gratefully acknowledges permission by Post Script, Inc. to reprint them here. He also wishes to thank Joseph Baum, former program director for the Maryland Film Guild and the Baltimore

Film Forum for permission to originally publish the dialogues with Louis Malle, Sydney Pollack, and Robert Altman.

Every reasonable effort has been made to contact the owners of copyright materials in this book, but in some instances this has proven impossible. The author and publisher will be glad to receive information leading to more complete acknowledgements in subsequent printings of the book and in the meantime extend their apologies for any omissions.

Braudy, Leo, and Robert P. Kolker. "Robert Altman: An Interview, Part I." *PS* 1.1 (Fall 1981): 2–7.

———. "Robert Altman: An Interview, Part II." *PS* 1.2 (Winter 1982): 2–14.

Braudy, Leo, and Mark Crispin Miller. "Sydney Pollack: An Interview." *PS* 3.1 (Fall 1983): 2–18.

Dixon, Wheeler Winston. "No More Excuses: An Interview with Robert Downey, Sr." *PS* 21.1 (Fall 2001): 3–13.

———. "Jamie Babbit: An Interview." *PS* 21.1 (Fall 2001): 14–23.

Duchovnay, Gerald. "Don Bluth: An Interview." *PS* 1.3 (Spring/Summer 1982): 2–17.

Foster, Gwendolyn Audrey. "Barbara Hammer, an Interview: Re/Constructing Lesbian Auto/Biographies in *Tender Fictions* and *Nitratre Kisses*." *PS* 16.3 (Summer 1997): 3–16.

Friedman, Lester, and Scott Stewart. "Keeping His Own Voice: An Interview with Stephen Frears." *PS* 11.3 (Summer 1992): 3–18.

Gentry, Ric. "Vittorio Storaro: An Interview, Part I." *PS* 4.1 (Fall 1984): 2–17.

———. "Vittorio Storaro: An Interview, Part II." *PS* 4.2 (Winter 1985): 2–18.

———. "Francis Coppola: An Interview." *PS* 6.3 (Spring/Summer 1987): 2–12.

———. "Francis Coppola: An Interview, Part II." *PS* 8.1 (Fall 1988): 52–63.

———. "Oliver Stone: An Interview." *PS* 15.3 (Summer 1996): 3–15.

———. "Clint Eastwood: An Interview." *PS* 17.3 (Summer 1998): 3–24.

———. "James Woods: An Interview." *PS* 18.3 (Summer 1999): 3–23.

Harcourt, Peter. "A Conversation with Atom Egoyam." *PS* 15.1 (Fall 1995): 68–74.

Macksey, Richard A. "Malle on Malle, Part I." *PS* 2.1 (Fall 1982): 2–12.

———. "Malle on Malle, Part II." *PS* 2.2 (Winter 1983): 2–13.

Shea, Chris, and Wade Jennings. "Paul Verhoeven: An Interview." *PS* 12.3 (Summer 1993): 3–24.

Wood, Gerald C. "Horton Foote: An Interview." *PS* 10.3 (Summer 1991): 3–12.

INTRODUCTION

GERALD DUCHOVNAY

The interviews in this collection bring together major Hollywood directors and actors, independent filmmakers, screenwriters, an animator, a film editor, and several international voices. Even with this diversity and interviews that cover filmmaking in the last two decades, several motifs repeat themselves: the concern for quality films, the influence of business ("the suits") and money on filmmaking, the importance of the script, casting, and audience, and technology's impact on the filmmaking process.

When Robert Altman was interviewed in Baltimore, Maryland, on March 28, 1981, after a screening of *Health* and *McCabe and Mrs. Miller*, he spoke candidly about those films and ten others (*The Long Goodbye, Three Women, Nashville, Brewster McCloud, Images, A Wedding, A Perfect Couple, Quintet, Popeye,* and *That Cold Day in the Park*). Considered more of an independent than a mainstream commercial director, Altman would prefer to sneak in a good film, made by artists, rather than satisfy audience appeal for action and horror films. Speaking more than two decades ago, but echoing today's industry penchant for dollars over art, he observes that "there is so much money involved, and they [studio hierarchy] are so concerned about the money that they don't want to take a chance of just making a film that will maybe break even or maybe take twenty percent. In most businesses, if you turn out a product and you can make fifty percent profit, it's pretty good."

Cognizant of the profit motive, Altman takes great joy in crafting "small" films. While highly regarded among industry professionals, many of whom are willing to work for scale for him, Altman has had few of the commercial successes craved by studio executives. *M*A*S*H* did well at the box office, but films like *The Player, Gosford Park,* and even *McCabe and Mrs. Miller* (now considered a classic, but panned by most reviewers when it first opened), have done little to assuage studio executives whose offices, like the home in D. H. Lawrence's "The Rocking Horse Winner," shout out for "more money."

For all his maverick status in Hollywood, Altman bridges independent and commercial films. He created his own production company, Lion's Gate Films, in order to maintain artistic control over his films, but he turns to studios or distributors to market them. Sometimes, as in the case of *The Long Goodbye*, the marketing campaign does not capture the tenor of the film; in other cases *(Health)* studio management changes and the film is buried or given to a distribution house that will market it in limited release on university campuses and to revival houses.

Often described as an "actor's director," Robert Altman tries to eschew politics. Although he wanted *Health*, a film he describes as an "essay," to open during the Carter presidency, he most often delights in the accidents of production (eight days of snow during the shooting of *McCabe and Mrs. Miller* allowed a look and feel that would not have otherwise been possible), or actors who collaborate on "interior" films or films of observation. His goal is "to show you something or let you see something that I see. Obviously, I'm manipulating the audience every time I make a cut or by what I show, but I'm trying to leave enough openness there so that you can bring your own interpretation to it, because I don't think a film has any value, or that any work of art is a work of art, unless it's something that the beholder meets half way and brings his own experience to." He is conscious of those who have come before (Federico Fellini, Max Ophuls) and he is not adverse to borrowing from his own films (*Images* and *The Long Goodbye; McCabe and Mrs. Miller* and *Popeye*), but his fondest wish is that "all of the people who are in it for the money, would go into shopping centers and leave the making of the films to the artists."

Francis Ford Coppola's distinguished career has included *Apocalypse Now*, *Godfather, Parts I, II*, and *III*, and *The Conversation*, but when he spoke to Ric Gentry in 1987, he had just completed "Rip Van Winkle," an episode of *Fairie Tale Theatre* for Shelley Duvall and was anxious to talk about that experience and his desire to use new technology for an "electronic cinema" in an "electronic studio." Working in television, and specifically on this production, gave Coppola the opportunity to explore differences in acting and editing not normally open to him in film and recalled high school and college experiences in the theater, and especially his dream of becoming a playwright. In 1987 his goal was to become "a writer of original full-length dramatic material for an audio-visual medium" that would involve live performances. In "Rip Van Winkle" Coppla uses stylized aspects of Japanese Kabuki theater, especially the linking of scenery and settings to the story's ideas, to help convey the fairy tale.

Oliver Stone revels in how imagery, aided by technology, helps him to get at "fractured" biographies. In his discussion with Ric Gentry about *Born on the Fourth of July, Heaven and Earth, Salvador, Nixon, JFK,* and especially *Natural Born Killers,* Stone emphasizes how important the cinematographer is and how the camera "has been reflective of [his] subjective point of view." To Stone it is the tension between the close-up and the long lens that creates the dynamics of cinematography.

Robert Altman and Clint Eastwood are also interested in technology, but in more traditional ways. Altman often chooses his cinematographer and soundman early on in the process, gives them a sense of where he wants to go with the picture, and collaborates with them throughout. Eastwood knows what he is about, doesn't storyboard his films, and has confidence in his cast and crew to accomplish his goals. Altman, Eastwood, and Stone use some degree of improvisation, but that works for them because they place a premium on casting. Pollack is a director who acts, while Eastwood is an actor who directs. Altman is a director who more than Eastwood, Pollack, or Coppola, gives greater freedom to his actors, sometimes (*Three Women*, for example) working only with an outline and no formal script. Casting, then, becomes essential, with Altman claiming that it is 90 percent of his process. Eastwood sees the cast as a jazz ensemble: "They're very much like jazz musicians in that within the scene they're doing a lot of things that aren't scripted—where they go, how they give the line, sometimes changing the line to have it make more sense or become more natural to them though not necessarily changing the meaning."

In *Midnight in the Garden of Good and Evil* Eastwood encouraged the actors to "find the soul" of their characters by allowing them to improvise, to "reveal in a given moment or situation, something ideally only that character or personality would do or express." To get immediacy, spontaneity, and energy from his actors, Eastwood rarely does extended takes: "The best takes are usually the first ones, before the actors fall into a pattern." He likes to work instinctively, but even with allowances for improvisation, there is only one person in charge. Not unlike his Man-with-No Name character, to Eastwood the director's view of the film is *the* view: "There only needs to be one perspective and that's the director's, not that I'm unresponsive to someone saying they think they could've done something better." There is collaboration and trust, but his role of director embodies the traits of many of his characters in his films—"independence and isolation and, by necessity, . . . moral autonomy."

Oliver Stone tries to build in time to rehearse before going in front of the camera. Because actors "bring enormous contributions," there is room for improvisation. Nevertheless, because he frequently has been involved in writing the script, because he thinks visually, and because he plans what his shots will be, "improvisation comes out of preparation." Like Sydney Pollack, Stone is trying to work out new combinations in order to make room for new perceptions, for enlightenment during the process. Each film is a test in which the director is a warrior-athlete, competing with himself, but also with actors and studio executives.

The importance of money, the influence of the studio and the ratings system, and the power of actors and producers make filmmaking a dangerous sport for directors. Stone considers the director vulnerable to not only the whims of the supporting cast, but also to critics who want him to "hit a home run" each time at bat. *Heaven and Earth* was a home run to its director, but not to the critics. To Stone it is "OK to hit a single or a double. Or a triple. You don't have to hit a home run every time." Other directors in this collection attest to Stone's belief that filmmaking is not a "certainty business. . . . It's not like a science. It's an art."

During the making of and shortly after the release of *Tootsie*, there were tabloid-type television and print stories about difficulties on the set between Sydney Pollack and Dustin Hoffman. Pollack claims that while Hoffman can be "very trying and very difficult," the differences of opinion were professional and based on their perceptions of Hoffman's character. While Altman, Pollack, and Eastwood are known as being "actors' directors," Pollack, more than the other two, places greater emphasis on the script and sees himself engaged in a "benevolent dictatorship." The movie is the director's. While there is some collaboration, he takes on projects because he wants to work out some idea, some armature, a subjective point of view that is clarified for him in the filmmaking process.

In its original form, *Tootsie* was a drag comedy. After turning down the studio's offer to direct four times, Pollack was allowed to restructure the script to his liking. Using one intriguing line from an early version of the script, "Being a woman has made you weird, Michael," Pollack worked with six screenwriters (primarily, though, Elaine May and Larry Gelbart) to reshape the text to where it had a spine, the organic idea that made the script work for him.

Not unlike *Mystic River* (2003), the script was the hook that got Clint Eastwood involved with *Midnight in the Garden of Good and Evil*. After screenwriter John Hancock, with whom Eastwood had worked before *(A Perfect World)*, gave him the screenplay, Eastwood told the studio he would be interested in directing the film. The studio greenlighted the project. The diversity of Savannah's population, its idiosyncratic characters, history, and relative harmony also attracted Eastwood to the project. After reading the novel and visiting Savannah, Eastwood found some of the characters and scenes to be "memorable and unusual" and reshaped aspects of the screenplay to accommodate them.

After having established his acting career in action-adventure films, Eastwood now finds it "rewarding to do a story about people—people who are unique, who aren't like you and me." Eastwood, Pollack, Altman, and several others interviewed in this volume give high priority to interpersonal relationships. In the *Bridges of Madison County*, for example, while the Streep/Eastwood relationship is central, how Streep's children respond to their own family situations after they find out about their mother's secret is also important to the resolution of the film. In *Absolute Power*, Eastwood had the script reworked to eliminate the emphasis given to the daughter's career and love relationship in the original literary text in order to emphasize the father-daughter conflict and his attempts at reconciliation.

The concerns and stresses of independent filmmakers are very different in degree from those who work for the studios and have big budgets. As Jamie Babbit explains, the first hurdle for the independent is to get the equipment, money, and crew to make a film. Once completed, the filmmaker has to find someone willing to distribute or even show the film. Jamie Babbit, Robert Downey, and Barbara Hammer discuss the difficulties of working on small-budget films that will have limited screenings. Don Bluth and Downey started with small films, but they eventually found audiences who made their works commercially successful. Bluth benefited from our culture's demand for more G-rated fare and a renewed interest in quality animated films.

Robert Downey has been making personal films since the 1960s. While spending some time in a stockade with pen and paper, Downey began to write. When a friend who owned a camera offered to shoot a script Downey wrote, he began making films. Influenced early on by Fellini and Preston Sturges, Downey began making films with $3,000 budgets. Sometimes the film was written, directed, and delivered in a week's time. Not until 1966, with *Chafed Elbows* (a $25,000 product) did he have his first underground success. But it wasn't until *Putney Swope* (1969), with a budget of $250,000 and a promise of national distribution, that Downey achieved national recognition. He has worked on a variety of projects since, including an adaptation of David Rabe's *Sticks and Bones*, and the cult favorite *Greaser's Palace* (1972). For much of the 1970s Downey battled a drug problem, but has been clean since 1982. He has appeared as an actor in films *(The Party's Over, The Family Man, Magnolia, Boogie Nights, To Live and Die in L.A.)*, but primarily at the request of directors who are friends or who like and have been influenced by his films. Like many of his commercial counterparts, Robert Downey is intrigued more by the process of making a film than the film's success. His most recent film is *Forest Hills Bob* (2001) with Philip Seymour Hoffman, but only *Putney Swope* has had wide distribution. Nevertheless, Robert Downey remains a highly regarded filmmaker by a coterie audience that appreciates his humor and irreverence.

As both audience member and filmmaker, Barbara Hammer and Jamie Babbit, like Robert Downey, are not concerned with the "programmed and predictable" story line of traditional cinema. In a career spanning approximately eighty films and videos, Hammer prefers experimental film that presents ideas and images "in a new and changing light either through content, formal concerns, or exhibition practices." In films such as *Nitrate Kisses* (1992) and *Tender Fictions* (1995), Hammer constructs lesbian autobiography and biography through history, memory, archival footage, and personal documentary in order to "confront and to challenge and to celebrate." As Hammer notes, "The challenge . . . is to find the boundaries (my own as well as community limits, systems rules, institutional demands) and then confront them. Confronting these constructed boundaries and deconstructing them is hard political work made possible through play or fun."

Gwendolyn Audrey Foster's edited transcript of extended correspondence with Hammer focuses on the construction of lesbian biographies and autobiographies in *Tender Fictions* (1995) and *Nitrate Kisses* (1992). Whether it is pursuing her own sexuality or uncovering Willa Cather's hidden sexual preference, Hammer wants to answer the questions, "What is it I am afraid of? How has this fear been constructed? And, by whom? Then what am I going to do about it? [and] How can I turn it into play?" While many consider her work as lesbian, she disdains categorization while proclaiming that what she does is "experimental or documentary or . . . dramatic, or any combination of the genres. Some of the work deals with lesbian representation, some of it is purely formal, and some of it confronts death or the fragility of film. Categorization is unidirectional, linear and unlifelike." Hammer is most concerned with engaging her audiences intellectually in the process of "what it is like to investigate, to look for traces, to uncover and find forgotten or misleading paths."

Jamie Babbit is the "youngster" in this collection, having made her first breakout film *(But I'm a Cheerleader)* in 1999–2000. She was an actor and stage manager as a young adult in Cleveland, and then went on to study film at Barnard and NYU. As she tells Wheeler Winston Dixon, she came to film through acting, and finds working with actors "essential" to the success of any of her projects. After graduating from college in 1993, she took a variety of jobs, from production assistant (for Martin Scorsese on *The Age of Innocence* and John Sayles on *The Secret of Roan Inish*) to script supervisor (*The Journey of August King* for John Duigan). After additional experience in experimental film, Babbit moved to Los Angeles, where she worked with David Fincher on *The Game* (1997). That experience and connection, and some assistance from Michael Douglas, allowed her to make the twelve-minute film *Sleeping Beauties* (shown periodically on the Independent Film Channel). Wanting to make the jump from short to feature, and using all her connections, Babbit moved on to *Cheerleader*, which focuses on "how gender expectations define our lives." Unlike other recent lesbian films such as *Go Fish* and *Boys Don't Cry*, Babbit sees her film as different because she "wanted the femme to be the pursuer, not the pursued" and that a "femme can be strong, and a femme can get what she wants." At the time of the interview (October 2000), Jamie Babbit was working on two television shows (*Popular* and *Undressed*) for the money (and experience) to help her make her next film.

Don Bluth was director of animation at Disney Studios when he and several of his coworkers left on September 13, 1979 (Bluth's birthday) as a result of creative differences. Bluth's first full-length film after establishing his independence was *The Secret of NIMH* (1979), which is still regarded as his best film and the focus of the interview included in this volume. Budgeted at seven million dollars and a thirty-month completion deadline, Bluth had hoped that if the film did well at the box office, it would open the doors to the financing of more animated films. Praised by critics for its revival of classical animation and later well received on home video, unfortunately the film did not do well in theaters. Nevertheless, Bluth's very presence in the industry but outside the Disney fold encouraged the studio to reenergize its animation department. Bluth's foray into the field led to new interest in and discussions of animated films. That interest has exploded in the last decade with audiences and studio executives as a result of new technology and box office successes such as *Toy Story* (1995) and *Finding Nemo* (2003).

To Bluth "the important emphasis should be on . . . the play, the story, the [audience] identification." What attracted him to *The Secret of NIMH* were the questions it asked: "What if a species here on earth became more intelligent than man himself. Would they be wiser than us? Would they be self-destructive like us? Would they manage to save the world from us? How would we, as man, as the human race, how would we get along with them?"

The two decades following *NIMH* saw Bluth team up with Steven Spielberg for *An American Tail* (1986) and *The Land Before Time* (1988), and develop several other independent projects. He even moved his production studios to Ireland for a time, highlighting his independence from Hollywood, while at the same time trying to save on production costs. With *Anastasia* (1997) and subsequently *Titan A. E.* (2000), Bluth has received a modicum of commercial success, but it has been his independent spirit and his desire to "help the art of animation to continue to grow" by challenging the industry and stimulating an interest in the animation process that have been his greatest contributions to the craft.

When he spoke to Gerald Wood in 1990, actor, screenwriter, and especially playwright Horton Foote emphasized how it has been easier for him to adapt his own works to the screen than those of others. Having lived with his characters for some time, his emotional connection is much greater to them than to those in somebody else's work. While he has been pleased with a few screened adaptations of his works and a few others (most notably *Dodsworth* and *The Dead*), he finds Hollywood adaptations lack the texture revealed in the specifics of a written text. Instead, the Hollywood film "seems to me overblown; it seems to me pretentious in the wrong way, and too loud, too overemphasized and vulgar. There are, of course, a million exceptions, but I almost dread going to films because the minute you go in they begin to manipulate you." A good film and a good writer will involve and enrich the audience, not manipulate it.

As one might expect from someone who has spent the better part of his life crafting the written word, Foote champions the writer as the key player in the process: "In spite of the Hollywood custom of believing that anybody can edit, or cut, or arrange a film, I think the architect is essentially the writer, and he's the one who can make the best decisions."

Dede Allen would agree that not anyone can edit a film, and her thoughts on the current filmmaking process are not that far removed from those of Horton Foote. After a stellar career as a film editor, and collaborations with directors such as Robert Wise, Elia Kazan, Arthur Penn, George Roy Hill, Sidney Lumet, and Curtis Hanson, Allen was invited to become vice president, and later senior vice president of Creative Development at Warner Bros. Known as the "truth person" for her candor, Allen had the unique opportunity to engage in the development of a project from its inception. Bringing to her job the unique perspective of over fifty years in the business, she was able to refine her social and economic vision of her profession. After changes of management at Warner Bros. made her tenure less stable and her colleagues less collegial, and with a greater emphasis on franchise pictures such as *Lethal Weapon* and *Mission Impossible*, Allen had enough. She returned to editing, working on Curtis Hanson's *Wonder Boys* (2000).

Ric Gentry's lengthy and substantive interview with Allen traces her early career in industrials, the difficulty she had as a woman in the film industry, how she got involved in all parts of the creative process, including sound, color, and story editing, and how she won the respect of directors like Robert Wise and Robert Rossen, Warren Beatty, and Arthur Penn by conveying her unique perspective and editing skills in her work. Along the way Allen comments on her editing of and interactions with directors of such films as *Odds Against Tomorrow; Bonnie and Clyde; Rachel, Rachel; America, America; Little Big Man; Slaughterhouse Five; Reds; The Addams Family;* and *Wonder Boys*. Understanding the characters in a film, feeling the way they do, and living in their world are essentials to Allen's dialectic of editing. By engaging in these elements, she is able to get in her editing what Foote would call "texture." Getting to that point, though, involves trust, the key element between the director and the editor. To Allen, "the important thing . . . is that you have to establish the same relationship as you would with any director, whether it's Bob Wise, Elia Kazan, or a first-time director. You have to have the same kind of openness to whatever they are going to do and whatever their ways are."

What alarms and depresses Allen about today's pictures is how so many of them are determined by eighteen to twenty-five year olds during market screenings in malls and by bean counters in studio offices who have no understanding of film history or the creative process and are only interested in making money. Echoing Robert Altman and Louis Malle, Allen is frustrated by their myopic concern for the bottom line: "There's no such thing as profits being enough anymore. Whatever the profits are they want more." As a result, films that Allen considers exciting or interesting, films like *Dog Day Afternoon* or *Bonnie and Clyde*, would be poorly received by contemporary test audiences: "The kids from the mall wouldn't know what they were about. They never would have opened well. It's very frightening."

The importance of light to Vittorio Storaro is "of the essence" and the subject of *Writing with Light: Vittorio Storaro* (1992). Recently Storaro has worked with Carlos Saura on *Tango, Goya in Bordeaux,* and *Flamenco,* and with Alonso Arau on *Picking Up the Pieces* and *Zapata*. At the time of the interview with Ric Gentry, the cinematographer had completed shoots with Warren Beatty on *Reds*, with Francis Ford Coppola on *Apocalypse Now*, and with Bernardo Bertolucci on, among several, *Last Tango in Paris, The Conformist,* and *1900.* His closest collaboration has been with Bertolucci, and that collaboration has influenced much of his career.

Storaro's goal as a cinematographer has been to have "a parallel story to the actual story so that through light and color you can feel and understand, consciously or unconsciously, much more clearly what the story is about." In *Spider's Strategem* and *The Conformist* the color of choice was blue; in *Last Tango* the colors were yellow-orange and red. Sometimes images are influenced by serendipitous events. While shooting *Last Tango,* Bertolucci and Storaro visited an exhibition of Francis Bacon paintings. The way that his works were often viewed through translucent material worked its way into several scenes in the film.

To Storaro, the director is a conductor, and it is the conductor's orientation, language, and style that he (and the other orchestra members) must follow. He gives visualization to the director's style, much in the same way that Dede Allen collaborates with her directors in editing sound and image and Robert Altman encourages improvisation from his actors. At the same time, throughout his work, there is dialectic, opposing forces that are constantly at battle. This could be natural and artificial energy, day and night, white and black. "Always two things in collision. And when they are brought together, into harmony, there will be a balance, which is the level all things seek. It is a very beautiful moment, but it is very hard to attain."

Beautiful moments were especially hard to attain on the difficult assignment of *Apocalypse Now,* where artificial and natural energies clashed. Exhausted after *Apocalypse,* Storaro took time off to read and write. Early in his career Storaro responded instinctively to his choices. Eventually he came to realize the importance of equilibrium and after extended research, he was more acutely aware of the physiology of color as it impacted images and characters. Unfortunately, at the time of the interview, he was having more success in attaining consistent results from the film labs and manufacturers in Italy than he was in the United States, where "technical functions and procedures" were often inconsistent and unpredictable.

James Woods has made more than sixty films and is brash, vociferous, highly competitive, and demanding of himself and those who perform with him. Educated at MIT, he left school for the stage, and has since worked with directors as varied as Oliver Stone, Clint Eastwood, Martin Scorsese, and Sofia Coppola.

Woods lives to act. He fervently believes that an actor must "do good work, every time you act." When he found out that CAA (Creative Artists Agency) was keeping scripts and parts from him (for example, Tarantino's *Reservoir Dogs*), he left them in no uncertain terms and joined ICM (International Creative Management) with the command that he be given the opportunity to read "every script that is out there." Woods's passion for acting, whether it be in a cameo *(Casino),* as a supporting player *(The General's Daughter),* or a starring role *(Salvador)* may best be conveyed by Alec Baldwin's complimentary description of

Woods as "the actor as terrorist." Whenever he has the opportunity, Woods wants to push his coactors and push those behind the camera to make every scene the very best possible. This is nowhere more apparent than his comments on *Another Day in Paradise,* a small, $4.5 million film that Woods produced and starred in.

The interview with Ric Gentry was, in large part, an effort to share ideas about his craft, but also to sell a film that had his total commitment. As he explains to Gentry, he produced and acted in the film because he loved the script. To get Melanie Griffith to costar, when writer-director Larry Clark *(Kids)* and writer Steven Chin said they couldn't afford her or get her the script in time for an impending deadline, Woods skirted Griffith's agency (CAA) and called her directly, offering her half of whatever he was getting for the film if she would read the script and commit in the next twenty-four hours. She read it and agreed to do it, and the film, with a thirty-eight-day shooting schedule, was on track. As detailed in the interview, the battles on and off the set were intense. Egos clashed (Woods and Clark), and while Woods's focus as both producer and actor did not prevent a bloodbath, the film was completed on time. Woods, however, did not want to go into the editing room to finish the cut because he believes that he "can't be objective and [didn't] want to influence the performances" that way. He also recalls with much sorrow how the studio cut an hour from Sergio Leone's *Once Upon a Time in America:* it was "like someone cutting the arms off your infant child. And I vowed that that would never happen to me again, never in my lifetime."

After much pleading and cajoling, Woods was able to get Clark to reedit his cut before it went to the studio. Thinking no doubt of his career and his battles with Clark, Woods remarks, "It's a necessary condition to have raw talent to be a long term success as an actor [and director], but it's also a necessary and imperative condition to be professional. It's not enough to be talented." Of his own preparation Woods says he generally reads a script once, looks at it before shooting a scene, and then goes with instinct. But not always. In *The General's Daughter,* his character was "a very clever, accomplished warfare expert who's engaging in a game of psychological chess," so, unlike *Another Day in Paradise,* there was no room for improvisation. This need to marry form and content, to be "word perfect" was also the case in one scene in *True Crime.* When Eastwood wanted an exchange where there was not a moment of silence between his character and Woods, both actors nailed it on one take—without rehearsals. When Woods asked if they should do another take for "insurance," Eastwood brushed it off with, "If it's great, why fix it?"

In his interview in this collection, Eastwood tells of Meryl Streep's observations that Eastwood includes "mistakes" in the finished cut. Woods sees the same thing when he recounts, "You're doing the rehearsal and all of a sudden you're shootin' the scene. And [Eastwood] said, 'I like it real and people make mistakes and I want to see human behavior as it is.'" Human behavior and honesty are what

James Woods gives us on the screen and in his interview. While he acknowledges he can be difficult to work with, whether it be asking Elia Kazan what it was like revealing names before HUAC, or battling with Larry Clark or Oliver Stone over an aspect of performance, Woods believes that volatility often helps to make a scene great or truthful, and he prefers the challenge of playing "enormously complicated, volatile, passionate characters." To Woods, "Drama . . . is about shocking the audience and electrifying them through real confrontation. And that means you push the other actor as hard as you can and they come back to you as hard as they can. No one wants to watch a fixed fight."

During two visits to the Ball State University campus between 1990 and 1992, Paul Verhoeven discussed the impact of living in bombed-out neighborhoods in The Hague during World War II, how he got started in filmmaking, the differences between pursuing his career in Holland and then the United States, and his views on censorship and violence in film.

The seeds of his views on violence took root as a child when he watched Allied bombers trying to destroy German rocket launching pads in The Hague and then witnessed misdirected English bombs killing twenty to thirty thousand people in his neighborhood. His home was spared in the errant bombing. As a child, Verhoeven was fascinated by the "special effects" of war and developed a strong sense that war and violence are normal and that peace is abnormal. To his father's delight, Verhoeven missed the opportunity to enroll in film school by a month. He eventually took a doctorate in mathematics. When he was drafted after graduation, he searched out a position in the navy's film department, where for two years he made documentaries. This training allowed him to secure a job in television when he was released. By the 1970s he shifted to feature films.

Holland, like many other European countries, has government subsidies for filmmakers. The government puts up the money or a substantial portion of it, and then if the film is successful based on the grosses, the filmmaker pays back the government and adds an additional 20 percent. Verhoeven flourished for more than a decade under this system. Working with the same producer (Rob Houwer) and screenwriter (Gerard Soeteman) for about thirteen years, Verhoeven's films *(Turkish Delight, Soldier of Orange, The Fourth Man)* were successful. Success drew offers from the United States, but he turned them down several times. Then, in the late 1970s and early 1980s, the political climate changed on the script committee that reviewed his proposals and funding for his films dried up. During this period, "entertainment was not enough, [the film] had to be politically or sociologically or culturally relevant." Most of Verhoeven's films were based on autobiography, newspaper articles, or real events, so when he was offered the opportunity to direct the fantasy *RoboCop*, he found it "too silly" and was not really interested. Neither were about ten or twelve other directors who had turned it down. But with no funding for future projects in Holland and with the encouragement of his wife, he eventually accepted the offer and moved to California.

RoboCop and the later *Total Recall* are very different from Verhoeven's dialogue-filled, realistic films, where he was able to work out the blueprints of the film with the screenwriter. These two projects, with already completed screenplays, gave him an opportunity to revisit his youthful fascination with special effects and comic books, while at the same time trying to push the soul issue by adding colors to what were the black and white paintings of the scripts. They also gave him time to improve his English so he could take on scripts with more dialogue. Wanting to move away from doing only action-science fiction films, which he feared would typecast him as a director, Verhoeven refused to do a sequel to *RoboCop*. When he was offered the opportunity to direct *Basic Instinct*, he accepted. He liked the script and the opportunity to work more closely with dialogue and actors and less with special effects.

Censorship and violence are two topics that often haunt discussions of Verhoeven's films. He has thought about both and concludes that violence in movies "has nothing to do with violence in society," and that rating boards are a hidden form of censorship that prevent artists from conveying the full impact of their works. Even though he has edited his films to secure the necessary "R" rating, he finds this form of censorship "extremely unpleasant."

British director Stephen Frears finds self-censorship the predominant mode in England in the 1980s. When asked about Clause 28, which limited the representation of homosexuals, Frears expresses concerns about the social and economic pressures placed on artists by the Thatcher government, which he directly attacks in *Sammy and Rosie Get Laid* (1987). Whereas Dede Allen was depressed about the quality of contemporary films and how some of the finest films made in the United States in the 1960s and 1970s would not see the light of day because of studio economics and a dumbing-down of movie audiences, Frears laments how government regulations and political grandstanding against the BBC influence what gets made. To Frears, "the world isn't quite the way everybody thinks it is in the movies" and it is sometimes necessary to "create a subversive message." Unlike the Thatcher government, Frears champions the changes brought out by the influx of immigrants: "England's success in the last forty or fifty years is due largely to immigration. . . . It's extraordinary having a colonial past, which is what all of my films are about."

Unlike many American filmmakers, Frears does not believe he needs to spell out the theme or key ideas of his work. Audiences have to decide for themselves. For example, he says *My Beautiful Laundrette* "does not avoid moral responsibility, but I don't see why the film should do the work for you. That's to say, you show it and allow the audience to form its own opinion." While there is much that he likes about the United States and its film industry, he is cognizant of how few British films make money: "It's particularly difficult to be a British film director because it's a very small market. . . . Over here, you can make a decent film and not get your money back. . . . You also depend on becoming an export. I've become an export, like Scotch whiskey or something. I can now get my money because my films have sold in France and America."

The pull of all things American is great. When casting *Dangerous Liaisons*, he considered British actors, but he thought they would be too reserved. He wanted to make a film "about emotion rather than manners. . . . I wanted the film to be vulgar, so I gradually began to see that casting British actors would be less interesting and less irreverent, in a way more respectful to customs practiced." In addition, the box office appeal of American actors to audiences in the United States and Europe is greater and would bring in more money. But when asked why he doesn't move to the United States to make his films, Frears says it boils down to whether he wants to make films about life in this country or in Britain. "If you want to make films about life in Britain, then the Americans are not very sympathetic to it." To Frears, then, whether it is the subject for his films, the angles of his shots, or the setting for his films, it all comes down to perspective.

Peter Harcourt's conversation with Canadian filmmaker Atom Egoyan ranges from his interest in film as a child to specific uses of color and setting in several of his films. Egoyan found the Hollywood film truly mystifying as a child, but he readily connected with the Canadian film *Nobody Waved Goodbye* (1965) about a teenager's frustrations. In reflecting on the creative process, Egoyan comments that so many of his characters are creating their own images and scenarios, but that by placing too much faith in the creative process we can lose sight of what we are doing and why we are doing it. This is reflected in characters in his films who are often out of touch with others, their inner selves, and their sexuality: "People talk about why can't there just be normal sex in the films and for me it's very clear that the situations are so unusual and people use sexuality to reflect what is gong on inside of them. So if they are dysfunctional, I think their sexuality becomes dysfunctional."

One of the ways we are able to bring order to our lives is through art. The process of creating allows the artist to bring order to chaos. At the same time, the process isolates the creator, both in the process of creating and often as a result of not having an audience with whom to share the creative product. Egoyan's greatest affinity is with the "creative person who has a tremendous source of inspiration but is not able to articulate it properly." That lack "could be a metaphor for the whole immigrant experience as well—for a person who, you know, never finds that language, never finds the complete control of his new environment."

The late Louis Malle was interviewed in Baltimore, Maryland, in March 1982, after the screening of *Pretty Baby* (1978) and *Lacombe, Lucien* (1973). He discussed his infatuation with film, his difficulty in working in another language, his recollection of certain films, and his responsibilities as a director. Malle's early work for Jacques Cousteau offered him the opportunity to engage in all aspects of the filmmaking process. What he learned about cinematography, sound, and editing assisted him throughout his career. A case in point is how he used the camera in *My Dinner with André* to achieve certain effects on his audience. Like Barber Hammer, who often slips into the theater to hear how audiences respond to her works, Malle would also drop in to "hear people laugh and participate and really react."

Malle generally preferred to write his own scripts, but enthusiastically accepted *My Dinner with André* after Wally Shawn pared it down from 7,000 pages of transcript to a "great" 180–page script. Like Eastwood, once Malle decided on a project, he allowed collaboration but final responsibility rested with him: "I very much think of a film as a film of mine; I always take complete responsibility, and I'm the one who makes the final decisions, so it's my show." This is clearly seen in his comments on the use of music in his films. When he was twelve, Malle was enthralled by jazz. Making *Pretty Baby* in New Orleans allowed him to revisit his early love and make it an integral part of the film, but generally he used music sparingly. When his friend Michel Legrand wanted to add music to different segments of *Atlantic City*, Malle gave him the okay but told him that he might not use the additions. He removed almost all of what was added.

On *Pretty Baby* he had to improvise some due to the material and actors. Unlike Oliver Stone and Robert Altman, who like improvisation, Malle preferred precision. Like Altman and Pollack, and several of the other directors interviewed in this volume, casting was an essential element in the process. To Pollack casting is 90 percent of the process; to Malle it was 50 percent of directing: "Sometimes through experience and a lot of work and a little manipulation in the cutting room, you can save a performance or sometimes even make it work, but basically you're always trying to save it, which is wrong." He comments on how he recruited Pierre Blaise for *Lacombe, Lucien* and his tragic death a few years later, and talks at length about the casting of *Pretty Baby*. To Malle, seeing a film again after several years can bring to focus a performance that might not have satisfied him years earlier but now works well on the screen.

Malle's harshest comments are directed at those in charge of the studios, executives who are not interested in making better films, but in films that make money. *Pretty Baby*, which Malle considers a B-movie, cost three million dollars to make, but would not fit into the paradigms of sequels and remakes so common in Hollywood. To those in power, a few blockbusters would better serve their purposes than a number of small pictures. As noted earlier, Dede Allen, speaking to Ric Gentry almost twenty years after Malle's remarks, but from the perspective of editor and ex–studio executive, says almost the same thing.

If we are to believe Malle and Allen, filmmaking is in ill health. The interviews in this volume with other filmmakers suggest the patient is healthy, but could be in better spirits.

PART I

Hollywood Voices

CHAPTER ONE

Robert Altman

LEO BRAUDY AND ROBERT P. KOLKER

The following interview took place after a screening of *Health* (1980) and *McCabe and Mrs. Miller* (1972) in Baltimore, Maryland, on March 28, 1981. The screenings and discussion were sponsored by the Maryland Film Guild and funded in part by the Maryland Committee for the Humanities. The interview was conducted and moderated by Professors Leo Braudy, then of Johns Hopkins University, now of the University of Southern California, and Robert P. Kolker of the University of Maryland. Members of the audience also participated in the exchange.

ROBERT ALTMAN: I have no opening remarks because I have nothing to say.

ROBERT P. KOLKER: What happened at Fox that *Health* did not get out when it should have and the way it should have?

RA: The film was made in 1979 and the Fox management changed about the time we finished editing. Then I was off to Malta to shoot *Popeye* [1980]. The new management came in and they agreed to wait until I came back to discuss the release plans, which was to be late summer of 1980. I wanted it to come out during the political conventions. They got a new head of sales, who I had the same problem with on the film I produced and Alan Rudolf directed for Columbia called *Remember My Name* [1978]. He chose not to release that because it was made under different management, and I ran into him again. They

FIGURE 1. Robert Altman and Kim Basinger on location for the film *Prêt-à-Porter* (1994). Courtesy: Jerry Ohlinger Archives.

chose not to release it, so they bought a film for that time slot instead and released it, a film called *Oh, Heavenly Dog!* [1980]. I don't know whether that was a comment or what. *Health* was given to Films Incorporated, so it will be seen. It's being played in universities and revival houses and that sort of thing. It never got a full release nor will it.

RK: Could you tell us how Lion's Gate [RA's production company] works and how you carry on your negotiations with distributors?

RA: I work as an independent company. We will develop a project, take it to a major distributor, they will finance the film, I'll guarantee the completion of the film, and they will release it. Usually we work in concert like that.

LEO BRAUDY: I wanted to ask something more about *Health* and, also, since you were preparing *Popeye* at the same time, about the two of them together. In some ways it seems that *Popeye* has such a more benevolent view about what a community is like and what's possible—personal statements and personal eccentricities—whereas *Health* seems much more satiric and has a pessimism about whether things work or not.

RA: When I make a film it's not my opinion of the way I think things should be. It doesn't reflect what I would like to see. I'm criticized severely for being very cynical. I feel I'm very optimistic, but an artist is not a politician, not a philosopher. I'm not a philosopher. I try to show what I see, the way I see things. I'm really saying, "Come over here and look at what I see through my distorted view," and it is distorted and it's going to be a little different from yours, but that's the whole point. For *Popeye* we went back to the 1930s, to the Segar comic strip, and tried to take the same philosophy that he put into those comic strips about that particular time. We created this oppressed community that was run by a dictator that they never saw and about people who were afraid. Then in comes this sort of I-am-what-I-am man and it's just a different subject.

LB: Many people saw *McCabe and Mrs. Miller* this morning and there was a kind of situation in which an I-am-what-I-am man comes into a town and gets lost.

RA: *Popeye* and *McCabe* are very, very close. I mean there are not only a lot of unintentional resemblances, but there are a lot of intentional resemblances.

LB: Could you tell us a little bit about them?

RA: The town drunk in *McCabe* did the dance on the ice. He not only played the same character in *Popeye* in that town, but we had him in the same wardrobe. It was the same actor.

LB: Was it the same set designer?

RA: No. But, we had a church and a kind of mad preacher, and there were a lot of similarities.

RK: The cutting in the first part of *Popeye* was very similar to the opening of *McCabe*, particularly when they first gather around the table, talking back and forth.

RA: Yes. But, I don't do those things consciously. Some things you do. The reason I don't like interviews or I don't particularly like to answer direct questions of "Why did you do this and what did this mean?" is that I really don't want to know. The minute I find out then it becomes mechanical with me and it prevents me from doing that. We were at the University of Maryland in College Park, and I met with some reporters before the *Health* screening, and they said, "What is this thing you have about every time somebody gets shot or hit or something, they fall in the water?" I said, "I don't know what you are talking about." They said, "Well, the cowboy in *McCabe*, when he got shot off the bridge, he went into the water." I said, "Well, hell, he was on the bridge," and he said, "Well, you did this even when the young gunfighter got killed; he went into the bathtub full of water." And I said, "I don't know, I don't think I'm doing that." Then he started naming other pictures and how many times this happens and I said, "Maybe it's because when you watch somebody take a punch or a shot or fly backwards, it's easier to have them fall in the water than on a pile of rocks. They don't get hurt, it makes a nice splash and is good visually, but there just isn't any other connection. You have seen something that I don't have any feeling about at all." Then we went on and an hour later we ran *Health* and there was Henry Gibson getting punched into the Jacuzzi.

RK: But, at the same time, you plan things very carefully. You plan the shots and the movements in the cutting in particular.

RA: Yes, but I don't know and, as I say, I don't want to know why I make those choices because it narrows my choices. It takes a lot of my freedom away from me; in any film I make in the future, when I have to have somebody hit, I'm going to look at that water and say, "Wait a minute, do I really want to do this or don't I?" So something has been taken away from me because of that. Now that has to happen. If I talk about it to you and I say what *Health* was about and what *McCabe* was about or *Popeye*, I'm limiting now your way of looking at that because you have to say, "Oh, that's what he meant," rather than figuring out in your mind what it means to you. It doesn't have to mean the same thing to you that it does to me. It shouldn't. Fellini made a film called *Casanova*[*] [1976], and when I saw *Casanova* I felt like I was a ten-year-old boy who had found the key to a museum that had been locked up for five hundred years and was able to wander around in there. I was just fascinated by that film. The film was crucified. What happened, I believe, was that there was so much money in the film—everybody is worried about money now—that they told Fellini he had to do interviews. Well, Fellini is not going to tell them what he thinks, because he is too smart and they wouldn't believe him if he told the truth because it's a joke;

---

[*]ED: Full title is *Fellini's Casanova*.

so he said he made comments about *Casanova* and his feeling about that kind of man and womanizing and these different things and the critics read all this and they got it so that when the picture came out instead of being able to accept it on the value of what they saw, they suddenly had to accept it within the bounds of what Fellini had said and, consequently, the picture became a limited piece of art.

LB: I wonder if action seems to be characteristic of your style. There is a hoveringness about it or an exploratory quality—about *Popeye* or *McCabe* or *Health;* the camera wanders around a lot. It seems that you are consciously trying to leave questions open about what things mean. You juxtapose different things and mix them, including sound. There is a sense that we are not supposed to listen to any one thing. We are supposed to take it all in.

RA: I'm trying to show you something or let you see something that I see. Obviously, I'm manipulating the audience every time I make a cut or by what I show, but I'm trying to leave enough openness there so that you can bring your own interpretation to it, because I don't think a film has any value, or that any work of art is a work of art, unless it's something that the beholder meets halfway and brings his own experience to. Some people ask me about *Three Women* [1977]. They'll say, "What was that supposed to mean?" I can give five very, very valid answers and they are all different. And I don't care. If somebody says, "Gee, I didn't understand it that way, I thought it was this way," then they feel disappointed. People will see a film together, go out and argue about what it meant. And the weaker debater of the two will say, "Well, I didn't like that, I thought that was kind of silly." They feel that they didn't get it. There is nothing to get. I mean, you will get it. In the case of an essay film like *Health*, you don't have any protagonist or person to get involved with, you are sitting there observing people. I can understand why the people don't like it. It's about a fifty-fifty split between those who enjoy that kind of thing and can bring something to it and say, "Oh that was terrific, that was funny," and those who say, "I thought that was a bore," and that's perfectly all right with me.

LB: It almost seems as if Cavett is designed as a character who is trying to figure it out.

RA: He is your tour guide. I felt that the real window to what was going on there was the publicity girl in the hotel, the public relations girl, the black girl. It was really through her eyes that I kind of saw what she saw.

RK: What is the future of that kind of film, a film of observation and laughter at pomposity, the kind of thing you do so well?

RA: It doesn't look very good right now. The patient is critical. A few good films will be made and be snuck through, and I think you will have to go underground again and lie a little bit to the people who put the money up and say, "This is really a nice action automobile race kind of picture" and sneak something underneath that to get them to do it, which happened in the early days of film making. But there is so much money involved, and they are so concerned about the money that they don't want to take a chance of just making a film that will maybe break even or maybe make 20 percent. In most businesses if you turn out a product and you can make 50 percent profit, it's pretty good.

RK: Do you see any new ways of financing coming about?

RA: I don't think there really are going to be new ways. There are the tax shelter things which they have in Canada, and the trouble is that that just encourages a bunch of opportunists to come in, and so good films aren't made that way. I think the only real cure is if we could get my salary cut down to nothing and take all the profit out of it, the high profit out of it, and if suddenly people couldn't become millionaires by being in the manufacturing or the process of making films—actors, producers, everything—if it just became a kind of a tough business, all of the people who are in it for the money would go into shopping centers and leave the making of films to the artists. I think it has to come to that to really work.

LB: Do you think that tapes or videocassettes are a separate area that might . . . ?

RA: It's going to be an offshoot. I'm very interested in it. We're doing it now. We are hampered by the length of films—that they have to be a certain length or within a certain area. I'm doing a play now that I finished mounting, but we don't quite know what to do with it. It's too short. It's an hour and five minutes. It's too strong a play to put something else with it, and so we have this kind of bastard length. Some people will pay eight or ten dollars for a ticket and they are out in an hour. I think that video, the whole use of videocassettes and box office and pay television and all that can help destroy that necessity for length, so that a piece can become what it should be and be as long as it should be. I saw a little film that was made in Canada. It's five minutes long and it's the best film I have ever seen. It's called *Why Me?** It's an animated thing. I think it's been released theatrically occasionally, but the Canadian Film Board makes these films and they don't know what to do with them. They just keep making these films and they put them under their arms and they take them out and show them at colleges, and occasionally they will run them on television late at night, but they don't make any money off of them.

LB: What do you think of possibly some alternate distribution network or some alternate funding that comes out of, say, the college circuit, if it ever got organized, or out of video disc companies or tape companies that weren't just picking up commercial releases?

RA: The video disc can be very valid. It's like book publishing. Poetry is still published. You can go into a book store and find books of poetry and buy them and

---

*ED: Created and directed by Janet Perlman, and written by Derek Lamb and Janet Perlman (1978).

most people are not going broke by doing this or they wouldn't do it, but you don't see them in the airport in those stands with the paperbacks. The video disc offers the same kind of thing. It offers the possibility of doing a piece for an elite audience and that's a small high.

LB: I think that in all your films you have used actors in a way that is different from most commercial directors. You emphasize improvisation a lot in working out the scenes and allow people to create a kind of ambiance between them that is very rare.

RA: It seemed the only logical way I know to work. The actors are the main artists, interpreters anyway, of a film and they're the people who perform it. I feel 90 percent of my creative work is finished when I have cast it; then it's up to them and I'm there to sort of keep the peace and boundaries because eventually these films take on their own life. By the time they are finished I really don't have much to do with it anymore. It's like fathering a child. You don't have to work very long.

LB: You do get them to do things though.

RA: I allow them to do things and that's the point. The improvisation is something that we use in rehearsal, but not necessarily when we go to shoot a piece; then it's set and it's very, very controlled. Now, if it has the illusion of being improvisational, that's great.

LB: I think it has the illusion that there is some kind of connection between the characters—a kind of intimacy, a kind of ambiance—that isn't just because of the script or because of the lines that they are saying. There is a kind of feeling. The improvisation creates that.

RA: That's why an actor is playing another character, but I try to set it up in such a way and even in casting so they can draw on their own experience and their own feelings and things that they know that I don't have to know.

RK: But you go in with a finished script.

RA: Sometimes we get into the finished blueprint and sometimes that will be a very complete script, dialogue, etc. Other times it will be outlined. *Three Women* was done with a thirty-three page outline. I knew the scenes that I wanted to shoot and how they were going to go together. I didn't dialogue them until the night before we were going to shoot a scene or I would get up at four or five in the morning and write the scene for that day. Because we shot in sequence I was able to take advantage of what had happened before, so the script grew as the film grew, and yet I knew how it was going to begin and end and what was going to happen.

LB: Robin Williams always comes across on television at least as being incredibly manic, yet in *Popeye* you managed to underplay that. Was that created between the two of you?

RA: He managed to underplay because we certainly took advantage of that. He's a master of improvisation. He could come up on a stage and entertain you for an hour with this coat and with just what would come to his mind, but he was playing *Popeye* and he confined his flourishes to the boundary of that character. In fact, a lot of times I would have to kind of kick him loose a little.

RK: *Health* seemed to me very much a film about the end of the Carter era. If you were going about it now, where would be your locale?

RA: I don't think I could make it now. I think *Health* could only have been made when it was made, and that was the end of the Carter era. I did want the film out during the conventions. All I can say about it is that, now that it's after the fact, we were right.

RK: It's almost a documentary.

LB: Exactly, which at that time was a satire. Now it's a documentary.

RA: I got credit for inventing Carter in *Nashville* [1975] and I felt it was my obligation to get rid of him. I didn't mean to do it quite in the way it was done.

RK: Do you shoot with one camera or do you cover?

RA: I shoot with two cameras a lot. *Health* was shot with two cameras; *Popeye* was shot with two or three cameras. In a film, what I call an interior film, like *Three Women*, of course, there is no point in that.

AUDIENCE: What are you working on now? What do you have in the can or what is coming up in the future?

RA: It looks pretty bleak. I'm working on a script. I had a film I was going to do for United Artists called *Lone Star*. We should be shooting right now. We had Howard Booth and Sigourney Weaver and were ready to go. Then the management of United Artists changed after Mr. Cimino's *Heaven's Gate* [1980] and they pulled the picture.

AUDIENCE: It was going to be a cheap picture?

RA: Yes, six million; that's as cheap as you can get now. But, the point is the man who became the president was head of foreign [distribution] and he said, "This picture won't work foreign because of *Urban Cowboy*." I said this isn't *Urban Cowboy* [1980] and he said, "Yeah, but they wear the same kind of clothes and it won't work in the foreign market because *Urban Cowboy* didn't work in the foreign market." So the picture was killed and I'm working on an original screenplay, a property* (I'm bringing in a writer, a playwright, to work on it with me) which I think we are going to do with Malcolm McDowell and Mary Steenburgen.

AUDIENCE: What's the nature of it?

---

*ED: Something bought or optioned to be made into a film.

RA: It's called *The Smith County Widow*.* It has to do with people who are the same but, because they come from different parts of the world think they are different, and the conflict that sets up. It's sort of a serious, mystery, comedy, farce.

AUDIENCE: What kind of preproduction plans do you make?

RA: When we start, when we think about a project and get it to the point where we say we are going to make a film out of this, the first decision I'll make will be the cinematographer. I'll set that person or at least do a lot of thinking about it and try to work out what my limitations are, or, in other words, what is out of my control. Then I decide what the visual and audio style of that film is going to be. For instance, in *Nashville*, or *Health*, or *Brewster McCloud* [1970] we were dealing with a real city and real places and we couldn't control what people wore. We couldn't say, "All right, nobody in St. Petersburg can wear a red shirt tomorrow." We have no control, so I know I have to change the style of how that's going to look, and I have to blend my film in with what is there. A lot of times that will determine the type of cameraman I want to use. In the case of *Popeye*, *Three Women*, and *Images* [1972], where we control, and *McCabe and Mrs. Miller*, where we create the whole environment, then we can decide how we want this to look to the audience because we do the wardrobe and the construction. Then we start putting our crew together based on what we can't control and how we are going to do it, and we cast it.

AUDIENCE: What kind of control problems did you have with *McCabe and Mrs. Miller*? I'm thinking of the snow in the last ten minutes of the film.

RA: Well, that was the best accident that ever happened. We shot the film in sequence. It never snows in Vancouver. I mean it snows, but it disappears the next day. The last scene we were shooting was at night, when Julie Christie comes out, leaves McCabe in the whorehouse, and starts across the bridge. It started to snow then, which we thought was terrific, and we took advantage of it and lit it, but when I say snow, it was snowing flakes that were the size of breakfast cereal. That night, when we finished, it was about ten or eleven o'clock, and we had been there so long that I got really cold, and I could feel it in my bones, and I got our special effects guy and I said, "Find out what the temperature is, I think it's going to freeze." It was twenty-eight and then it got down to twenty-seven. The next morning we were to start shooting the chase—where McCabe comes out and sees the town empty. I said, "Let's freeze the town," and so everybody stayed up all night and we got hoses and we just sprayed all the trees and the roofs. It froze and we made icicles, and the next morning it was beautiful.

It snowed all night and we had this beautiful vista there. The reason we had all that water is that the whole town had been rigged when we built it so we could

---

*ED: Steenburgen and McDowell teamed up in *Cross Creek* (1983), based on the life of Marjorie Kinnan Rawlings, directed by Martin Ritt, but Altman never made *The Smith County Widow*.

have rain. The original plan was to shoot the whole end of the picture at night. Then we realized we didn't have the light to do it and it would have taken us forever, and the shortcuts would have lost something. So we decided we would just do it with rain, but then it rained through the whole damned picture. I didn't want to continue it with rain, so I said, "Okay, we'll do it in a wind storm." I ordered up a bunch of those big Ritters,* airplane propellers to make wind. I thought I would use the wind to take away the element of hearing and use that as a suspense value in the chase; but then this snow came along and it kept snowing. I said, "Let's shoot it in snow." We knew we had two weeks or a week and a half to do that in—it would take that long—and Warren Beatty said, "Let's just take five days off because there is no point in starting this in the snow, because the snow will not be here by the time we finish." I said, "That's probably true," and he said, "Then we will have to redo everything." I said, "It's snowing now and we got nothing else to do, so let's do it." It took a lot of convincing to get him out of his trailer, and it snowed constantly for eight days. I mean it did not stop. The snow at times was up to my waist. The nature of the snow is such that as soon as you run a truck through or when an electrician walks through or a grip, there are the footprints and it's all screwed up. So we set up barriers. Suddenly we realized it didn't make any difference; we could walk through the snow and in five minutes it was covered up. We finished the last of that chase scene and we went up to start the church burning, which we did last, and it started to rain and in six hours you couldn't have gotten a bushel basket of snow. That was luck. I'll never forget Rex Reed's review. Not only did he hate the picture, he said, but when he got to that fake snow . . .

LB: In your other films, I don't think you used pastels as much as you do in *Health*. Is this also a matter of control?

RA: In *A Wedding* we had total control and we did the pastels and those colors to separate the characters from the back ground. In *Nashville* we had the opposite problem. If we had dressed our main characters the way that those people really dressed, you would have said, "Oh, this is silly, I don't believe that." So we had to actually become conservative with our main characters, and if you will look at the background you will see that.

AUDIENCE: Did the people who cut the music for *Nashville* take the movie too seriously?

RA: No, they didn't like it because we didn't use their music, and I tried to point out that in *Nashville* I wasn't interested in good music. I was interested in the whole spectrum of the kind of music that comes out of there and a lot of it is very good and a lot of it is very bad. I wasn't interested in creating songs, and so we

---

*ED: Ritter is the name of the company that makes these wind machines.

didn't use Nashville people or existing songs. They didn't like that because they like to keep a little mystique about. It's always been curious to me that people will go look at Bufford Pusser and those road running pictures about the South* where they make these people cretins, and they'll laugh at that and think that's just great and that's good old boy stuff, and because it's exaggerated, far enough away, they say, "That ain't me." But in Nashville they took offense. They felt that I was making fun of them and we got a backlash, but a lot of that came from the critics, too.

AUDIENCE: Was the soundtrack recorded and was it boycotted by the distributors?

RA: Yes. No, ABC at that time had the thing. The guy that had the record company was forced to take it. He didn't like it, didn't want it, and it was just not successful.

Braudy: What about *Popeye*? Has that been recorded?

RA: That was released, but that did nothing either.

LB: Actually, one of the things that offended me most about the critical response to *Popeye* was how people put down the music, which I love, and which seemed totally suitable to the film. In general, do you use music as a bridge, a connector between things? I am thinking of the guy playing the fiddle in *McCabe*.

RA: I always have to come to the position that I'm not making music. In other words, I'm not making a record. I'm not producing music that an audience is going to hear directly. I'm making a film, and so I use music in the film, behind the film, in any way that augments that film the most, and sometimes I purposely use bad music or bland music. I didn't want *Popeye* to look like a Broadway musical. I didn't want suddenly everybody to start dancing, so the people who did the dancing were not the good dancers and we didn't go for voices. We wanted simplicity. I have used a word which is misinterpreted and I should be able to think of a better word, but I want the picture to be "tacky" and kind of rough around the edges and torn up and not slick, and that's why I felt that the music worked so well. The album of *Popeye* that would be a great success and a work of art in itself would be if [Harry] Nilsson sings *Popeye*, if he would do all those songs.

RK: *Nashville* is musical in its structure, with scenes and characters emerging and coming in and out and moving like a musical arrangement, so in a way it echoes the songs themselves.

RA: The people just didn't like all of the songs and some of them were pretty bad. I think the best film I have made in terms of structure—the most outgoing kind of structure or the newest or most adventurous—was *A Perfect Couple* [1979]. We took very bland, I mean soft, middle-of-the-road rock kind of music and used it with a semisuccessful group, but we used the music in that to displace

---

*ED: *Walking Tall* (1973) and its sequels.

obligatory scenes. In other words, the music carried you emotionally through a scene, prepared you for the next one, yet you didn't actually see the scene. The film didn't last because it came so close after *Quintet* [1979] that the theater owners didn't even want it, but the audiences felt that it was probably the most conventional, satisfactory, happy-ending kind of film that I had made.

RK: How did you handle your feelings after *Quintet*, a very experimental film which most people didn't like very much, and *A Perfect Couple*, a very lovely film, a very different film from *Quintet*, a small light film that didn't go either?

RA: You mean, how do I feel? I feel bad, I cry. But that can't be helped. In other words, that doesn't diminish the film in my mind or for the people that I have made the film with. We just feel, well, that didn't work commercially. There are lots of reasons for it, but that doesn't mean the film is any the less.

RK: Do you use the commercial failure as a way of examining what you did and making different selections for the next film?

RA: No. With every film I have started and when I have just finished the film, I think, "That is going to be a blockbuster. *Three Women* is going to win all the Academy Awards, it's going to win everything, it's going to be the biggest film, it's going to knock *Star Wars* off the map." I felt the same way about *Quintet* and I'm always shocked how wrong I am. But it doesn't change my affection for the beast.

AUDIENCE: Was *Three Women* based on a dream and how did you cast it? I think it should have won awards.

RA: Thank you. It did, though. Shelley Duvall did win best actress at the Cannes Film Festival for it and the film itself came awful close that year except for three women who were on the jury: [director] Agnes Varda, who felt that the film was dangerous to women and should not be released, [actress] Marthe Keller, and [film critic] Pauline Kael, who loved the first two-thirds of the movie and hated the last third. I tried to point out to her that I don't make movies in sections, but she just hated the film. But anyway, it did happen from a dream. I dreamed that I was making a film in the desert with Sissy Spacek and Shelley Duvall and that it was called *Three Women* and it was a character stealing, personality theft kind of thing. I woke up and made some notes on this yellow pad next to my bed and went back to sleep, and then I dreamed some more that I was sending my production manager out to look for desert locations and I woke up and made more notes on it and went back to sleep. Then I woke up and realized that I don't keep a yellow pad next to my bed—the whole damn thing was a dream, but it was a dream about making a picture, not of what the picture was, but suggestions came from it. The next day was Sunday. I was depressed at the time. A film had been cancelled that we were going to do, or I chose to step out and cancel it myself. My wife was in the hospital and she was very ill at the time—we didn't know how seriously. (She is fine now.) I called up the girl who does the casting for me and wardrobe and is probably the top creative associate I have, and I said I read a short story last night and let me tell you what it's about, and I kind of faked through the thing. I said, do you think it could make a good movie and she said, "Yeah, can you get the rights?" And I said, "Yeah, I think so." Within nine days of that time I went in to Alan Ladd Jr.* That was the first film I did with him and I told him that story. I said I won't write a script, but I'll do an outline, and we had the deal for making the picture.

LB: You were talking about actors before and the large creative input that they give to films. In *Three Women* and *Images* you were attracted to themes about people turning into other people, robbing personalities. I wonder if actors inspire you that way, the ease with which they go from role to role. Is there something fragile about the actor's temperament?

RA: I don't know where that comes from. It is very easy in retrospect for me to see that I make those kinds of pictures. *That Cold Day in the Park* [1969] was that kind of a picture, *Images* was that kind of picture, and so was *Three Women*. They are all very closely akin, what I would call an interior film—where I am dealing with the inside of the person's head, and what they see or what you see or what I show you that they see may not necessarily be what's happening. I have some fascination with that. Obviously, I don't know what it is and I don't want to know because I keep dealing with that.

LB: When the camera at the end of *McCabe and Mrs. Miller* goes into Julie Christie's eye, are we to take that as the film having been seen in some great part from her point of view?

RA: No. I don't know what that was. I was trying to do the opposite of the normal ending because there is no way to end a film. I mean, life doesn't stop. The only way I really know to end a film is with the main character's death. That is the easiest way, so usually you do this big pull back, but I thought why not just go inside of somebody's head. That little vase that she was using and looking at—we brought that into a studio or garage in order to shoot it, to get as close as we did with that—suddenly it seemed to me when we shot it that it looked like another planet. It's just the idea that occurs. I'm sure you didn't see it in *Popeye*, but if you see *Popeye* again, you will notice that when Popeye first comes in to the bordello looking for Wimpy and Sweet Pea, we go around that room and in one of those bottom bunks you will see the woman who I call Cinderella, the wash woman, the raggedy woman who is kind of around in the background, who also I think is probably Sweet Pea's mother. She is lying in that bunk. The preacher is above her smoking an opium pipe and she is looking at this same vase, and that's just fun for me. If it became obvious to an audience, it would be destructive.

---

*ED: In 1977 he became president of 20th Century-Fox, only to leave a few years later to form The Ladd Company. Later he became president of MGM/UA Entertainment (1985–1988).

AUDIENCE: How much fun did you have making one of the characters in *Health* read the *National Enquirer* with what happened with Carol Burnett?

RA: The *National Enquirer* was just a magazine that I personally deplore and I had to have something going on there. I just decided to take a shot at it, but I didn't know anything about Carol—I didn't even know about her suit at that time.

AUDIENCE: Was *The Long Goodbye* [1973] difficult to make?

RA: That was a successful film and should have been much more successful. That film was hurt originally because United Artists wanted to release it as a serious film. They had a poster of Elliot with a cat on his shoulder and a smoking gun and it looked like the ad for *The Postman Always Rings Twice* [1946]. People went in to see that kind of a film and they were disappointed, and they didn't like it. We got them to pull the film, and we redid the campaign, opened it several months later in New York, and had that been the original opening, it would have been a very, very successful film. The real dyed-in-the-wool Raymond Chandler fans didn't like it because, they said, it wasn't true to the book or to Raymond Chandler, that wasn't Philip Marlowe. But they weren't thinking about Raymond Chandler, they were thinking about Humphrey Bogart. I would love to show that film to Raymond Chandler because I think that what I tried to do in *The Long Goodbye* was the same thing he did in the book. He used those crappy plots that he couldn't follow himself—I never finished that book either, by the way—but he used them as a device to hang a bunch of thumbnail essays on, observations, and that's the approach that we took on that picture.

RK: Visually it is your most elaborate film. There is not one shot in that film in which the camera is not moving.

RA: That was another experiment we tried. The camera is constantly moving, but not moving with something, not moving the way it should. You know how you would be in a crowd. You are trying to watch something and it moves and somebody is here and you are just always kind of at the wrong place at the wrong time. That was the kind of tension or attitude I was trying to get in that film. The idea came from a small sequence that we did in *Images*, where we did the same kind of thing in a short slice, so I felt safe with it, but it seemed to work so well in *Images* that we thought maybe we could do a whole film that way and *The Long Goodbye* was the film that followed *Images*.

AUDIENCE: Have other directors had an influence on you?

RA: Oh, sure. Yeah, of course they do. The bad ones. The bad films have an influence. I mean, everything you see is a part of what you take and nothing is new. Of the ending of *Brewster McCloud*, several critics said, "He just stole the Fellini ending." But Max Ophuls used that ending in *Lola Montez* [1965], so who stole what from whom? I was aware of it. It seemed to work for my film, and why not borrow from my friend? I say Fellini is my friend because I love what he does. I love his approach to film.

AUDIENCE: Why do you do lectures if you don't like pre- or postfilm analysis?

RA: I'm not doing a lecture tour. I was invited to speak at the University of Maryland and here, and this was tied in to two days and I happened to be free at the time. I like to do this sort of thing because I usually come away learning more than anybody in the audience. I learn from the questions and I learn from hearing myself talk, although I try not to listen. People don't remember that when *McCabe and Mrs. Miller* opened, it was one of the worst bombs of all time, it was crucified by the critics. Two or three major critics went the other way, but the audiences hated it, it lasted no time in the theaters, and it was a big, big flop. People like Vincent Canby, who now is talking about *Quintet* or certain films that they made a bad review of—I don't know if *Quintet* was the one—say that something has happened to RA, he doesn't have the same kind of poetic feeling that he had in the marvelous masterpiece *McCabe*. Well, I have his original review, and so I don't feel that *Health* is dead. From a commercial standpoint, as a regular theatrical release, yes, but the next picture that you are going to see start playing the most in these retrospective and revival houses will be *Quintet*. That picture was maligned, but I feel it has a long, long life. We look at it occasionally and I love it, and I think audiences after a period of time will be able to sit with it without the hype and without having to say, "Well, gee, this is the next RA, what's it going to be like?" and be able to look at that film. I think it's quite prophetic and whatever the opposite of that is. I hope that *Health* will be played in this kind of situation and I will do everything I can to promote it being seen because we made the film for audiences to see. I don't have to go around and do this for *Popeye* and *M*A*S*H* or *Nashville*, but the other films . . . I also have a responsibility to the actors. The really evil thing is that studios violate the people that they need and that really make their business work. In *A Perfect Couple* there was Paul Dooley, who nobody knew, and Marta Heflin, who nobody knew, but we also had Carol Burnett, Glenda Jackson, Betty Bacall, Jim Garner—all of these people came in on that picture at about half their normal price. They came in to do it because we were doing it together. They wanted to do it and they're the ones who have been hurt by it.

AUDIENCE: What is your opinion of blind bidding on the part of theater owners?

RA: Blind bidding is an attempt to stop what block booking was. I think it hurts now because, even with *Popeye*, we set a release for December 12 and we hardly made that. We could have been hurt because we didn't have the editing time we wanted or felt we needed. We got it opened, but there were nineteen states where we couldn't get theaters until we had a print to show them, so I had to make a scratch print or a print that was close enough to what the final thing was going to be, so we could take it around and show it to them. That cost us a great deal of money which added on to the cost of the film and also took a great deal of our editing time. In that respect it hurt. The ideal thing would have been to say, "The picture won't be ready until the summer." But they felt, and I agreed with them, that it was and should have been a Christmas picture.

AUDIENCE: What is your attitude toward your own films? Are there things you would change in them?

RA: The only answer to that question, and I have said this before, is that these films take on their own life. They are like your children and none of your children is alike; none has the same success in the world, but you love them all for themselves and equally, and I love all of my films. As far as changing anything and saying, "Gee, I wish I had done that," at the risk of sounding arrogant I don't have any of those feelings because if there are mistakes in those films, if there are things that didn't work, they are also part of that film and that film doesn't have anything to do with me anymore. It's there and I'm here. My affection for my films is genuine and each of them has different memories and different things, but there is nothing I would change.

AUDIENCE: Have the public's artistic standards risen, with films like *The Elephant Man* [1980], *Raging Bull* [1980], and *Ordinary People* [1980], or will we continue to spend our money on trash?

RA: I don't know what's going to happen in the future. I think those films you mentioned are certainly excellent films, especially *The Elephant Man,* and I think that a few pictures like that will continue to get made, but not very many because people are still going to look for, well, *Friday the 13th* [1980]. I'm not condemning that film, or the whole mass of horror and action films. But somebody is always going to sneak a good one through. And I hope I'm one of the sneaks.

CHAPTER TWO

Francis Ford Coppola

RIC GENTRY

Francis Coppola is an ardent advocate of new audiovisual forms and technology. While he directs such mainstream films as *Peggy Sue Got Married* [1986] and, more recently, *Gardens of Stone* [1987], Coppola nevertheless proceeds to invest time and money in promoting video and, ultimately, in an entirely new, largely electronic means of production for storytelling. And he makes no bones about it—if he could revolutionize the film industry and all current means of popular entertainment and mass communication, he would do it. Not only that, he sees such an opportunity as one that would thoroughly revamp society and the prevailing political structures, both of which he is eager to do. Yet, as grandiose as these aspirations are, Coppola is clearly not interested in power and influence for its own sake. As this interview shows, Coppola is nothing if not a humanitarian and an idealist.

Coppola was able to realize his ambition of directing drama with video as the medium of record, as well as to direct specifically for television, after he met with Shelley Duvall, executive producer and the imaginative force behind the highly acclaimed *Faerie Tale Theatre,* produced for cable's Showtime. The result was the twenty-sixth and, at least tentatively, final episode of the *Faerie Tales,* "Rip Van Winkle," televised on March 23, 1987. This conversation was conducted in Coppola's office just as the postproduction editing and sound were being completed for "Rip Van Winkle."

FIGURE 2. Francis Ford Coppola shooting *The Cotton Club* (1984). Courtesy: Jerry Ohlinger Archives.

RIC GENTRY: In your work, are you more interested in the form and the technology than in the content?

FRANCIS FORD COPPOLA: I am. In particular, I'm interested in what kind of content the technology can produce. I've been trying to find a way to create new narrative patterns based on the times and the technology for a long time. It's also very difficult for me to maintain an interest in the traditional stories of old that get recycled into things we see today.

The climate of our times is very tired. It's not that we have fewer ideas so much as something in the culture that doesn't allow itself new approaches. Technology is delivering new values that have yet to be tapped. We've got all this new stuff and people aren't looking at the obvious, which is that something totally new in terms of stories can come about. Instead, we use the advances in technology to reproduce and reiterate what we've already seen, what's been done in terms of form for centuries. I think it's time we catch up with the tools that have been invented.

The truth is I am interested in a content that I cannot get at. I yearn to be able to move into a world where my ideas connect into a pattern that could be identified as a story. But I truly cannot get there. It's equally difficult for me to recycle the old stories of the past as most movies do today.

RG: So in a way you're saying that advances in technology are synonymous with new ways of seeing and thinking, and therefore our traditional stories, structurally at least, are sort of culturally redundant and, in every way—sociologically, psychologically, artistically—unvitalizing.

FFC: What I'm saying is that technology, if used in new ways, might break up the monopoly certain imagery, certain icons, have on our attention. I think we could see a less homogenized view of things, and we'll have to if there's going to be a shake-up in our current political thinking. There's something in our politics as old, as dated, as those stories from ancient times that get endlessly recycled.

With a new technology comes a tidal wave of new givens, new ideas, new beliefs, and most important, a new group of rulers. I hate to use such an archaic word for it but that's what they are—rulers. Whether they are the high priests of the powerful and entrenched world religion, or the lords who control the land and the agriculture, the merchant seamen, conquistadors, the captains of the Industrial Revolution, they are our rulers. They and their ideas move out when progress moves them out by changing the nature of where power comes from.

I am beginning to have the thought that my primal interest in technology is a temporary phase—a vehicle—not unlike the ships of ancient explorers taking us from the Old World to a new continent of content and story. At that time I fantasize of leaving the old ship and moving into still another area of art and thinking.

RG: I get the impression, and *Faerie Tale Theatre* seems to confirm this, that artificial situations, theatrical ones, are better suited to creative video than location work, which is better for a movie. So ultimately, video is less spontaneous.

FFC: In the case of movies, like *Rumblefish* [1983], you can do wonderful neat stuff. Those of us who were first attracted to movies always had those few shots that, when they came back from the lab, you were more anxious to see how they came out. It's just that I reached a point, not long ago, where I was no longer interested in that. I was very much interested in the new medium that was going to be approaching as the years went by, a kind of electronic cinema. Not quite television, but some modern version of that—advanced video, or high resolution, whatever you want to call it. I got involved with "Rip Van Winkle" just so I could continue to learn, try out a few ideas, and do my best.

Also, the process is very enjoyable. It didn't take very long—like a week of rehearsal and then you were shooting—and that meant the focus was more on acting and ideas than on this kind of slow molasses method of making some movies. Personally, I really enjoyed myself a lot. It was like doing a play in college. But I would love to do a fable that was very realistic and then one that was realistic and maybe live, without any cinema editing at all.

RG: Do you have any ideas of how to implement that?

FFC: No. I mean, if someone said to me, "Francis, how would you like to do *The Caine Mutiny Court-Martial* on TV and do it live?," I would do it. Of course, I'd rather do something original from a book or some story. But I would take any opportunity. I would love to direct for even a few months. I can't, but I'd like to do a soap opera. That's my dream.

RG: Just because you could work quickly?

FFC: Just to learn about it, basically. They say that a person really has one idea or two in his lifetime. I am working up to mine, and I feel it has very much to do with television and live-style television and twenty-four-track recording style. It has to do with a type of television evolved because of advances not only in video, but in computer science and all sorts of systems and electronics.

RG: Maybe you could have a group, maybe *Faerie Tale Theatre* is a prototype of such an organization.

FFC: They just did the fairy tales, but they were able to turn out a full-blown dramatic production every six weeks using the resources of video, cinema, matting, and all the aids to production and then, of course, found a way to sell it, to get sponsorship. That's a really exciting thing to be connected with.

RG: But what about this idea that you're working toward? Do you think there's an idea that is synonymous with the new technology that isn't evident yet?

FFC: I don't talk about the types of work I would do because it's easier to talk about the technology. The idea is very hard to explain. I could probably explain it to you very well if we spent hours and hours and said, "OK, let's start from the beginning." But the truth, it's still coming into focus for me.

Basically, what I'm really interested in is becoming a writer of original, full-length dramatic material for an audiovisual medium, whatever it is. I'd be very interested in being a writer who could sit down, as I'm doing here, to explore to the best of my ability whatever my ideas and fantasies are, and then to know that I have a way to do it and to actually produce it for a cost that is not prohibitive, that is not so much that they won't let me do it. It's like a writer who wanted to have the theatre company of his dreams.

I went to college, a little one,* and you'd see, oh, my God, they have a radio station. Well, then you could write radio plays. Somehow the fact that you had the radio station or the little theater came first, and then second, what you could do with it. In a way, it is as important. The theatre has always had those people who loved what it was in terms of the greasepaint, the fly system,† the lighting board, the scenery, and the actresses. What's the difference why you love something, if you love it? So, I do very much come to television with a love for it because it made its impressions on me. I mean, I'm a kid, born in 1939, and in 1945, I was six and saw this thing. A Motorola television. In 1946 we had one. And so I fantasized about television for almost as long as I can remember.

It's interesting. When I was fifteen, I wanted to be a playwright. I didn't know if I could be a good playwright, but that just suited me to a tee. And I tried writing plays, and they were never any good. But finally, just being good at science, I was the guy who ran the light board for the shows at school, and that's how I got to be in that crowd. And then, putting up the lights on the ladder, I would look down and watch them rehearsing and see the director and say, I could do as well as that. So I started directing, but I started directing sort of on the same level as starting on the light board.

But what I really wanted to be was a writer. I had a big success during college when I was young. I directed a Eugene O'Neill play that I won an award for and I became the new student director at Hofstra College. But I wanted to be a playwright.

But then one day I went to see a movie at four o'clock in the afternoon. It was Eisenstein's *Ten Days that Shook the World* [1928]. I had never heard of him, but I was so overwhelmed by this film that I said, I want to be a movie director. So, I did. I became a movie director. But then, a few years ago, after *Apocalypse*, what I really wanted to do was a kind of super television. Television taken to its full potential to be able to interpret dramatic subjects. That's why I want a studio and I want to make that studio an electronics studio, so that some day it would have a company of actors, and it would have a means to essentially be a glorified *Faerie Tale Theatre*. I tried to have that studio and maybe it got pretty much out of hand, it was so big. But even so, whether it's big or small, now I know that I want to work in this new medium and learn about it.

---

*ED: Hofstra College, now Hofstra University, in Hampstead, New York.
†ED: The system that controls the movement of the scenery.

RG: I get the impression most filmmakers have some kind of phobia about video, that there's something they think they might lose in the transition. Maybe that's because video is in some sort of incipient stage of development.

FFC: It is in a new phase of development. More importantly, people in their time are ruled much more by social conditions. It's enough to turn people off that video is considered kind of second class and cinema is the big deal. Television has been regulated and it's been said that we don't have exciting original work done for television so much, that people shy away from it. But that shouldn't give the medium itself a bad name. I almost wish we had a new name for television because it's waiting for the new artists in the country—writers and actors and directors. It's going to be their instrument.

RG: Do you recall when was the first time you saw or used a videotape recorder?

FFC: I remember very vividly because I was a real child of television and just obsessed with learning about it. My dad was on television in the symphony once a week. At one point, they called me in and said, "Look, Daddy's on television." So I ran to see it and there he was on television. And I couldn't believe it, because he was right over there in the room. And of course, it was videotape. I had never seen videotape. It looked so real. This was about 1956.

But after that I went to visit the UCLA film school and they had an early tape recorder there. And just the idea of having access to a videotape recorder seemed to me like having a rocketship. Then, when they began to come out with the first reel-to-reel home recorder, I would get every one. I have every model of every one. I even had the little one-quarter inch that Akai put out. When I was a little kid, we had a pretty big house for a while, with these big recreation rooms. I was always given a place for a shop. When I was eleven or ten, I built, on a full scale, wooden TV cameras and sound booms. I had in the basement recreation room a window that had a square in it and I used to play television. There was a wooden board you could hold for the microphone, and you would get the kids over and pretend you were videotaping. So I always had the idea of having a television capability. And I always had an audiotape recorder. I had been stricken with polio so I got a lot of gifts the year I was paralyzed.

So I did follow very, very carefully all of the developments, and knew a lot about it. I knew about Philo Farnsworth* and Dr. Zworkin.† I had my own systems that I used to put down on paper. In fact, I worked very hard on a color system in the days when the first color systems were pioneered. The system I devised as a child was very similar to the RCA system, except it had lines of color phosphors rather than dots.

---

*ED: Inventor who patented process of electronic image analysis and synthesis that we know as television.
†ED: Vladimir K. Zworkin tried to buy Farnsworth's patents without success. Developed television camera.

RG: Were you building any equipment yourself?

FFC: No, but I did build a television, when I was fourteen, from a kit. I knew that in the early days of color television there was a dispute on the CBS color wheel. I was one of the kids that followed that stuff and understood how it worked. I built a mechanical television with a large rotating drum, covered with a spiral pattern of pieces of mirrors. When it rotated a beam of light would scan the subject and be read by a photoelectric cell.

RG: How does this lead up to your use of video for *Apocalypse Now?*

FFC: With *Apocalypse Now*, since we were in those very difficult jungle locations, we found that we were never able to view any of the work. Dealing with projection was very tough. So we started to transfer the rushes to video. The video was actually transferred in L.A., but we bought a couple of those very first Beta 1 machines. I had one in a little hut and I used to get these cassettes and plug them in and see it. After a while, I was lugging this Beta around. I even put it on a houseboat floating down the river so we were able to see material and make decisions for reshooting and that kind of thing. Then a very interesting use developed when we got this job of making *Godfather I* [1972] and *Godfather II* [1974] into a special television feature for NBC. They were willing to pay a lot for it. I was in the Philippines, so the editor arrived with all the *Godfather I* and *Godfather II* on tape. It was funny because there were big typhoons and we were running around with this Beta machine in helicopters. Whenever we stopped we would use the Betamax to make decisions since we didn't have editing capabilities. At one point, we landed in some bombed-out place in the helicopter. We couldn't get any 110 [electrical current] because we didn't have a transformer. So, a helicopter pilot went into the kitchen where there was a washer/dryer and literally ripped the transformer off the wall. We plugged it in and that's how we made that NBC special.

RG: Do you think there will be the money and the channels, literally and figuratively, for the number of aspiring writers and video makers to get into and make an impact?

FFC: To predict how it's going to be for artists in the future.... It's not so much, "What could it be for the artists?" Because you have to go back and wonder about the history of the industry itself. It depends on who's running it, but it seems that the new video is something like television after World War II. It's something that really would connect with the writing talent, the design talent, the acting talent of the country if only there was a way for the three to come together. Right now, television is controlled, if not by the networks then the big cable companies, and if not by them, then by the big video cassette companies. It's a business like fast food. It's not like a national cultural interest. So it's hard to predict what's going to happen.

RG: Getting back to your story concept, the one you're working toward. Aren't there any contemporary issues or stories that stimulate you enough to say, "This is a new story," even if it's told with traditional beginning, middle and end? For instance, the nuclear threat.

FFC: No. I'm so bored with all those kinds of political films. I don't think it's the way to change the world and I don't think it's the way to deal with the issues. I feel that it's chipping away with a spoon at a wall so big. All the well-worn political issues that people choose to think they're being relevant and constructive with do not interest me. It's mainly that they announce themselves as political films. I like political work that sneaks up on you. I admire, to a small extent, those people. But I feel, in a way, that it isn't revolutionary work at all. That's like establishment revolutionary. We all know, at any given time that there are worthy causes related to either disarmament or peace. And then there's establishment press and movie business—but it's all entrenched, even the political areas. I'm interested in an area that is perhaps so radical that people don't even see it as political yet.

RG: Have you always felt this way? Or has it evolved over the years?

FFC: I've always been really turned off by the current political issues of the day. I find that people who gravitate toward that are, for the most part, just another version of the people who are in the establishment. I find them inordinately interested in power, fame, and money. I feel that they just see that as an area that's available and they go in there and rabble rouse. I don't respect them for the most part.

RG: After *One from the Heart* [1982], Vittorio Storaro told me that he thought everything you were doing was already ten years ahead of itself.

FFC: That's why we're so broke. That's why I'm in such trouble. *[Laughter.]*

RG: Do you still think we'll be able to beam pictures through satellite for movies rather than using film projectors in theaters as we know them today? And do you look forward to that?

FFC: I never talked about the kind of distribution methods. But there have been some breakthroughs. One of them is the writable videodisc. That has been a missing link, the write/read disc. The way it works is that each disc can have, say, twenty to thirty minutes each. I mean the discs are that fast. Right now, we organize a cassette for it to be simple. We have really gotten good at the librarian aspect. We don't put a lot of information on a cassette, so your random access is the old random access. But with the disc, the speed is extraordinary. With one hundred discs, you might have the rushes for a whole movie with one or two changes. Let's say you don't have any changes and instead you have twenty discs and each one has an hour [of rushes]. You don't have to worry about searching out the right scene, take, or time code because it's all available to you. The disc is capable of getting it so fast that your editorial time is going to be almost immediate.

RG: And then on a screen, you could add words, and the scene would appear on the monitor, parallel the sound track. You could also pull up or parallel the sound track.

FFC: That goes into my interest. So far, few people are interested in it, for some reason. I've done so much work in scriptwriting that I know the value of being able to put your hand over there and have that line for that take. That's what I'm after. There would be text connected to image and sound. So whether you move the image or the text around—or move the sounds around—each of its fraternal cousins will move accordingly. So that if you take control and you want to run the image forward, the script will be going forward, too.

Now the area that there hasn't been a big breakthrough is, and of course it's eagerly awaited by many people, a large-screen television format that's got clarity and luster. That would make a big difference to the field.

RG: Would that be something comparable to what we see at a closed-circuit fight, or better?

FFC: Yes, but that's the point. The best ones, Eidophor, cost $700,000 and the one under that is $100,000. There's got to be a time when people have large-screen televisions that are really sharp and clear like a monitor and don't cost that much. When that exists, then start talking about distribution.

We know, in terms of distribution, that cable satellite, microwave beams, and fiber optics are all ways to transmit images and sounds. They all work great and what they then have is a television set at the end of that. And the image of the television set is inferior to the transmission process. Right now, I look more to finishing the show on television and then transferring it to film because there are 35mm [film] projectors all over the world already. They're cheap and people know how to use them.

RG: What would be an ideal TV format to shoot on to achieve that transfer?

FFC: The new high definition format which they're pushing as a world standard, which is definitely improved television.

RG: You mean like the European PAL television system?

FFC: The NHK, the Japanese system, with 1,125 lines. I'm talking about the very best television image and transferring it to film. I believe the image would be acceptable for a movie.

RG: And by the time you get to a release print the quality is just as good?

FFC: It looks like film. It is film, because in the end that's what it is. You're projecting an image through light. I've always been interested in doing that and doing productions electronically and then releasing them in film. I don't think that the big-screen, quality television screens are going to be around for maybe another four to eight years, but we've got all the other parts—the writable disc, high-definition. . .

RG: Why is there this continual lack of standardization among countries and within the industry?

FFC: It's greed. There's no reason other than that and vested interests and political interest trying to control something that belongs to people. Technology is the product of humanity and belongs to humanity. I mean, how is it that some small, little vested group is going to determine how technology is used? It's bad enough that big groups like Eastman Kodak and IBM do it by using their wealth to buy up all the research talent and then release it as it benefits the company rather than the public. I'm tired of companies using technology, which is supposed to benefit mankind, to benefit their profit position.

And then with high-definition, I read these letters from people who own television stations. You know that all they're saying is, "Look, we had a great thing that made millions since 1946 on television, and now if you change it to make it better it's going to affect us. We would rather still make the dough than improve television."

Television in this country is a disgrace. We're stuck to that 1956 NTSC nonsense. We should have television that is as gorgeous as any image you can have in the world. And we're capable of doing it.

RG: Ultimately, is it safe to say that what you're looking to achieve, at least personally, is something in the new technology that will be a marriage between film style and video technique?

FFC: Except, to be more accurate, I see it as a marriage of film and television, in particular of live television. When I say "live television," what I mean is television at its most elemental form, which is multicamera, live television production. Combine that with twenty-four-track audio production; which is to say, treat the video images that you get that way and be able to bounce them around on your video tracks in a way that you are treating the video pretty much the way audio is treated in sophisticated record production. Combine that with theater with its visual tradition of lighting effects and live action performances. Then add cinema with its great tradition of camera angles and editing. Take all of those mediums and put them into one super medium: Super Television.

RG: Do you ever get the impression that the communications industry and the film industry are afraid of the progress you're pursuing, or that they're afraid of you?

FFC: Yes, I do get that impression. They're afraid that if I ever got the chance, I'd change their lives. And they're right. But I'm only one representative of the times. You can be sure that other people are going to be doing the same kind of stuff, and the world is going to change. Right in our lifetime.

RG: How did you get interested in *Faerie Tale Theatre?*

FFC: I was interested in *Faerie Tale Theatre* because as a child I was interested in fairy tales and felt especially close to them. Then later, when I was a little older, there was a program on the radio called "Let's Pretend,"* which was a fairy tale anthology series that I thought was really great. As a little kid I just liked those kind of stories. Many kids are like that, but for me it was my special interest.

When I noticed that Shelley [Duvall] started to do the fairy tales, I saw that it was a less expensive way of doing television. I saw several of them. So when the chance arrived, I was very anxious to do one, although it was on very short notice for everyone. I just figured that this was my opportunity to experiment with something in the television format, which I'd always wanted to do.

RG: Was "Rip Van Winkle" your choice?

FFC: It was theirs. They offered me several possible stories.

RG: In your preparation for "Rip Van Winkle," was there anything technical that you wanted to experiment with that you hadn't before?

FFC: Yes. I wanted it to have a number of different areas of experimentation. For one thing, I wanted the landscape visuals to become an important part of the story. In other episodes of *Faerie Tale Theatre,* they approached the shows in a somewhat realistic way. They usually build little sets, and in a couple they experimented with Ultimatte†—its background capability. I wanted to see if I could come up with a way to use those facilities in a style unique to this show.

"Rip Van Winkle" doesn't have much of a story. We all know something of it, but there isn't this whole complicated narrative with conflict. So I thought, this was an American fairy tale, and the mood and the environment we could create visually might be really something to work with. In particular, when I talked to the company, I said, "I want to make a Kabuki fairy tale. I want to use Kabuki techniques."

RG: You've been interested in that for a long time. *One from the Heart* was a project you made reference to as having Kabuki elements.

FFC: Kabuki, as I use it, is really that point at which the scenery and the settings connect with the main ideas of the story in a freer way, almost as though the scenery is a character. In other words, if I say, "They walked for twenty-five miles," there might be a way that Kabuki would move a curtain a little bit, or do something that shows they had walked twenty-five miles. So it was a way that

---

*ED: Created, written, and produced by former Vaudeville and Broadway actress Nila Mack, the series began in 1929 as "The Adventures of Helen and Mary." Mack joined the Saturday Morning Show in 1930 and was responsible for the re-enactments and adaptations of classic fairy tales and fantasies.
†Ultimatte is a device by which the points of view of two or more video cameras can be "matted," or, essentially, superimposed. Unlike matting processes for film, which are carefully planned and completed in a laboratory, the effects of Ultimatte are visible immediately.

the scenic element and the cast complement and reinforce one another. We have one scene, for instance, where Rip Van Winkle is out there sleeping on the mountain and he's freezing and you see the mountain shiver.

Several years ago, I directed the play *Private Lives* in San Francisco, and I did a kind of unusual production, the seeds of which, really, were where *One from the Heart* sprang from. I treated the play so that a lot of the songs commented on the action, although they weren't sung by the performers. But then I also liked the notion that the performers could, at a certain moment, burst into song. It didn't have to be so unified. And I think that that, along with some investigation of Japanese theater I've been doing over the years, influenced me. Specifically, the notion that in Japanese theater, all the elements—the scenery, the music, the dancing, the singing—step forward to tell that part of the story which each element can best tell. So if someone is going to take a journey for so many miles, maybe the curtain would move. You can get at emotion in Oriental theater in a lot more different ways than just Freudian naturalism.

With "Rip Van Winkle," I did some of that. You know the settings are not real, but you accept them as not being real, and in return for their not being real, they are more animated and they tell their share of the story. It seemed that since this was a fable, sort of whimsical, without a lot of plot, I thought all that would be appropriate.

Also, I don't know why, but I associate America and Japan. I always do. Something of what America had in those days, the magic of the Indians and the Catskill Mountains and something really new, virginal and exciting. Somehow I thought we might be able to express that as well. It just seemed a lot of things to try to do in one little story.

RG: Did you have any kind of Kabuki orientation in *The Cotton Club* [1984]? There are the elaborate, beautiful sets, and a sense of convergence between reality and fantasy, of things happening in the streets or the train station that would ordinarily take place in the club, and vice-versa.

FFC: *Cotton Club*, in my mind, always was related to *One from the Heart* somehow—the theatricality of it, artifice of it. I tried to make *Cotton Club* within that theatrical style but relatively realistic. There was nothing in there that was strange, that you couldn't explain. Whereas *One from the Heart* had walls that became transparent and stuff that was extremely theatrical. "Rip Van Winkle" is even further in that direction. I'm just very interested in that subject and those techniques and trying to learn more about it. To put it in the simplest way, I wish I could work by having a great big stage and video capability and just make up movies and stories.

"Rip Van Winkle" is extremely theatrical. It's a little stylized thing, like a little operetta, but you could also make films in which their impact would be a lot more interesting and dramatic if they moved a little bit more in that direction. If they said, "OK, you're going to get what you want," I'd rather go in and experiment with that than making movies in a conventional way. Because I feel that, for the cinema, not for other filmmakers but for me, my real interest is somewhere else. Always has been.

RG: Video, because of its technical nature, seems to lend itself best to overstated, exaggerated theatrical imagery, "hot" imagery in a sense. Film is more adept at picking up subtlety and texture. Did you find this to be true with "Rip Van Winkle?"

FFC: I think you can work a tremendous variety of all sorts of styles to either a great degree or a lesser degree, depending on the needs of the story. Video has great range. It's like comparing a synclavier music synthesizer to a piano. The piano can play piano like nothing else can, and nobody can play a piano like a piano, but a clavier can do piano and everything else. The electronic medium is like that. If you want to work in a style of theatricality, you can. "Rip Van Winkle" is that, but it wouldn't have to be, though it's hard to play a fairy tale like *On the Waterfront* [1954]. But it could have been a story depicted in a very realistic way of acting.

But you know what it is? The first time out, when you get the chance to work in it, you're almost a little brainwashed to think that it has to be that kind of theatre or style because you certainly can't do that in the movies. I wish that I could do six of them in a row, or a soap opera every day. I'm not kidding when I say you have to learn about it. You've got to see how the medium responds.

RG: Did you use three cameras* when you shot a given scene?

FFC: We did use three cameras because the three cameras came with the package, and we really weren't quite sure how the mattes were going to work. In other words, the show was conceived for the Ultimatte, and it was a new edition Ultimatte. One of the abilities the Ultimatte had was that you could add dimensions to the background live. We had five dancers under the blanket [to form a moving] mountain, for example, and we photographed them and then put the mountain in, and then we could have another camera on the painting of clouds and Ultimatte that in. Technically, you could do that ad infinitum. You could create the frame of your movie the same way you'd add in a collage. You'd put your main actor there and possibly another actor. The frame becomes really plastic.

So we did run three cameras, but we very often had an Ultimatte-keyed preferred shot, and then other cameras would get anything else they could. Sometimes they got useful stuff, sometimes they didn't.

RG: Did you work from a storyboard so that you knew what kind of Ultimatte effects shots you wanted?

FFC: No, because, number one, we hadn't been preparing the show long enough to make a storyboard. They were wonderful over at the Theatre because we were

---

*Three cameras is customary for television production, whereas for film usually one camera is used.

a week away and we're talking about human mountains and stuff they hadn't even built. It was just a free-for-all. And I didn't know for sure what it was going to be, with the matted camera and everything.

You know, it looks good. If it hadn't looked so good, maybe we would have done something else, tried to get at the problem a different way. But in the overall, what we were hoping for was that the show had a style or a patina all its own, was unique and that was attractive and good for the story.

RG: They were pretty unflappable about having extraordinary or unusual ideas because they deal with that all the time.

FFC: That was what made it so nice for me. They were so trusting in so short a time. They could have said, "How about a little less far-out approach this time?" But a lot of it worked. Some of it didn't.

RG: Was there any difficulty or period of adjustment in moving from film to television work? The limitations of the [screen] ratio for example.

FFC: My experience was that once we were off and running, I was just out there yelling, "Get the thing in." You're only concerned to get done. You're out there and that's a wonderful kind of work because everyone is operating at their pitch and no one really knows what's going to happen. We just worked together.

My only thing is that when something happens with the actors that you feel is really lively and interesting and it doesn't conform to that, what do you do? You have to make a decision: am I going for the live version or the canned version? I go for the live version, and I always know that usually in the cutting room you can fix any problem you might have. The only thing is that the cutting was a difficult thing and it had to be done so quickly. I'm usually a little freer in the editorial process because you normally have so much more time.

RG: And here there's so much material to work with, considering the three cameras.

FFC: Yes. Television was a phenomenon of broadcasting, and broadcasting has a tradition of its own. The television tradition [of editing] comes from a guy cutting a little radio tape with a razor. That's editing in the broadcaster's mind. In the film person's mind, editing is Sergei Eisenstein.* So editing techniques and attitudes for video aren't really up to handling the image and sound in the same, very expressive way.

Film has been edited for sixty years by some of the great geniuses of our time, whereas video evolved more as an offshoot of broadcasting and had more mundane purposes. In other words, the tape recorder was invented by Ampex not so much as an incredible creative tool, but so they could do programming in New York and rebroadcast it. That is why they built it.

---

*ED: Russian film theorist and director, best known for *The Battleship Potemkin* (1925).

They didn't think they were ever going to sell more than ten of them. Somehow, video editing equipment has to be conceived more by film editors than by video editors. I feel that (as far as the equipment goes) someone has to take the gigantic technical advantages of video, but not lose sight of the tremendous literature or methodology of film. I feel that the video mentality when applied to editing is very limited compared to the film mentality, and rightly so. We have Eisenstein and we have [G. W.] Pabst.* We have all the great minds and they are the founding fathers of the medium. People who became video editors descended more from the technicians and broadcasters who were not really into the art. So, what I'd really like to find is a video editing system designed by a film mind.

My impression of a lot of good television, like *Faerie Tale Theatre,* is they do a scene in something of a set, and when they do it they are running several cameras. Those cameras are the legitimate coverage of that scene, so that if you just give them that tape [of the footage by the three cameras], it's crazy to cut that together. Whereas in "Rip Van Winkle," every shot was a different kind of idea, so it didn't all just fall in as though you've got a master shot and close-up. The shots were much more odd and not done in that way. It made it more interesting, but it also made it more time consuming.

RG: The footage I saw was gorgeous. It was hard to believe video could look that rich.

FFC: It was an attempt to make nice-looking television, to show people that the reason television looks so simplistic put side by side with cinema isn't the medium, but time and attitude in the way it's produced. And if you had a great lighting guy and a wonderful camera guy and a director who was anxious for the video to look beautiful. . . . You see in the videos they do for rock 'n' roll how gorgeous the stuff is, and some of that is video.

RG: Are you interested in rock videos?

FFC: I don't know. I'm not being modest, but I'd be a little scared to . . . all those guys with guitars.†

RG: I remember reading that you were very impressed and influenced by *A Hard Day's Night* [1964], which as a style is a kind of precursor to rock videos.

FFC: I thought *A Hard Day's Night* was fine, but those videos are so spectacular and fanciful it would be hard for me to sit down and think how I could do one that would be so good. You always hope you know how to do it. All these hip, young rock and roll guys. Kids would be able to do it better than I.

---

*ED: Austrian-born German stage and screen director, much influenced by Eisenstein and his theories related to montage.
†Coppola has since directed the 3-D "Captain EO" with Michael Jackson, one of the most popular attractions at Disneyland and Disneyworld. "Captain EO" was produced by George Lucas and photographed by Vittorio Storaro in the film medium.

RG: How close did you work with [*Faerie Tale* lighting director] George Riesenberger on getting light levels for "Rip?"

FFC: He was wonderful. A lot of times people get the picture of what you're trying to do, but decide they're going to pretend the whole time that they don't. It's their way of protesting the picture.

But George understood that I was trying to work with lighting in a way related to the scenic thing—very strong colors, people going into gold or to red or artsy mood lighting. He was just wonderful and quick and the whole thing was just done so fast.

And that's another thing. When you do production the regular way, it always goes faster. Everyone is used to the procedure. Whenever you start doing things in a weird way a little bit, then it takes a bit of time to get everyone on the team and for them to understand exactly what you mean. They were kind enough to let me do the show in this sort of way and were pretty supportive, because definitely it was a tougher way to do it and without assured results.

Some of it is always bound to be interesting. There's nothing worse than when you get a movie and you realize you got what you expected and there's not one wrinkle in it. I watch movies a lot on cassette at home because we don't get television here. You have to buy a dish and we have not. It's an advantage. What I like is when you get a movie with something really interesting in it. It might be something that you want to watch a second time. That's a thrill when you get a movie that you want to watch a second time.

RG: What are some of your favorite movies? What are the ones that are most important to you?

FFC: I was very impressed with *Ashes and Diamonds* [1958], and with films like *I Vitellone* [1953] by Fellini. As I said, I was very impressed the first time I saw Eisenstein, and also Kurosawa, Kubrick's *Dr. Strangelove* [1964]. But I also loved *Lawrence of Arabia* [1962] and movies like that. Of the directors of my generation, I like Billy Friedkin's *The French Connection* [1971], George Lucas' *THX 1138* [1971] and *American Graffiti* [1973], Scorsese's *Mean Streets* [1973], and I enjoy Spielberg's films.

RG: Was there anything about the "Rip Van Winkle" production that surprised you, or that you benefited by, unexpectedly?

FFC: It's hard for me to put them into something like nice quotes. You know how sometimes when you're learning, say, the piano or the typewriter or the automobile, you start to get the knack of it more through the way you feel, the feeling of competence you get. I would say that as a result of this opportunity with *Faerie Tale Theatre*, although I could make fifty statements, it's more what I feel—comfortable and having something of the hang of it. I want to go back to my next lesson. You know, so many things turned out to be exactly as I expected and so many were not.

RG: For instance . . .

FFC: Well, the manipulation of the three cameras. And the fact that when you're doing very general types of lighting you create a lot of latitude of what it looks like with three cameras, because it's in a way destroying the directionality of depth of the light and it sort of makes it easy to shoot. But the more we gave the thing a look with the angle and the light and the other techniques, the more the other cameras had no place they could get a shot. And I'm confirmed in my feelings that just to rely on long lenses, when you want to reach out and get a close shot, you only get a very low level close shot. You don't get a beautiful close shot, which is much better with a slightly shorter lens put in the right place with the lighting being right. We tended to get them with the other, the B and C cameras, by reaching out with the long lenses.

So one of the things I would really want to think about carefully and one of the reasons I would like to do a live show is to work on my camera work. I would like to do a show with four cameras like John Frankenheimer did when he did live TV* to see if I could do it. That's why I would like to practice and maybe even do a soap opera, a dramatic story without the fairy tale stuff.

Something I did learn was not to let television fool you into thinking the performance should be simply broader or more theatrical. The performance should be extremely realistic, just like film. If I had to do it over again, I would have played it more realistic. I was so involved in so many elements of it that I almost wasn't thinking. We just started doing it that way because the script was written. But I think if I was going to criticize myself or to say something I learned, it would be that video responds to that same kind of believable, realistic acting style. Harry Dean Stanton is such a naturalistic actor, anyway. And the best ones are the ones who are the movie actors.

I could go through one hundred things that I learned. But just as I thought, it's a plastic, versatile, tremendous new instrument that no one has felt. It's like music, and music has Mozart and Beethoven, who have written masterpieces. But here's a medium that's so new that there isn't anyone who has even written anything for it or done anything with it yet compared with what is going to happen with it in the next fifty years. It's the instrument of youth. The young people are going to make it come alive.

RG: You've always been a pioneer in the use of sound for movies and sound technology. Is there anything unique in terms of sound for "Rip Van Winkle"?

FFC: We were going to try something a little novel. Instead of the regular video sound that economics and time force on the production, we were going to give it a slightly more developed soundtrack, more the way a movie soundtrack is done with someone really working to design a combination of music and sound

---

*ED: Frankenheimer directed *You Are There* for a time, and over one hundred television plays, including many for *Playhouse 90*.

effects. It will be very expressive. It will underscore the visual style. They are making it possible to get Richard Beggs [Academy Award for sound for *Apocalypse Now*], who does my movies. He's going to take it and see what happens.

RG: Was there anything unusual about the editing?

FFC: Murdo [Laird, Zoetrope's chief engineer, Electronic Cinema Division] edited and did an excellent job. He didn't have a lot of time to do it, and a lot of it was spent in the nightmare of video editing.

    We ourselves have a project at Zoetrope, a video editing system we hope will someday be available to us. It's a piece of software that uses disc editing. The disc is going to make a big difference. Laser Edit in Burbank, where the on-line was done [for "Rip Van Winkle"], has a disc installation system. I sense that video editing still has the big road to go to come close to what you can do in film editing, as I was saying. Film editing is totally mechanical and infinitely more precise. Video takes you through a series of elaborate rerecordings to get at it. But I'm really confident that in the near future the right methodology will be found. I think that's what it is—methodology.

    There are some people who have some formidable hardware for doing various jobs, but the television editor's mind and people designing the video systems pretty much design them for broadcasting people, the networks and the big companies that buy them. But that kind of so-called television network editing is very different from motion picture editing and very different from what it has to do, what its job is and how it manipulates the soundtrack. We're just not there yet in terms of a real editing system that can really cut like a movie editor can. So we're dreaming that up. We're working on one.

CHAPTER THREE

Sydney Pollack

LEO BRAUDY AND MARK CRISPIN MILLER

The following comments by director Sydney Pollack were made in Baltimore, Maryland, in May 1983, after a screening of *Tootsie* and *They Shoot Horses, Don't They?* The exchange, including questions from the audience, was moderated by Leo Braudy, then of Johns Hopkins University, now of the University of Southern California, and Mark Crispin Miller, then of Johns Hopkins University, now of New York University.

LEO BRAUDY: You have directed a lot of the top actors in Hollywood, the biggest moneymakers, and you are known, in fact, as a performer's director. Do you choose projects in that way? Are you more attracted to working with particular performers or are you more attracted to scripts?

SYDNEY POLLACK: Working with name performers, as you call it, is more of a habit than anything else. The first film I did was in 1965, and it had two of the previous year's Academy Award winners in it. It was kind of a fluke that I got to do it. I'd been directing television and the project was offered to me with them already in it. Actually, one of the original stars of the movie was an ex-student of mine when I taught acting, Elizabeth Ashley, who was subsequently replaced by Anne Bancroft. The two people were Sidney Poitier and Anne Bancroft. By the time I was halfway finished with that I was asked to be interviewed by Natalie Wood. She was looking for a director for her next film, *This Property*

FIGURE 3. Sydney Pollack during production of *Havana* (1990). Courtesy: Jerry Ohlinger Archives.

is Condemned, and there was this new star, Robert Redford, whom she'd found in a play called *Barefoot in the Park*. I had an interview with her. She chose her directors. This was 1965–66 and she was at the zenith of her career. By the time I had done those two then and gone ahead and done a couple of pictures with Burt Lancaster,* I just got used to them. I didn't pick a picture for a star necessarily, although I've done five films with Redford and quite often we'll just get together and look for a film to do, as we're doing now. In that case, I would be very specifically looking to see if there is a role for him to play. But normally, I'm looking for a particular film as a film, and what happens with the stars becomes secondary. Curiously enough, I don't think I've ever made a film without stars, but quite often I started to do it.

LB: So many of your films have a strong central character, or one or two strong central characters; that seems to make them films that concentrate on character rather than, let's say, a total directorial vision in which characters are subordinate.

SP: I would say I've made films that are not precisely in that category: *Three Days of the Condor* [1975] is more of a narrative film, a film which is carried more by narrative drive, let's say; and *They Shoot Horses, Don't They?* [1969] has a certain sort of visual energy and style and is an ensemble kind of a picture, although the leading characters are very much the leading characters and it does rely on those performances. I think that's again because of my background as an acting teacher, and so the areas I was most comfortable in initially were areas of performance. What I had to learn when I went to Hollywood was which end of a camera to look through. I used to ask for close-ups with the feet in them. I didn't know what the hell a camera was about when I started. It took me a long time to learn that. But what I was always comfortable with was working with the actors.

LB: You would engage, then, in a collaborative endeavor with the actors in a film?

SP: It's a benevolent dictatorship. You still have to be the final arbiter of what happens, but the way that you have to coax a performance is largely psychological, too. You want the actors to feel as though they are creating as much of the performance as you are.

LB: Do you want to talk about *Tootsie* along these lines, or are you sick of talking about your relationship with Dustin Hoffman? We all heard that there was a duel going on between the two of you, and you incorporated that into the script. Is that inaccurate?

SP: No, no, no, no, no. That didn't get incorporated into the script at all. It happens that there's a scene where I say as an agent to him, "You're difficult, nobody will work with you." Sometimes life and art cross a little, but the stories are greatly exaggerated. You couldn't make a movie with as much ill will as has been reported in the newspapers. We would've killed each other. We did argue sometimes, but

---

The Scalphunters (1968) and *Castle Keep* (1969).

I can remember only one time when voices got raised. We never argued on the set. If we were going to have an argument, we'd go off in a room somewhere and argue, and that was not a regular happening. The directorial work itself went very smoothly. He's a wonderful actor to direct, and moment by moment on the set we got along fine. We had slightly different points of view about what the picture was going to be, and that was usually the basis for one of our several arguments. Only one got vocally out of hand, where there was some real yelling going on, but again I say never in front of the cast, or anything like that. I think Dustin wanted to make more of an homage to actors while I wanted to do something more about men and women, if you will, more of a gentle love story that really probed what the similarities and the differences precisely are, if there are any. I mean, other than plumbing. And I would say that Dustin has a slightly more outrageous sense of humor than I do. I don't say one is better than the other, just different. Dustin's sense of humor is more bawdy than mine, so occasionally something that he would think was funny, I would think was not funny, or I would think was in bad taste, let's say. And we might argue about that. Our way of solving a lot of these problems was the way any adults try to solve a problem. That is, I tried to convince him my way was right, he tried to convince me his way was right. One of us usually succeeded in convincing the other. If we could not come to some sort of agreement, we would shoot it both ways, in which case I had the clear advantage because I had the final cut. So it was very easy for me to pretend to be benevolent and say, "OK, we'll do it your way if you'll do it my way," and I could just cut out what I didn't want. He had lots of wonderful ideas, and we used lots and lots of his ideas. I don't say for a moment that I was right and he was wrong or he was right and I was wrong; that's not what happened. I do think it would've been a different film if we had done it his way and I don't know that it wouldn't have been better, it just would've been different. It would've been a more bawdy film, more outrageous, slightly more crude, let's say, more in the direction you would think you're going to go when you've got a guy with false breasts and a false bottom on.

LB: Did you ever find that your scenes with him derived some of their energy from your continuing . . .

SP: No. If that were true, I wouldn't be able to play Oedipus unless I slept with my mother. That's not the way acting works. It makes a good story, but that's about all. Yes, it's true that Dustin does not want to be told by anybody that he's difficult, and, yes, it's true that I occasionally found Dustin very trying and very difficult, but it is also true in some cases that it can help your acting if a relationship has certain elements of tension. For example, one of the reasons I got talked into that role is that most of the actors suggested for the role Dustin begged me not to use because he kept on saying, "They are peers of mine, they are equals. I do not look on them as authority figures. When those people say, 'You are never going to work again,' I don't believe it's going to make me put the dress on. But if *you* say to me, 'You're never going to work again,' I think I'd probably put the dress on." That's really how he talked me into doing the role. It's not something I wanted to do, it's not something I would ever do again if I were directing. The start of our argument, to tell the truth, was that he kept saying please do it. He sent me two dozen red roses with a note saying, "Please be my agent. Love, Dorothy." We also had a problem with the picture in that we didn't have what we always refer to as a gun. In *Some Like it Hot* [1959], you literally had a gun to force them into the dress. Those two guys were going to be killed by mobsters unless they found a way to get out of town. But here we had a problem. It took us months and months and months and we tried it one hundred fifty ways, saying what in the hell is going to make this guy put a dress on? At one time, we were actually going to have him see *Some Like it Hot* on television and click, the light bulb goes on. Finally, we ended up doing it just by threatening him that he would never work again.

LB: It's funny that you talk about the direction that way because you frequently have in your films a nasty director, a bad director, the one who tells people to do bad things, or forces them into some kind of mold, who makes Redford put on all those electric lights [in *The Electric Horseman*, 1969]. Does the idea of semibenevolent director in the film follow a certain line of interest?

SP: Yes. They are cast as villainous roles except I always try to make them relatively sympathetic because I don't really believe in black hats and white hats. Gig Young in *They Shoot Horses, Don't They?* is clearly the guy who is profiting from all this misery, but on the other hand, I think you have a certain odd sympathy with him in the picture. I tried to keep him from coming off as a cold-blooded, unfeeling villain. There's something almost pathetic about him; you feel that he's as much a victim as they are.

MARK CRISPIN MILLER: Sure, now he's just as much in it as they are. He just has that kind of momentary power over them.

SP: Exactly, exactly.

LB: This theme runs through many of your films, even though it sometimes becomes abstract in, say, *Three Days of the Condor*.

SP: I always feel like I'm defending dumbness when I get asked a question like that because the hardest thing is to be correct and accurate in analyzing yourself; it's very,very hard for me to look at my work with any real objectivity. Most of the things I think about my work have come from reading critics. I read people who say, well, Pollack is preoccupied with so and so and I say, yeah, I guess so. I guess that's what I'm preoccupied with. I have to find what I would call an "armature" when I work. In sculpting, an armature is something that's hidden from view, but really supports the piece of work. Sometimes it's a wadded up ball of paper, sometimes it's a piece of hanger wire that you bend together, then you put clay over it and sculpt it into shape It's holding everything up, but it's invisible to most people who are watching. I come to a picture with my own subjective point of view, and then I quite often am shocked when I read what it's about from an objective point of view. Sure, certain things we all know. We know that *They Shoot Horses, Don't They?* is an existential picture which deals with man's inhumanity to man. You don't have to be a genius to know that. But my armature had to do with a certain kind of courage, which is what interested me. There was no reason whatsoever for those people to keep coming back every time the siren went off. And the fact that they did was very moving to me, which is why I did the film. Certain characters must have some sort of psychological significance to me that I don't precisely understand, because I keep using them, but I don't do it on purpose. It happens unconsciously, and I think that's part of any real art. You can develop a technique and understand what choices are possible, but you cannot develop the mechanism that makes you make the choice, which is talent, and that is largely a function of your unconscious. I don't like to mess with it too much because, if I start getting self-conscious about those choices, then I'm going to start imitating myself. If I read over and over and over again that I make circular films and that the people end where they began then I start thinking, "Jesus, now I've got to make this thing end the way it began because otherwise it won't be a picture like my other pictures." I do believe very much what T. S. Eliot said: that the purpose of all our wandering is to arrive at the point where we started and know it for the first time, which is a line in *Four Quartets*. I do think that's a preoccupation of mine and I do think it's in the films.

LB: *They Shoot Horses, Don't They?* has a political dimension, it is a vision of-the American system . . .

SP: It's a film of the sixties. I made it in '69. I was considerably younger myself then, and it's a young film of mine and it's an angry film and it's very much a product of the sixties. I wouldn't go off and do that film today necessarily, and if I did, I wouldn't do it that way.

LB: So you didn't see it strictly as a period piece when you made it.

SP: Oddly enough, the seven films I made before *Three Days of the Condor* were all period films, again for inexplicable reasons. Then I did *Three Days of the Condor* and since then I have not done a period film. Maybe I got to a certain age where I wanted to deal with or speak more directly to contemporary problems, I don't know, but I did think of *Horses* as a period film that was relevant to the sixties.

LB: Would you compare it to *Castle Keep* [1969], which also has a kind of heavy irony?

SP: Yes.

LB: And chaotic sixties techniques?

SP: Yes, they're both films of the sixties for me. I think of *They Shoot Horses, Don't They?* as an antiwar film, oddly enough, and I did think of *Castle Keep* as the same kind of film, but I was in my late twenties, early thirties, when I was making those films, and now I'm a little bit embarrassed sometimes that it gets laid on pretty thick in some spots.

LB: In your more recent films, your heroes tend to beat the system: Paul Newman in *Absence of Malice* [1981] and Dustin Hoffman in *Tootsie* [1982]. It's more exhilarating than the end of *Horses!*

SP: That is *not* a real laugh a minute.

MCM: The earlier films are more pessimistic in a way. The line that Jane Fonda has in *Horses* about "Central Casting has it all figured out before you come there" seems to sum up the tone of many of those earlier films. But with *Absence of Malice* and *Tootsie* and *Jeremiah Johnson* [1972], the films become much more positive and open and not so fatal and circular.

SP: Yes, I think *Tootsie* is the most optimistic of the films. All the films are love stories. I've never made a film that isn't a love story. But I've never done a love story where the two people end up together; again, I don't know why. In *Tootsie* they almost do, that's as close as I could get them. I thought about it and I said, "No, I don't believe they would actually walk off together but maybe they're getting along." Maybe in the next one, they'll end up in each other's arms.

MCM: Is that too much ending inside the film, you want it to go outside?

SP: It's partially that. I get asked the question often and first I try not to answer because I say, "Look, I don't know how to answer," but then I think about it and I say, "Why do I keep doing that, why do they not get together?" And usually I have to go back a ways and say I do a film because I don't understand something. That's the only way I can get motivated to do a film. I would never make a film that says something that I wanted to tell you because I would be bored and so would you, if I had to spend a year and a half doing something I already knew the answer to. I would probably end up lecturing you in some way. I do the films because they're a way of exploring an argument that I'm not quite sure of the answer to. In *Tootsie*, it has to do with masculinity and femininity: are the similarities more important than the differences finally? What precisely are the perimeters of masculinity and what precisely are the perimeters of femininity? I don't know the answer to those questions. If I did I wouldn't have made the film. What happens is that usually the metaphor for the question is placed in the hands of the male and female protagonists, and in trying to mine as deeply as possible the differences and be sympathetic to both of them, I usually end up creating such a rift that they can never reconcile it believably.

In other words, take a film like *The Way We Were* [1973]. In a certain way, I have great guilt about the fact that I don't leap on more barricades, go around with placards, give money to causes, and do all that. On the other hand, I also have great contempt for lots of my colleagues who at the drop of a hat are on any barricade for whatever reason. They have no life except to find some cause to join. This business of precisely what commitment is and what commitment is not and commitment versus noncommitment—you begin to argue that out on a deeper level and, say, give the Redford character a longer-range vision than the character that Streisand played, where she sees only as far as the cause and not what will happen two years from now or three years from now.

At a certain point, if I wanted those arguments to be equally compelling, and I try to defend both of the characters as strongly as I can, I get myself into a corner and at the end I say I don't believe these two people are ever going to be together. That's so even in a frothy little comedy like *The Electric Horseman*. Here are two people who would never spend five minutes together outside of the mountains somewhere. He can't even pronounce the name of the city she lives in. But up there away from all the external distractions, they have a terrific relationship for a short time—which I also believe in and offer a lot in the films, like *Condor*. Under this pressure cooker, what seem to be differences aren't really differences, they're cultural or they're moral or philosophical or racial or sexual as in *Tootsie*. But they're not basic differences. What *Tootsie* says finally is that he's not that much different than she is. They were good friends when he had the dress on; he was still himself, and they were capable of being terrific friends.

MCM: What's underneath then when all these things are stripped away?

SP: Human beings.

MCM: But is it that courage you were talking about before?

SP: It's courage and a kind of humanity, which means a real ability, I think, to care and encourage and nurture and reach out. Culturally, racially, morally, and philosophically, society or various societies keep piling on layers which destroy that. And you keep wanting to break through that. The perfect breakthrough occurs when he puts a dress on. If you were to ask any man to list the qualities most appealing in a woman, forgetting anything physical, most men would list qualities which we would all find most appealing in men. They would say patience, understanding, a sense of nurturing, empathy, sensitivity, or whatever. All of these are qualities that I certainly respect in men but they're not the qualities that society asks you to cultivate at the expense of strength, leadership, whatever, as a man. This guy is a good enough actor to know that he makes the role out of himself. So when he puts the dress on, something gets fired up in him and he makes contact with that part of him which is what society might say is feminine. It's human in a certain way, so when she says, "I miss Dorothy," he says, "You don't have to—she's right here." He is right, he has learned a lesson.

LB: It sounds as if you've worked with some of the best screenwriters in Hollywood, as if you really work with them.

SP: Very much so.

LB: You don't just wait for something to come over the transom.

SP: No, no, no, it doesn't happen that way. Sometimes something comes over the transom that's the germ of an idea that you can start with, but then it's a long, long, process of passing it through your own sensibilities so that it can be about what you're trying to make it. *Tootsie* was not at all about any of this when I got the script. *Tootsie* was a drag comedy, period. Teri Garr didn't exist as a character. Bill Murray, the roommate, didn't exist. George Gaynes, the lecherous soap opera guy, didn't exist. None of that stuff at the farm existed; the Julie character hardly existed. Her boyfriend was not the director of the soap opera, and he was not at all a chauvinistic, lecherous guy. But what was there was the situation of a guy who, in order to get work, had to put a dress on.

And when I first got the material, I turned it down. In fact, I turned it down about four different times. But every time I said no, they would come back and finally they proposed a situation which I could work with: would I take a two-week period and see if I could restructure the picture in a way that I liked? They would pay me for the time, and at the end of the two weeks, if I didn't want to do it, at least I would've given it a shot, they would have the benefit of whatever good work had been done in the two weeks, and I might convince myself to do it, which is precisely what happened.

As soon as I started to work, I encountered one line in the piece in which one of the characters says near the end of the film, "Being a woman has made you weird, Michael." I started thinking about that line and I thought, if the line were "Being a woman has made a man out of you, Michael" that irony would be an interesting place to work backwards from. And that got me kind of excited, and I said maybe we can do this film about a guy who learns how to be a man by being a woman and in the course of it really changes all the other lives around him.

What happens in a well-constructed screenplay is that if you find the nerve of it, the spine of it—I call it that, some people call it the "theme" or the "bones"—you will find that it permeates every character in one form or another, if it's organic. That is, he not only changes himself, but everybody around him changes as well. "I have trouble with anger," Teri Garr says early on, "I have a hard time with anger." He has to coax her to get angry, she's such a doormat. He says to her, "Stop being a doormat." She lets everybody push her around. She's finally able, on her own, at the end of the picture, to recreate herself, to recreate that same degree of anger and more at him in real life.

Julie, the character whom Jessica Lange plays, is finally, for the first time in her life, able to stand up for herself and break off with the character played by Dabney Coleman. She says, "Oh, you don't think I do this by accident, do you? There's a lot of guys out there. I wait 'til I find the guy who can do the most damage, and that's when I make my move." She knows she's self-destructive, but she can't do anything about it. Even the father, Charlie Durning: Julie says that he hasn't gone out with another woman since her mother died, and at the end of the picture he says, "I got myself a real good woman now, I checked her out, in the bar."

So everybody changes. In *Three Days of the Condor* a man moves from total trust to total paranoia and through his relationship he moves a girl from total paranoia to total trust. You start to play these games with thematic ideas and then it starts to all be like a tree with branches on it.

To return to *Tootsie*, once I found this idea, this spine, then I knew I wanted to make that film.

MCM: Given these considerations, what do you think about the other kind of big money makers, in fact the dominant big money makers in Hollywood, films like *Star Wars* [1977] and all the genre films in which character is probably the least important element?

SP: I'm very grateful for them. It would be awfully boring if everybody made the same kind of film. It's a genre that I would not be very good at, I don't have any particular skill in that area. I enjoy watching them occasionally, but I'm more interested in the other type of film because I feel closer to them.

Just recently, I went up to San Francisco and spent a couple of days with George Lucas going through the whole facility and watching those computer-generated graphics and things. I was blown away by it, but I couldn't be as creative as he is in that area. He thinks that way and he see it that way. I am a pre–computer-generation person. I'm in my late forties; I had a different childhood. I make films that come out of whatever my character is which was formed by my childhood, which is just different than the more modern generation of movie makers.

MCM: How much of your style and interests were formed in New York and New York theater and television?

SP: A lot of it was, but I still think that I make very traditional films basically. They're all romantic in a way, and that's a reflection of films of the late forties and the fifties, which was my formative period. I was a teenager in the late forties and early fifties, and my taste for what real romance came from the movies of Debra Paget and Louis Jourdan or whomever. And so my idea of movies got formed by those movies. I went on to New York and worked in the theater, which elevated my taste somewhat, I suppose, but my roots are still in the films I saw as a child.

AUDIENCE: What is your relationship with the screenwriter on the set?

SP: For economic reasons, the screenwriter usually is not on the set. As a rule, most screenwriters are off writing their next picture. I have occasionally had a screenwriter on the set and it's a great luxury when it happens, but it happens very, very rarely.

AUDIENCE : As you know, in the history of the Academy Awards, no comedy—and I think it's unjust to call *Tootsie* just a comedy—has ever won the best picture award. Why has comedy been relegated to a second-class status?

SP: That's a good question. There are two genres that are always considered second class genres: westerns and comedies. We've broken a lot of those rules however, with *Tootsie*, and I'll show you why in a second. There is no film in the top ten grossers of all time that's a comedy, there never has been, except for *Tootsie*. We were the first comedy that ever broke those bonds. I don't know why, but comedy is just considered a less major form than drama. At Cannes, for example, there's never a western, there's never a comedy. Actually, *Jeremiah Johnson* was the first western ever invited to Cannes because it was an oddball kind of western. I don't know the answer to that question, because quite often comedies are much more serious than dramas and in a way that sometimes is more affecting. I don't think I could've spoken to the questions that *Tootsie* speaks to as well in a drama. I think you accept the ideas in a much more organic way than you would had I tried to do it seriously. But for some reason or other, you're quite right—it is a second-class genre.

AUDIENCE : How much of the screenplay for *Tootsie* is your contribution? How much came from others?

SP: It's hard to say; it's hard to measure in percentages. The screenplay went through lots and lots and lots of revisions.

AUDIENCE : Are the screenwriters contacted when there are revisions?

SP: Yes, I would call. Elaine May did a lot of work on this film without credit, as she did on *Reds* [1981] without credit. She doesn't take credit when she doesn't do the whole film. She never has. Elaine is a real genius and she did an awful lot of good work. I think that Elaine and Larry Gelbart did the bulk of the work, but this screenplay was written first by Don McGuire, next by Bob Kaufmann, next by Murray Schisgal, next by Larry Gelbart, next by Elaine May, and even I spent the week with Baltimore's own Barry Levinson. He didn't do any writing, but he held my hand for a week when I was ready to jump off the roof. Because I couldn't get it all together. It was a mess of different screenplays, some of them so disparate in style, that finally I had to sit down in a room with scotch tape and scissors and glue it all together. And then keep rewriting it myself. Dustin kept on rewriting his part, and then he and I would fight about those. I wrote the last scene—that scene about "I was a better man as a woman as a man" or whatever—I must have written that thirty times. And I didn't really get it the way it was shot until the night before we shot it. It's just constant work. So you can't measure it exactly. There would be no film without Larry and Elaine and they wrote 90 percent, but we changed a lot of it.

AUDIENCE : When supporting actors were nominated, were you disappointed that you weren't nominated for an Academy Award?

SP: Oh, no. I prevented them from submitting me for a nomination because I think there would've been a lot of bad feeling from actors if that had happened. I'm a director; that's the way I make my living. I don't need a job as an actor. There are other actors who need the work. I think they would have been very resentful if all of a sudden I had taken out ads in the papers saying, "For your consideration for best supporting actor." It would have been a little bit arrogant. So I wouldn't let them do that.

AUDIENCE : You did a film about six years ago called *Bobby Deerfield* [1977] which I enjoyed very much.

SP: You and me and that's about it.

AUDIENCE : How do you respond to a lot of the criticism that seemed to come down about that film.

SP: I cry and do other things. I have to be philosophical about it; I get criticized a lot. I would be lying to you if I told you it felt good to be called an idiot in *Time*, or whatever. You're in the public eye if you direct a film; they can say whatever they want to say about you. And, boy, they sure said it about *Bobby Deerfield*. It doesn't feel good; your instinct is to want to hide, well sometimes, if they get really mean, which they did on that one. But you just get used to it, you get to a point where you have to know better somehow. If you believe it when they call you an idiot, then you have to believe when they call you a genius, and both things aren't true. So somewhere in the middle is the truth. I'm not as good as I've been told in the successes, and I'm not as bad as I've been told in the failures. There's a body of work there. Twenty years from now or thirty years from now, after I'm dead somebody will figure out where I belong. I've got to try and believe that, and most filmmakers try to believe that and so you don't get so caught up in the moment because, if you did, you would make only one film. If it didn't do well, then that would be the end of your career. But you can't do that, you have to make a body of work. As we talked about earlier, we can see changes already in my work over the years. That's the interesting part for me. Everybody is asking now, what are you going to do after *Tootsie*? I'll do another film, and it probably will be a flop! Sometimes it goes like that. You have a hit, you have a flop, you have a hit. I worked just as hard on *Bobby Deerfield* as I did on *Tootsie*. I did the same kind of work, made the same kind of choices; something worked on *Tootsie* and something didn't on *Bobby Deerfield*.

CHAPTER FOUR

Clint Eastwood

RIC GENTRY

Clint Eastwood frequently refers to an aspiration for "realism" in his films. He was attracted to *Midnight in the Garden of Good and Evil* [1997] because it was about "real people, people whose differences make them interesting." Savannah, where the film is situated, is depicted "realistically, as if a character in the story." The actors and the camera perform in tandem to capture "immediacy and spontaneity," discovering rather than imposing a view on the film.

Norman Mailer once said of Eastwood, "You can see the man in his work just as clearly as you can see Hemingway in *A Farewell to Arms*." What Hemingway sought to achieve with language, Eastwood similarly endeavors with unobtrusive camerawork—that is, to address the world as it is, clearly, with the least mediation.

To see things and others as they are is to hold a standard against a homogenizing world. Eastwood's acceptance of others, regardless of how eccentric, and "the economy and directness" of his visual style, as director Barry Levinson (*Tin Men*, 1987; *Wag the Dog*, 1997) notes, becomes a moral imperative against dissolution into the generic, artificial, or predictable.

To go on location, as Eastwood invariably does for each film; to determine his shots only when he sizes up the setting at that moment; and to encourage the actors to go for the take, are methods of seizing experience with spontaneity and in the present tense. As the shot unfolds, Eastwood determines if it is satisfactory or not—that is, what is revealed by and through the shot itself, not according to an inflexible predesign. "I think a film is seeing it," Eastwood says,

FIGURE 4. Clint Eastwood directing *Midnight in the Garden of Good and Evil* (1997) on location in Savannah. Courtesy: Jerry Ohlinger Archives.

"when you see it there live, when it's happening right there in front of you." Video assist, used by other major directors in Hollywood to view the shot afterward on a monitor, is not used by Eastwood. He is fully at home with and trusts his senses. Ultimately, Eastwood is a naturalist in the truest sense of the term, faithful to the moment and the environment but idealizing neither.

Unlike Hemingway, Eastwood obviously has the advantage of encountering the quotidian, or physical world as he records it—this is the special prerogative of the camera. As such, one might imagine the envy of an artist like Hemingway or Eastwood the filmmaker when the former identifies the three most difficult impediments to writing: "knowing what you truly felt rather than what you were supposed to feel"; putting "down what really happened in action"; and then finding "the real thing, the sequence of motion and fact which made the emotion." The idea is to reach beyond precedent to one's inner reserve of instinct and feeling to address the new experience with authenticity—for instincts and feelings, like Nature itself, do not lie: they are the truest part of a person. Again, Eastwood's way with the camera may very well comprise the logical extension of Hemingway's own ambitions with prose.

Eastwood's characters, often peripatetic riders or drivers, men without homes and rarely with families, escape the usual restrictions of routine, conventional education, dogma, mundane responsibility, and society itself so that, keeping their own counsel, the true impulses of the self beneath anything artificial may emerge.

His antipathy to bureaucracy, "where everyone's afraid to make decisions and everyone's afraid to make a move," is as much as anything an antagonism for all in our present era that threatens to mechanize or thwart idiosyncrasy, feeling, and spontaneity. When he ran for mayor in his hometown of Carmel, California, in 1985 it was to fight bureaucracy at the local level.

Eastwood's advocating the individual has at times been confused with some kind of conservative or right wing sentiment, but it is not left or right that Eastwood is implicitly for or against. Rather, it is the abstract regulations and artificial calls for order that suppresses the best, most unique in each of us. After all, nothing represents the violation of immediacy and natural rhythm more than bureaucracy.

Eastwood's forty-five films in the last thirty-four years (with another presently in preproduction) also indicate, especially in view of the methods he employs, not only a passion for filmmaking but a way of maintaining a sense of renewal and vitality which is as authentic as it is uncompromised.

The independence of Eastwood's characters as well as the man himself draws from within but corresponds with the seclusion and purity of life outside, beyond ordinary borders, both physical and psychological. Eastwood is quintessentially American, a pioneering spirit that goes ever forward into "unchartered territory." As Mailer writes, "There is perhaps no one more American than Eastwood."

We met at his suite of offices at the Burbank Studios, which Eastwood has occupied since the beginning of his relationship with Warner Brothers in early 1970s. He was in the final editing stages of *Midnight in the Garden of Good and Evil*.

RIC GENTRY: You've said before that one of the reasons you enjoy living in Carmel is for the diversity of the local populace and one of the reasons you ran for mayor was to restore a greater sense of tolerance in the community.

CLINT EASTWOOD: Well, it's a community with a great deal of history. It was originally established as a refuge for artists, many from the Bay Area, such as Jack London, Robinson Jeffers, Edward Weston, Ansel Adams, and George Sterling. A lot of others, a very diverse group, some who just came to retire there, but it was the differences in the people that made it interesting.

When I ran for mayor I felt things in the community had become a little too restrictive. It really became apparent to me when I wanted to do some construction in town and the city council couldn't tell me what the building requirements were. I said, "Tell me what they are. I'll make it work accordingly." But they just couldn't or wouldn't tell me. And I just began to sense that a very unneighborly and restraining atmosphere had begun to prevail.

So, yeah, I ran for mayor and I just wanted to see if I couldn't bring more of a community spirit back to Carmel, create a better relationship between the business and residential community and just enable people to enjoy themselves and each other more, see if I couldn't bring back some of the previous spirit.

RG: And from what I understand, from people I've spoken to or what I've read, you were quite successful at that.

CE: I think it worked out. There was a pretty good sense of that spirit at the time.

RG: I sense that it was something similar that attracted you to *Midnight in the Garden of Good and Evil*, the diversity of Savannah and the broad tolerance in that community.

CE: That's true. Savannah is one of those communities in Georgia that is so distinctive that people almost consider it another state. The area has always been renowned for its diversity and for people living there in relative harmony.

The book is not so much driven by plot as the fact that this writer visits there and decides to stay because he's fascinated by the people and the beauty of the city. The longer he's there the more he forms relationships with many of them. Along the way a murder is committed by one of the leading citizens and the writer begins to document all that. In the book that doesn't happen for about 180 pages and we bring that in much sooner for the film. But the book is built around characters and the scenes with characters are the ones that were most memorable and unusual.

Even the history of Savannah is interesting. It was very carefully laid out around a series of some twenty-four squares or plazas, each of which has a name and a kind of theme. The citizens were very proud of the city and during the Civil War, when so much of Georgia was pillaged and burned by Sherman in his march to the sea, the city administrators went out and met the oncoming Yankee troops before they got to the town and persuaded them to spare Savannah by escorting them in and showing them how beautiful it was and to join them in some impromptu festivities, you know, a big party. It was the Savannah way of disarming an antagonist, with charm and civility instead of resistance or aggression. But even their race relations were different, progressive by comparison to most of the South. And it's still that way today, a familiar and very diverse community.

I think the book and now the picture show how everyone can live their lifestyle in a relatively small world but I think it's a good model for people everywhere, a fairly democratic ideal. The murder tends to divide people but it's not a crime story. The city of Savannah and the whole atmosphere there is really what it's about.

When you go there now, there's a whole cult behind the book. In fact, when you pass bookstores you'll see signs that read, "The book on sale here." They don't say what book. At first you think, "What? The Bible?" But, no it's *Midnight in the Garden of Good and Evil.* That's how it's considered there.

RG: How did you become involved with the *Midnight* project?

CE: Well, about a year and a half ago the writer—this was before *Absolute Power* [1997], as a matter of fact—John Hancock was here on the lot (at Warner Brothers) working on the screen adaptation of the book [by John Behrendt]. He'd written the screenplay for *A Perfect World,* which I made a few years back [1993]. And John came to me one day and asked if I would have a look at the *Midnight* adaptation and tell him what I thought. I hadn't read the book, though I knew it was a bestseller. John said he thought it was an interesting story and that he had the feeling they were going to take him off the project for some reason and put another writer on. He was developing it for the studio and wanted to get it going as a project, not for any particular producer.

So I said, "Sure, I'll have a look at that." I read the screenplay and I really liked it. I called John and said, "I think you did some very good work here." So I called the studio; I think I spoke to [president] Terry Semel, and I said, "This is a very good screenplay. Are you unsatisfied with it in some way?—because I think I'd be very interesting in directing it." He said, "Well, that's great. We'd probably be interested in that. Let's see what we can do." I said, "OK, let me know. In the meantime, I'm going to go back and read the book itself."

So I did, and I liked the book, too, but I appreciated the screenplay even more because I saw how difficult it was to translate all that material from the prose. There were a few things omitted from the book that I thought might go back in as well as a few other changes but once we all agreed that I would direct it we did a rewrite and then got ready to shoot.

RG: What were some of the changes you recommended?

CE: The protagonist was originally an attorney and I thought it should be changed back to the writer. I thought that was a bit more faithful to the book. Since part of the story would involve the courtroom, an attorney's background and allegiances might muddle the point of view.

And then I wanted a few more of the characters back and a bit more detail in general about several of them. It seemed to me that the idiosyncrasies of the characters were important to the book's appeal and that those who had read *Midnight* would feel more satisfied if they encountered some of those characters on screen. Obviously, when you're working with material that's so popular, you don't want to tamper too much with what made it that way. At the same time, 90 percent of the movie audience isn't going to be familiar with the material at all, so it has to be something that will attract them, too. Though presumably, if it was compelling to the readers of the book, why wouldn't it be to movie viewers as well?

RG: And what was it that most attracted you to *Midnight?* Was it the characters?

CE: It really was. There are so many action-adventure films these days, and I've done my share of them, it's just rewarding to do a story about people—people who are unique, who aren't like you or me, whether it's a woman who practices witchcraft, or a guy moving from place to place who wants to open a saloon or another guy who takes his pet flies into town on miniature leashes *[laughs]* or an antique dealer, eccentrics some of them obviously, but people in a very interesting and unique region of the country as subjects in themselves for a movie. The fact that they were all real people, people whose differences make them interesting, people from recent Savannah history attracted me. Most of them are still around. Some of the characters are composites but in the composites they still seem real.

RG: Did Luther Driggers really take his pet flies out on threads attached to them?

CE: Yeah, he really did. *[Laughs.]* I met Luther Driggers. You first read about him and you think, "Taking flies for a walk? That is so bizarre. Why would he do that?" But he's also very intelligent, a biologist and chemist and the whole thing came out of his background in the sciences. He actually ended up on the jury for the trial of Jim Williams, as it is in the film.

RG: And Minerva, who practices witchcraft, or at least works to mediate between the living and the departed, is a great character.

CE: Yeah, she is. In the film she's actually the composite of two witch doctors. I never met the real Minerva. She doesn't like to feel important. She just goes her own way.

RG: And then there's [Lady] Chablis, the actual female impersonator, as "she" likes to be called, who plays "herself" in the film.

CE: Right. The temptation of course is to have someone play the part of Chablis, and an actor might think this is quite an opportunity, cross-dress and just cultivate all this wild flamboyance—you know, really ham it up something fierce. But Chablis was already a stage performer [who does a stand-up routine, much of it interacting with the audience, regularly at the Pick Up Lounge in downtown Savannah] and she lives this life all the time. She could be very spontaneous and you wouldn't have to worry about the usual clichés or pitfalls an actor interpreting her might be prone to. She would just come off as much more credible, much more real playing herself.

So I thought, "Let's cast her." You can't do that with most of the actors of course, but with her you could. John Behrendt wrote most of her dialogue while attending her shows and she's been that character, you might say, all of her life. There was nothing for her to prepare for, nothing to study up on.

I first met her on the set of *Absolute Power*. She came out to visit while we were shooting on the lot over at Paramount, and right away I thought she could do it.

RG: When she visited you there, she was dressed—how?

CE: As Chablis. She's just always in that mode so you don't think otherwise. Just as you would see her in the film, that's how she is in life. She can also be serious and thoughtful, though all those gestures are real. By the time we wrapped I think she said she would be pleased to accept an Academy Award for either Best Supporting Actress or Best Supporting Actor [smiles].

But the idea was to keep it all very real, with actors who were very unmannered in their approach to performing and could go with the moment—John Cusack, Kevin Spacey—a good ensemble who could impart something very natural and develop the relationships among the characters.

RG: There tends to be idiosyncratic, even eccentric characters in many of your films. *Bronco Billy* [1980], *High Plains Drifter* [1973], *The Outlaw Josey Wales* [1976], *Escape from Alcatraz* [1979], *Bird* [1988], *Unforgiven* [1992] come readily to mind.

CE: I like individuals. I'm drawn to that, I guess. And I encourage actors to bring themselves into the performance, go for the take and try to be instinctive with their characters. I often like to be surprised by what'll occur before the camera.

RG: John Cusack mentioned that there was a lot of improvisation on this film.

CE: There was. Quite a lot. There was a lot between his character of the writer and Chablis, for example, who were really great at just amiably provoking one another and really getting the most out of a scene. But there always is improvisation to some extent. I really like the actors to find their characters as we go along, not so much the dramatic direction but the soul of the character and in that respect what they'll reveal in a given moment or situation, something ideally only that character or personality would do or express. Not think it out too much, but make discoveries as they happen right there in the scene, often as we're doing it.

RG: You mentioned that you like to be surprised and John said that at one point he started to tell you what he was going to say to Chablis in a scene, something that wasn't scripted, but you promptly told him not to tell you what it was he wanted to say but just to do it once the camera was rolling.

CE: I think a film is seeing it, when you see it there live, when it happens right there in front of you. Say John walks in and then Chablis walks in and the scene just goes, right at the instance of the first take. You know, a lot of times it's a shock. You think, "Jesus, that worked terrifically." At other times it doesn't and you have to work until it does happen. You might have a little scene you think you're going to get done in no time, with very little effort and before you know it you've spent a good part of the afternoon on it. But I like to keep everything moving and keep the actors from tiring and I think the best takes are usually the first ones, before the actors fall into a pattern. You see and feel the energy and immediacy of the first takes.

After Meryl Streep had a look at *The Bridges of Madison County* [1995], she said, "You know what I really like? You used all my mistakes, too." And I said, "Yeah, but they were genuine mistakes." In other words, they were human mistakes, not an actor's mistakes. They're more like how people really behave.

RG: As a director you don't like to overplan. For instance, in terms of your camerawork, you don't decide what the angles and composition are until you come to the set and to accommodate that, Jack [Green, the cinematographer] will light the set virtually 360 degrees so the camera can go in any direction. There's never any fixed shot list or storyboards.

CE: No, because it's a similar thing from that side of the camera, where you size up the moment as you encounter it. I come to the set knowing what we need to do and with very clear ideas of what I think will work, but I don't like to walk in and impose on the setting with a lot of preconceptions. I like to see what we've got on that day, what the lighting is like, what's in the environment, what's interesting or can be made to become interesting and then to see where the actors are going to go. You size it up and work it out and figure where all the coverage is and I'll confer with Jack [Green] and then shoot.

A lot of times I'll have thought something out when we scouted the location, which may have been a month before, maybe just the night before. Sometimes all you've seen of the location are photographs the art director has brought in, a house maybe for a minor sequence. But nothing is ever the same the day you go out to shoot and so I like to be open to what I find. The light is never the same. You've got actors in the environment now, and they are going to be influenced or stimulated by the environment and they're going to be doing the scene as a character or as characters they've been developing for the first time in that situation. I like to respond to all that, work with it and bring it into the film.

RG: Is there a certain heightened awareness that occurs while you're shooting?

CE: Yeah, I think so. I think you become hyperaware as you work, as a director especially. I think you do see in a heightened way, with the adrenalin going, coming to terms with what's in front of you and around you, kind of coming together with it all while you're out there. I think that's one of the virtues of working with film, really, that immediacy and that interaction.

RG: Why the many locations. For atmosphere?

CE: The idea was to capture what's there and Savannah's a very unique place, in appearance as well as in personality. I would like to think the look is very atmospheric, yeah. The city is depicted realistically, as if a character in the story.

There are two cemeteries, actually. The Bonaventure, which is more upscale you might say, and then there's the one a little more on the outskirts where the writer and Jim Williams go with Minerva to the grave of Dr. Buzzard, where she appeals to the spirits and performs her rites and where what happens before midnight is the time for good and after midnight is the time for bad. We had to reproduce that in a section of the Bonaventure but it still has that eerie kind of feeling about it. Henry Bumstead was the art director and he did great work for making it all realistic and historically accurate. Henry's just great, terrific.

RG: In another vein, I understand that the gay community is preparing to endorse the film.

CE: I don't know how any one is lining up or preparing to endorse the film. It's hard to know with any audience. It's hard to know how the gay community would feel about it. I would venture to think that they would feel positive about this story, though, because it treats Jim Williams, who was gay, as a real person, without clichés. Even with Chablis, despite everything else she is, she also has her perspective on things.

As I was saying, I like them to be portrayed as real people and not caricatures to illustrate who they are, not some facile misconception of the gay community. You know, we don't play Jim Williams to affect a gay presence. He's just a guy who has that lifestyle, though it does get him into trouble with the [murder victim] Billy Hanson character. But I think the gay community would appreciate that realistic element, a guy with personality beyond some surface suggestion of this other part of his orientation.

There are three trials in the book and we've condensed it to one, but the jury is inclined against him initially because he's gay. But there is a bit of a "Rashomonesque" element, in the sense that there's more than one interpretation of what exactly happened with the murder. At one point during the trial and while he's still being held, as things begin to look rather bleak for him, in an effort to change the nature of the defense, he offers an explanation that apparently didn't happen at all. Along with that, you never really know whether Jim Williams acted in self-defense as he claims to the detectives, who bungled the evidence gathering at the murder scene. So there's really more than one plausible point of view on what happened.

But by and large there is that realistic approach to it. You try to remain faithful to the story and just tell it and hope that people enjoy it. The book was well received by straights and gays equally. It didn't seem like there was a demographic that indicated there was a particular attraction one way or the other. You can't have a best-seller by excluding either one. There has to be a broad appeal. But again, Jim Williams and his lifestyle are part of a collage of personalities that lived in Savannah at that time, ten years ago or so. It's the whole collage that makes for that broad appeal.

RG: And of course, your idea of civil rights, which you've always championed, extends to gays as much as anyone else.

CE: Absolutely. If you're a true individualist you should believe that everyone else should be an individualist and enjoy people who are not like yourself precisely for that reason, because their differences make them interesting and the community itself more interesting.

RG: I think because of your distinctly American male persona, your view on that and the fact that you're making this film might very well be a positive influence on men still less certain or comfortable with accepting the gay community.

CE: I think "macho" is a kind of outdated term. I'm not sure what it means. Kicking over tables, exuding testosterone? It may have to do more with being secure and confident, accepting of others, and being very gentle. I remember meeting Rocky Marciano. He took your hand very gently yet he was a world heavyweight champion. He didn't have anything to prove.

RG: You did a considerable amount of work on the screenplays to *The Bridges of Madison County* and *Absolute Power* [1997].

CE: *Bridges* was very popular. It hit a nerve out there with a lot of people and you can't fault something that works so well for so many. Some of the writing did strike me as self-indulgent and beyond flowery. But if you distill it to what takes place, a man who's rather rootless and a rural housewife who are both lonely or unfulfilled in their own ways and who are attracted to one another, it's pretty simple. You take that and strip away what's superfluous and try to work on the relationship.

RG: You worked with the writer, Richard LaGravenese, a bit?

CE: Actually, Steven Spielberg (whose Amblin Entertainment had first optioned the novel) and I both worked on a screenplay based on Richard's first draft. There were actually several other drafts after that but we went back to the first one and did some work on that and then gave it back to Richard, who wanted another pass at it and by then it was in really good form. Anyone who wasn't too enamored of the book seemed to like the translation.

RG: Including Meryl Streep.

CE: Yeah, she liked what we showed her. She wasn't especially taken with the novel. We had to ask her to reconsider the material based on the screenplay.

RG: And then she received an Academy Award nomination. You got a great performance from her.

CE: Well, she's not too hard to get a great performance from. She's wonderful.

RG: What were some of the changes you and Steven Spielberg suggested?

CE: Richard in his first draft had worked in a tremendous number of flashbacks. He had it written very densely. There was just a lot of material, a bit overly complex. I thought it should just go straightforward. The book starts out in Washington State and is more from the man's point of view. I thought it should be told more from the woman's point of view, because she has the greater dilemma, the dilemma of the family. And LaGravenese and Spielberg thought the children should be brought back at the end. They make this discovery and then they reflect again on it later.

At the end of the book he goes back to Bellingham [Washington] and there's a saxophone player who remembers this man, an itinerant photographer who sometimes worked for *National Geographic*, to someone who's looking for him only to learn that's he's passed away, and it just goes on and on. There were so many conclusions. And I said, "No, no. There should be one ending. One good ending. And it should really end when he drives off." I thought we should really stay with that, at least in terms of the relationship.

But in the screenplay we go back one more time to the children, who are adults now after their mother has died, who've found these letters and they've not only learned something about her which they never knew but it affects their lives personally. The daughter decides to reconcile with her husband and the son to be a better man to the wife he has, all because of this experience with the letters. The conclusion is much more satisfying and meaningful, I thought.

RG: And then there's the final scene where the children are dispersing the ashes at the bridge. That wasn't in the book either, this mingling of the elements at this place where they both once were and whatever the bridge invokes about ideas of transition.

CE: Yeah, that worked well. I liked that, too.

RG: I thought the film really captured the tenor and feel of that region in Iowa, the look and the way of life.

CE: You try to be responsive to what you find. You get impressions when you prepare and when you scout the locations and by the people you meet. You visualize a story but you discover so much when you start to absorb the environment and the personalities there, which reflect each other in a way. You just have to be open and engage yourself as the project goes on.

RG: The character of the photographer in *Bridges* must have appealed to you as well—not atypical of a lot of your other characters in many ways, an independent guy without a firm idea of home, no family to speak of, a kind of drifter really, who exercises his own values and manages time in his own way. He's a throwback, in that sense, to a less encumbering America.

CE: Yeah, I liked that character. It's a lonely life though seemingly a romantic life. He's used to working on a solitary basis and then he meets this woman and everything turns around on him. And yeah, sometimes the price of independence is isolation.

I sometimes find myself attracted to characters in search of some sort of redemption, some sort of reconciliation with their soul. I'm not sure if it's a common quality. A lot of them are outsiders, a lot of them in mutiny against social conditions. A lot of them have been lonely for one reason or another, either by fate or by choice. The character in *Bridges* is a loner. I guess I relate to those kinds of people.

It interests me though when a character has something driving him, something he needs to overcome, something in his background that's painful. Through some pain, some trial and error, through some suffering in life, they come to what they are. They have to have something going on to bring them to that point. The character in *In the Line of Fire* [1993] had struggle and pain. *Josey Wales* or William Munny in *Unforgiven*, they experienced it.

RG: The character in *Absolute Power* is another solitary character, this time on the other side of the law, though considering who the antagonist is, his morality is in many ways superior to the lawmakers. You worked on that script as well.

CE: When Castle Rock asked if I would be interested in that, I said, "Not particularly." I liked the character and I liked the excitement, but it didn't seem to be going anywhere. The protagonist gets killed off prematurely, I thought. There should be someone the audience is pulling for that has a better resolution and I wanted to know more about his daughter, who's a promising young attorney. I thought she should be developed differently. She has this romance with another lawyer in the book. I thought, What about not having that romance? Why not have the relationship she's struggling with be more with her father, the master thief, who was never there when she was a kid? That's what I'd like to know more about. I want to see them come to terms with one another. I didn't want everything to be futile.

Though some things are. Some things are futile. *Bridges* once again. You know, the feeling is that you want her to get out of the truck or find a way to rejoin him when she's riding in town with her husband when he gets back and she sees Kincaid, the photographer, driving behind her. But she doesn't, because she's correct when she says that in three years everything will be different than it was for them in this brief period when they were together. She has the children. She has a husband, who's a good man. She has all the practical dialogue in the story. She's the realist. There was one version of the script that even managed to have a so-called happy ending.

RG: Where they go off together?

CE: Yeah. The husband conveniently dies and she goes off to meet him in Rangoon or some place. But that was too much. Because part of what makes the story so effective is that sustaining what they have is impossible, that their relationship was special because it was fleeting, an accident of fate in a way that nonetheless gives each of them something, a more piquant sense of life or its potential that they'll always carry with them and ultimately influences her children positively. So it was not at all in vain. For them it was a taste from a deep cup that not everyone gets.

RG: You know, I really loved the camera work in that film. The sense of just watching, observing. And the editing. It was very patient and lingering and unrushed.

CE: There was real time in it. That was what we were striving for, to make it kind of "real time." Because the era we live in, there's such a preponderance of jagged, nervous energy in trying to get somewhere with the cutting or for its own sake. This movie, you wanted it to reflect something more durable, something you can get a hold of.

It's also in the scenes themselves. A lot of it is just the two of them talking, telling each other about their lives. He's telling her jokes, just the kind of actual things people might do. This isn't action. It's not there. It's not supposed to be there. *Midnight* has a little of that because it's a character story, even though there's a greater number of characters and many more relationships with one guy sort of traveling through it. It's important to move along, but as with the book, you want to make the whole journey.

RG: You mentioned the "real time" element in *Bridges*, which strikes me as exactly the right way to describe it. And what's interesting about that, too, is that because so much editing these days is so hopped up and fragmented, as you were saying, it takes the viewer a little while to adjust to the rhythm of that film and yet by the time you leave the theater you've surrendered to it, to the rhythm of that world.

Your editing pace in general tends to be unhurried, relaxed, with a fairly strong sense for real time, maintaining a certain fidelity to the way things happened before the camera. I always felt that was one difference between your films and Don Siegel's [who Eastwood worked with as an actor for five films], whose editing pace was more abrupt. It's also very different than Sergio Leone [who Eastwood worked with on three films], who dilated time, in the sense that by sometimes providing more shots than the actual event on screen could bear, in terms of how one would experience it if he or she were actually there, it not only slowed the pace but inflated time, distended it.

CE: Well, yeah. And I would agree with a lot of what you said. Sergio did like to really look at things at times. He loved faces. A face was a kind of landscape to him.

RG: But sometimes you do accelerate the time, like with *Play Misty for Me* [1971], when he knows his girlfriend's in danger and he's driving to her house. There's a shot of him in the car, back to her with the other girl who's the threat, back to the car, back to her—bam, bam, bam. While most of the picture is more how time would unravel naturally, you pick it up there. Or in *Absolute Power*, Luther had to get out of the house before the Secret Service Agents find him inside. They go up the stairs, into the room, out the window, after him through the field, until he gets away. That's not real time but it's real adrenalin.

CE: But I think I am drawn to having things edited in a frame of time that seems probable. Things arise out of the material, too. In the trial sequence in *Midnight* there are a lot of characters and you can't neglect any of them. There are three or four principle characters and then some minor ones and still others. Minerva's there. Jim Williams' mother, Billy Hanson's mother, the lawyer's assistant, Luther Driggers, the judge himself, who's played by Sonny Seilor [Williams' lawyer in the actual Savannah case]. Just a lot of characters. You don't want to be condescending to the audience by overdirecting their attention but by the same token you have to tell the story. And you're trying to resolve what happens in the book over three trials in one. There was a lot to manage there.

RG: Did you use the Steadicam* much in *Midnight?*

CE: Yeah, we used the Steadicam. Not much for the trial sequence, but in a lot of other places. All prime lenses [no zooms].

RG: It always struck me that your use of the Steadicam [used for a record number of shots in *Heartbreak Ridge*, at 25 percent in 1986, and later for a third of *Absolute Power*] was really a way of narrowing the gap between fiction and what might also be called a "real" or "authentic" moment on film, in that the camera is working freely to cover the actors who are moving through the scene, often very spontaneously. It's really a documentary style camera in those takes used in a way that's acceptable for a major commercial film.

CE: It's so much easier than laying dolly track, which not only takes time but is something on the set the actors and everyone else has to avoid stepping into. It's a practical thing. But it does enable you to catch the moment. Sometimes you can get reverse sides [in the same take].

---

*A camera mounted on a gyroscope for fluid handheld moves and a favorite Eastwood device.

RG: What's equally astonishing, really, is that you'll use the Steadicam, with the camera operator moving almost at random with the actors, who are doing the scene for the first time and maybe once or twice again, and never use video assist to be sure you've got what you expected.

CE: The video assist just slows things down. I used it on my first picture, on *Misty*, and I found that after each take everyone would gather around the monitor and it was almost like shooting it twice, in the time that it would take. And everyone would have an opinion, but an opinion based on what they were supposed to do in the shot. They were only looking at themselves or their responsibility and it starts to become a decision by collective. There only needs to be one perspective and that's the director's, not that I'm unresponsive to someone saying they think they could've done something better. So for me it's much more efficient to do without the assist.

I'll tell the [camera] operator what we're looking for—"We've got to be here when she gives us that look, then she'll turn around toward the camera and I'd like a medium close-up. After that, she's going to walk over here and it should be a medium over-the-shoulder on him." You know, something like that. From there, you trust your operator. He knows when he's got it.

RG: Doesn't that put an extraordinary responsibility on the operator?

CE: It does, but I cast the crew just like the actors. These are talented people from behind the camera, too.

RG: By nature, though, these kinds of shots are bound to be a little uneven. My impression is that you often consider that a virtue.

CE: Oh, definitely. I don't like things to be composed too perfectly. I prefer a little coarseness, like the grain in wood or the lesions in leather. Those flaws or qualities have character. They've been made from natural materials rather than manufactured from something synthetic and overly slick.

RG: So the liability with video assist is that it costs too much time and it slows the production momentum, thereby infringing on creative spontaneity.

CE: Yeah, exactly. Both.

RG: There seems to be an aversion to high-tech equipment and the look that produces, though the Steadicam is a pretty modern device. Joel [Cox]* once told me that he liked working with the KEM† and the Moviola‡ because it enabled him to keep his hands on what he was doing. I was quite surprised when I learned that he was working on the Avid,§ though from the footage we looked at (of *Midnight*) it seems he's become very adept at it. But working on that system doesn't change your shooting, for you in particular, in any way, does it?

---

*Veteran Eastwood editor and Academy Award winner for *Unforgiven*.
†KEM is a flatbed editing system.
‡A moviola is an upright, very traditional system, both of which use celluloid.
§Avid is a nonlinear video system of editing.

CE: Oh, no. The Avid only becomes a factor later. As you could see, you take all the elements and transfer them to tape and then you put all of that back into the computer digitally and you edit from that. You never have to handle the workprint. The film isn't touched until you decide you've got the cut you want. Then you start conforming,* though we will take the workprint and using the [computer] codes, have that put together for a look on the big screen before we decide on a final cut, because I like to see it in that format before we finish, though it's been just a few touch-ups here and there. You really have a pretty good idea of what the final cut is by the time you finish on the Avid.

RG: You don't like to deliberate when you're working.

CE: No. I find that usually the first decisions are you're best decisions. You don't want to overthink things because you can just talk yourself out of whatever it might be. I just try to work instinctively.

RG: Do you ever change the script once you start production?

CE: If it appeals to you or if it does by the time you've tinkered with it before you're ready to go—why start wondering about it later? Just because it becomes more and more familiar to you through the course of making it doesn't mean it loses the originality or whatever it was that appealed to you when the audience sees it for the first time. You have to believe it's going to have the same impact on them as it did on you when you were first impressed with it.

That doesn't mean that on a day-to-day basis we aren't chiseling with the look or putting the dialogue into words that the actor is more comfortable with or improvising a little, maybe even a lot, as with *Midnight*, but the direction of the story and the structure stay the same. You can really get lost when you start that kind of thing, because I've seen it happen on other films, when the director starts second-guessing himself.

RG: One of the crew on *Absolute Power*, who'd been in the industry for some thirty years or so, told me that the only director he ever worked with who ever finished ahead of schedule was Clint Eastwood. And I remember so well, when I visited the set for *Absolute Power*, someone told me you were twelve days ahead of schedule, and I said, "Say that again?" And by the time you were finished it was almost three and a half weeks ahead of schedule, which turned out to be some kind of record for a major commercial film and all the more noteworthy in this era of huge budgets and cost overruns.

CE: Well, *Absolute Power* wasn't scheduled realistically. *Midnight* would have been three and a half weeks ahead of schedule too except that I said before we started, "Let's budget this the way it should be." We were actually behind schedule for awhile on *Midnight*. I was tending to the characters and some scenes took just a little more time. No matter how many years you've done it, there's always something

---

*Arranging the negative in two rolls that are later merged in the lab.

that surprises you. Sometimes the actors fall right into it and it goes great and sometimes not quite as much. Or, as I was saying before, you think, "This scene should take no time," but five hours later you're still messing with it. There's always a factor X when you're scheduling but we were pretty close with *Midnight*.

With *Absolute Power*, Castle Rock said, "We'll schedule it the way we think it should be." Then I looked at the schedule and I said, "I don't need this much time." And they came back again and told [Eastwood executive producer Tom] Rooker, "Well, this is how much time we think it'll take." And I said, "Well, to hell with it then. Let 'em put down six months, but the fact is it won't take as long as they say it will." I don't like to make a false budget or a false schedule. Some people will pad either one or both so that they come in under, or if they go over it doesn't look as bad. To me, if you're a skilled organization, the ideal is to make it exactly what you think it is, though it never turns out quite that way. If you finish early, fine. That happens too.

RG: Let's go back a little. With *A Fistful of Dollars** [1964], you influenced Leone to eliminate the name of the character, the exposition about the character's background, and a lot of the dialogue. Did you feel that this was a little closer to your own nature, or something you simply wanted to play after the more chary character of Rowdy Yates?† Do you recall your feeling about that?

CE: Well, I went over with certain ideas. One of them was that there should be more of a mystique about the character. There were pages and pages about his background, a lot of which came when he helps reunite the family and the father asks, "Why are you doing this?" And I said to Sergio, "No one wants to stop the movie at this point to find out what's happened with this guy. Let's keep the mystery of the character and just allude to what happened."

RG: All the character says is, "Something happened once."

CE: Yeah, something like that. "Something happened once and there was no one there." Sergio argued with me but then he finally went with it. But then the producers thought something was really awry. They said, "Christ, this guy, he isn't doing anything. He isn't saying anything. He doesn't even have a name! *[Laughs.]* He's just got that cigar, sitting there burning." They didn't know what the hell was going on. They were so much more familiar with the hellzapoppin' school of Italian performances. Of course, when they saw it all assembled they realized what it was and then how it went over with the public. The "No Name" guy soon became a very imitated character.

RG: Yeah, there were hundreds of spaghetti westerns after that, few of which ever made it to the U.S. But what also intrigues me about that character and many of your

---

*The first of the Leone trilogy of Italian westerns and what made Eastwood an international figure.
†Eastwood character on the TV series *Rawhide* from 1959 to 1966.

understated characters that followed is how many critics misunderstood the omissions and the subtlety of the performance, even when that film and the others were so successful, even when some of those critics admitted they rather begrudgingly liked the films. Sometimes they went so far as to call it "nonacting" or "wooden."

And then I read something that Marshall McLuhan wrote in *Understanding Media*, published the same year that *A Fistful of Dollars* was released. I don't think he was referring to film particularly but he said something to the effect that by offering an incomplete image or process, the artist can now involve his audience in the creative activity. It allows the audience to participate in depth because of the peculiar requirement of completing or closing the artist's creation. The more literal minded and the literary brahmins "just can't see it." They've accommodated themselves to the completed package in prose and in verse and in the plastic arts.*

And I remember you telling me once before, "Let the audience participate. Let the audience write with you. Let them imagine with you. You don't have to tell them everything." And I came to think that there was a correlation between what you felt and what McLuhan put his finger on and that in that respect you were way ahead of your time. It took the critics a long while to catch up with what you were doing.

CE: I'm not acquainted with that passage but if I were, even at that time, I would have thought, "Yeah, that adds up to me." I think a little bit of ambiguity goes a long way, though there was quite a bit of it in that character. But there are deletions I'll make in the material, in the dialogue or the exposition or how it concludes.

At the end of *Josey Wales* [1975], for example, I remember an argument I had with the editor about how that should end. He thought I should literally show him returning to the girl and the group after he has the talk with the chief and rides out. And I said, "No, you don't have to show him going back. You see him riding him off at sunrise and that's enough." He said, "Yeah, but how is the audience going to know that he's going back to the girl and the chief and the others?" And I said, "Because they're willing him to go back there. The audience is taking him back there." The imagination of the audience is an ingredient there. You don't have to spell it all out for them.

With *High Plains Drifter*, a lot of people, including those who worked on the film, wondered about the protagonist. They asked, "Is he the brother of the murdered sheriff that was whipped to death and has come to town to enact some kind of retribution, or is this guy some supernatural demon or an avenging angel or what?" I said, "Well, it could be all three." Originally it was written that he was the brother but I played it as if he could have been some apparition.

The only thing you see is that the protagonist lies down in the hotel room and has these images of the sheriff being whipped to death and you know from

---

*ED: An edited and somewhat abbreviated version of the statement. See *Understanding Media*. New York: New American Library, 1964, p. 282.

there that he's tied in with the murder in some way, though you don't know how, just that he's very interested in having this town pay for passively standing back and letting this happen. But that's all you know. That way you keep the mystique alive and the whole atmosphere is mysterious. If the Drifter comes to town and immediately says, "I'm the brother of the sheriff you let get killed," you draw your conclusion right there. But as he comes to dominate the town and humiliate them through various means, the audience asks, "Who is he? Why is he doing this?" And you never really find out.

RG: *High Plains Drifter* opens with that great shot, of the rider emerging from the desert through this dance of light and haze that, through the view of that extreme telephoto lens, almost gives the impression that he's almost gliding through the sky. It's the virtual arrival of an apocalyptic horseman.

CE: The visuals at the beginning were to set up the mood of the rider. I took a piece of the heat wave out of the corner and blew it up so it was the same texture in the whole frame. As it was initially I couldn't get back far enough with the lens to get the rider out of sight, so I just started with a blank screen and dissolved through it. With the heat wave you don't notice the dissolve. Things like that just set the tone for the film, but from the beginning I saw it all very clearly. It was the reason I decided to direct it.

RG: The cinematography in *Drifter* really works to create the mood. There seemed to be unusually open [camera] apertures to intensify the outdoor brightness, so that everything in the town appears visibly scorched by the light [precipitating the later incident when the Drifter coerces the citizens to paint the exterior of the town red and retitle it "Hell"], which contrasts with the interiors, which are all dark browns and sienna and burnt orange, with a tendency toward underexposure which gives this sense of decay.

CE: Yeah, that was part of it, too. It was originally written for Monument Valley but that wouldn't have corresponded with the mood I got from the story. I finally decided on Mono Lake [in northeastern California]. It's a dead lake. It has some very interesting outcroppings and the colors change almost moment by moment, so it gave the look an elusive quality.

And then the relationship between the interiors which were built at the location and the exteriors, that was part of the elusiveness too. The colors changed, the clouds changed and the exposures jumped at you. In one instance we started with the Drifter in the saloon, a very dark room, and then had him walk out the door into the light, so there's a huge exposure change. As you get to the door you have to start changing it or you get a massive flare. It was a bit tricky to pull off but in the film it worked quite effectively.

RG: Critics later called *High Plains Drifter* the first metaphysical western, just as they came to consider *A Fistful of Dollars* the first existential western. Omissions in the character were obviously significant to both.

CE: Well, you know, that character was not so easy to play. On the surface it looks very easy, like the guy's just standing there or walking around, but you take an economy of dialogue and build a whole feeling through attitude and movements. It takes a very concentrated thought process to do that, provided of course all the other elements are there—if it's directed and edited in such a way that you can transmit that.

RG: You've come to represent an archetypal personality in many ways. Have you ever pondered just what that is?

CE: Having the audience respond or identify with a character . . . I don't know if it's something you learn or whether it's inbred or what it is. I really don't know. And I probably don't want to know.

RG: What the mystique finally is?

CE: Yeah. People ask, "What do you attribute your success to?" There's two ways of answering that. You could go into all kinds of intellectual things about the characters you play, be superanalytical about the things you're trying to get across. Or you could say, "I really don't care. I don't want to know about it." *[Laughs.]* I don't want to know about it because I don't want to lose it. I've always done it by instinct.

RG: The No Name character was also this independent, morally nonaligned guy. As he looks over the town, beginning to strategize how he might make a little money out of the situation, he says, "The Rojos on one side, the Baxters on the other side, and me right in the middle."

CE: And this is a plot paradigm that follows in so many films, with the character acting on his own between two sides, either mutually exclusive morally or legally or equally corrupt. *Joe Kidd, High Plains Drifter, Josey Wales, Firefox, Bronco Billy,* all the Dirty Harry Callahan films, *The Gauntlet, Tightrope, Heartbreak Ridge,* right down to *Absolute Power,* and *In the Line of Fire.* What that does is emphasize his independence and isolation and, by necessity, his moral autonomy.

RG: I think that when the No Name character first appeared, he struck a chord with so many people, consciously or not, because of that, too. It was 1964, and here was this very male character so different from anything a John Wayne character would portray. Is that something you look for in a script or cultivate or add?

CE: That is something a lot of those characters have in common. Sometimes it's in the script but sometimes it's added. It does emphasize their isolation and the fact that they have to make decisions on their own. But that's not to say that these characters are morally correct just because they're morally separate. Everyone has moral limitations. They have principles of some kind and out of their individualism they may draw a line as to how far they'll go.

All that may have connected with people. It just felt right to me or struck me as interesting. And yeah, it was different than the John Wayne tradition.

Sometimes I got flak for that early on, that I was tampering with what the western should do. White hats and black hats didn't mean much anymore. We entered a different world where traditional authority made less sense. There was just a lot less faith in our institutions. We see that today just as much.

You know, there was a time when you were led to believe the FBI was a great organization, for example, the great "G" man, the government man, the protector of the country and the American way of life. In recent years, there's been so much brought to light. It seems like every day there's a new incident where they falsely accused someone of something. Right up through today, Richard Jewel in Atlanta, they [falsely] accused him of the bomb at the Olympics. It's kind of a scary time.

RG: One of the things you've always been opposed to is bureaucracy, which is one of the misunderstood themes in your films, especially the Harry Callahan films. Can you trace the source of your feelings about that, the antibureaucratic sentiment.

CE: Well, I remember, I was out job hunting when I was a kid and I had an offer from a trucking company, a big organization, Pacific Intermountain Express as a matter of fact. And they said, "Sure, we'll hire you. All you have to do is join the union." I said, "OK, I'll do that." So I went over to the union and they said, "No, you can't join." And I said, "Why not? I've got a job. They told me they'll put me to work." They said, "Sorry, you just can't. We've got too many people unemployed." And I just thought, "What the—?"

And you know, you're raised very naively as a kid, thinking it's a free country and there's a certain amount of sense to how things are handled. But you start realizing there really isn't. There's always a bureaucracy to wrench things around. That was my first experience, the first I can remember. It sorts of sticks with me because, [though] I was never antiunion after that, I was never prounion either, though I've belonged to quite a few over the years in entertainment and music and what have you.

And then you just start noticing bureaucracy as you go on, not necessarily parallel situations to that. Anytime you do things related to government. Or in the military, you may find a guy with the rank of corporal but he can't really make any decisions. Or it may be the second lieutenant. He can't say yes but he can say no. And then you get to the captain, who can sometimes say yes. Then the colonel, who can say yes a little more often. But you find that everyone's afraid of decisions and everyone's afraid to make a move. It's an endless food chain of bureaucracy and nothing's getting done.

Now of course it's even worse. With government you see so much paper being thrown around. Jesus, the amount of paper circulated over every little thing, even minute things. How many forests could be saved right there? The legal profession, they've designed everything to be a conflict. You know, everyone is just looking to litigate. And it's because there's so many lawyers and they've got to work and all the congressman are lawyers and all the senators are lawyers and the president's a lawyer and Mrs. President's a lawyer. They're all lawyers and there's no way around it.

It's like the game you see being played with the tobacco industry. I don't smoke [off-screen], never have. I like the fact that there's no smoking in restaurants and government buildings. That's fine. But that being said, all this litigation with the tobacco thing is a racket.

Or, you know, Dan White kills the mayor of San Francisco (in the eighties) and one of the board of supervisors and he gets off with a very minor sentence, seven years and he gets out, on the "Twinkie Defense." He ingested Twinkies and it threw his system off (because there was too much sugar in his blood) and he went on a murder spree. Now why aren't they putting disclaimers on a Twinkie package? And you could say the same thing—I know, it sounds like I'm on a soapbox—people could say the same thing when they have a heart attack. The cheese industry, it's their fault. Or the beef industry, it's their fault. Or any fast food chain that serves a lot of fat foods, it's their fault. They could just go on and on.

Everyone talks about how much apathy there is out there, but as long as you can litigate, why would you want to take responsibility? Every accident has to be someone's fault. It's like little kids in the playground: I didn't do it, she did it. No, he did it. That's the way adults are behaving, like little kids. And our political system is pretty much the same way, because everyone is pretty much doing the same thing. They're buying into all this stuff.

RG: You ran as a Republican for mayor (of Carmel) but you're more Libertarian, right?

CE: Yeah, I like the Libertarian point of view because it's more traditional American. It tends to be, as long as someone is not bothering anyone else, just leave everyone alone. Unfortunately, you can't confuse that with liberal because the liberals tend to want to legislate as much as the conservatives. Both sides, right and left, tend to want to dictate what everyone else does. And so would the Libertarians if they seized influence. Once you get in it all changes.

RG: That kind of makes you a perpetual outsider then.

CE: Maybe. I guess so. The Rojos on one side, the Baxters on the other. *[Laughs.]*

RG: After you ran for mayor, you were heavily courted for higher office by the Republican party and I remember that after George Bush was nominated for president, he was quoted in *Newsweek* as saying, because he hadn't selected anyone yet, that for vice-president on the ticket he wanted Clint Eastwood. Were you surprised?

CE: I really don't remember that.

RG: Would you ever consider running for office again?

CE: Making movies is more satisfying. You actually have more contact with the public. Politicians really don't have as much. Not when you get to a certain level. They make a speech now and then but they don't really mingle.

RG: What you've always done is avoid a bureaucratically tempered film. You've never had studio interference and your production methods and aspirations are more like, if anything, improvisatory jazz, really.

CE: Yeah. As long as everyone knows what the melody is, you can reach out. We were speaking of the actors before and they're very much like jazz musicians in that within the scene they're doing a lot of things that aren't scripted—where they go, how they give the line, sometimes changing the line to have it make more sense or become more natural to them though not necessarily changing the meaning. They're improvising on the melody in a way.

And that's why I like first takes and to shoot the rehearsal, because over the years I'd see an actor do something interesting and not always be able to quite make it happen again. A good actor can conjure it but it may never have the same spontaneity. But everyone has ideas on the set, not just the actors or the director or the cinematographer. You know, a director is not just some guy moving through the set with a viewfinder setting up shots. You try to set up an atmosphere that's comfortable for everyone and in which each person can be proud of their contribution. And everyone contributes.

RG: And jazz has always been important to you. You were a jazz musician as a kid and still play. Many of your musical scores are jazz based or inflected. The character in *In the Line of Fire* is a big Miles Davis fan. And then there's *Bird* [1988] of course.

CE: Well, it's the true American art form. It's freedom as idealized through sound, in a way, the music itself. And then early bands and the players were not only musical pioneers but pioneers of a new society, a more integrated society. Whether black or white they played together. It was a subculture of what was to be more generally accepted only much later on.

RG: The character of Chan in *Bird* was an extremely progressive woman, one of the most fully liberated and independent characters I could ever remember seeing on screen. She's reflective of many of your female characters, who are usually strong and independent. You also seldom feature females who are glamorous or attractive in some stereotypical way.

CE: If you play up the glamorous girls, all of a sudden it's a Hollywood picture. You don't want some Barbie doll up there, I don't think. You can just ruin a movie with glamour and all that, with gloss.

As for the integration issue in *Bird*, we just didn't try to make any kind of deal about a mixed marriage, though again it was to society at that time. Basically, Charlie Parker and Chan were just two people in love. That's how we looked at it.

But Chan was just a free spirit who did whatever compelled her. Social pieties and all that didn't mean much to her. She was a strong individual, and definitely the stronger of the two (between her and Parker). But again, we weren't going out of our way to make a statement with that character. That's how she was, a very different person for her era.

RG: Do you have a favorite of your films?

CE: Jeez, I don't know. I liked doing them all for one reason or another. I loved, liked *Bronco Billy*. And *Josey Wales*. And I liked *Unforgiven*. Those are ones I've appeared in (and directed). *Bird* is a favorite.

RG: Steven Spielberg says that one of his favorites was your first, *Play Misty for Me*. And that is a very well-constructed first film.

CE: Well, it was nice and it was done very spare, on a modest budget and I was proud of that. No one spoiled me and said, "Here, take twenty weeks and have a good time." But you know, back in the early seventies, there weren't too many actors that were directing. In fact, very few. There were precedents of course—Chaplin, Welles, and even Olivier. And John Wayne tried it. Marlon Brando tried it. Some tried it and never continued with it. William S. Hart did a number of them. Stan Laurel. There was precedent for actors becoming directors but it was in a kind of dormant period in the sixties and seventies. A few tried it with television or on a television series in the sixties. In fact, I wanted to [on *Rawhide*] but they wouldn't let me. Too many other actors who started to direct television hadn't done so well with it.

RG: What attracted you to *White Hunter, Black Heart* [1990]?

CE: The madness of the main character, driven by this obsession with the elephant, throwing everything aside to go out and kill this magnificent creature. It was a gripping premise. You just didn't know what this man would do or what he was capable of because of this fixation, this obsession. All of that got me hooked right away.

RG: Peter Viertel, novelist and screenwriter of *White Hunter, Black Heart*, confirmed that you caught the style and essence of the John Huston kind of character* without really trying to impersonate him. Did you ever have an opportunity to meet Huston?

CE: No, I never did. What I did was research his character through various readings and by watching films that he appeared in—*The Treasure of Sierra Madre* [1948], *Chinatown* [1974], things like that. I also watched an interesting film that Orson Welles was making but never finished† in which Huston had a very prominent role.

---

*Viertel based the novel after his work with Huston on *The African Queen*.
†*The Other Side of the Wind*, started in 1971.

Another thing was that a long time ago, when I was in the army (during the early fifties), I was a projectionist for some classes. And in one particular class, I always had to run *The Battle of San Pietro* [1945], a film Huston made during World War II by assembling combat footage which he also narrated. I must have seen that film a hundred times if I saw it once. I just watched and listened and became fascinated with his rhythm of speech and his delivery.

RG: Through your research, did you come to any conclusions about what kind of person Huston was?

CE: He was a real dichotomy, a guy who would stand up and defend the less privileged and the oppressed, for example. I think when he arrived in Africa in 1951, he was appalled by the way black people were treated in their own country, and that's the way the Wilson character (the protagonist of *White Hunter*) is depicted. He could be very charming, very winning, but also very antagonistic and cruel to his friends and associates. He was a very complex man, with a lot of contradictions.

RG: One of the more interesting contradictions in the film I thought was his preoccupation with the creative process, writing and preparing for the film, while at the same time dwelling, as you said, obsessively with killing, with the hunt.

CE: There's a scene that kind of addresses that. He's working on the script with the writer (based on Viertel, played by Jeff Fahey) on the veranda of the hotel in Africa. The writer, who is kind of the conscience of the film, is seated behind a typewriter at this table, and they're talking about the scene they're working on. Wilson begins to describe what he wants from the scene, but all the while he's handling a bore rifle, because he's also thinking about getting on with his pursuit of the elephant.

RG: Would that indicate some kind of analogy between the two, some common impulse between creativity and destruction?

CE: Maybe, at least with this guy. He's kind of megalomaniacal, the way he conducts himself, both with the hunt and the production. He admits that killing the elephant is "a sin" he wants to commit. You can start to draw your own conclusions, that the way he lords over the world of his movies isn't enough. He's got to intrude on the world that doesn't belong to him, that he can't lord over in the same way. The elephant kind of embodies Nature, creation in a more divine sense. He's ready to violate that.

RG: It's a little like Ahab meets *Heart of Darkness*.

CE: Yeah *[laughs]*, along those lines in a way.

RG: You must have enjoyed shooting—or maybe I should say "working"—in Africa.

CE: Yeah, all we "shot" was film. But it was great. We were in Zimbabwe, June through August, which are the winter months, as Zimbabwe is quite a ways south of the equator. And it was very beautiful there that time of the year, not too hot and the skies are clear. One night on the terrace of the hotel in Cariba we could see these three elephants in the lake, just playing in the moonlight. That was very nice, though there are hazards, too. The big cats came out at night, lions and leopards, and you couldn't leave the hotel compound on foot or without an armed guard.

Peter Viertel told me before we went that Africa would not leave you "unmarked." And he was right. The Zambezi River, for example, these big whirlpools that are like fifteen feet across, just pulling everything in. Something could go down inside and come spewing back out maybe hundreds of yards away. It's just an incredible force. And it's kind of what Africa's about. After awhile you feel like you're where it all began. It's a great place to make a movie.

RG: Do you see *Unforgiven* as your last western?

CE: At the time I thought so, that it might very well be the last one. I was quite conscious of that while making the film. It seemed like the appropriate one to finish with. But who knows? When good material comes along it doesn't matter what genre it's in.

There were a lot of different qualities about the script, which I recognized when I got hold of it, back in '83. Francis Coppola had it for a while. But I just thought, "I'll hang on to this. It'll be better to play when I've aged a bit more." Finally I felt the time was right.

RG: Critics have mentioned how generous you were with your fellow actors in that film, in the sense that the other characters are as developed as the William Munny protagonist and that most leading men would have rewritten it to put more of themselves on screen, if for no other reason than to please the audience that comes to see that actor. As a matter of fact, I think it was [screenwriter] David Webb Peoples who said that, early on, that was why the film wasn't made. It was too dispersed or something in the usual commercial way.

CE: That could've been, but I liked it how it was. You don't want to tamper with something that well written. That was not a script I thought needed work.

RG: I really love the scene where William Munny wakes up the morning after he's been terribly ill and has all these hallucinations of death worked in with the haunting memories of the mayhem he produced in his earlier life and finds himself in the corral or the stable with the prostitute who had been maimed and thinks for a moment, in his confusion, that's this is now the afterlife and this scarred woman is an angel.

But what really made that scene for me is the snow, the snow over the landscape, the beauty but also the purity. After that horrible night Munny has the night before, it seemed like he'd rid himself of both physical and spiritual sickness in a way, or some of it or comes to terms with it. And I wondered, was that in the script or did it just happen to snow or—how did that work? It was so perfect.

CE: Well, it did snow. We were up there in Alberta and it came down one night. We were getting close to that scene and though I like to shoot in sequence I thought, "Let's move ahead and do that now." Actually, it would have broken the continuity for most of the other scenes but for that one it would work. And it just felt right, but it works in the ways that you mention. I thought the snow would complement that scene rather nicely.

RG: It's like the second of two visions of the afterlife, one of hell and one of a serene heaven where everyone, even a maimed woman can be beautiful or a killer can find peace. But really, the title of the film seemed to suggest, among other things, that this man felt he would never be forgiven for his sins, that he would never see the wife he loved (and had reformed him and then died) in the afterlife because she would go to one place and he would go to the other, so to speak, that he was damned no matter what he did, that Munny was therefore about as unforgiven as you could get.

And just before he pulls the trigger on the sheriff, the Gene Hackman character, after the shootout in the saloon, the sheriff says to him, "I'll see you in hell, William Munny," which they both seemed to take as very literal. So it just seemed that the whole idea of being unforgiven worked on several levels, including the most meaningful one of all, that this man's life was unforgivable, that he was condemned and he knew it.

CE: Well, basically, there was no way out for this guy. He'd tried to do better and then hardship compelled him to go back to the only thing he ever knew how to do well, which was killing and shooting. He'd failed as a hog farmer. He felt he was failing his children. Along comes this opportunity and he seizes it, though he's not sure at first if he's up to the task. He can't even get up on his horse. But he resigns himself to it for the bounty involved. It seems fairly straightforward—do the job and get paid—though exactly what happened in the brothel has already been exaggerated to an extent by the time he hears about it. Seeking justice never becomes a part of the situation, though. If anything it's about conscience, about coming to grips with what he's done and then just how violence has consequences in every direction, even for the perpetrator who has to live with his deeds, or misdeeds. Violence doesn't solve the issues. It just complicates the issues and there's no end to it or escape from it once it starts. The Rodney King incident was rather current at the time and there was some kind of analogy there, I felt.

But Munny sees his past before his eyes that night, all that death, and in a way sees the future too, because seeing the decomposing bodies of one of his victims is something like what could become of himself for his actions. It could be looked at that way. It's a kind of death without hope of salvation. He's frightened there, and for good reason. But it was a vision.

RG: As I understand it, *Unforgiven* was finished just before a storm that lasted weeks.

CE: Yeah, we just managed to stay ahead of that. The last few days were pretty tough. A lot of night shooting. I'm not sure what we'd have done had we not got the last scenes in the can before then.

RG: Is there anything else you'd still like to achieve?

CE: I enjoy watching my kids doing their things and I enjoy watching and being with the family. I just enjoy doing a lot of things now. I may not make as many films back to back. When *Unforgiven* started to have a nice release, I never really got to enjoy it. I was off making another movie.

RG: I remember around the time of *Bird*, you made maybe five films in two and a half years.

CE: Yeah. *[Smiles.]* But I began to think maybe I should take a little more time between films. I guess the old cliché is "smell the roses" a little bit. Of course, I say that now but I could read a script tomorrow and go, "God, I've got to do this immediately." Though I doubt it.

But I'm always looking for projects that are different. I probably won't do sequels that take given characters in different directions like I did in the seventies. I'm just looking for material that's unique, though whether it is in the eyes of the beholder or not is another thing again. But I'm always looking for that.

CHAPTER FIVE

Oliver Stone

RIC GENTRY

Writer-director Oliver Stone was in the final weeks of postproduction on *Nixon* when this interview was conducted. Under unavoidable pressure, appearing a bit weary, Stone was nevertheless spirited, buoyant, and often jovial, prone to laughing frequently and heartily, including at some of his own foibles. In retrospect, I have the impression that he welcomed the opportunity to emerge from prolonged, intense work on the film to begin reflecting on its processes as well as preparing himself for how *Nixon* [1995] would be received. Stone was also very generous with his time, despite several necessary interruptions.

While projecting twentieth-century U.S. history through the biography of the thirty-seventh president, Stone also projects a veritable history of the film medium through a profusion of techniques—from the associative metaphors of Griffith to the high-tech digital matting of Industrial Light and Magic; Soviet construction to the deep focus of Welles; the experimentation of the 1950s and 1960s to the Saturday afternoon newsreels of the pretelevision era. Though a "calm, thoughtful" film, as Stone describes it, the freewheeling incorporation of techniques and formal devices works to hypercharge, indeed transcend what is usually one of the most staid of genres, the solemn historical biography.

Nixon also enables Stone to amplify themes at the crux of several of his other films: the ascent and influence of the military industrial complex, the Vietnam War, the CIA-organized crime coalition, the JFK assassination, how power and avarice corrupt, how mass media pollutes American culture and society, how the 1960s were a turning point in our historical destiny, how individuals must struggle for their own redemption. The issues in *Nixon*,

FIGURE 5. Oliver Stone (left) with Kevin Costner and Donald Sutherland during the shooting of *JFK* (1991). Courtesy: Jerry Ohlinger Archives.

however, are viewed from the apex of power, which in part shades the steep, abrupt fall of the protagonist.

Nixon begins with the beam of a 16mm projector cutting through the confines of a dark room to show a cheerfully ingenuous 1950s-style sales training film, then moves to Nixon in the firelit gloom of the Lincoln Sitting Room in the White House pondering his own involvement in the Watergate quagmire. Stone once remarked that what each of his characters had in common was the fight for identity, integrity, and the fate of their soul—sometimes losing it, sometimes regaining it—and that he felt the highest virtue was the Socratic one: to know thyself. The juxtaposition between a lesson in self-promotion and the psychological disability of the uncomprehending and unrepentant chief executive indicates that, by this criterion, Nixon committed the ultimate error. The confusion and doubt at the core of Nixon's success is Death of a Salesman raised to something like the tenth power.

Coupled with Nixon's own neurotic relationship to the media, which he alternately courted and disdained, the film is also a deconstruction of how modern history is chronicled. When Nixon confronts the press after losing the 1962 California gubernatorial election and remarks, "You won't have Richard Nixon to kick around anymore," a volley of crosscuts from a multiplicity of perspectives and formats virtually simulates an execution by firing squad. Once Nixon has resolved to seek the Republican presidential nomination in 1968, there is the sound of tape recorders whirring, stopping, starting again. Erasing the eighteen and a half minutes of potentially incriminating conversation on one of the tapes subpoenaed by the Watergate special prosecutor, a series of visual images runs backward. Paradoxically, facts dependent on recording devices can be distorted, yet Nixon's refusal to acknowledge the evidence on the tapes borders on delusion. The ontology of the image is revealed to be suspect if not an implicit lie, yet representation is increasingly how truth is determined in this century. Nixon before the miles of audio replications is like a man hopelessly in search of his own identity, one that an outraged American public now claims to know in essence better than he does.

It is perhaps worth noting that in addition to the stylistic echoes between Natural Born Killers (1994) and Nixon (not only in the audiovisual extremes but in the dense texture of spoken language, as it is with virtually all of Stone's films), there are also thematic complements, such as murder and derangement at each end of the psychosocial spectrum. Whereas the disenfranchised Mickey and Mallory are unrepressed media-made pop heroes who kill with immediacy and intimacy, Nixon is a priggish, nationally elected official whose bombs wipe out masses from a distance (there is no staged violence in Nixon) and whose sarcastic soubriquet of "madman" by Secretary of State Kissinger is exploited (as it was historically) to inspire in Hanoi fear of nuclear retaliation. One may wonder of the characters in each film, which are more evil? Which more twisted? Which more lethal?

Epic while psychologically intricate, hotwired with ideas and experiments, Nixon is riveting, provocative, and masterfully orchestrated, and reaffirms Stone's position as an important, audacious, intelligent, and masterful filmmaker. Certainly no writer-director has ever before so affected our political debate or our struggles with national self-awareness. The *Los Angeles Times* once referred to Stone as "the most dangerous man in America."

We met at his company, Ixtlan Productions, which maintains an entire fifth floor, replete with extensive editing facilities, at a corner of Second Street in Santa Monica, California.

RIC GENTRY: Why did you use the anamorphic (2:35 to 1) widescreen rather than the 1:85 to 1 (spherical) format on *Nixon?*

OLIVER STONE: I always felt that when we went to anamorphic in '89 with *Born [on the Fourth of July]*—late '88, '89—that we felt we would be imprisoned by that medium. And I remember a very strong feeling of wanting to liberate that medium, to take the widescreen format and to jar it, to shake it up, to make it more dynamic and immediate. So we did a lot of handheld and we did Steadicam.* We did stuff I've never seen, honestly, in anamorphic.

I grew up looking at Sergio Leone, and was very impressed by him. David Lean, his use of the wide screen. *Lawrence of Arabia* [1962]. Even as early as *The Robe* [1953], the Roman films, when I was a kid. *The Fall of the Roman Empire* [1964]—great film, great use of scope. I loved those films as a kid. In fact, I told Robert Wise at a party about a year ago, "You know, when I was a kid, I can't tell you what *Helen of Troy* [1955] did for me." It really turned me on to mythology and it turned me on to history and beautiful old ancient ruins—although the film was probably panned by critics at the time, to a child, it was a great wonder. And it's hard to believe that Robert Wise did *Helen of Troy*.

And I wanted to come into this thing, [cinematographer] Bob [Richardson] and I, and just liberate the hell out of it and just not be intimidated by the scope of Sergio Leone. So we made it more like a home movie and we've done things that are very intimate and very documentary with anamorphic.

RG: So you didn't want to observe the sort of stateliness or grandeur you associated with anamorphic.

OS: Yes, but on the fly. Stateliness on the fly.

RG: There's some extraordinary stuff on—*The Doors* [1991].

OS: We went crazy, right at the start of that film. And by the time we hit *Natural Born Killers*, we didn't have any need to prove anything to ourselves, I guess,

---

*A gyroscopic mount that enables a handheld camera to move fluidly.

so we went back to 1:85, because it also had its own sense—we wanted to liberate 1:85. So we bounced back to 1:85, liberated that—for ourselves. I'm saying, just for ourselves. I don't expect anyone to follow in this path, unless they're particularly attracted to this kind of cutting style and shooting style. Because it is different. And it does commit you, in a way, to a concept of thought that you don't see in ordinary films. So, once you're on that path you can't go back. I mean, people ask me, Why don't you do this, do that, go here?

On *Nixon*, we went back to a more classic style. I would certainly say it's a quiet film. A calm, thoughtful film about a thoughtful, devious man. A man hunched, repressed. Physically hunched. Physically and mentally repressed. The conventional thing is to shoot inside traps, rooms, prisons, apartment buildings, city blocks. Lots of confinement and containment and one space boxed in by another space. I mean, the German Expressionist style, sort of modernized, would be interesting for that, to keep the figures small in the frame and sever his head, sever his body. Do fractured compositions, and keep the head space high. Keep a big head space between the top of his head and the ceiling, and just work him into a corner. I can't say we stuck to that but certainly that was predominant. And we studied the Russian pictures: Eisenstein, his portraiture. But then, even von Sternberg to some degree, the Dietrich films. All of them are shot in that kind, there's something German about . . .

RG: Because of the predominance of the artificial?

OS: The sets are, among other things. The lighting is artificial. But they were glorious, those films. But we're working in color now. It's a whole other ball game. You can't get away with some of that stuff in color. You have to recreate it. Color's very treacherous, I think, and tricky. I think it's great to be a black and white cameraman but the palette, the choices are more with color.

RG: Did you start to say that you essentially sought to partition *Nixon* at the frame line?*

OS: Oh, yeah. That was a given. We did some of that with Ron Kovic [in *Born on the Fourth of July*]. I do believe that the camera, at least in my films, has been reflective of a subjective point of view, that it crosses the boundaries. It stays outside and yet I think sometimes it collapses the boundaries to the character.

Do you remember Kovic? We went low on Kovic. I was shooting low cam (low and upward angles), which nobody [was doing.] They were afraid of doing it. I was saying, "Let's shoot more of this of, the low mode [angle and height] of Steadicam. " And it was great. I mean, we were pickin' up shit on the move with Steadicam in his wheelchair. It was fabulous—and we kept Cruise very low. And we worked the angles a lot. We put him on sides of frames. [Considering] the challenge in *Born*, I thought we succeeded. I'm so proud of that achievement; we

---

*ED: The horizontal border that separates one frame from the next.

took this Massapequa house you could barely walk ten feet in, and carpets and ugly design, by the standards of movies, and we went in and turned it into a magic kingdom. And we liberated that little house. On a set. It was on the stage. So obviously everything was flying [removable walls that lift]. But when we did that, we created a world. You remember all the movements in that house? And, they were like crabs on a bucket on top of each other, these people [the Kovic family]. That's the feeling we got. That's very tough to do. It's much easier to work outdoors, you know, in big spaces. The challenge is to work wide when you're tight. To work wide and tight indoors. That's really the challenge. Then you get that tension going.

I think that's the trick of—that to me is the dynamism of photo—I was going to say "photojournalism." Anything. Any—cinematography, essentially. The dynamism of cinematography. And what makes a great movie cinematographically for me is a tension that exists between the long lens and the close-up, or to put it wide and tight. To keep the tension enormous and the background huge. The tension tight, the background huge. That's great! There's like—how do you call it? There's like a yin/yang thing going.

RG: *Natural Born Killers* is just a cornucopia of energy and surprises and . . .

OS: Yeah, *Natural Born Killers* is very weird and a misunderstood film. And I hope it will, I think it will, survive twenty years. I think it was much maligned. The subject was misunderstood.

RG: I don't think people really know how to talk about that film yet. I don't think I do, though I know it was unlike anything else I've seen.

OS: There's no vocabulary for it. It's depressing. As long as there are people who understand that, you can get past the enormous amount of mediocrity we have around us. That thinking process, right? Liberate ourselves from that thinking process.

RG: How do you prepare for your shot?

OS: Basically it's a changing process. It's somewhere in between improvisation and planning. In writing, or cowriting the material, I absorb every single line, totally, as a writer. So it's set, in my head. It's visualized. It's seen. I come to the set. I'm not Hitchcock. I wouldn't be able to function under that tedium, of shooting something prearranged. So I'm always trying to refine it in my head. So as the day goes, perception happens, enlightenment occurs. That's what makes it interesting.

Let's say you come to a scene and you think it out in twelve to fifteen shots and all of a sudden—it clicks. You can do it in seven. Or nine. Or four. That's when it's interesting because suddenly you thought you had it preconceived, you thought you had it figured out and you were wrong. So you're obviously testing yourself and it's a game you play, a warrior-athlete kind of thing. It's interesting. It's fun.

I don't use storyboards unless it's ultra complicated and something involving armies and a lot of money. (Where there's) a lot of money (involved), you might have to do that. But if you can shoot it—within my confines, it's in my head—I come up with it, my shot list, shot for shot, and that's the one that's ready. That's my fallback position. Rehearsal occurs. Actors bring enormous contributions and changes. This is the second set of rehearsals by the way (on the set). The first set's already occurred before the production. This is organized. We're very organized. We improvise off preparation.

RG: How long would you rehearse your actors?

OS: On *Nixon?* Three weeks. It was hard. I rehearsed as early as I could. I didn't have the money to make the picture until about five weeks before we were shooting. Think about that. I was preparing the whole movie, out of my own pocket—out of my own pocket—with no guarantee that it would be made. I was basically saying to Tony Hopkins, "You know, we're paying you and we're making this movie." Thank God he didn't ask me to send a bank draft to him or something. Or I would've been fucked. Seriously. Five weeks before, so by the time we really had the dough, then we really started to break our chops, in the last five weeks.

But I rehearsed before the five weeks, maybe seven to eight weeks because I wanted to do some more rewriting, with (cowriters) Steve [Revele] and Chris [Wilkinson]. So we rehearsed, stopped and then came back again, rehearsed another two weeks, so about three weeks total. And then stopped for a week so I could work some of the revisions at the end, just before we started shooting. So we invest, we've always invested in prep here [at Ixtlan]. We feel very strongly that prep is really important because it saves you problems on the production floor. Tremendous problems.

One mistake: in hindsight I can look back and say, yeah, if I'd have cut seven scenes, that weren't in the (final cut of the) movie, I could've saved $500,000. But you can't look at it that way because in some way you needed to shoot those seven scenes in order to know where the balances really lay. In other words, you have to go through that truth of experimentation.

I consider filmmaking a bit like research science, where you need money from a grant kind of situation, where you have to be supported to make mistakes. You know, you've got to spend $2 million going wrong on an experiment. And development money, I look at the same way. It's not a waste, as long as it's intentioned well. And if you intended to make the movie, it makes sense to develop because you can develop five, six things but if none of them has the right touch, allure, sexiness that makes you want to really just do it, get out there and make it happen.

RG: How is *Nixon* structured?

OS: The film is the most complex structure I've done. More so than *JFK*. *Natural Born Killers*, if you study the structure, is also complicated. Because there are things that happen inside time, and inside of that. In *Nixon*, we're outside time, inside time, outside time, inside time, it goes back and forth. I love it. It's like going into an architecturally modern building and being surprised at every corner. Because we do things . . . there's a newsreel in the middle of the picture *[laughs]* which retraces his steps. We retrace his steps two to three to four times in the movie. It is extremely complex.

RG: So you might want to go back over the same event, looking at it from a separate perspective?

OS: Yes.

RG: Like *Citizen Kane* in a way?

OS: Yes. It's the totality of his life. It's an interpretation of his life. It's a myth about his life. *[Laughs.]* It's what we choose to see Nixon as. Nixon is a prism for us, too, and looking at him we can only judge ourselves. Each person can stand in a different position and look and see and reflect and be reflected on.

RG: A man who was elected president and reelected by the most decisive margin in our history has to be a reflection of his country.

OS: That would be an indication. And just his years as a politician. A great many years in public life. One person described it nicely to me in saying, in each scene you never know which Richard Nixon you're going to meet. So, in other words, sometimes you think he's contemptible and sometimes you think he's magnificent. And you go to the things between. So I would say, it's purpose is character study. When I was pitching it at Warner Brothers and they turned us down, I said it was a character piece, a portrait. And I implied that they could look at examples like *Patton* [1970] or *Gandhi* [1982], and consider it that way. That's why it was called *Nixon*, as opposed to *JFK*. *JFK* was not a biography. *JFK*'s a code. I imagined it like *Z*. A code for something else. *JFK* is not featured. I've done biography, with [Jim] Morrison *[The Doors]* and Kovic and lately [Le Ly] Hayslip [*Heaven & Earth*, 1993]. And Boyle, Richard Boyle, to some degree [in *Salvador*, 1986].

RG: And the *Midnight Express* [1978] character.

OS: Yes.

RG: The Tony Montana character in *Scarface* [1983, which Stone wrote] is situated in the context of real events. I think one of the great things about your films is how they impinge on or parallel things that have occurred, often examining political situations or cultural institutions through drama. Even the style sometimes strives to make that political or cultural situation more deeply felt with a documentary kind of camera.

OS: I've been fracturing biography for years. And now with *Nixon*, I think the first hour and a half of the movie is the antecedents of the man. It's all the threads that lead to him. At the halfway point, you come up to the Republican convention, national convention (in 1968). Halfway, and that is when he gets the power, so we enter into another arena now. What does he do now, now that we've seen the antecedents of the man? What are going to be the consequences? And the second part is more linear. And proceeds in more linear fashion for that reason.

RG: So that's his administration.

OS: Yeah, but I feel the antecedents are complex. And I'm not sure that we even got them all. I think there's more stuff we could've done. But given the limitations of my mind and the script—the opening is intended as antecedent.

RG: What are some of the features of the antecedents?

OS: The threads of his life: loss, death, class warfare, bitterness, Quakerism. These are some of the antecedents. Also great idealism. We must not forget. Great idealism. Invoked by his mother. But, an idealism that is more image than reality.

RG: Is the movie too complex, too confusing to an audience?

OS: I don't know. Maybe it is. This is a gamble again. I was afraid on *Natural Born Killers*. That was one of the few movies I ever took out and previewed. I had time to. But I took it out quietly to Seattle and showed it two different nights to younger people, admittedly a music audience, so it was favorable in our direction, but I was enormously relieved that they understood the effect of the film, because it was extremely fast, at that point.

This was probably the first film with that amount of imagery that quick. And I thought, maybe the synapses were just going to collapse. *[Laughs.]* It was scary. But—it worked. I mean, we pulled back on a lot of the chaos. There was more chaos in that cut. And we pulled back on the chaos a bit.

RG: In a sense, pacing it out a little less intensely or dynamically?

OS: Yeah, yeah. And pulling out some of the wild cutting, the juxtaposition of imagery is pretty insane. And we pulled back. And we pulled back even a little more with the MPAA.* So by the time it came out and everyone was saying it was such a radical film, I was shocked because we made 150 cuts for the MPAA. And on top of that we'd peeled it back a bit for Warners.

I'm glad to say the director's cut will come out now. It was a struggle for awhile because of Senator Dole† to get it out, but we're going to get out this director's cut of *NBK*. Nobody has seen that film. Those are my rhythms with my editors. That's the way the film was submitted to the MPAA. And we're going to add another twenty minutes of scenes on the back of the video, scenes that were never even submitted that were shot. Some of them—crazy. *[Laughs.]*

---

*ED: Motion Picture Association of America, a self-regulatory trade association, which instituted in 1968 (revised in 1972 and 1984) the current movie classification system (G, PG, PG-13, R, NC-17).

†One of a number of politicians to speak out against violence in contemporary films.

With *Nixon*, I guess I would say that although the plot is complex, the camera is quieter. More classical. Containing Nixon. And being contained by Nixon. You understand the duality. And Nixon controls much of it. Although, there are overlays, I think, of good air. You need a breather in a word film, a film about the word. This is a dialogue movie. And character movie. Character and dialogue movie. But you need air in these things. I never liked the kinds of movies that go for Academy Award performances by putting the camera on the actor and letting the actor just like run with the ball.

RG: Just follow the actor.

OS: Yeah, it becomes to me—they say that's nondistracting. I find that distracting. *[Laughs.] Scent of a Woman* [1992] is a case in point. It's made by a very good director but because it's Al [Pacino], he just puts the camera on Al and that's it. There's no judiciousness in that. So I think that attitude is important.

Directors are faced with a tremendous temptation, and choice, each moment of each day. Directors are tested in a sense—their souls are being bought and sold every day. Are they going to sell out or not? The power resides with the actor because he's being paid more money by the system. The actor therefore dominates or can dominate. And the director ultimately must keep him happy and sometimes suit his style; he cuts his own style to fit that of the nature of the producer, or the nature of the actor, or the nature of the studio, or the nature of the story.

And then other directors maintain their own style but it takes enormous strength to do that. Because you have to resist the power. You know, directors have limited power. They do. I mean, all this nonsense about the megalomania of the Hollywood director, it's just bullshit because the director is very vulnerable. It takes a long time to make a film. Each time a film comes out you're judged and cut to shreds, or it's dismissed, it's nothing. An actor can do three films a year, if he has to. A director, no way. Plus the whole process is mentally exhausting. It really drains you. It takes your body and soul.

So megalomania? Hardly. Vulnerable. "Megalo-vulnerable," I would say is the right word. And [a director] knows it. Anyone who is sensitive would know they're vulnerable. I mean, how many directors have been run out of the business? Some of the directors who were my heroes aren't even working anymore. It's a very dangerous sport. And the more times you put your head in the block, the more chance you take [of getting it chopped off]. Sometimes I think I'm crazy to have to have made ten films in the last nine years. Crazy. Why? I didn't have to. It's like this energy, that I wanted to be honest to my energy. But not necessarily to expose myself, my genitals on the chopping block.

RG: *Heaven and Earth* had beauty in its visuals, the landscapes, the textures. The performance from this unseasoned young actress, getting a performance from her like that, aging over a period of time.

OS: I love *Heaven and Earth*, too. You hit a tender spot for me with that movie. *Heaven and Earth*, I really love. I'm very happy with my progress, mentally. But the thing is that the critics are saying, you know, because my last two pictures didn't do as well as, say, *JFK,* that I've slipped. They don't understand that it's OK to hit a single or a double. Or a triple. You don't have to hit a home run every time. I consider *Heaven and Earth* a home run but I guess it was a single by their standards. Or not even. It was an out. But definitely *NBK* was at least a triple, if not a home run.

It delivered commercially. An extremely radical film, and it made money. I was happy we even opened the film. I was thinking, this thing could be hard. This could be a miss. And so what? We did it. That was my attitude. Anyway, I'm proud of those two. I know I've grown. Maybe one of the next two films will be a big hit, but if it is a big hit, you know what? It won't be a big hit by itself. It will be a hit because it's a part of a family of films and that depended on me working on films that didn't make money. So you have to support the concept of a filmmaker over time if you believe in him. You can't depend on the last one, either way.

RG: You seem to be coming up with the budget for your films most of the time.

OS: I came up with it at the last second on *Nixon*. We may not make money on it. I don't know. That remains to be seen. But it was worth the try. It's a valuable film.

RG: Do you think that Richard Nixon ever knew his own soul, or lost his soul, or if he did, did he ever regain it?

OS: In our film he regains it. He starts to gain it. In real life—in real life—I don't think the Richard Nixon that I saw in documentary, in television, had the same awareness that the actor has in the film. I do think that awareness came to him over his long twenty-year exile. See, that was the greatest test of his life. That was the ultimate crisis for Richard Nixon.

RG: Where do you go after you've been exiled from the highest office in the land?

OS: Exactly. There's no higher power he wanted in the world than the presidency. What can you become after president? He has to reconstruct his entire being, his character, in order to become an elder statesman, a respected figure. It's very hard to do that when you've been disgraced. So it was another battle. And one that he won, definitely won. He was a fighter. He never quit. But I think that in his interviews with (David) Frost and in his own home movie, with Gannon, he was acknowledging, more than ever, some of the problems. But he never apologized for Watergate.

Even with Frost, he said, "I fucked up because I didn't take responsibility, earlier." That's horseshit. I mean, he's basically saying his aides did it and he had nothing to do with it. He should have fired them sooner, is what he's saying. That doesn't cut it. He knew. He knew and he covered. But there were a lot of contradictions in the man.

RG: I have the feeling Nixon lied and dissembled because he thought he was so disadvantaged and implicitly inferior in some way, assumed he would be rejected for who he really was, that, personally—consciously or not—to reveal himself was worse than lying.

OS: Yeah, that's some of the conflict. But it is complex. He was secretive, phobic, paranoid, defensive. Lies came easy to him in a way because he was always reinventing himself. He could not accept himself as culpable for anything. He was a victim, always a victim. When you're a victim you're on the offensive. When you're a victim you've done nothing wrong. You've been abused. Anything you do is justified because the situation is not equitable to begin with. You level the field with less than honorable tactics to compensate for your lack of advantage at the start. Or at least that was sort of characteristic of him.

There is no doubt that he was also brilliant. He was a self-made man who came from nothing, who came from squalor. His wife came from squalor. Less than squalor. He could not see himself as the product of his gifts, but as the product of deprivation and punishment. Therefore his self-destructive streak was strong. He did not deserve what he did achieve. He was suspicious of his success. After all, he must have known or felt that he achieved it by a measure of deceit, by never showing who he really was, because down deep he never really deserved to achieve anything. It was a cycle, an oppressive cycle within the man. Yet, it drove him. It drove him to become president.

Yes, he was voted in by the largest landslide in U.S. history and even that could not ensure him that he was accepted. As the votes were counted, he was already beginning to contend with the seeds of his demise, the break-in, the petty criminal overture to make sure he did win the election. So he wins the election and yet there's the element of not really winning it somewhere inside of it. That you win, not by popularity but by tactics, questionable tactics. In his own heart that was the only way he could win, considering the person he felt he really was, who was someone who could not win or be accepted. It's complex. And sad and tragic. Horatio Alger tainted at the root.

RG: And he alleges that Kennedy stole the election from him in '60.

OS: Yeah. I believe those allegations. I think Joseph Kennedy was corrupt, and John too. People think I'm idealistic or naive but I consider Kennedy a pretty toughminded politician. But there was a significant evolution between '61 and '63, between the time that he was elected and the time that he was killed, which I indicate in *JFK*.

RG: Bob [Richardson] said there was a complication with that lighting.

OS: We had to save money, so we couldn't print [the film to view on a projector or traditional editing equipment]. We printed occasionally. I printed the first week. I looked at it with Bob. And then he printed selectively. But selectively, he'd look at a couple of shots. So we were on video, to save the dough. We saved a couple of hundred thousand. And we were tight on the budget.

RG: Was that method worth it?

OS: Well, Bob said that we'd pay the price later on because on a rush schedule, we'd get surprises in the workprint. And the workprint was all over the place. It was pretty shocking. In fact, it was pretty devastating and depressing screening the workprint like that for the first time.

But no question that we reprinted. Fixed things. Sometimes. And originally we wanted it dark. We discussed it. We talked about shadows. I wouldn't say Gregg Toland,* but that kind of a deep throw (of light to create harsh shadows on opposing walls). And we were going big. We were going high. It was a stately film about big spaces. There were a lot of interiors.

RG: When you say "shadows," you mean a slightly expressionistic touch?

OS: If you want to call that expressionistic, absolutely. We were expressionists and realists. Unless you go around studying shadows, you never really see them. But I guess if you hang out in a room long enough and you keep an eye out for them, you can see shadows that lengthen. So I don't know if you call that realist, but it's probably true. Expressionist is realist, in that sense. It depends on what you see and what you're looking to see in a way.

RG: I think Bob just mentioned that you were just hoping to move more quickly with fewer lights, perhaps?

OS: Oh, yeah. We didn't have enough money to buy the big lighting package, believe it or not. You have no idea how sometimes, $42 million is supposed to be such a huge budget. Believe me, considering the size and the period piece of this film, no. No. It's not. It's tough. So we cut down the lighting package. And time, too. Although definitely being in the studio situation we could have taken more light. It was purely money. Purely money. I mean, we talked about it, Bob and I, and basically he asked for more at the beginning. (Producer) Clayton Townsend, too. We cut them down and he accepted it. So, yeah, we suffered sometimes. Absolutely. But on the other hand, we had to move fast because we had a 180-page script and sixty-one days. That's not easy. In fact, the script expanded in prep and I didn't add any days. I was just jamming more shooting into less days. We had the issue of prosthetics [to transform Hopkins to appear more like Richard Nixon]. If we had prosthetics on Mr. Hopkins it would slow us down even more. It would be a two-hour (per day) slowdown.

RG: So that was part of the reason to restrict it to hairline and maybe dental adjustments.

OS: Yes, that was part of the reason. But it looked good. It was more convenient in every way but it certainly was a factor. Imagine putting a nose on every day?

---

*ED: Illustrious cinematographer known for his work with deep focus photography, complex compositions, and collaboration with directors such as Orson Welles, William Wyler, and John Ford.

We shot very fast. But we rehearsed every day. The actors were never short-changed. They were well treated. And well rehearsed. And we had a wonderful experience. It was a growing experience as we shot. Bob and I have a relationship a bit like a husband and a wife now. I mean, we know each other like husband and wife do and it's an easy communication. He's very sensitive. We fight. We disagree. But I think we fight well and we don't let it get emotional. It's like a good married couple who can fight without losing their bond and their sense of humor about it too.

I offered *Salvador* first to James Glennon, who shot *El Norte* [1983], because he was cheap and he was fast and he knew low budget. Glennon turned it down. His wife wanted him to shoot a commercial feature in Chicago, he said. So he went to Chicago. And then Juan Ruiz Anchea turned me down.

And I said, "Do you know somebody that you could recommend?" And he said, "Bob Richardson." I think he mentioned him. But you know, off the cuff. We called him in. And the moment I met Bob, I liked his eyes. I liked the way he saw things. I liked him. It was like when someone walks into a room and you know he's going to be connected to you in this life. It was just that kind of a feeling. It was wonderful.

RG: It wasn't a big budget film?

OS: *Salvador* was very cheap. That was my Nixon period. I lied to get it made. *[Laughs.]* I told [Hemdale Films] I could make it for $2.5 million. And I really didn't know what I was talking about because I had the shoot in Mexico, the United States, international type crew, special effects warfare. I was crazy. I just said, "I can do it." It ended up costing $4 or $5 million. But that extra $2 million killed us. It was just a nightmare. A tough shoot, financially.

RG: Did it make its money back?

OS: No, it died in the theatrical box office. It only did some business on video. And then it never really got back because Hemdale went out of business. So the best I could do right now is a laser disc kind of release. I'm sure the negative on that is in jeopardy right now, because the negative is owned by a company that doesn't care about making movies.

RG: Are you trying to get a hold of the negatives?

OS: I can't. I'm trying to do it. It's hard. I tried, but I haven't tried hard enough maybe. But definitely the negative after ten years is going to be in bad shape.... We all die.

RG: Did you ever have to make any concessions in terms of coverage because of the budget or because of the size of the story or anything along those lines?

OS: Sure, because of time. Two days to shoot the Lincoln Memorial (meeting with student demonstrators). I would have liked three, in hindsight. It's just time. But you know, I've always worked within those limits. On a Sunday before the week I've generally decided—I go through each day, mentally, what I'm going to shoot that week. Sort of a Sunday routine I've gotten into over seven or eight pictures, where I just really think it through on a Sunday—take three hours and go through it shot by shot, the week ahead. So each day I have sort of an idea how that day is going to go. So by the time I get to the day, whether it's a Thursday or a Monday, I'm ready with a concept of how I'm going to get it done. I have to achieve fifteen shots in this day. So that's the way it goes. And that dictates the whole approach to the scene.

It might become sticky, one of those sticky ones where you get lost. Sometimes, not often, I do get lost in the scene and I can't get out and I have to retreat. You know what I'm trying to say? You retreat. Try to get out alive. Get something that will work and leave. That's basically it. You don't, you can't achieve what you set out to do but you can get enough to get out. You don't have to achieve the tonality of it.

And honestly, sometimes you shoot a scene, and you think it's great, and it ain't great. And sometimes you shoot a scene and you think it's shit and it's great. It's not like it's a certainty business. It's not like stocks and bonds. Well, it is maybe. It's not like a science. It's an art.

RG: And sometimes you discover something in the editing room that you didn't pick up on the set?

OS: Oh, tons of times. Tons of times. Any director who tells you he knows everything is full of shit. I admire Alfred's confidence. *[Laughs.]* That's what made him famous. Express great confidence and people will believe you.

RG: What was most challenging about the film for you?

OS: To go inside a man's mind, and make it believable. Yes, that's very difficult. The *Natural Born Killers* stuff, the concept of using "counterimages," let's call them, in either color or different frames, comes from trying to achieve an inner state for a piece of dialogue or a look. An inner state. Everyone has an inner state. When we speak. We have exterior actions but we have an inner state. So often the style that governs the scene is based on that desire to know and to express. So that's where it comes from essentially. Like every moment has what's above the sea and what's under the sea. So we're trying to kind of show the surface to see both.

RG: That's a washing machine kind of motion you're making with your hands now? Or just to turn something over?

OS: It's called a lunar effect.

RG: Tide in, tide out.

OS: Yeah.

RG: Are there certain types of imagery that you think of as having emotional connotations or in juxtaposition of those types of images which . . .

OS: Both.

RG: Both?

OS: I think a symbol can exist on one frame, on its own frame and I think a symbol can achieve synergy and more power through association. And the association's intense. I mean, it's not just one shot to another shot, it's also one shot within a five-shot scene or ten-shot scene. And sometimes you see an image earlier in the movie and you see an image that lays a seed for later. Much of *Nixon* is truly a setup for the second part. Most of the first part, the antecedent section—it all pays off. A lot of movies are cheats, I think. They put a lot of seeds in and nothing happens. *Crimson Tide* [1995] is the kind of movie where (there's) the seed of all these bad guys, right, but none of that pays off. The plot goes in another direction. So it's all a misdirection, a red herring to get you set up for suspense. *Nixon*, I think, seeds a lot of ideas in the first hour and a half and then they do pay off.

RG: And that's in the text and in the imagery? Visually as well as in the spoken elements?

OS: Of course. I don't think they're necessarily divorced, words from image. That's a duality that doesn't interest me. I think that they're the same. I think Godard proved that. Or tried to prove it.

PART II

Independent Voices

CHAPTER SIX

Barbara Hammer

GWENDOLYN AUDREY FOSTER

Filmmaker Barbara Hammer's *Tender Fictions* (1995) and *Nitrate Kisses* (1992) work to re/construct lesbian autobiographies and histories. Both are highly experimental feature films that interweave archival footage with personal documentary evidence of lost and found lesbian history. Since the late 1960s, Hammer has been making personal films which combine the evocative and the performative in a haunting blend of images and sound in a style which is uniquely her own. I corresponded with Barbara Hammer about her latest work over a period of some time; here is an edited transcript of our give-and-take correspondence. In all of her works, Hammer is most interested in the creation of lesbian biography and autobiography, and it is these questions which she addresses in her first feature films. At once sexy, erotic, and confrontational, Hammer's work operates at the margins between truth and fiction, memory and history, opening up a web of discourse for a new conceptualization of lesbian auto/biography.

GWENDOLYN FOSTER: It seems like the central theme of *Tender Fictions* is the constructedness of biography, autobiography, and the self. At the beginning of the film, you introduce the theme that you wanted to write your own biography before one is constructed for you. I'm fascinated by the way that you dance around this question in all its complexities; the way you almost immediately

FIGURE 6. Experimental filmmaker Barbara Hammer. Courtesy: Jerry Ohlinger Archives.

introduce performative selves and performativity as a means to self-construction. For example, at the beginning of the film there is a sequence in which you are dancing on the star of Shirley Temple at the Hollywood Walk of Fame. At once, you destabilize the notion of an integrated self that is constituted through the manifestation of the cult of the individual. You intertwine your selves with those of Charlie Chaplin, D. W. Griffith, Shirley Temple, and others. You also use the voices of critics such as Hélène Cixous, Sue-Ellen Case, Roland Barthes, Trinh T. Minh-ha, Barbara Smith, and many others. I wonder if you would elaborate on the idea of construction of selves?

BARBARA HAMMER: First, let me say that it has been over two or three years that I began the research on autobiography that helped me with ideas and ideology on that subject. I think each of the writers I quote, each of the cultural heroes I show or quote or refer to, are all the different constructions I hang on the skeletal scarecrow of the "self," the "constructed self." For instance, the quotes in *Tender Fictions* about D. W. Griffith came from his memorial service at the Masonic Temple on July 27, 1948. Charles Brackett's words are used on behalf of the Motion Picture Academy and the entire industry. As a pioneer of lesbian avant-garde cinema, I sympathize and identify with Griffith, as one of the pioneers of American narrative cinema.

As Brackett wrote, "I'm afraid it didn't ease his heartache very much," talking about the Academy Oscar Griffith received in 1936, during dark days for him. "When you've had what he'd had, what you want is the chance to make more pictures, unlimited budgets to play with, complete confidence behind you. What does a man full of vitality care for the honors of the past? It's the present he wants and the future."

Now, you may wonder why this quote has resonance for me? I am fifty-seven years old, have made over seventy-seven films and videos, am full of creative ideas and projects for new work, yet I had to take a full-time teaching job to assure myself of health insurance, basic needs, and a social security monthly income. Real basic stuff. This is just an example. The use of "he," the application of the moustache over the Griffith soundtrack, further increases the identification. Perhaps the self is made of the cut-and-paste applications from historic and contemporary culture as much as anything. Today I awoke with the idea that I should go to my studio every day that I work cross-dressed as a man. What are the power implications that the gender construction would lend to the work?

GF: In *Tender Fictions* you create new ways of looking at truth and its constructedness in autobiography and biography, yet you are careful to point out that history and biography are important political tools; that for example, when you looked back through your mothers, so to speak, you saw no lesbians. You underscore this point with a very touching and playful use of sound and voice. When we hear you singing a fragment, "looking for lesbians," it strikes me as a stunning use of humor for an important political statement. This might be a good place to begin talking about your use of humor and strategies of opposites to make the viewer or listener want to look again. In an interview with experimental ethnographic filmmaker Trinh T. Minh-ha that I did,* she talked about how some audiences did not seem to be able to approach her films with a sense of humor. I wonder if that happens with your films and I wonder what you think about using humor as a performative political strategy?

BH: Humor in a film leads to instant gratification for the filmmaker when she is sitting in the audience. No one has talked about receptivity theory in regards to the maker as audience member in an audience community. When I hear laughter or giggles or murmurs at junctures in *Tender Fictions* and other films that I enjoyed, laughed out loud at while editing, I am rewarded, pleased, feel connected to the community that is my audience. Similarly, when the film falls flat, and I am greeted with silence, I feel anxious, not sure that the film has been read with the intention with which it was made.

Humor is a great way to make a point. I like to pleasure myself while working, so it was with great surprise and joy that I found the over thirty-year-old black and white super 8 roll of a kitten playing with my ex-husband's penis. Yes, it was directed!

Filmmaking can be such hard work. When you work as an independent using your own resources or limited grant monies, you are spending time that is your life. I want to enjoy myself as much as possible within the limited time and resources I have, even with a life expectancy of eighty-four. If I am working on a subject that is not humorous, I want to feel deeply.

GF: I'm interested in your theories about performative gestures between lesbian couples, and how lesbian couples develop a complementary set of movements and gestures.

BH: I thought that was so funny, to notice the carefully precise back and forth movement in the footage I found of Sally Cloninger and Marilyn Frasca in their motorboat on the Puget Sound. I noticed that within my own relationship I was sensitive to the nuances of body gestures of my partner and myself, nuances that I didn't have with my friends. I imagine if someone were filming Florrie Burke and myself today they would find in the footage the same careful acuity of sensitivity to emotional and intellectual variations of each of us to the other. This borders on the phenomenon of couples picking up each other's habits, ways of wording phrases, even laughter patterns. And, of course, the ultimate is finishing your partner's sentences. "Till death do us part," but it may be sooner, if sentence completion sets in!

GF: Another section in which you cut together a performance of your cross-dressing with a voice-over describing an entirely different, if related, scene strikes

---

*"Character Zone: An Interview with Trinh T. Minh-ha." *Countervisions: Asian American Film Criticism*. Sandra Liu and Darrell Y. Hamamoto, eds. Philadelphia: Temple University Press, 2000. 204–220.

me as an enactment of the slippage in biography itself, between the referent and the signifier. You also embed the notion of multiplicity in the voice-overs which are sometimes read by two or more people of different genders. You have, in postproduction, changed the pitch of your voices so that we can no longer read gender and we are confronted with our own participation in what Kate Bornstein calls "the cult of gender."* You move across subjectivities here and elsewhere. Aren't you, in a way, enacting the call for politicization of location in the words of, for example, Barbara Smith, whom you quote as saying, "White feminists and lesbians should render their own histories, subjectivities, and writing complex by attending to their various implications in overlapping social discursive divisions and their histories"?†

BH: The voice is my own but the frequencies are changed. I first used this technique (of course, Laurie Anderson used it long ago) myself in a performance at the Women and Technology Conference in April 1994 at the Yerba Buena Gardens in San Francisco. In a live performance I noted in my script arrows going up or down (up for feminist theorists, down for male cultural analysts, and normal for my "I stories") and I gave it to the sound person with instructions to lower or raise the frequency according to my directions. This was so successful with the audience *[laughter]* that I incorporated the technique throughout the film as a way of using theory and poking fun at it at the same time.

When I repeat the story of driving around the world on a motorcycle and use a different pronoun with every telling, I am suggesting the patriarchal incorporation of power and words. I heard that the "she" pronoun carried less significance in the story than the "he," and that when I used the first person singular, "I," there was a greater suggestion of truth telling. All these attached conditions interest me. This is the cultural baggage, be it a pronoun or a moustache.

GF: I wrestled with the question of the role of biographer as I was writing an encyclopedia of women directors.‡ I must admit I reexperienced a sinking feeling when you talked about biographers telling other/s stories in *Tender Fictions*. I was highly aware of constructing selves, highlighting one thing over another, putting things in a positive or negative light, trying to write women directors into a history which has traditionally excluded them. These women had extraordinarily complex lives, as we all do, but I had to look at them primarily as filmmakers.

To some extent I see a parallel in your story of your selves. You include a section on your father and another on your mother. I'm sure you were thinking about the politics of telling another's story and you do fascinating and moving things with their stories. In the section on your father, who is remembered as

---

*Gender Outlaw: On Men, Women and the Rest of Us. New York: Routledge, 1994.
†Smith is a feminist theorist speaking in *Tender Fictions*.
‡*Women Film Directors: An International Bio-Critical Dictionary*. Westport, Conn.: Greenwood Press, 1995.

being many things, including suicidal, you demonstrate the constructedness of truth and biography by having his photograph framed and reframed with mattes that a hand moves in the frame. In the sections on your mother, you capture the elusiveness of the truth or truths of her existence. According to the films multivalent planes, she was either a product of her times, which demanded women to act in horribly confined ways, or she was a woman who controlled her own destiny and own self. Your work with the dualities of constructions of selfhood here is profound; between the culturally defined self of the televisual and fashion culture, and the self-defined person. Are you working toward a self that can be experienced across subjectivities and therefore a different way to look at the familial construct?

BH: Definitely, and the placement of the individual within the community is important here. I see myself as defined and defining myself alongside of and sometimes within the burgeoning feminist movement of the late 1960s and early 1970s. These were formative years for me as an artist as well as a political woman. If the rising surge of lesbian feminism hadn't been happening at that time, I don't think I could have identified myself as one (a lesbian feminist) without the community. I have always read that a biographer needs to look at the context of an individual's life, but looking back on mine it seems even more profound. More like a tribal context, something we read about in some African cultures where the individual (as such) isn't even a construction. He or she is there only as part of a long tradition that includes ancestry, tribal rites, and histories, and so on. In many ways, I can see those of us participating in the early culture making of women who were self-defining, as part of a tribe/community. That's the new family. The "old" family, the "natural born killers," is to be understood, then, left. A few hinges will remain but they are easily seen and so accounted for as the woman springs into her newly defined being (this takes years of course and is a slow-motion spring!).

GF: I love the way you weave in a reference to *The Flower Thief* [1960], a classic queer film by Ron Rice. It is one of the incidences that we know may not be true (but by now we are questioning whether or not it matters if everything be factual). This is how I read it, and of course every viewer constructs their own truths. You tell a story about being in an audition and not doing well and being shamed by having to wear a sign that says, "I am a flower thief." It made me think of the classic Freudian case, the one referred to as the "Child is Being Beaten"* scenario and of course all the Freudian baggage of childhood: questions of safety, pain, pleasure, and punishment. But by bringing in the reference to Ron Rice, it moved your subjectivity into context with an icon of queer sixties freedom; therefore I read it as you having control over the memory, control over the manner in

---

*See *On Freud's "A Child is Being Beaten."* Ed. Ethel S. Person. New Haven: Yale University Press, 1997.

which you wish to reexperience the memory. I was wondering if you were working around this, and were you doing something different in the "I saw a meese" sequence, in which the child Barbara Hammer is forever associated with a tale that is retold in your family, until it becomes as much a part of oneself as a name?

BH: In editing I find tremendous control, ability to shake things up, reconfigure, and by doing so, make references to my own thievery as well as Ron Rice's. Memory is reconfigured through context and this is important. I recently saw a show at the African Museum here in New York. The Luba use a memory board to attempt to make exact recall of historic events and figures. The board is carved with raised symbols, beads are attached, a few human figures are carved (standing in for gods and goddesses). They remember through touching. I don't know if these locators affirm an exact and ongoing retelling as I believe they are meant to do, or if each history teller embellishes or in some way interprets the event, figure, or icon from their particular frame of reference. What do we have here in the West as locator boards? Scrapbooks, but mainly, snapshots. Snapshots in the form of photographs or in the form of stories. When the "meese" story gets attached to "Barbara memories," the yoking of personhood and familial story become a kind of tribal family memory. This is a bump on my memory board.

GF: In *Tender Fictions,* you utilize several quotes having to do with postmodern experiences of truth, memory, and subjectivity. You have a voice-over from [French critical theorist] Hélène Cixous: "Her speech, even when theoretical or political is never simple or linear. She draws her story into history." You include another voice-over in the film from Roland Barthes, stating, "The one who speaks is not the one who writes and the one who writes is not the one who is." One of the most profound quotes, however, is from Barbara Hammer: "I is a lesbian couple." Can you place this in the context of your developing theories and experiences as a postmodern filmmaker?

BH: As a developing postmodern filmmaker, I must give credit to the many, many literary sources as well as my own lived experience that prompted the statement "I is a lesbian couple." The statement that continues to make me uneasy and confirms my emotional ambivalence to, perhaps, any definition. The chapter "A Signature of Autobiography: 'Gertrice/Altrude'," by Leigh Gilmore in *Autobiography and Questions of Gender* as well as Biddy Martin's "Lesbian Identity and Autobiographical Difference(s)," in *The Lesbian and Gay Studies Reader,** were especially important to me. In all my research, these were the only two essays on lesbian autobiography I could find. Shocking.

So "I is a lesbian couple" addresses the dilemma of self-naming and polarities. Since taking a class on ethics at UCLA in my undergraduate years, I have

---

*Edited by Henry Abelove, Michele Aiva Barale, and David Halperin. New York: Routledge, 1993.

been perplexed by the idea that one cannot understand "freedom" without constraint. Similarly, if one accepts the "genital definition of lesbian" (Tee Corinne), rather than the intellectual definition (T. Grace Atkinson),* one knows one's lesbian self in relationship. There are a whole lot of selves, however, that are unknown in relationships and continue to be important functioning, creative, artistic, and other parts of play that exist outside of the couple. This has yet to be addressed in essay literary form, but I address it in my film with all the material, and image and sound, conjunctions that come before the introduction of "the couple." As a postmodern filmmaker, I draw from everything I see and read and taste and hear and smell and hold and delight and suffer from and with and more.

GF: You problematize the notion of an essentialized, easily defined notion of lesbian versus hetero, butch versus femme, self versus models, and so on. It seems to me that you continue to transgress boundaries, that one of your goals as an artist is to confront and to challenge and to celebrate. How do you manage to combine a celebratory energy with a radical political energy and how can we continue the work (and the play) of *Tender Fictions?*

BH: I do take on goals like confrontation, challenge, and celebration. The challenge for me is to find the boundaries (my own as well as community limits, systems rules, institutional demands) and then confront them. Confronting these constructed boundaries and deconstructing them is hard political work made possible through play or fun. Take any problem as a challenge and turn it into play while you confront it and you find out you are having fun, celebrating your life energy. Hey, what else is it about?

Ask yourself these questions: what is it I am afraid of? How has this fear been constructed? And, by whom? Then what am I going to do about it? How can I turn it into play? *The Lesbian Primer, or How to Return to My Preadolescent Roots and Reclaim My Preheterosexual Self,* by Barbara Hammer.

GF: That's an important concept. Let's talk about your preheterosexual identity.

BH: I call my preheterosexual identity the years up until thirteen, or more like fifteen, when I became acutely aware of my interests in the adventures of having boyfriends. Of course, the heterosexist training and cultural conditioning started with my name and from day one, I'm sure. However, what I'm talking about is the time when a girl thrives on just being herself in all her fullness with imagination galore, fear unknown, and turning a blind eye to prescriptive behavior. That was my life until fourteen or fifteen. I lived without a mind to femininity, restrictive clothing, ideas on what a girl should or shouldn't do. Even when I became interested in boys, I chose the ones who were rebels, older than me, and sometimes out of school. During high school and college there is such pressure to date, to attract men, that I can imagine even the hardiest of

---

*Corinne and Atkinson are feminist theorists.

girls in the fifties trying to conform to some precast mold of docility, and so on. So, when I became a dyke, at the ripe old age of thirty, I felt like I was back inside the "old" me of thirteen and now I could keep on growing. It felt like a continuum that had been broken and was restored. It felt absolutely great and still does.

GF: *Nitrate Kisses* begins with some words from poet and essayist Adrienne Rich about the importance of recovering what has been "unnamed." Both films deal with the issue of loss, recovery, and retrieval of lost histories and narratives of lesbians, gays, bisexuals, and others. Going back even further in your work you were already, of course, exploring these issues. I'd like you to elaborate on that and talk about how you came to this material, particularly the sections on Willa Cather.

BH: It wasn't easy. Everything at the Cather Foundation was under covers, but I found a sympathetic person there who pointed me in the direction of some articles she Xeroxed for me, and a host of archival photographs that included the ones I eventually purchased for use in the film. I had a thick biography of Willa Cather by James Woodress, yet I could not find "lesbian" in the index. This was the initial impetus that eventually became the beginning of *Nitrate Kisses*. After Sharon O'Brien published her biography on Cather, I felt better.*

I attended a lecture Sharon O'Brien gave at the New York Historical Society. When I asked her about her courage in writing of Cather's hidden sexual preference, she gave the frank answer that she had no intention of doing so and was going to continue the tradition of secrecy until she talked with noted Cather scholar William Curtin, who absolutely knew Cather was gay from firsthand knowledge and who encouraged her to publish the lesbian facts.

GF: I am especially drawn to the beginning of *Nitrate Kisses* in which you perform an active and living biographization of Willa Cather. Living here in Nebraska, I am familiar with the way many literary biographers, teachers, historians, and Nebraskans in general choose to erase her lesbian lifestyle. What I am struck by is how you turn this appalling situation around and make her history alive again. I'm interested in the way that you bring out the visual evidence—what should be quite obvious evidence, photographs of her crossdressing as a young girl, calling herself "Will," the testimony of her lifelong lesbian relationship—but instead of simply stating these things as fact you reenact them in a way, onscreen. How did you arrive at the strategy of exposing the uncovery/recovery process?

BH: Traditional cinema uses a storyline of ever changing events to keep audience interest. This is boring because it is so programmed and predictable. Experimental cinema presents film in a new and changing light either through

---

*James Woodress, *Willa Cather: A Literary Life*. Lincoln: University of Nebraska Press, 1987; Sharon O'Brien, *Willa Cather: The Emerging Voice*. New York: Oxford University Press, 1987.

content, formal concerns, or exhibition practices and awakens me to myself, stimulates my ability to perceive, gives me pleasure of process and imagination. That's why I like to watch it and why I like to make it. I don't have to be a historian, or an expert on Cather, to let the film give the viewer the distinct experience of what it is like to investigate, to look for traces, to uncover and find forgotten or misleading paths. I try to make an experimental cinema of investigation. The viewing audience become the archeologists, the historians, piecing together the fragments, feeling the emptiness of blurred and overexposed film, seeing through the scratches of dated emulsion, and finding the memories to recover their own history. For if one history is lost, all of us are less rich than before.

GF: In this same section on Willa Cather, you use the visual image of torn photographs of Willa Cather that, for lack of a better word, "regenerate." You intercut this with on-the-road footage in which you go searching for the lesbian Willa Cather. Would you say this is in some ways comparable to what you are doing in *Tender Fictions* with auto/biography? I'd like you to elaborate on your feelings about how we can use experimental cinema to regenerate.

BH: Experimental cinema for me knows no scripting. Filming can take place through adventure, or chance proceedings, but develops with energy when "a way is found." I filmed the torn photographs in forward motion, but because I had put the camera on the copy stand incorrectly, the images came out backwards, making the photos being put back together rather than torn apart. I liked this much better than my original more traditional idea and incorporated it as is with glee. This was a metaphor for the copy-and-paste and put-the-puzzle-together method of creating the film, of finding the lost lesbian history of Willa Cather. It was similar to the road trip from Lincoln, Nebraska, to Red Cloud where I looked and saw only horizon lines and a broken down building as sites for Willa Cather. Ultimately, Willa Cather is a place in the imagination and represents the many lives that have been lost through a false but codified history.

GF: Both *Nitrate Kisses* and *Tender Fictions* feature the use of multiple narrators. One sequence that struck me as particularly self-reflective and performative was the section in which we hear a female voice-over intercut with what I assume is the male voice from a recording that one would hear at the Willa Cather home. This authoritarian voice gives us the "official" biography of Willa Cather and she is treated almost as an ethnographic subject. Naturally, the official version tells us nothing about Willa/Will that has to do with her sexuality. In this sequence, I get a sense that you are asking the viewer to participate in the regenerative process of the recovery of lesbian history, no?

BH: The tour guide's voice that you hear with the photos of Willa Cather's home in Red Bank is even further removed than you think! The guide's voice is piped in from a prerecording and as visitors walk through the house a different sequence is played. It was very funny. The feminist author who visited Willa's home herself and who wrote a book on midwestern women,* Sandy Boucher, is the other voice you hear telling the story that hasn't been told. I believe we need multiple voices to present multiple viewpoints. As light can be defined by neither particle nor wave theory, it seems to me varying phenomena need different approaches. There is no reason we can't hold several truths to be self-evident.

GF: Both *Tender Fictions* and *Nitrate Kisses* are political call-to-action films. In addition to all the other things that you accomplish with these works you encourage, demand, and insist that lesbians write their own stories. You also have a website that is a communal lesbian biography in the making. When you reach the site, you are asked to participate in the rewriting of lesbian, gay, bisexual, and transgendered history. What has the response been?

BH: The response to the *Lesbian Cyberspace Biography*† has been exciting. A few weeks ago I received a posting from a young woman in Korea who was in her late teens and who felt that she was a lesbian, but had so far found no place to explore these feelings. That was a good feeling for me, to find a way to communicate with someone with that need. I want to go deeper with the website, have more interactivity, more visuals. I want to hyperlink the stories, images, and countries. I want to print out the material and post it in a gallery space with a computer setup ready for visitors to enter in more data.

GF: What are the political implications of someone, like myself, who, though bisexual or heterosexual, is not of the lesbian community; how do you feel about nonlesbians working in the field of recovery and regeneration of lesbian history?

BH: A person who describes herself as a nonlesbian would have difficulty in understanding and interpreting cultural innuendoes, just as lesbians from different generations can easily make errors of interpretation by not knowing the coding, the subtleties, the distinctions that are generational differences. Anyone can be a lesbian, but I still agree with identity politics, in that difference is best illuminated by those members of the self-inscribed group.

One of the more challenging ideas that has come from the Internet is the possibility and practice of assumed identities. These masked selves can be heroes, personify inanimate objects, project sexualities. Anyone can be a virtual lesbian in cyberspace. This is so different from the seventies, when we limited our identity to particular women who wore particular clothes and hairstyles and who practiced a particular type of sexuality. There is such strength and sureness now in identity practices around sexuality that the door can be opened, the reins loosened, that the sexual horse can canter into the field without fences. I hope that

---

Heartwomen. New York: HarperCollins, 1982.
†http://www.barbarahammerfilms.com/

metaphor didn't run away in all its freedom! If everyone can be a virtual lesbian than there are no nonlesbians and everyone can work in the recovery of marginalized peoples, their history as well as their contemporary contributions to late-twentieth-century politics, economics, and culture. Of course, I still think Tee Corinne's "genital definition" of lesbian practice is the criterion for the card-carrying type. Do I contradict myself? Well, well.

GF: In *Nitrate Kisses* there is a recovery of a tremendous outpouring of lesbian testimony, especially that of older lesbian women. There is a lot of hot sex and eroticism and playfulness between these women that makes the film, again, a performative vehicle. Your camera-eye finds pleasure in the beauty of age itself, as well as the retelling and staging of lesbian auto/biographies. This film must draw a strong response, especially from older lesbian women, but I am sure all women. I watched it with a friend of mine who is gay and he could not stop talking about the beauty of these scenes. I think he liked them even more than the scenes of gay male sexuality and storytelling. I want to ask you: what has the response been from various members of different communities?

BH: I have admired older women since I came out at thirty. The wrinkles and loose skin tell me about experience that goes beyond my own. Everything can be eroticized, and it is especially exciting to take the more maligned physical features of aging and find them erotic. When various people think they are complimenting me with a "You don't look fifty-seven," I respond to the ageist remark with "This is what fifty-seven looks like."

The responses to the older women making love have been universally the most talked about and impressive images of the film. This surprised me. I didn't make these images to create the amount of attention that they have drawn. In fact, it was late in the editing process when I realized that I was leaving out an underrepresented sexuality. I had included black and white couples, S/M sexual practices, sex between women of color. I am conscious that as members of lesbian communities, gay communities, we also sometimes marginalize and leave out of the history of many members of our own communities. I saw that I had left out old lesbians.

I'm glad you see the older women making love as performative, as, indeed, it was. Many viewers immediately believe what they see and inscribe notions of relationship longevity onto these bodies. In fact, these two women had never had sex before. They were friends and were willing to be directed by me in the shoot. One of them is bisexual and the other is a lesbian. So stop it, girls and boys! Stop reading in the narrative you want to see, the myth-making propaganda slipped into your bedtime reading materials.

This response of seeing these women as a stable couple who continue their erotic practices is very common. Another response was from two young women, perhaps in their late teens, who left the film as soon as the sexual expression of the older women appeared. I confronted them in the lobby of the theater and asked why. They weren't able to articulate their feelings. I flashed on the thought that they might have seen the women as their mothers and this was the greatest taboo: don't watch your parents having sex. When I suggested this might be the cause of their discomfort, they agreed.

Gay men are often amazed and provoked in different ways than women at the older couple. Gay culture is vastly different from lesbian culture. There is such an emphasis placed on the fit and youthful-looking body. Some guys just can't even imagine that two old gals could go to town in this manner and that the camera could so lovingly celebrate their wrinkles. Hey, when does lesbian culture get to influence gay and heterosexual culture?

I am very interested right now in the construction of the closet, both by deceased female artists who were lesbian or bisexual or by the contemporary institutions that "protect" or "represent" the artists and their work. I think I have to understand the contextual historical situation of the period of time in which these artists lived and practiced artmaking before I can make statements, judgments, or anything of the like. That means I have to talk to cultural historians and read people like lesbian film historian Lillian Faderman, feminist theorists Jennifer Terry and Terry Castle, and Adrienne Rich to increase my knowledge. It is more difficult to find historical societies, museums, and individual art collectors who allow a contemporary sexual reading of the artists whose work they own. This I fear is blatant homophobia and it is also based on economics. I think it is feared that if the photographer is considered to be a lesbian, her work will be worth less.

GF: As you know, my special area of interest is women filmmakers. I'm especially interested in recovering the history of early women directors. I find it really frustrating to deal with the erasure of sexualities in these cases, especially because looking through the photographic record and reading the biographies of and around these early women directors, it seems obvious to me that there was a strong lesbian community directing and writing in the teens and twenties. Everyone knows that [director] Dorothy Arzner was lesbian, but I think there were many, many more lesbians and bisexual women working in Hollywood at that time. I sure hope someone is writing a book called *Queering Hollywood*, because I think it is so important to recover as much lesbian, gay, bisexual, and transgendered sexual history as possible. And what about cases such as that of Willa Cather where certain lesbians go to extreme measures to hide their sexuality from the public and from historians? For example, it is strongly rumored that Ida Lupino* was involved in a long-term lesbian relationship. I guess this gets us into the politics of outing?

BH: The "politics of outing"? On that topic, I'm reading *The Sewing Circle: Hollywood's Greatest Secret: Female Stars Who Loved Other Women* by Axel Madsen.†

---

*1940s star and later director of feminist films, 1949–1966.
†New York: Birch Lane Press, 1995.

We don't consider politics involved in the uncovering of an ancient Scythian tomb, an archeological site where a slave to a prince is found buried next to his master. Surely our interpretation of class strata can be of no less interest and importance than our interpretation of sexual preference. Must we find two female skeletons entwined in embrace before we might tentatively be led to the important historic definition of these two women as lesbians? Do Willa and Edith have to be buried on top of one another before their importance and particular lifestyle is credited?

GF: I found the images of decay and loss equally compelling in *Nitrate Kisses*. For example, I wanted to discuss the black and white images of rubble that are reminiscent of W.W. II documentaries. The tracking shots along the rubble reminded me of the loss of the history of sexualities as well as the constant war our society wages against sexuality, especially lesbian, gay, bisexual, and transgendered people and practices. I was struck by the element of performativity in these strong images. You lay them as a bed under the voices of women and men who talk openly about their coming out and living in the world as lesbians and gays. It has a transformative effect. Do you generally preplan this sort of idea, or do you do this more intuitively in postproduction?

BH: I was living in a home in the Oakland Hills that was nearly destroyed by the catastrophic Berkeley-Oakland fire in October, 1991. Many people lost their lives or their life work in this fire. When I drove through the rubble a few days after the fire, I felt a terrible loss. A loss that could have been my own loss of work.

I think a distinguishing characteristic of my films is that they all come from deeply felt personal experience. An image will have personal resonance for me and I will use it. I trust that there will be enough of a collective reading of the emotional text in the image to be useful, to propel the forward movement of the film

In the editing as well, there are many personal meanings that I hope are understood. For example, in the older woman section, a dyke historian, Frances Doughty, is commenting on how people will inscribe history if there is a blank background. The image is of a naked older woman's back without clothing. To me that is the background onto which we viewers inscribe meaning: the lesbian body.

This work is not preplanned. I find meaning through the process of making. I use intuition to guide the research, filming, and editing of picture and sound. In these films I did not use a script, and only wrote the script afterwards from the completed film so that translations for subtitling could be made in Germany, France, Japan, and Taiwan.

By the way, I have just finished my first feature film script, *Nothing Could Be Worse Than Two Dykes in Menopause*, and I'm looking for a producer.* It's a romantic comedy. Kathleen Chalfont, the great Broadway actor, is interested in one of the leading roles!

---

*As of December 2003, this is still in production.

GF: Great title! In *Nitrate Kisses* you cover so much political territory in such a brief period of time: passing, coding, the history of the Village and Christopher Street, issues of lesbians and gays of color, pulp novel culture, butch/femme and beyond, coming out, being closeted, sexuality, and so on. Would you elaborate on how you manage to cover so much in such depth and complexity?

BH: There is so much covered in so little time because the lesbians I interviewed, who were in their sixties, seventies, and nineties, had so much to say, they had so much lived and felt experience. I only intercut four stories, each one rich with dense references. My idea was not to make a definitive film on any one of these issues, but to make a film about how history is made. Questions of who makes history and who is left out: the processes of history making is the subject matter of *Nitrate Kisses*.

GF: In *Nitrate Kisses*, while we are watching images from an early experimental gay film, *Lot in Sodom* [1933], a man speaks on the soundtrack about the complexity of sexuality and sexual categorizations. I think he speaks for a lot of us when he says that the categories don't always work, in fact they are boxes that few people fit. This brings up the unnameable again, and it is important to note that this is lyrically demonstrated or performed by the experimental film we are watching. Neither are easily explained. Both subjects are difficult. What would your position be on categorization?

BH: On categorization, I was teaching my Feminist Film Seminar last week at the Museum School of Fine Arts in Boston, when an African American student said she felt it was demeaning to have her work put in the context of a Black Film Festival or a Women's Film Festival. Films made by whites and men were not put into a White Film Festival or a Men's Film Festival. That's the catch. We get the screenings, but we're categorized. People think of my work as lesbian. I think of my work as experimental or documentary or now, dramatic, or any combination of the genres. Some of the work deals with lesbian representation, some of it is purely formal, some of it confronts death or the fragility of film. Categorization is unidirectional, linear, and unlifelike. Stop it.

GF: I would like to ask you to discuss the importance of the sequence in *Nitrate Kisses* dealing with the Motion Picture Production Code of 1930. In the film you run the text of the code as a crawl title over anal interracial sex. This strikes me as a performance of transgressive activism which works on a number of important levels. Not only is this funny and politically and sexually charged, but it has a visceral effect on the viewer that takes me back to what we were talking about earlier: the unnameable. The text is scored with an opera, and there are again multiple voices speaking about how the code itself was designed to work against the "Mixing of the Races" and a host of other social taboos, including homosexuality. This sequence has elements of the performative documentary; it reads like a postmodern opera, erotica with commentary, a poem. How would you describe this sequence?

BH: In selecting the four separate couples who would have explicit sexual relations in the film, I searched for couples that historically or contemporary lesbian, gay, bisexual, and transgendered communities might censor. We have our own issues about acceptability and presentability. No community is without its own censoring phenomenon. I chose old women, an S/M leather couple, two tattooed and pierced women of color, and the black and white gay male couple to represent some areas of experience the gay community, itself, might censor.

The most exciting element in the gay male scene was the beautiful shape of the rounded butts of different color, almost an abstract shot that went on and on. The Motion Picture Code completely forbid representation of "mixed races" on the screen for twenty-five years.*

I was making this film with NEA monies and trying very hard to not self-censor in the conservative time when the agency was under attack. The sequence became a perfect metaphor. The scripted code rolls up the screen and makes the viewer choose between looking at the beautiful sexuality or read the fascinating no-nos in the code. The code acts as a jailer to the image; we must see the under-represented, the disallowed, through the bars of censorship. I, as a filmmaker, must make the invisible, visible.

The operatic references come from the late and great experimental filmmaker Warren Sonbert, who directed me to Don Carlos, and suggested that the love songs between the Don and his best man could be appropriated and seen as gay. The two women of color make love to a duet between Octavian, a young gentleman dressed as a woman and often played by a female on the stage, and *The Marschallin,* Princess Werdenberg in *Der Rosenkavalier* by Richard Strauss.

GF: Another postmodern technique you use is the inclusion of texts themselves as images. Trinh T. Minh-ha, Su Friedrich, Sadie Benning,† and many other experimental filmmakers use this strategy. I love how you integrate a long quote for Michel Foucault, whose words almost read like a battle cry.‡ He called for us to free ourselves from repression and he said it would take what amounts to a full-scale overthrow of dominant ideologies, that we must transgress laws, lift prohibitions, and, perhaps most importantly, reinstate pleasure. This is exactly the kind of art you are performing and generating, both in yourself and in the audience. What is your philosophy when it comes to the role of the artist and the need to create "a new economy of power" (in the words of Foucault)?

BH: Artists should unionize! Artists should form their own code of ethics, have our own organization much as physicians and lawyers do. We should use our

---

*1930–1955, with a few exceptions.
†Su Friedrich is an experimental feminist filmmaker, and Sadie Benning is an experimental video artist famous for her pixelvision films.
‡This refers to Foucault's theory of sexual difference and freedom as articulated in *The History of Sexuality.* Trans. Robert Hurley. New York: Vintage, 1984.

physical presence in demonstrations, our monies to make political announcements. We should make a general attempt to raise the consciousness of the American public about the profession of artmaking, the necessity of imagination, and the life-giving source art is to the individual and society. When I first moved to New York City, I would feel I was a part of a profession when I was out and about in the city. I saw other artists on the street, collecting materials, posting their mail, buying supplies. I felt like a cultural worker, which is exactly what I am. There is a visible community of artists in New York. That community has never received the recognition and support it deserves from the general society. It is time to demand it and to organize.

GF: Finally, I have not really talked to you about your influences, and perhaps even more importantly, who you are influencing in the artistic and filmmaking, and performative community. I am thinking of figures going back to Alice Guy Blaché,* and up through Marie Menken,† Gunvor Nelson,‡ Jonas Mekas,§ Sadie Benning, Marlon Riggs,** Chantal Akerman,†† Trinh T. Minh-ha, Barbara, and so many others.

BH: I began to make films in my late twenties and it wasn't until I was thirty that I enrolled in college courses in filmmaking. There I saw for the first time *Meshes in the Afternoon* (1943–1944) by Maya Deren. I saw a cinema of difference, a cinema of woman. I felt that there was a blank screen in terms of women's cinema and I could try to begin to fill it. There were very few experimental film classes at San Francisco State University where I received my M.A., so it wasn't until I moved to New York City and saw the work of Marie Menken at the Anthology Film Archives that I was taken with the vigor and freshness of her films. I researched her life and films at the Archives. I had felt for a long time that art was energy, and here it was exemplified in the extraordinary and unpretentious physical and perceptive films by Marie. Gunvor Nelson's films, especially her early films, used symbolic imagery that influenced me. There is one image of a bicycle tied to a tree, wrapped round and round by a rope, that I will never forget. Yvonne Rainer‡‡ and Trinh T. Minh-ha challenged me to regard the possibilities of a "thinking cinema," a more complex viewing experience that challenged and engaged the audience intellectually.

I was aware after I made *Dyke Tactics* in 1973 that something unusual had happened. I projected it at Film Finals at San Francisco State University. Several

---

*Pioneering feminist filmmaker, who worked in France and America from 1908–1920.
†Animation and collage filmmaker (1940s–1960s).
‡San Francisco feminist filmmaker.
§Experimental filmmaker and entrepreneur.
**Gay video artist.
††Belgian film director.
‡‡Experimental narrative filmmaker.

professors ran up to me afterwards with exclamations and congratulations. Later, I was told that this was the first lesbian lovemaking film made by a lesbian. Coni [aka, Constance] Beeson* confronted me when I repeated that statement, and said that she was the first with her film, *Holding* [1971]. *Holding* did precede *Dyke Tactics,* and is a beautiful film. Connie told me she identified as a bisexual, so I continued to think the pronouncement was right on. Now, I don't think "firsts" are *the* important thing. Simultaneous invention, cultural constructions, the sexual liberty that was in the air all contributed to the making of both of our films.

I was aware that there had been none or little lesbian filmmaking before me because I looked for it and couldn't find it. I strongly felt that Maya Deren was bisexual, and later study has confirmed this, but at the time there were no biographies on her life. I decided quite intentionally that I would put my life on film (of course, in my own manner), so that at least one lesbian's life in the twentieth century would be known. Today I can laugh at that presumption: 1) that what we see on the screen could be considered "true" and "a life" and 2) that there is a wonderful flood of lesbian, dyke, and queer filmmaking now.

The entrance of the Independent Television Service on the scene made a major difference for me. There was an opportunity for major funding that would allow me to envision a much larger project than I had up to this point. In my first grant application to ITVS (one I did not get, nor have I been funded by them up until now), I wrote expansively, researched a large project of "searching for lost lesbian and gay culture," and proposed a budget to match the project's scope. In my usual manner, I couldn't wait to see if I was funded, but began to shoot almost as soon as I had conceptualized the ideas.

Immediately upon finishing the grant application I left for a tour of Germany and France with my films. In Hamburg, Berlin, and Paris I borrowed Super 8 cameras, hunted out the only source of black and white Super 8 films, cajoled transportation from my hosts, and began to film. By then I had found I didn't enjoy "touristic" travel and was much happier pursuing research even when I was on a screening tour. The days were intense, but I like them that way.

It wasn't until I began teaching Feminist Film Seminars that I found the forgotten history of the first narrative filmmaker in the world, Alice Guy Blaché, and the two hundred films she made in her lifetime. Barbara Kruger's use of text has always amazed me, especially the last show she had at the Mary Boone Gallery in Soho where the floor, walls, and ceilings were covered with her astounding red, black, and white image text. I felt as if I was entering a feminist church of the twenty-first century when I walked into the space that day. *Reassemblage* was the best film I saw in 1985. Trinh T. Minh-ha's sound and image cutting introduced a third space in film, the floating space between the soundtrack and the picture that does not have to correspond exactly, but that works as a third track, an area of disruption, an unsettling. Today I recommend

---

*Pioneering lesbian filmmaker.

the freely moving narrative in the optically printed masterpiece, *Chronic* [1997], by the young filmmaker Jennifer Reeves.

There are artists who achieve a certain level of recognition with a particular body of work and who spend the rest of their art making redoing, refining, rethinking that work. That seems the easy way out. Art making for me is a commitment to a lifetime work of exploration and process. I could continue to make the optically printed work of the eighties (*Optic Nerve* [1985], *Endangered* [1988], *Sanctus* [1990]), but I chose to attempt a longer form, a more documentary form, a form that used text as image *(Nitrate Kisses, Tender Fictions)*. With the feature narrative *Nothing Could Be Worse Than Two Dykes in Menopause*, I would like the opportunity to direct and bring a narrative vision of issues around aging and commitment to a large screen near you!

CHAPTER SEVEN

Robert Downey Sr.

WHEELER WINSTON DIXON

On March 3rd, 2001, I had the opportunity to talk once again with Robert Downey Sr., the father of actor Robert Downey Jr. and a gifted filmmaker in his own right. I first met Robert during the spring of 1969, when his film *Putney Swope* (1969) was a breakout hit and he was finishing up postproduction on *Pound* (1970), a film that unhappily never received the attention or distribution it deserved. I was working as a writer for *Life* magazine at the time, covering what was then dubiously termed "underground cinema." Unlike some other filmmakers I interviewed, Downey welcomed me into his cutting room with true generosity of spirit, and we spoke for at least two hours of his plans for the future, which at that point were pretty much up in the air. Now, some thirty years later, Downey has amassed a deeply personal body of work, despite a hiatus of nearly ten years, when, by his own admission, he was unable to work due to a combination of drugs and alcohol. Clean since 1982, Downey has come back with such remarkable films as the memorably hallucinatory and yet still profoundly human *Hugo Pool* (1997), and is currently preparing *Forest Hills Bob* [2001], starring Philip Seymour Hoffman, which Jonathan Demme will produce. Although we hadn't spoken in some three decades, Bob Downey was immediately there for me, and answered my questions directly and honestly, without any pretension or evasiveness. In addition, Downey has fully embraced the new digital filmmaking technology, and seems equally at home using both conventional and cutting-edge methods of production. One can only wish the best for Robert Downey Sr.; he is

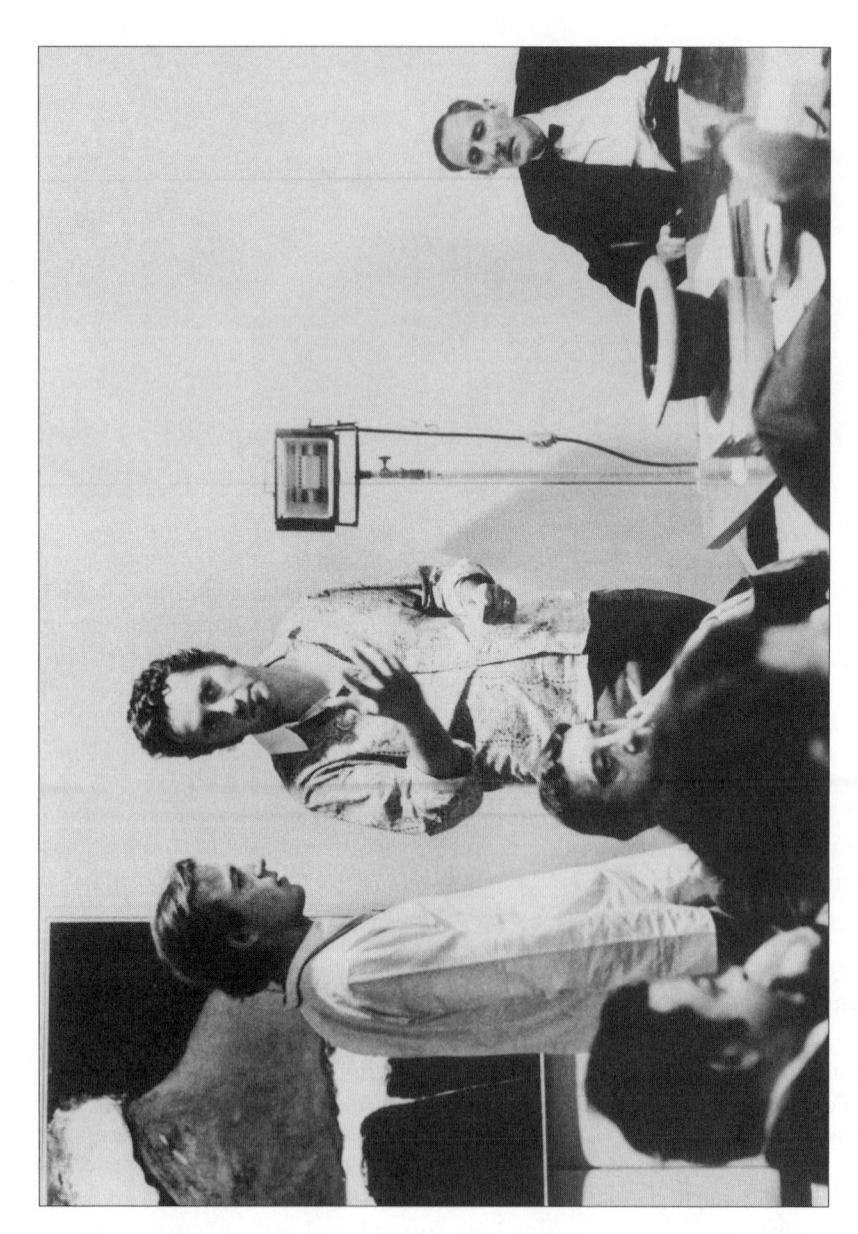

FIGURE 7. Robert Downey Sr. (center, gesturing) on the set of *Putney Swope* (1969). Courtesy: Jerry Ohlinger Archives.

a true survivor, and a true independent, one of the last of the 1960s mavericks who sought to remake the American cinema. Downey spoke with me by telephone from his home in Manhattan.

WHEELER WINSTON DIXON: Hello, Bob, it's me.

ROBERT DOWNEY SR.: Hey man, how you doing?

WWD: I hope I'm not too punctual.

RD: No, you are. That's good. What do you want to know?

WWD: Well, for a start, when and where were you born, and what can you remember about your early life?

RD: I was born June 24, 1936, in New York City. My mother was a model for magazines and stuff; she was one of the twelve Powers [a then-famous modeling agency] models in the beginning; she was quite famous. My father did a lot of things, mainly motel management, restaurant management. My main interest when I was a kid was baseball. That's it. Boxing. *[Laughs.]*

WWD: Was it during this period that you acquired what I might call the "cheerfully nihilistic" view of such films as *Putney Swope* [1969] and *Greaser's Palace* [1972]?

RD: I can't analyze that. I don't know the answer to that, when, or if . . . I don't look at my stuff that way.

WWD: Well, how do you look at it?

RD: Most of it I'm bored by. You know what I'm saying? So how can I even go try to figure it out if I'm bored by it?

WWD: Been there, done that?

RD: No, I'm just changing the way I do things, and my writing, and leaning more towards documentaries. That's the new stuff I'm doing now.

WWD: You dropped out of high school; why'd you do that?

RD: Well, let me see. Well, I think I ran into geometry or something! I just knew that it was something I wasn't interested in, and that you had to pay attention, so I was happy to get out. And I joined the army.

WWD: What did you do in the army?

RD: Served a lot of time in the stockade for being a drunk!

WWD: So did you get an honorable or a dishonorable discharge?

RD: Bad conduct, three years later. Then for one summer I was a pitcher in semipro baseball. It was in Pennsylvania. I forget the name of the team, but it was in Brookline, Pennsylvania, near Pittsburgh.

WWD: Were you any good?

RD: Yeah!

WWD: You still like to do that from time to time, just go out and pitch a few balls?

RD: Well, I just went to the gym the other day for the first time in forty years, and I'm still hurting. So I guess that's behind me.

WWD: What drew you into filmmaking from this background?

RD: Well, my first inspiration . . . when I was in the army, I was in the stockade, and one of the guys who ran the stockade gave me a notebook and a pen and said, "When you have nothing to do, maybe you can amuse yourself." So I started writing, and when I got out, I wrote a little bit and I was an off-off-off-Broadway playwright. And when one of my plays was done, this fellow I was working with said, "Look, we can make a movie." I said, "How can we do that?," and he said, "I have a camera and you have a script, so let's just do it." Simple.

WWD: What was the play you were doing?

RD: It was called something like *What Else Is There?* The actors played missiles, in silos, ready to go off. It was kind of wild, pretty ahead of its time. The guy with the camera was William Waering, who later photographed *Babo 73* [1964] for me. So we shot the film, and that was the start of that.

WWD: I almost hate to ask this question, but when you started making films, did you have any idols, anyone you admired as a filmmaker out there?

RD: Well, I was beginning to pay attention to Fellini, and Bill [Waering] turned me on to Preston Sturges. Those were my two main influences at that point.

WWD: Was this first film *Balls Bluff* [1963]?

RD: Yeah. It was silent, about thirty minutes long. It was about a Union Civil War soldier who wakes up in the twentieth century in New York City. I had to play the soldier, because the actor kept quitting! *[Laughs.]*

WWD: And then *Babo 73* came out of that.

RD: Yeah. Taylor Mead [the legendary underground film actor] was our leading guy. He played the president of the United Status *[sic]*. And Tom O' Horgan, who later went on to do *Hair*, did the music. That was shot in 16mm, and we just basically went down to the White House and starting shooting, with no press passes, permits, anything like that. Kennedy was in Europe, so nobody was too tight with the security, so we were outside the White House mainly, ran around, we actually threw Taylor in with some real generals, who were appalled by what we were trying to do! It was an hour long; the budget was about $3,000.

WWD: And then you jump straight into sexploitation with *The Sweet Smell of Sex* [1965], which was pretty much a 42nd Street type of movie, that you directed for someone else. I thought it was kind of a parody of *The Sweet Smell of Success* [1957; directed by Alexander Mackendrick] in weird sort of way.

RD: If you say so! Barnard L. Sackett offered me that. He produced it, and I directed it. I needed a payday to do what was considered kind of a porno film, but it really wasn't. We made a film that was a satire of that; it was funny. I had to write, direct, and deliver the film in a week! But when Sackett saw it he wasn't too happy. It wasn't porno enough for him. It was shot on 16mm, and then blown up to 35mm. It played on 42nd Street, and places like that. I actually did *Sweet Smell of Sex* to pay for the birth of my son [actor Robert Downey Jr.], because when my daughter was born it was tough, it was in Bellevue. Because of *Sweet Smell of Sex*, I was able to put his mother [Elsie Downey] in a decent hospital, and that's what that was really about. It didn't mind doing it fast, either!

WWD: Now we come to *Chafed Elbows* [1966], which was your first substantial underground hit. That played at the Gate Theatre for months, and got reviews in the *New York Post*, the *Times* . . . even Bosley Crowther liked it.

RD: Yeah, that was kind of amazing! We shot it in 16mm and 35mm, for $25,000, and my first wife, Elsie, played all the women characters in the film. The live action I shot in 16mm. But it was mostly stills, and we photographed the stills on an Oxberry Animation bench in 35mm. The whole thing was in black and white, but just like *Babo*, there was one color sequence when the lead character, Walter Dinsmore [George Morgan] goes to heaven. Then we blew the whole thing up to 35mm. It was about a guy who married his mother, and then they go on welfare. It was kind of a musical.

WWD: I remember the last line, "I don't want to spend the rest of my life on welfare . . . but it's a start." Great stuff.

RD: Yeah, we had a lot of fun making that film. Anything seemed possible back then.

WWD: Were you consciously trying to break away from the underground film scene and go into commercial theatricals at this point?

RD: Not really; I never really analyzed it that way. I mean, I was happy to have anything shown.

WWD: *No More Excuses* [1968] follows this. You used sections of *Balls Bluff* in that film, am I right?

RD: Well, actually what I did was take five little shorts that I'd worked on, five little things, and intercut them all.

WWD: That seemed pretty much designed to come up with some product quickly. I remember it had a guy in it, Alan Abel, who was pretty much a professional prankster, posing as an outraged citizen, protesting that all animals should wear clothing; otherwise, it was indecent exposure.

RD: That's right. How do you know all this?

WWD: Well, actually, one of the times we met was at Douglass College in New Jersey in the late 1960s, when I ran the film for a student group and you were the guest speaker. At first you tried to pass him off as "a very sick guy" to play along with the gag, but later you copped to it.

RD: You've got a good memory.

WWD: Now we get to *Putney Swope*.

RD: That was my first film in 35mm. That was put together by a company called Cinema V. The budget was $250,000; it was the first time I had a shot at something that was really going to get major distribution. Donald Rugoff put the whole thing together.

WWD: The plot revolved around Putney Swope, the token African American on the board of directors of a huge New York advertising agency, who is accidentally elected the new head of the agency when the chairman dies of a stroke in the middle of a pitch meeting. What interested me in that film is that everyone is corrupt; as soon as Putney is voted in, he begins stealing everyone's ideas, starting with using Nathan [Stan Gottlieb], the token white guy, to pitch an advertising idea for the "Get Outa Here Mousetrap" to electronics mogul Wing Soney [Tom Odachi], and then immediately firing Nathan when the pitch is successful. By the end of the film, Putney is completely selling out, pushing war toys, the Borman Six [a huge gas-guzzling car], and even marrying a woman he doesn't even like [Laura Greene] just to get ideas from her for ads! Are you saying that everyone is equally rotten and on the take?

RD: I should hope so! That's what I was saying; how else could it be?

WWD: You dubbed Putney's voice yourself; why?

RD: Arnold [Johnson; the actor who played Putney] never learned his lines. He couldn't. He just didn't, he couldn't, so the cameraman [Gerald Cotts] one night said to me—he knew I was upset—I said, "Jesus, I can't make any fucking sense out of this," and he said, "Well look through here," and I looked through the viewfinder. He said, "You see that beard moving?" I said, "Yeah," and he said, "You can put anything in there. Including what you wrote. But you gotta do it later. Don't waste your energy now getting upset." So I would come in every night—we shot most of the film at night—and [Arnold] would say, "I've got the lines." And I would say, "Oh, good," and then I knew he didn't. He would get pieces of it. But we just kept shooting after that, and then I dubbed the whole thing in later. But it was my voice all the way through. It had to be. It sounded like it was coming from Canada [because it was so obviously dubbed in]!

WWD: Where did you get into what I call "repetition humor" in your films? You take certain gags and use them over and over again, essentially running them into the ground until they stop being funny, and then after a while, the gags start being funny again because they simply won't quit. When the ad agency executive in Putney Swope dies of a stuttering stroke in midsentence, the other board members at first think he's playing charades, and even after he's clearly dead, one of his acolytes [Joe Madden] keeps shouting endlessly, "How many syllables, Mario?" Later in the film, when Putney is trying to come up with an angle for the Borman Six ads, one of his assistants repeatedly admonishes the other staff members that "Putney says the Borman Six girl has got to have soul!" And in *Greaser's Palace* [1972], Allan Arbus's Christ character Jessy continually asks, "What's going down here?" for no discernable reason at all. So what is going down here?

RD: I don't even think about it as repetition humor. It was just the moment. I just wanted to hang on to the moment, and stretch it out as long as possible. But that's a good name for it.

WWD: Another example in *Greaser's Palace* is the card sharp [Ronald Nealy] who tells Vernon Greaser [James Antonio] to "pick a card, any card . . . don't show it to me . . . now put it back in the deck. Is this the card?" Greaser replies, "No." "Is this the card?" "No." And on and on and on, all during a long tracking shot in the desert, for at least five minutes.

RD: Well, that's based on a real thing that happened, where somebody did a real card trick, and kept asking, "Is this the card?" and it was always the wrong card. I was with the guy who ended up doing that; he was the line producer of the movie. So we put a hat on him, and a coat, and said, "Let's do it again." The thing was, he kept trying that trick on us, and he never could find the fucking card.

WWD: You use a lot of dwarfs in your early films, like President Mimeo and the First Lady in *Putney Swope* [Pepi and Ruth Hermine] and Hervé Villechaize in *Greaser's Palace*. Why?

RD: First of all, in *Putney Swope*, it was written that the president of the United States should be a midget. For obvious reasons. The tough part was this one guy showed up with five midgets, it was a family of them, and he was their manager! And we had to pick the husband and wife, so we picked them, and then they turned out to be brother and sister! *[Laughs.]* So it made it twice as funny. But they were lovely people.

WWD: Another running gag in *Putney Swope* was a man who ran around the agency exposing himself, and Mr. Bad News (Alan Arbus) would constantly have to confront Putney with the problem thoughout the film. When *Putney Swope* opened in New York at the Cinema II theater, I remember that the guy who played the flasher would appear in the lobby at the end of each performance, clad only in a raincoat and shoes, pretending to flash the exiting patrons!

RD: Yeah, that was a great piece of street theater! That was Rugoff's idea.

WWD: *Putney Swope* was your biggest hit to date, and really broke through for you nationally. At that point, it seemed like you could get funded for anything.

RD: You're right. *Chafed Elbows* never left New York, except for one time it played in Boston and got banned. It was playing on a double bill with [Kenneth Anger's] *Scorpio Rising* [1964]. *Putney Swope* got real distribution; it was a big hit, particularly when you consider how little it cost.

WWD: But you followed up *Putney Swope* with *Pound* [1970], which is essentially about a bunch of dogs, played by human beings without any makeup, waiting in the pound to either be adopted, or put to sleep. Not exactly an upbeat subject.

RD: Well, the irony of that one is that when I turned it in to United Artists, the head of the studio said, "I thought this was gonna be animated." They didn't even bother to look at the script!

WWD: Oh, no!

RD: Oh, yeah, which I thought was hilarious. Then they finally put it out on the bottom half of a double bill with [Fellini's] *Satyricon* [1969], which was all right with me. That's good company, at least.

WWD: That's where I first met you, in the cutting rooms on 55th Street, I think, in New York, at Floyd Peterson's place [the producer of *Pound*], when you were cutting *Pound*. I remember you explained the whole idea of *Pound* to me, and it was clear to me, at least, what you were trying to do.

RD: Yeah, but they didn't pay attention; nobody read anything! The same thing happened with [Downey's adaptation of author David Rabe's anti-Vietnam war stage play] *Sticks and Bones* [1972] when I did that with Joe Papp [as a TV movie for CBS]. Nobody paid attention to the script.

WWD: With *Pound, Putney, Chafed Elbows,* you're still pretty much working with New York actors, the whole New York theater group, right?

RD: Yeah, absolutely. They were great to work with.

WWD: And *Pound* was Robert Jr.'s debut as an actor.

RD: That's right; it was his first film.

WWD: How did *Greaser's Palace* come about? With *Greaser's Palace,* you had a much larger budget. Where was it shot?

RD: It cost about $800,000; it was shot in New Mexico.

WWD: So what made you want to tackle a western?

RD: This woman Cyma Rubin came to me, and said, "What do you want to do next?" and I said, "Well, I have this thought about Christ coming back in a western," and she said, "I'll finance that," and she did, the whole budget! When the film was completed, she gave it to Cinema V to distribute; he didn't give her any money for it, but he took it over, and put it in theaters, and ran this huge ad in the *Village Voice* for the film, with one letter per full page, spelling out G R E A S E R S   P A L A C E; pretty amazing. You couldn't miss that.

WWD: *Greaser's Palace* deals with the exploits of Jessy [Alan Arbus], who appears in the wilderness as Christ, and his interactions with Vernon Greaser [James Antonio], a corrupt land baron, and his band of cutthroats, who hold court at Greaser's Palace, a local saloon. Vernon runs the town with an iron hand; anyone who commits even the most minor infraction is shot to death by Vernon or his hired guns. The entire film takes place in a desolate wasteland, punctuated only by the small town where Vernon reigns as a virtual king. The film opens up with Vernon's wife, Cholero Greaser [Luana Anders], singing a dirgelike song praising virginity and condemning adultery, which her husband, Vernon Greaser, loudly applauds. What were you trying to do in that scene?

RD: I did that basically to show that she can do whatever she wants. She's the only woman for a hundred miles, other than the Indian Girl [Toni Basil]. And that's what she does every day, she sings that song, and these same guys [Vernon Greaser's disreputable henchmen] applaud her every day. And she sings the same song the next day, and the whole thing keeps repeating itself. That's what I get out of it.

WWD: To please his public, Jessy does a few pathetic miracles—walking on water, healing people with the phrase "If you feel, you're healed" . . . but then he tries to avoid his ultimate crucifixion, and tells everyone he's working for "the Agent Morris." When Jessy finally does his rather lame song and dance routine for Vernon and his boys, dressed in a zoot suit, no one is impressed until he displays stigmata on his hands. Do you see Christ as a confused showman?

RD: That's absolutely right!

WWD: The Holy Ghost [Roland Nealy, who also plays the ineffectual cardsharp described earlier] is shown as a guy with a derby in a white sheet; and poor old Lamy "Homo" Greaser, Vernon's son [Michael Sullivan] keeps getting killed over and over again . . . What's going on there?

RD: Well, Lamy's a stand-in for Lazarus. He gets raised from the dead again and again by Jessy, only to be killed by his father over and over. And then there's the final father-and-son bonding scene, where Vernon finally accepts Lamy, and tells him, "You're not a homo; you're a greaser!" It's their big moment.

WWD: A particularly sick running gag in the film involves a family crossing the desert so that the wife can audition as a dance hall singer for Vernon Greaser.

RD: That's Elsie again, yeah.

WWD: When her husband and son get killed, she has to bury the two corpses on her own. Then, for the rest of the film, we keep cutting back to her "progress," as she continues toward her dubious goal, despite getting blasted with a shotgun, shot repeatedly with a bow and arrow, and otherwise abused and manhandled. Does this mean that life is going to kick you in the teeth no matter what?

RD: Absolutely! She's Job. It's all pretty straightforward, in a way.

WWD: How long did it take to shoot *Greaser's Palace?*

RD: It took six, seven weeks to shoot, and it was a lot of fun to do, because I'd never been outdoors that much before, with such beautiful light for shooting. We shot a lot of it with natural light, and we used as much of the desert as we could. It was a whole new experience for me.

WWD: But it wasn't a hit.

RD: I don't think so, but through the years it's become quite a cult favorite. And Joe Papp saw it, liked it, and that led to my next job.

WWD: Tell me about *Sticks and Bones,* your next project. This was a change, because it was made for TV.

RD: Joe Papp* saw *Greaser's Palace* and offered me *Sticks and Bones.* It was based on David Rabe's play, which I really liked, and I said "sure, I'll do it." We shot on two-inch tape, which was then the standard. But we transferred the whole thing to film, cut it on film, and then transferred it back to tape for broadcast, so we could cut it in a way that was more fun than just having to wade through those rolls of tape. Two-inch was completely primitive at the time, so we used a KEM† to cut the thing and then conformed it back to two-inch. And we mixed the sound on film, too.

WWD: Were you happy with the end quality?

RD: Yeah! I liked it. And I liked that there were no commercials for two hours. It was on CBS, and when they first saw it, they panicked. They couldn't get anybody to buy any commercials, so it went out commercial-free. It was great. I was happy to work with Joe Papp, have some fun, and make David Rabe happy, because I'd never been able to do anybody else's stuff. Then, or since then. I always do my own scripts better. David was always there, on the set, and we didn't change any of his stuff; we just took an hour out of the play. We had a pretty good schedule for that: five weeks. CBS financed it because they thought, "If it's Joe Papp, it's gonna be Shakespeare." They didn't even bother to read the thing! They didn't know what it was. And then when they saw it, they panicked.

WWD: Then there's a huge gap in your filmography, between 1972 and 1980. Other than writing for *The Gong Show Movie* [1980; directed by Chuck Barris], what did you do?

RD: Yeah, *The Gong Show Movie.* Well, I worked on something called *Jive* [never completed], which was a black and white film that went to Telluride, and I was a mess on drugs. In the 1970s, I was a mess. Not heroin, but a lot of coke and pot. It was a disaster. Coke is such a waste of time. A total waste of time.

---

*Famed New York theatrical producer. Papp was famous for his "Shakespeare in the Park" series in New York's Central Park each summer.
†Flatbed editing machine.

WWD: And so when we get to *Up the Academy* [1980], a rather lame satire on militaristic boarding schools, that doesn't seem like it's you at all.

RD: No, it's not. I was called in to do that, and I said, "The best way to do that is to have these kids be nine and ten years old." They said, "We can't do that." I said, "Why?" They said, "You can't work kids all day," and I said, "Well then work them half a day, but don't use fifteen and sixteen year olds, because it's not going to work." And they basically said, "If you don't like it, you can get the fuck out of here." No, I'm not really involved in the film at all—you're right about that. Not a pleasant experience. Then about 1980, I began to climb out of the whole drug thing, and I got sober in 1982, and I've been that way ever since.

WWD: You did some *Twilight Zone* episodes in the 1980s, when the show was briefly revived on CBS.

RD: Yeah, I rather enjoyed those. One was called "Tooth and Consequences." It was about a paranoid Jewish dentist who has a visit from the tooth fairy, and he can't believe it. It winds up with the dentist on a train to nowhere with a lot of other dentists; it's kinda weird. "Children's Zoo" was about a little girl who was so tired of her parents she wound up putting them in a zoo! I didn't write them; I was just the filmmaker. These were short pieces, very short; one was ten minutes, and the other was maybe twelve. But they were a lot of fun to do.

WWD: The next credit I have for you is *America* [shot in 1982; released in 1986]. It had a great cast: Zack Norman, Tammy Grimes, Michael J. Pollard, Richard Belzer, and a lot of other ensemble actors, and centered on the crew of a wacky cable TV station in New York that accidentally bounces their signal off the moon, thus gaining international fame. But it didn't really work, I don't think.

RD: That was horrible; it was the end of the drugs. It wasn't a failure on every level, and there were some good things in it, but it never really focused. It was shot and shelved for a long time. It was released in 1986, but it was shot a long time before that.

WWD: *Rented Lips* followed in 1988. Again, an enormous cast: Martin Mull, Dick Shawn, Jennifer Tilly, Robert Downey Jr., June Lockhart, Eileen Brennan, Shelley Berman, a host of others. It's a remarkably twisted film about two industrial filmmakers [Mull and Shawn] who get tricked into directing a porn film by their crooked boss [Berman]. The situation is rather funny: two hapless filmmakers go from producing such harmless films as "Aluminum, Our Shiny Friend," to making Nazi-themed porn films for hire. Were you happy with this movie?

RD: That was Martin Mull's film, really. I was just the filmmaker on it. It was all right; it had a couple of moments. But it's always fun to work with my son, who was in that film, on any project. He played an out-of-control porn star [named Wolf Dangler]. When we work together, he more or less comes up with characterizations, and then we kick it around a bit, and then we shoot it. That's it.

WWD: *Too Much Sun* [1991] was another ensemble film, with a huge cast: Allan Arbus, Howard Duff, Eric Idle, Ralph Macchio, James Hong, and Andrea Martin, to name just a few. The plot is typically twisted: a brother and sister compete to see who can have a child first in order to inherit a fortune from their father; however, the son is gay, and the daughter is lesbian, so this complicates matters. Are you happy with the film?

RD: That was somebody else's script, which I wrote a screenplay out of. It was all right; but it didn't really come together as a whole.

WWD: *Hugo Pool* [1997] is your most recent feature to date, a very beautiful film, with an unusually relaxed and mellow feel to it. The plot is more straightforward than some of your films of the late 1980s and early 1990s: a young woman, Hugo Dugay [Alyssa Milano] has to clean something like forty-five pools in one day, while putting up with her coked-out, alcoholic father [Malcolm McDowell] and her gambling addict mother [Cathy Moriarty]. It's a day-in-the-life film. There are the usual star-studded cameos: Robert Downey Jr., Sean Penn, Chuck Barris, Michael Lewis, Ann Magnuson, and many others. But the real focus of the film is the relationship between Hugo and Floyd Gaylen [Patrick Dempsey], who is afflicted with ALS [Lou Gehrig's Disease, a neuromuscular disease].

RD: *Hugo Pool* came out of a real experience, because my second wife, Laura Ernst, had ALS, and she died of it. We wrote that while she was ill. Actually, I'm doing some ALS films now, which I enjoy—documentaries, and films for patients.

WWD: How did you get the funding for such a personal film? Not to mention the services of Sean Penn as an actor, who would much rather direct these days? Some people find him difficult to work with.

RD: Well, not for me! When Hal Ashby,* who was my best friend, was dying, a friend of both of ours gave Sean a couple of my films, and I guess he liked them because when I called and asked him to do this, he said, "Let me read it," and then he called up and said, "I like this little part; I'll be there." It was because of him it got [funded]. He worked on it for a week, mostly with Malcolm McDowell, as a hitchhiker who's obsessed with his shoes. He was an absolute gentleman to work with.

WWD: The thing that stays with me is that the film seems less narrative focused than people focused. It's not so much interested in what will happen next, as 99 percent of Hollywood movies are today, but rather how people will interact with each other.

---

*ED: Film editor and director (*Harold and Maude*, 1971; *The Last Detail*, 1973; *Shampoo*, 1975; *Coming Home*, 1978; *Being There*, 1979) who died from cancer in 1988.

RD: Well, I wouldn't know a narrative if I saw one! And that's a good thing. You know a film I saw recently that's really good, a really good relationship film? *Last Resort* [2000; directed by Paul Pavlikovsky]. I also liked *Croupier* [1999; directed by Mike Hodges]. I just saw *Last Resort* [1986] yesterday; it's refreshing to see a good film. There's really so few good films these days; it used to be there was always one or two.

WWD: In the meantime, you've also carved out a second career for yourself as an actor, in such films as *The Family Man* [2000], *Magnolia* [1999], *Boogie Nights* [1997], *To Live and Die In LA* [1985] and other films. How did this come about? What do you think of your work as an actor?

RD: I'm not really an actor. It's just that guys like Paul Thomas Anderson and Brett Ratner like my films and want me to show up. But I can't learn lines or anything; this is all just improvisational stuff. I just show up, do it, and I'm gone.

WWD: When you look back on all the work you did in 16mm and 35mm, the technology probably seems very clumsy, compared to the digital stuff you're doing now. You've told me that you embrace the new digital technology. Why, and what kind of work are you doing with it? How is it a departure from your earlier work?

RD: Well, what I like about the digital technology is that people, especially if you're doing documentary stuff, they don't even know you're there, even though you're with them. They don't think of it as a movie, so they're totally real. We use a Sony digital camera for a lot of stuff, and we just helped out a guy in Philadelphia who was shooting some stuff on high-def of the Mummers on New Year's Day. Even high-def technology is still so unobtrusive. The key to digital filmmaking is you gotta pay attention to the sound; you can't use the mike that sticks out of the camera. You either gotta get a boom man, with a DAT recorder, or at least stick the plug into the camera and just hold up a mike! I just use the mike in the camera as a second mike, to pick up background. But most people think, when they start out, you can just use the mike on the camera.

WWD: What's next?

RD: Well, I'm doing a lot of the ALS stuff, and I'm working on a new script, which I'm very happy with. It's just about done, and Jonathan Demme is going to produce it. It's called *Forest Hills Bob*. I don't want to tell you about it, except that I'm very happy with it, and Philip Seymour Hoffman and Blythe Danner have both agreed to be in it. This is my favorite one, because it's totally real. I don't have a dime yet, though. I've just had two readings, and Jonathan and his partner are trying to get me the money, but I'm about a month away from finishing the next draft. On this one I'm going through a lot of drafts. In the past, I've been a little bit lazy, I think. But this one is really good. As Godard said, "A film has a beginning, a middle, and an end, but not necessarily in that order." And I've finally figured out the order on this thing, and I'm really excited about a project for the first time in years.

WWD: I love Philip Seymour Hoffman; he was the best thing in *The Talented Mr. Ripley* [1999; directed by Anthony Minghella], and the rather indifferent remake of *Purple Noon* [1960; directed by René Clément].

RD: You know, it's funny you should bring that up. I wanted to do that ten years ago with Robert Jr. . . . I took the book around, and people said, "Are you crazy?" And then they didn't do it right. It was supposed to be really frightening, and they made it too cute. Philip Seymour Hoffman is also a wonderful stage director, you know. I've seen two plays he's done in the last year, and they're both great.

WWD: Speaking of recent digital movies, have you seen *Celebration* [1998; directed by Thomas Vinterberg]?

RD: Of course! I love it.

WWD: What did you think of James Toback's *Black and White* [2000]?

RD: It was all right. I thought the scenes with my kid and Mike Tyson were great.

WWD: I read that in that scene, Toback simply told Robert to come on to Tyson sexually, and see what happened. Completely improvised. Robert said, "What if he kills me?," and Toback replied "Well, at least we'll get it on film."

RD: That sounds about right.

WWD: When you look back on your body of work as a whole, what do you think?

RD: It's odd, thinking about them. I have to lecture tomorrow at the School of Visual Arts, and I've had to put together a clip reel to illustrate my talk. I used some ALS clips, and a little piece from every film that I could find on tape, and the one that surprised me the most in being better than I thought was *Hugo Pool*. At the time it didn't have any good distribution. In fact, *Putney Swope* is the only film of mine that ever had any real distribution. But that's all right. I love the idea of getting them done, but not worrying about what happens to them later.

CHAPTER EIGHT

Don Bluth

GERALD DUCHOVNAY

The following interview was conducted with director Don Bluth on May 28, 1982. After joining Disney Studios in 1971, Don Bluth animated studio releases such as *Robin Hood* (1973) and *Winnie the Pooh and Tigger Too* (1974). He was promoted to directing animator for *The Rescuers* (1977) and director of animation for *Pete's Dragon* (1977). Dissatisfied with the creative direction being taken by Disney Studios, Bluth, along with Gary Goldman, John Pomeroy, and numerous animators, assistant animators, and a special effects assistant left Disney Studios in September 1979. *The Secret of NIMH*, an MGM/UA release, opened in July 1982, and is the first major production of Don Bluth Productions. The interview was conducted by Gerald Duchovnay, the General Editor of *Post Script*.

GERALD DUCHOVNAY: When you were growing up in El Paso and you milked cows and you picked tomatoes, how did you first get interested in animation?

DON BLUTH: It's a hard thing to know what attracts anybody to anything. I just know that when I was living on the farm we used to go to the Saturday morning movies. We rode our horses into town because we lived three to four miles outside of town. I loved those Saturday morning cartoons. It just so happened that whenever a Disney film would come, we would go into town on the horses, and we would look at those films and the magic of those films was just . . . captivating. I got carried away with those and I thought, "Wouldn't it be wonderful if you could work on things like that?" So I began to dream that when I grew up

FIGURE 8. Don Bluth (standing on left) with some of his staff on the animated film *The Secret of NIMH* (1982). Courtesy: Jerry Ohlinger Archives.

maybe I could become part of something that would help create those films. I got all the Disney comic books and all the paraphernalia that spins off from a film, and I began to learn how to draw with the dream that one day I would work for Walt Disney. It was just something that took my fancy and became so much a part of me that I had to do it.

GD: How did you make your first move into animation?

DB: Well, of course, I knew that Disney was in California and by then I was in Utah and until somehow I got a chance to go to California, it would never happen. I believe I was in tenth grade; I went out to visit an aunt and uncle who lived in California. My aunt knew someone who worked at Disney studios and they got me through on a special tour. It was when they were making *Peter Pan* [1953]. And that was my first real taste of the place. I knew where it was located and I knew what it was all about, so I just said, "When I get out of high school, I'll be back." I didn't do that; I went to a year of college before trying to convince my parents that I could not study in college while that dream was still waiting for me. So I went to Disney in 1971.

GD: When you were at Disney studios you were considered by many to be the heir apparent. Why did you decide to leave about three years ago?

DB: I think it was mainly because my fixation with those early Disney classics was so strong—the production values, the beautiful things that I saw on the screen when I was a child, the stories themselves, which were so strong. They were full of threat and horror and scary and everything and then they rescued you from that. All of these things were not there by the time I got to the studio, and so I said, "Gee, maybe we can fix it, maybe we can at least start making pictures that have that in it." I went to the Disney studio first in 1965; Walt was still alive and I worked at the studio on *Sleeping Beauty* for one year. There was a feeling in the building when Walt was there that you were doing all this for him. There was a feeling that he was the paternal figure; he knew what he was doing. You had a pride in the film you were making because he was there. Then I left the studio and in 1971 I returned, and of course he wasn't there anymore. There was a vast difference. I tried for a long time to roll up my sleeves and just make the best of that situation, hoping that we could rebuild Camelot, slightly. It became more and more obvious to me and to the fellows I worked with that we couldn't put Humpty Dumpty back together again. So we said, "Why not just, instead of fighting with all the people who are trying to run Disney studio, go off on our own and start brand new? We know what we want to see; let's make it to the screen that way."

GD: You resigned on your birthday, September 13, 1979. Was that a symbolic gesture?

DB: I wanted to remember that date, and I have a hard time with dates; that seemed like a good birthday present, so I said, "Let's get out of here on my birthday and let's go start our film."

GD: When you left, sixteen others left too. Did it bother you that you were gutting the Disney studios of some of its best talent?

DB: I didn't really feel that we were. They led us to believe so much around there, while we were there, that we weren't that significant to their operation. Disney Studio itself was so strong that nothing in the world could touch them. All we had better do was get in line or we wouldn't be in sync with what they were trying to do. It was not my intention to hurt them at all. The intention was simply to help the art of animation, the industry to continue to grow, not to continue to slide downwards until all that was left was Saturday morning cartoons. We wanted it to get better and to become even more artful, if possible, than Disney had achieved. It was on a slide downwards. So our intent was not to harm; our intent was to simply help build the future of the animation industry. When we left, we knew that they were in the middle of *The Fox and the Hound* [1981], that they had a great deal of money, that they had Cal-Art students to choose from, and that they would quickly recuperate. We also felt that by providing some competition, maybe it would cause them to worry a little and to work harder, and maybe they would get better. I think that's really what has happened; we did more good for the Disney Studio out than we did when we were in there.

GD: Your last project was *The Small One* [1978].

DB: Yes, that was the last picture I did while in Disney Studios.

GD: Was that followed by *Banjo, the Woodpile Cat* [1982]?

DB: No, *Banjo, the Woodpile Cat* was an exercise that Gary Goldman, John Pomeroy, and myself and a few other people did at night and on weekends in my garage. The reason we started doing *Banjo, the Woodpile Cat* was to educate ourselves as to how to build an animated picture. We were not being schooled in how to do that at the studio. We were being taught maybe how to animate, but not how to put the whole picture together. So we were trying to teach ourselves, and by doing *Banjo, the Woodpile Cat*, questions would arise which we would immediately run back to the studio and ask the old veterans there. We'd say, "How did you do this?" Then they would tell us. But it never occurred to them to just offer the information because they assumed that everyone knew what they knew.

GD: This was all preparation for *The Secret of NIMH*?

DB: It turned out that way. But it didn't start with that intention. We were really just trying to get better at what we did. I was at that studio for nine years hoping that maybe I could at least get high enough in the administration of the animation department to effect some change for the better. Later on, after we finished *Banjo*, we finally realized, towards the end of *The Small One*, that we were not going to make the studio do anything different. They were going to continue to do what they wanted to. We said why not take *Banjo*, use it as a portfolio, and see if we can't fund our own picture? So *Banjo* then became a different reason for being than it had been.

GD: Did you find much difficulty in financing *Banjo?*

DB: *Banjo,* yes. That was hard because that came out of our pockets. Yes, that was our paychecks and everything. There was nobody putting money there.

GD: How many people worked on that and how many in comparison to *The Secret of NIMH?*

DB: On Banjo I would have to say about thirteen or fourteen. It took us five years. *The Secret of NIMH,* on the other hand, had maybe sixty-five, and at our highest production moment we had 120 on crew.

GD: *The Secret of NIMH* is being heralded as the second age of animation. Why is that?

DB: That's an expression that we coined ourselves. I have found that there are many, many young people, college age and even younger, who would be delighted to get involved in the animation world. But there is no place for them to actually go to be schooled. Even if they school themselves, there is no place for them to work except in one of the TV houses such as Hanna-Barbera or Filmation or Saturday morning cartoons. So what we did by starting this new studio was we said we were going to go back to the classical look, which up to this point maybe has been called Disneyesque, but we were going to a classical look for animation and we were going to begin again. What we were going to do was make sure that this grows now to a very, very mature point. So that the stories are better, not just cartoons for kids. The stories will be animated for the teenage audience and for the adult audience. Kids, there will be something there for them, but it's for the whole range of the human being, not just for children. Because of the interest that we have felt from all sides, we have said there is indeed, I think, a renaissance going on in the animation world. I can name several other studios that are starting up right now, with much the same idea—to get back into the storytelling business with a classical look, rather than a very artsy look, which we saw in pictures, in some of Bakshi's pictures or in *Heavy Metal* [1981].

What is important to remember is telling a story which an audience can actually sit through for eighty minutes. If I ask you to look at a piece of film, an animated piece of film, that was three minutes long, it wouldn't matter exactly how it was done or anything because three minutes is not much of your time and it can hold your attention. If I ask you to sit through a half hour's worth, the animation has got to have some kind of content that will hold your interest. If I ask you to sit through eighty to ninety minutes worth of animation, I've got to have something so strong to hold you there that you won't get up and walk out. Now if I can't hold you there, I don't have any box office draw; if there is no box office draw, it is not commercial, and there is no way that it will ever come into being. No one will put up money to fund a failure. So the important thing we have to do in animation is create audience interest.

Now it is no secret that the way you get an audience involved in a play is that you get them to identify with what's going on in the play, you get them to have a catharsis with the character on the stage and on screen. With animation, that has not been the approach. Most animation producers simply are up there doing the very artsy thing, and they're being very self-indulgent about their craft, their designs, and their far-out colors. But all of that is technique, it has nothing to do with identification in a play. All of that technique will simply bore the average man or woman who goes to see it. What the important emphasis should be on is the play, the story, the identification.

GD: From your perspective, does the average moviegoer consider animation to be cartoons?

DB: The only thing that I find a frustration in speaking with many people is that they do not realize that the term "animation" is not definitive enough to cover what is there. If we speak of the term "music," there are many, many, many categories of music: jazz, classical, rock, disco, impressionistic, atonal. There are many kinds of music. In animation we have the same kind of thing. We have many categories, much of them dependent on how long you want the audience to watch it. But that division is never clear in people's minds, they just simply think all things that are drawn and move are cartoons. They don't even really use the term "animation." We're not quite that clumsy, we're not quite that . . . primitive. In the animated world, there are many styles of animation, and many times people turn against each other and they simply say, "Our way is best" and then another group will say, "No, our way is the best." But each group actually has something to offer. The people that do the old Warner Brothers shorts, you know, the very zany style like Chuck Jones.* That is, I love that animation; that's great animation to do for three, four, five minutes and you'll love it sitting there. But if I had to sit there through an hour of those, I'd just go crazy.

GD: How did you come to select *Mrs. Brisby and the Rats of NIMH*?

DB: It had many of those elements I mentioned before. Also there was a concept in that book that I really, really liked—it had to do with what if a species here on earth became more intelligent than man himself? Would they be wiser than us? Would they be self-destructive like us? Would they manage to save the world from us? How would we, as man—as the human race—how would we get along with them? The concept there is fascinating to me. I've always been fascinated with the idea that maybe the porpoises are very intelligent, it's just that we haven't figured out how to talk to them yet. And also when you say if a species were to become extremely intelligent; does that mean they would also be moral? It asks that question—would they want to do the right thing? Or would they take

---

*ED: Jones helped create such characters as Daffy Duck, Porky Pig, Wile E. Coyote, Road Runner, and Bugs Bunny for the Warner Bros. Cartoon department.

advantage, using that intelligence as a tool to actually dominate other species? Which is what we as humans do, a lot. We use our intelligence to hurt each other rather than to help each other.

GD: How early in the production process did you choose the voices for the characters? Once you had the characters set?

DB: The voices are all recorded first, before we draw the animated figure. We design the character. We kind of know what they're going to look like. We've written *reams* on their characterization. We want to know how they think, how they interact with each other, we want to know what their fears are, what their dreams are; all of this we kind of explore. Then we start talking about people's voices that we've heard that seem to fit the character. Once we've come up with a candidate for a part, we start listening to the voices, looking at some early character design. If the design and the voice seem to fit together, then we call the agent of that actor or actress and we see if they are interested. Then we bring them in for a reading. We explain to the actor what the character looks like and he usually hooks on to the whole characterization. He will give it something which will cause us to go back and change our original character design to even be stronger than it was. So, it's a ping-ponging back and forth—the developing—and it's done very early.

GD: Then the character voices add to the dialogue, or sometimes they alter the script, similar to the way actors work with directors?

DB: That's exactly it, exactly.

GD: In *NIMH* there are a number of special effects. What are some of the ones that we can look forward to seeing?

DB: Most of the special effects that you will see in *NIMH* have to do with things that we can do on the animation stand itself. Some that are easily explained are contact shadows under the character. We put this back. They have been removed from many of the later Disney films. There are a lot of little things like that—sparkles that you might see on the water, reflections of the character in glassy surfaces or in the water. There are multiple passes through the camera of a certain scene, so that it has a double exposure, creating transparent looks. There's one scene I'm thinking of when Mrs. Brisby goes into the tree of an owl. There are cobwebs hanging all over it. All those cobwebs are many, many passes through the camera, so that they feel very filmy and ethereal. That takes time because every time you pass the film through the camera again with another level of drawing, that's double the amount of work, double the amount of hours and double the money. But some scenes have as high as twenty-five passes through the camera, or more.

GD: In the classical animation mode, there are twenty-four drawings of each animated character, special effect per second. In *NIMH*, are there as many as ninety-six drawings in a second of film?

DB: That might be a mistaken idea. There are twenty-four frames a second, and that's standard in any projector. Now, for every character that you see on the screen, we draw twenty-four forms for that second. If there are two characters on the screen, then it's doubled to forty-eight. If there are three, then we just go another twenty-four. So that is where that kind of figure comes from.

Now there may be many levels of animation. There will be a stack of drawings, say, for the character Mrs. Brisby. If she is reflected in the water, there will be a stack of drawings that are Mrs. Brisby upside down, and it's her reflection. If there is a sparkle on the necklace she has around her neck, that will be another stack of drawings. So each one of these stacks is another twenty-four drawings for each second on the screen. So, sometimes it does mount up so that you have many, many drawings for each second on the screen.

GD: When you began the project, how many years did you anticipate it would take?

DB: About two and a half. We were on a very strict budget of $7 million and we had two and a half years to complete it. So we regulated that time and that money extremely cautiously.

GD: So while it's complex, you were very much aware of the cost and you've been able to do everything you wanted to do within the budget?

DB: Yes.

GD: Is it difficult to find financing for animated films? And was it difficult to find financing for *NIMH?*

DB: I think it has been in the past very difficult to find financing because traditionally if you talk to a banker or private funder, he will say the only person in the world who has ever made animation profitable is Walt Disney. And no one else has ever done it, and he is correct. No one has successfully made a box office smash out of an animated film except Disney Studios. So, they're all afraid of it. They shy away from it. Our biggest problem here was to convince the backer that we could indeed make him a picture that would get his money back and many more dollars besides; that we could indeed make a picture that would make as much money as any Disney picture, and once he saw that possibility, then the funding, of course, became very, very easy. But it's not easy because traditionally there might not have been many box office successes in animation. It's because of what I previously explained; most animated producers do not understand that for ninety minutes no one wants to watch graphics. It's just not interesting.

GD: Do you believe that the video and disc markets will increase or alter the funding that will be available for animated features?

DB: It should have some effect on us, but I don't know how much. Animation is not understood by the average public. Animation is called "cartoons" by the average public. The sophisticated animation that holds your interest for ninety minutes is not a cartoon. At that point, if you are cartooning and expect to hold someone for ninety minutes, you are fooling yourself because you have to go way beyond what is just the broad cartoon look. It has to be subtle, the colors have to be graded down, it has to be believable, and for a moment the audience has to think that this isn't drawn, this is really happening. When they suspend their disbelief and start buying what you're selling them on the screen as real, then that's not cartooning.

GD: From the things you've been working on and what will appear in *NIMH*, what changes, what improvements do you see in the next decade in animation?

DB: A lot depends on the final outcome of this movie. If *The Secret of NIMH* will go out there and make several million dollars in the box office, and luckily if it will get itself up there in the top ten, or even top twelve, the gross, then that provides hope for many people. They will say, "Look, it can be done." If indeed we can make a picture make that kind of money, that means Disney isn't the only one. *The Fox and the Hound*, for example, was, I think, number twelve in box office gross when it came out last year. It made a great deal of money—wasn't that good a picture, but it made a lot of money because it was animated. Now that just simply underscores one fact: Disney knows how to make an animated film. It isn't my cup of tea, but I know they know how to make an animated film. So, what we're saying is if another producer can make that kind of money or get into that bracket, then I think that loosens up the purses of many, many financiers. They'll be more anxious to invest in animation films, they'll actually seek someone to make them a film. Animation when it works is extremely lucrative. *Rescuers* [1977] in Germany outgrossed *Star Wars* [1977].

GD: Do you see differences in European animation?

DB: Yes, it is different because our cultures are really quite different. But they are very much art oriented and they love animation. I just got back from Frankfurt not too long ago and the group I spoke with had marketed *The Fox and the Hound*, and in Frankfurt alone they managed to get the Germans to pay $16 million to go see that picture, just in Germany. Now that's the negative cost, almost the entire negative cost back, in just one European country. They are very much a fan of the animated work; they love it, they really do. And those people I talked to there, the Germans, were excited and could hardly wait. They are looking forward very much to this picture.

GD: Do you find yourself having to sell *NIMH*? For example, you went through a four-hour grilling at the American Film Institute. Do you see this as a necessary part of the filmmaking process?

DB: No. Most of the seminars that I've been giving have been to small groups. Those seminars, ranging from 250 to 300 people, are not really selling tickets. Those seminars are an effort on our part to try and get the college age, the young students, to stimulate an interest in them in the animation process and to instill hope in them that if they really want to get involved in the animation world, that it's a very fine world and there are a lot of opportunities for them. So, I haven't really had to sell too much; in fact, it has been just the reverse. When I talk at one of these places, I find out that most of them already know their homework; the questions they ask are very relevant, and they know what is going on. They're anxious to see the picture, they want it to work, which means financially.

GD: Do you recommend New York or Los Angeles or can they do animation anywhere?

DB: There are only one or two places you can go. I was talking to the New School of Animation in New York in May. Most of those young people said there was just nothing going on in New York. If any of them wanted to get involved in animation they thought they had to come to California. I said, "Well, if you really want animation, that's not too bad; California isn't too bad a place. Come on out."

GD: Can the industry absorb them right now?

DB: No. That is why so much hangs for me on getting *NIMH* to work. If *The Secret of NIMH* will be measured correctly by the yardstick of finance, if it does well, that will cause more growth. We are already funded to go into a second picture so I can absorb a little bit of that and we have a better budget on the second picture than the first.

GD: Can you say something more about the next project?

DB: Yes, it's a story that is original. It's based on a Norwegian fairy tale called *East of the Sun, West of the Moon,* and we're funded for $11 million.

GD: And what's your target date on that?

GD: In thirty months we'll have it finished. Two and a half years is ample time to build.

GD: We'll look forward to that.

DB: Thanks a lot.

GD: Thank you.

CHAPTER NINE

Jamie Babbit

WHEELER WINSTON DIXON

Jamie Babbit's *But I'm a Cheerleader* (1999) was one of the breakout independent film hits of the 1999–2000 season. Babbit, a surprisingly assured thirty-year-old from Cleveland, Ohio, came to filmmaking though amateur theater, and went on to direct a series of short films, including *Frog Crossing* (1996) and *Sleeping Beauties* (1999), before making her debut as a feature director with *Cheerleader*.

Cheerleader tells the story of "femme" Megan (Natasha Lyonne), a young woman who doesn't realize that she's a lesbian until her parents stage an "intervention," which results in Megan being shipped off to True Directions, a deprogramming center for gays and lesbians who are forced to be straight. True Directions is run by the monstrously repressive Mary (Cathy Moriarty) and her in-denial gay son Rock (Eddie Cibrian), with the assistance of camp supervisor Mike (RuPaul Charles, in his first nondrag role). At True Directions, Megan meets and falls in love with the butch lesbian Graham (Clea DuVall), and despite all of Mary's threats and machinations, Megan and Graham's love triumphs over True Direction's worst efforts to make the two girls straighten out.

Babbit stages *Cheerleader* as a bright, "popped out" comedy, with bright colors and heavily stylized sets. At the same time, Babbit's experience with actors allows her to seamlessly handle a large ensemble cast with practiced efficiency. Babbit also works in television, where she directs the WB television series *Popular* (1999), and the MTV series *Undressed* (1999). Honest and open about her

154

FIGURE 9. Jamie Babbit directs the low-budget independent film *But I'm A Cheerleader* (1999). Courtesy: Jerry Ohlinger Archives.

work and her lifestyle, Jamie was pleased to have a chance to talk about *But I'm A Cheerleader* in detail. She is already at work on her next feature film, tentatively titled *Conjugating Niki*.* I spoke with Jamie on October 21, 2000.

WHEELER WINSTON DIXON: How did you get started in the business, and what was your childhood like?

JAMIE BABBIT: I came to filmmaking through theater. I was born in Cleveland, Ohio, and I started at the Cleveland Playhouse when I was about seven years old, taking acting classes and then moving on to stage managing. There are a lot of elements of *Cheerleader* that are autobiographical. I never went to a homosexual rehabilitation camp, although such places do exist, like the Exodus Project, but my mother runs a treatment program for teenagers in Ohio called New Directions, which helps them beat alcohol and drug problems. My father is more like the Bud Cort character in *Cheerleader;* he's really sweet and supportive. He doesn't really want to talk about my being lesbian, but he's always been there for me. He's a lawyer. So I'd always wanted to do a comedy about growing up in rehab, and the absurdity of that atmosphere. But I didn't want to make fun of twelve-step programs for alcoholism and drugs, because they really help people, but when you turn it into Homosexuals Anonymous, then I felt that was a situation I could have fun with.

WWD: Did your parents support your work in the theater?

JB: My parents were very supportive, doing the car pool thing, taking me all around, so I continued all through high school doing a lot of acting. Even though we were in Ohio, it was a really avant-garde theater program; we were singing Leonard Cohen and Tom Waits songs, not the usual stuff. Gradually, I moved more into being a stage manager, and doing lighting, which I enjoyed more. Then I was lucky enough to go to college at Barnard, and when I was there I did theater, and I started taking film classes. So I really came to film through acting, and working with actors. I really think that's essential, and I love working with actors to this day.

WWD: How did you get involved in film? At Barnard?

JB: I didn't take the film classes at Barnard; I took them at NYU during the summer. I got a Centennial Scholarship, which basically gave me money to pursue something I was interested in. So I wound up taking film classes at NYU. My film teacher was named Boris; he was pretty tough on all of us. He'd look at my films and say, "Jamie, I don't like this at all. It's terrible. Make babies, not

---

*ED: Sandwiched between numerous television shows (*Ed, Malcolm in the Middle, Gilmore Girls,* and others), Babbit has directed *Stuck* (2001), a seven-minute short film.

films." Pretty hardcore! *[Laughs.]* But he would do it to everyone. He was brutal, but really, really talented. He was a great teacher, and he really put me on the right track.

WWD: The importance of lesbian identity is a central issue in *But I'm A Cheerleader*. When did you come out yourself?

JB: I came out to myself as a lesbian in high school, but it was one of those things that you kind of know, but you're not really sure. I think I had lots of pictures of women in my locker at high school, just like the character of Megan in *Cheerleader*. Other people would say to me, "Hey, you're a lesbian" and I would think, "Hmm, you think so?" And I was still thinking about it in college and then fully came out after college, when I was twenty-two. I was very lucky; my mother and father were very supportive of my decision, and so that made things much easier.

WWD: What were your first short films like?

JB: I made a lot of short films before *Cheerleader*, for classes, just exercises, but there's one I'd still like to expand into a feature, which I made in college in Super 8mm, called *Discharge*. It was just two minutes long, the first thing I ever made in Super 8mm. It was simple: this woman is walking down the streets of New York, and some guy is harassing her, some construction worker type, played by my brother, incidentally, and she gets really irritated, and finally reaches under her skirt, pulls out her tampon and throws it at him.

When I screened it in class, the instructor was somewhat taken aback by the film; I remember he asked me, "Do you think this is a *feminist* film?" So then I did some other short films, which were awful, and then I made *Frog Crossing* in 1996 with a friend of mine, Ari Gold. It was a short film we made in San Francisco, about an animal rights activist who protects frogs as they hop across the highway. It was about twelve minutes, but it's very similar to *Cheerleader* in that it's very stylized, and there are only two colors in the whole movie; it's very constructed in every sense of the word. It's got a real pop feel to it.

WWD: How did you make the jump from college to working within the industry?

JB: When I graduated from Barnard in 1993, I needed a job. I had worked as an intern in the industry when I was in college, while I was making my own short films on the side, but I wanted to jump into a real film. My first job was as a production assistant in Martin Scorsese's office on *The Age of Innocence* [1993]. I actually never met him, because it was such a huge production. I would run errands, and his mom would knit booties for Steven Spielberg's new baby, and I would go over and pick them up; that was my job.

But it was a good office to work in, because Marty has such an encyclopedic knowledge of film, and an enormous personal archive of films; he really knows film history inside and out. It was a good lesson for me, because I still had a lot to learn about the history of film, and how valuable it can be in the day to day production process. Marty would phone the office from the set, and ask me to get some Italian film from the 1940s from his archive and send it to set, so Daniel Day Lewis could look at it to help him work on his character. Marty's knowledge in this area is so vast, and I thought, "This is something I really have to get on with." That was fifty dollars a day, but it was a start, and I was learning a lot.

WWD: That's a good entry point. What happened next?

JB: From there, I got a job with John Sayles on *The Secret of Roan Inish* [1994], also as a production assistant. It was a much smaller movie, and there were three people working in the office: Karen Kusama, who has just directed her first big hit, *Girlfight* [2000]; one was Jasmine Kosovic, who produced a film called *The Adventures of Sebastian Cole* [1998]; and one was me! It was just the three of us working in this small office, and we were all saying, "We want to be filmmakers, someday!" Working with John Sayles is great; he's just a wonderful person. His whole philosophy is, if you're going to make a movie, just do it. And that goes back to his first film, *The Return of the Secaucus Seven* [1980]. John is really down to earth, and working with him made me realize that I really wanted to get on the set, because I had been stuck in the office, and I really wanted to work with the actors, and be part of the creative process. I knew I really needed to learn from directors working on the set, so I decided to lie my way into being a script supervisor, and it worked.

WWD: In time-honored Hollywood tradition! Did anyone catch on?

JB: Well, my first job as script supervisor was with John Duigan, on *The Journey of August King* [1995]. I love John's work, especially *Flirting* [1991], which is one my favorite films. The director of photography on *August King* was a great guy named Slavomir Idziak, who also photographed Krzysztof Kieslowski's *Blue* [1993] and a bunch of other projects, and he was wonderful to me. The assistant director, Skip Cosper, was an old pro who had worked on huge films like *Days of Heaven* [1978], so everyone really knew what they were doing, and they helped me get away with it. I didn't know anything, but I pretended that I did, and they were so good, they didn't need me that much anyway, thank God! And then from there I worked with Su Friedrich* on her first narrative movie, *Hide and Seek* [1996].

WWD: That's quite a jump, from a more traditional narrative project to an experimental narrative feature.

JB: Well, I was taking what I could get! My next job, Nancy Savoca's TV movie *If These Walls Could Talk* [1996] was actually my first job in L.A. I fell in love with producer Andrea Sperling. I was going through a breakup, and Andrea lived in L.A., so I went there and wound up working for Nancy on that film, which was an incredible experience. I actually worked on only one segment of the film,

---

*ED: Since 1978, director, writer, editor, and producer of short films.

the "1974" sequence with Sissy Spacek, in which she plays a mother who decides not to get an abortion. After that, I went on to my first big-budget Hollywood movie, David Fincher's *The Game* [1997]. That was a fascinating experience, because I went from Nancy's movie, which was probably a $2 million, $3 million movie, to an $80 million movie, working with Michael Douglas, Sean Penn, and a real Hollywood crew.

WWD: What was that experience like?

JB: Intense. But David Fincher is so interesting; even though he's a Hollywood director, he's a real auteur. He really has a vision, and his command of the technical aspects of filmmaking is staggering. I learned a lot from him. And I was very lucky, because he was very supportive of my work.

WWD: That's surprising to me, because Fincher's films, like *Se7en* [1995] and *Fight Club* [1999] are really dark movies, and your films are exactly the opposite.

JB: Well, *Fight Club* was meant to be a comedy, actually. The whole time I was watching it, I was laughing, because I know him, and he just took the whole thing as a really, really dark comedy. It's not a typical Hollywood film at all. But it was David who actually gave me the chance to shoot *Sleeping Beauties*. We'd been talking about fairy tales on the set, and David was very interested in the project, so he wound up giving me some leftover film stock from *The Game*, about six thousand feet of 35mm film. That allowed me to shoot in 35mm, which made a big difference in the short, and also David's editor for *The Game* gave me the use of the AVID [editing machine] for free, so it was a real break. And to top it off, I met Michael Douglas while we were making the movie, and he was kind enough to write a letter to Paramount saying, "Please give Jamie Babbit access to the costume and wardrobe department for her film," and so I basically had free reign at Paramount. *Sleeping Beauties* cost about $10,000, which is pretty cheap for a twelve-minute 35mm color film.

WWD: You're quite a hustler.

JB: Well, I had to be! I was desperate! *[Laughs.]* I wanted to make *Sleeping Beauties*, and I was going to do it anyway I could. You have to do this sort of stuff when you're starting out, if you're ever going to get anything off the ground. You have to go for it, and that's what I did.

WWD: Tell me about *Sleeping Beauties*.

JB: *Sleeping Beauties* [1998] is a retelling of the fairy tale *Sleeping Beauty*, which in turn is inspired by the Disney version from the 1930s. *Sleeping Beauties* tells the story of a girl who works as a makeup artist at a funeral home, who is obsessed with unavailable women. And the metaphors for the unavailable women are the corpses that she paints.

WWD: Cheerful.

JB: Yeah. And then through her job, she ends up meeting a photographer at one of the funerals, played by Clea DuVall, who also plays the character of Graham in *Cheerleader*, and they wind up in a relationship, so it has a happy ending. It's only about twelve minutes long. The great thing about that film was working not only with Clea, but also with Radha Mitchell, who really broke through as the lead role in Lisa Cholodenko's *High Art* [1998]. I fell in love with Radha when I saw her in a film called *Love and Other Catastrophes* [1996], when I was at Sundance with *Frog Crossing*. She was at Sundance promoting the film, and we met very briefly. Then I came back to Los Angeles, and Radha had just moved there, and I called her up and asked her to be in *Sleeping Beauties*, and she was great. Then, a couple of months later, Lisa Cholodenko called me and said, "I'm considering this actress Radha Mitchell for *High Art*; what do you think of her?," and I said, "She's fabulous, you should definitely hire her!" So that's how that happened.

WWD: When and how did you decide to tackle a feature film?

JB: When I finished shooting *Sleeping Beauties*, I realized it was time to make the jump to a feature, so I wrote a three-page treatment for *Cheerleader*, and met with a bunch of writers who were recommended to me by friends, who would basically write me a screenplay for free. *Sleeping Beauties* was still in postproduction, and I had enough experience from *Frog Crossing* to know that when you screen something at a festival, and people like it, they're immediately going to ask you, "What are you doing next?," so you have to have something new in the pipeline.

My girlfriend Andrea Sperling agreed to produce *Cheerleader*, and Brian Wayne Peterson came on board as the screenwriter. By this time, Andrea had a produced a whole bunch of films, like *Desert Blue* [1998], *Fame Whore* [1997], and Gregg Araki's *Nowhere* [1997], *The Doom Generation* [1995], and *Totally F***ed Up* [1993]. So we said to Brian, "*Sleeping Beauties* will be done in four months, so you have four months to write the script, so let's do it, and we'll take the film and your script to Sundance, and see if we can get it financed." By this time, Andrea had become friends with the financier Michael Burns, who is now the vice president of Lion's Gate Films, but at the time was just financing movies out of his own bank account. We approached him and said, "We want to make this comedy about these two girls falling in love at a homosexual rehabilitation camp" and he said, "I love it, it's a great idea, I'd love to see the script" and so he ended up financing it himself.

WWD: What was your budget?

JB: The initial budget was $500,000, and when the film actually went into production, he agreed to give us $1,000,000.

WWD: How did you get your cast? It's really a superb ensemble: Natasha Lyonne, Clea DuVall, RuPaul Charles, Cathy Moriarty, Bud Cort, Richard Moll, Mink Stole—that's some pretty ambitious casting.

JB: Well, I simply pursued Cathy Moriarty. I simply wouldn't take no for an answer. You know, I'd pop out of the bushes with the script in hand *[laughs]* and I just pursued her until I got her. I needed a really strong person to play Mary, the head of True Directions, a person who could utterly dominate the frame, and Cathy was the perfect choice. She works really hard in the film; she makes True Directions real, and simultaneously over-the-top.

For the rest of the cast, I started with Clea, because Clea worked at a coffee shop in an art house theater in L.A., and Clea would give me free coffee for a while, so we became friends. I showed her my first film, and then I wrote *Cheerleader* with her in mind for the part of Graham, the butch girl who Megan, Natasha Lyonne's character, falls in love with. Clea was actually friends with Natasha, so that's how we got her in the film.

At this point, we got a really good casting director, who had worked on Tamara Jenkins's *Slums of Beverly Hills* [1998], Sheila Jaffe. She does at least five movies a year at Sundance, works on *The Sopranos*, and so she had access to a lot of excellent actors. I loved Doug Spain from *Star Maps* [1997], so I knew I wanted him; RuPaul was really excited about it, and really happy to do a role that wasn't in drag for a change. Mink Stole came in and auditioned; Bud Cort was brought in by Sheila. I loved Bud in *Harold and Maude* [1971] and *Brewster McCloud* [1970]; *Brewster* is Natasha's favorite movie, so she was really pleased to be working with him.

WWD: What about Jules LaBarthe, your director of photography?

JB: Jules shot *Frog Crossing, Sleeping Beauties,* and *But I'm A Cheerleader;* he's done all my films. He went to NYU as a filmmaker, and he was someone I met at a coffee shop in Los Angeles. He'd shot some "B" features before he did *Cheerleader,* but this was his first real independent feature.

WWD: You meet a lot of people at coffee shops!

JB: No, but it's true! Coffee culture, desperate filmmakers, alone in Los Angeles; you make some really good connections there. You have to keep working to keep your skills up, and that's the reason why I like directing television. I'm obviously still working on feature projects, but it takes a lot of time to put a feature project together, to put the financing in place, and get a script ready. Since I'm developing my own material, it takes longer. Some people say, "I'm a director," but they haven't been on a set for five years! That's the nice thing about television shows like *Popular* and *Undressed,* because you're not responsible for anything except working with the actors. The directorial style's been established, the writers really have the power, and the producers do the casting, so you're just really working with the actors.

WWD: And you have to work really quickly to get it in the can.

JB: Yeah, but they asked me when I started working on *Popular* [a weekly, hour-long comedy series on WB] and *Undressed* [an MTV series] whether or not I'd be able to keep up the pace, and I said, "Look, I come from independent filmmaking, so I'm working as fast as I can all the time on the set anyway." It actually feels really luxurious. Eight days to shoot one hour of programming is fine. And it's not even really an hour; when you get rid of the main title, end title, and all the commercial breaks, it's really about forty-two minutes.

WWD: *Cheerleader* is very much interested in performativity, defining gender through tasks: the boys play football, fix cars, chop wood, while the girls do household chores. It seems that the film is one enormous drag act, whether lesbian, heterosexual, or gay.

JB: Well, I definitely wanted to talk about gender roles, gender expectations, and the absurdity of them, and I think a lot of that came from my own life. When I was coming out as a lesbian, a lot of people made fun of me because I was bad at sports. I mean, I was terrible, an absolute sissy; I couldn't do anything. And one of the many bizarre gender expectations is that lesbians are supposed to be really good at sports. But I'm not; I'm femme, and that's it. I was doing an interview for *The Advocate* [the gay and lesbian magazine], and a lesbian reporter came over to my house, and the walls are pink, and there are Barbie dolls everywhere, and she was really upset. "Are these Barbies *yours?*" she demanded, and when I said "yes" she shot back, "I don't know any lesbians who have Barbie dolls!" So, maybe I was born as a gay man!

That's the kind of stuff I wanted to talk about in this film; how gender expectations define our lives, and how others see us. In some ways, that's where the title of the film came from. Because Megan is a cheerleader, she can't believe that she's a lesbian. But then, at the end of the film, Megan uses her cheerleading skills to affirm her lesbian desire, when she urges Graham not to buckle under to the True Directions manifesto, and to come out as her lesbian lover. I didn't want it to be a film about a lesbian who comes out, and then drives off on a motorcycle at the end. She was still a cheerleader at the end.

WWD: Why did you make the character of Graham, Megan's love interest, so butch, the archetypal "bad girl," smoking cigarettes and dripping with macho attitude?

JB: I just wanted to make her the antithesis of Megan, and Megan's such a good girl, and good girls always fall for bad girls, or maybe that's another autobiographical element of the film. Clea DuVall just has such a kind of raw, natural sexiness to her that she was perfect for the part.

WWD: What about Eddie Cibrian, who played Rock, Mary's gay son who is supposedly straight? He doesn't do much, but he manages to get a lot of mileage fooling around with a chainsaw, and stroking a rather phallic rake.

JB: Well, he's great to work with, and a lot of that stuff with the rake was just improvised on the set. He played the masseuse in *Living Out Loud* [1998], giving Holly Hunter massages throughout the film, playing a muscle-bound hunk who is basically a male prostitute.

WWD: When you run *Cheerleader* for a sympathetic audience, you're obviously going to get an enthusiastic response, but have you ever run the film for an audience that flat out hated it, because they were that homophobic? At several screenings I attended, when Megan and Graham finally kiss, a number of audience members simply got up and walked out, which astounded me. It's just two people kissing, but apparently, that's too much for some narrow-minded spectators.

JB: Well, I've never had a bad response at any screenings in Los Angeles, where I live, although I have shown it to some not as friendly audiences elsewhere, so I know what you mean. But the most bizarre screening was (and I'm going to kill my girlfriend for doing this to me) when Andrea made me show it to her ninety-six-year-old grandmother! *[Laughs.]*

She's really conservative, and I thought, "This is the most excruciating screening I've ever attended." She really didn't need to see the film, you know what I mean?

WWD: Why did she do that?

JB: Well, Andrea has produced a lot of really dark films, like *The Doom Generation* [1995], *Totally F***ed Up* [1993], a lot of dark, very gay movies. And this was the lightest movie that she's ever made, so she thought, "Well, my grandmother can see this!" She didn't think she could screen the other films, but she thought that *Cheerleader* was a *happy* movie, and I said, "Yeah, it's a happy movie, but there's lots of swear words, and there's girls kissing." I think Andrea kind of forgot the kind of levels there.

WWD: How would you differentiate your film from such recent lesbian films as *Go Fish* [1994], *The Incredibly True Adventure of Two Girls in Love* [1995], *The Watermelon Woman* [1996] and *Boys Don't Cry* [1999]?

JB: Well, they're told from the butch angle, and so they're films that I wouldn't make, but they're films that I like. But in *Cheerleader*, I wanted to make a conscious choice to have a femme protagonist. In *Go Fish*, Max is the femme character, but she's the love interest of Ely, the lead character, who gets the buzzcut. And when you deconstruct the film, Max becomes more butch, and that's how she gets the girl. And in *Incredibly True Adventure*, we're given a tomboy girl, who ends up going for the femme, the object of her affections. In *Cheerleader*, I wanted the femme to be the pursuer, not the pursued. Not only movies, but also a lot of lesbian fiction I've read, a lot of lesbian narratives, are told from the butch perspective. And it was important to me to not tell that story again, because I wanted to show that a femme can be strong, and a femme can get what she wants.

At the same time, one of the things I've been most interested in in the art world is the concept of "constructed realities," like Cindy Sherman, Red Grooms, Barbara Kruger—people who create an entire alternative universe in which everything is hyperreal, popped out, colorful, and utterly plastic. So at the same time I wanted to talk about gender constructs, and the absurdity of gender constructs, I wanted to explore the artifice and unreality of a completely constructed world, in which nothing is real. I really wanted the sets and the world that I created for the characters in the film to be something unreal, campy, and yet really colorful and vibrant. Lots of pinks, blues, and very artificial. When I was going to Barnard, Red Grooms did an exhibit at Grand Central station, which I really loved; I adored his papier-mâché cityscapes. As part of this Grand Central exhibit, Grooms created a fake subway car that you could really sit down in, and it was like living inside a cartoon. That's the look I wanted for the film. I'm also really fond of Derek Jarman's work, particularly *Caravaggio* [1986] and *Queer Edward II* [1991], in which all of his sets are transparently constructed in one location.

WWD: Were you at all influenced by the TV series *Pee Wee's Playhouse?*

JB: Yes, I love *Pee Wee's Playhouse,* and I also love Tim Burton's work, which is pretty much the same thing; the creation of a safe, or in Burton's case, menacing alternative universe. Actually, I offered a part in the film to Paul Reubens [Pee Wee], but he was busy on another project, and he had to turn it down. But then after the film came out, Bud Cort had a birthday party, and I ran into Pee Wee there. He came over to me and said, "I want you to know that I loved the script, and thank you for thinking of me," which made me really happy, because I'd felt rejected.

WWD: What about working with Richard Moll, who is probably most famous for his work on the TV series *Night Court?*

JB: He was great, because he's such a bear, and I wanted to cast him because he's such a huge, yet gentle guy. There was a scene that I wanted to do with him, though, that caused a big controversy on the set. Megan has just escaped from True Directions, and finds safety in Lloyd [Wesley Mann] and Larry's [Richard Moll] house. I wanted Richard Moll's character to offer Megan a platter of dildos when she walked in, and say, "Welcome to being a lesbian." Richard and I had this big controversy on the set; essentially, he said, "This is weird, Jamie. I don't want to do this." And then some other people on set agreed with him, and Andrea said, "You know, I think there's something weird about coming out as a lesbian, and then someone hands you a bunch of plastic penises." Eventually, I agreed, and we just said forget it. I think Richard thought I'd gone off the deep end! *[Laughs.]*

WWD: How long was the shoot?

JB: Twenty-eight days.

WWD: Did anyone give you any grief because of your relative youth? I mean, you look *really* young.

JB: I know what you mean, and a lot of people say that, but I didn't have any real problems. Sometimes, people would be a little shocked when they came in to audition. When RuPaul came in, he took one look at me and said, "you're twelve!," but during the shoot everyone was fine. I think a lot of it was that I was working with a lot of people who were younger than me, or slightly younger than me, so it all worked out.

WWD: Your film has a very childlike, innocent air, a place of safety and reassurance in which people can come out and be themselves. Is this the kind of world that your films try to construct in the real world, for real audiences?

JB: Well, in the film, True Directions is a really violent, horrible place, and I shot a lot of Cathy Moriarty's close-ups right in the camera, with a slight wide angle lens to make her appear *really* scary. One of the things that I said to the production designer and the costume designer, was that I wanted to be sure, as the film went on, that the materials for the sets and costumes became more artificial. So by the end, when all the kids at True Directions are graduating to the straight life in their plastic uniforms, I said, "I don't want cotton, I don't want polyester—I want pure plastic."

WWD: That plastic look is central to the film's overall vision and design.

JB: Absolutely. If you notice, in the beginning, Megan's clothing is cotton; in the middle, polyester; and at the end, everything is entirely plastic. I wanted the production design and the sets to follow the same pattern, because at the end of the film, when the kids all say that they're straight, that's the most artificial that they are; they're denying their true selves. In fact, everything that Cathy Moriarty wore was plastic from the beginning of the film to the end; the costume designers originally put her in a polyester uniform, and I said, "No, let's give her a plastic lab coat." I thought that her character should be really paranoid about diseases, AIDS, germs, and so we made everything sanitized. When she's outside cleaning her flowers, they're not even real flowers, because she doesn't believe in real sexual urges. To Mary, gay desire is unnatural, so let's go to a completely artificial place with her character.

WWD: Do you think that American society has changed much over the past ten years or so? Can you come out without dealing with an enormous amount of free-floating hostility? What are the risks?

JB: I do think you can come out, and I do think it will be OK. I'm an optimist. I think it will be OK because at least you will have love; Megan and Graham really love each other, and that love will carry them through a world full of problems and conflicts. The outside world may be hideous and horrible, and it may be a fight to stay alive, but if you have love, you'll be OK, no matter what happens.

WWD: A lot of people have compared *Cheerleader* to John Waters's films, sort of a camp aesthetic, but I don't see that at all.

JB: Nor do I. I like John's films, but to me, I'm doing something totally different, and the optimism of *Cheerleader* is one of the things that makes it something separate. Tim Burton and John Waters both go for the same kind of constructed hyperreality that I use in my films, but they both have a darker edge to their work, and I'm more interested in using the camp aesthetic to make a positive statement. Then there's the whole question of women doing camp, which I don't think has ever really been done before. I wasn't interested in doing a camp movie that was completely satirical. I wanted it to have emotion, and I'm a romantic, so I wanted it to have some heart. A lot of people got on the Internet and attacked me for it, saying in essence, "You wish you could be John Waters," but I'm not trying to do that. I think it misses the point. I love his work, especially *Serial Mom* [1994], but I'm doing something lighter, more romantic, and more positive.

WWD: What's next?

JB: Well, for the moment, more television, and then a feature, but that takes so much time to get off the ground, as I've said. Sometimes you just have to work for money, but even then, you should always give it your best shot. I hope I can get a feature off the ground in the next couple of years, and obviously, all the critical and audience response to *But I'm A Cheerleader* really helps with your next project. We'll just have to see what happens next.

PART III

International Voices

CHAPTER TEN

Paul Verhoeven

CHRIS SHEA AND WADE JENNINGS

Paul Verhoeven appeared twice on the Ball State University campus, in November 1990 in conjunction with the university's opening of an exchange with Groningen University in the Netherlands, and in September 1992 to join Millard Fuller, Bette Bao Lord, Terry Waite, Dennis Weaver, James Burke, and others as a "UniverCitizen" in the award-winning UniverCity project. In 1990 he had just returned from the European and Japanese openings of *Total Recall* and was three days into the casting for *Basic Instinct*; in 1992, he was fresh from a worldwide promotion tour for *Basic Instinct* and reading scripts for his next project.

In his 1990 visit, Verhoeven, who had trained as a university mathematics professor, graciously agreed to teach a class, as well as meet with the press and speak in a fully formal public lecture. The class of about ninety students and professors was a composite of fields represented by members of the University Film Committee: two advanced telecommunications classes on film technique and history, two classics courses (Classical Greek and the Ancient World in the Cinema), several senior English seminars, and the stray art historian, mathematician, or physicist. (Verhoeven's dissertation was on the mathematics of nuclear physics.) Verhoeven lectured, in royal academic style, and answered questions on his career and violence in film.

For the evening session, Verhoeven had opted for a question-and-answer format, and, to insure a steady supply of questions, the Film Committee had put up a display in the student center inviting questions for Dr. Verhoeven. But so far had Verhoeven gone to overcoming the students' midwestern shyness that, in fact, committee members read only six (of nearly a hundred) questions before

FIGURE 10. Paul Verhoeven on the set of his breakthrough American film, *RoboCop* (1987). Courtesy: Jerry Ohlinger Archives.

long lines formed at the auditorium's mikes. There were nearly eight hundred there that night, and most remained until, after three hours, we flashed the lights (the security staff was about to go into overtime).

In 1992 airline schedules and Indiana's rejection of Daylight Savings Time (we're on "God's Time") conspired to limit Verhoeven's time in Muncie to less than twenty hours. Although he again acted the "Man of Iron" (as the *Los Angeles Times* has it), taking questions for more than two hours, we were forced to break off a lively discussion for the run to the airport.

In general, we think what follows shows all the personae of this remarkable man: painter, Greek philologist, physicist—and poet and pirate, too.

CHRIS SHEA: What was your childhood like?

PAUL VERHOEVEN: I was born in '38 in Amsterdam and, as you know, the Germans occupied Holland in '40. So from when I was three until seven or eight, until '45, I was living in an occupied country. The first couple of years of the occupation were pretty mild, but the last couple of years were very violent, and I was living in The Hague, which was the center of the German government and also, even more important, the launching pads of the rockets, the V1s and V2s, which were invented by Werner von Braun, who later was head of the NASA program here. He'd invented these armed rockets which were being made in Peenemünde, in Germany, then sent over to The Hague, and the launching pads were about one mile from our house. So these rockets were always sent to London. And, because of that, the English and the Americans were continuously bombing the area. That was in fact the area around our house, because they wanted to get rid of these rockets and these launching pads to prevent the rockets from going to London.

So when I was living there, especially the last couple of years—it was '44 when they started sending these rockets around—it was an extremely violent situation because of the bombs that were falling down. And as a child I think I saw so much violence there, so many dead bodies. There was a lot of blood, and, strangely enough, the whole area around our house was completely bombed out because the English squadron leader at a certain moment reversed the map in his cockpit and so they bombed the wrong area, which was a civilian area, and twenty to thirty thousand people were killed. And that was just, let's say, one hundred yards from my house. The whole area beyond the back of the house was completely destroyed, and so that part of The Hague was completely in flames.

CS: Did this help shape your view of violence?

PV: It's very astonishing when you are a child and your perception of the daily routine is dead people, violence, bombing, fire, day in, day out. I think that gives you a very strong depression which probably sinks into the subconscious later when it's all over and the war is over and peace starts. For me, to be honest, the war was a great time. I mean I was a child and I loved it. I don't know if you've ever seen the movie by John Boorman, *Hope and Glory* [1987]; it was exactly like that but worse. I mean that was not so violent because there was not that much happening in London. There was bombing, but not like in The Hague, which was absolutely, extremely violent. But for a child it was kind of fun. It's amazing to say so, but that's what I felt. It was like every day was a big adventure. Of course, if your brothers and sisters or parents are killed, that's a different situation, but in my family nobody was killed. So as a child you don't look much further around you—you're not aware of the one hundred thousand Jewish people who are sent away and never come back—you realize all of that after the war, but during the war I never realized it. For me, it was like the most fantastic special effects you've ever seen. Every night when you look up at the sky you would see burning planes coming down. And the next day my father would bring me for a walk, about half a mile, and we would look at the plane that came down. I remember, for example, that the Germans were picking up pieces of meat, which was the English pilot, and putting them in a little box. These things are so strange, in fact, but so normal for me at the time that I think that's responsible for a lot of the violence in my movies, my feeling that violence is normal, and that peace is anormal, that war is the natural state, and that peace is an anatural state—which of course is not true, and of course I'm not making propaganda for war—to the contrary.

CS: Has your attitude changed?

PV: When you get older and you have your own kids, it's the worse thing that can happen to you. But there are things which can be learned in an intellectual way from bad or good, moral or not moral—you are a child and you are open to everything and accept it as it is. And I think that's basically why my defense system against violence is very limited. When I make a violent scene in a movie, all these images of the war or similar images come to my mind, and I portray them as I saw them when I was a child, without any moral standards probably, because as a child you don't have them. You just look and see and think, "Oh, this is it." Well, you see a hand here, and a leg there. So I think in images like those in *Soldier of Orange* [1979], when they're walking in the military complex and they see part of a leg on the ground. That's basically based on those images that I saw when this English pilot was downed. And so that's what I feel is the ultimate background of the violence that's in my movies.

Now it's a wonderful theory, and certainly what I'm telling you is true. I don't know whether it's the ultimate truth, or that I'm basically bad that I like violence in the first place. That I don't know. But I have a little bit the feeling that to a certain degree violence is anyhow a very human situation, and that part of our brains, I would even say part of our genetic structure, part of our DNA chain, as it is genetically related to sharks and to certain apes, is probably violent in the first place. We are always trying to deny that; we always are pointing out that violence and evil are in our neighbors and not in ourselves, but basically I feel it's in ourselves probably more than in our neighbors.

WADE JENNINGS: How did you get interested in film?

PV: After the war, of course, we were liberated by the Americans, the Canadians, and the English, and the only films that were available, and the only amusement, entertainment we could get were American movies. So when I was a child of seven, eight, nine, I saw a lot of American movies, and these were probably not what you would call A-movies, they probably were B-movies. So, a lot of Westerns, action, science fiction. And as a child I thought that was great and when I got older I wanted to be a film director; very badly I wanted to be that. And I tried to get into the Institute for Cinematographic Studies in Paris, but, unfortunately, I was a month too late, so that didn't work out. And then my father told me that I was foolish anyhow to pursue a career in filmmaking because there was no film industry in Holland in the first place. I think at that time, which was in the fifties, sixties, they made one or two movies a year, which was not extremely promising for a career. So he said I'd be much better off to go to university, and as I was pretty good in mathematics, I just took mathematics, because I thought it was interesting and elegant and that I could do it.

So for six, seven years I studied mathematics, but I always felt that emotionally I was kind of warped. I think that mathematics . . . it's really an aesthetic situation, a challenge to your intelligence, and even your creativity, but emotionally it's difficult, of course, there's not much emotion around, and also I felt that although I could do all my exams I would never be really creative at mathematics. I thought that my brains were not really prepared to defend any new interesting theories, that I would not be able to do that, that my creativity stopped after my exams. And so, during my study I started as a hobby to do filmmaking and then I got very lucky. After defending my doctorate, I was drafted into the military and they wanted to send me to the air force, to the rocket bases in Germany. I talked to the government, to the state secretarial office, and I asked to be allowed to get into the film department of the navy, and for some reason that was possible. And so for two years, I was making documentaries about the marines—pretty boring, in fact. When I came out—this was after two years, because I was drafted—I decided not to pursue any mathematics anymore, but to try to make a career in filmmaking. And so I did.

Based on the work I had done in the navy, it was not difficult to get a job in television, and from television—this was at the end of the sixties, beginning of the seventies—I moved over to feature filmmaking. At that time, between '70 and '80, with a lot of subsidy of the government it was not so difficult. The movies that I made together with the same producer, that was Rob Houwer, and the same screenwriter, Gerard Soeteman, and whoever has seen *Soldier of Orange* or *The Fourth Man* [1983] can see that these are the same people who are throughout all my movies. There was a group of three people who always worked together for twelve, thirteen years, and we made seven movies together, which were all, by Dutch standards, extremely successful. In fact there was no reason at all to leave Holland until the beginning of the eighties. I mean, after I made a movie in '73 or '74 which was called *Turkish Delight* and which got an Oscar nomination in Los Angeles, I was invited several times to come to the United States. Especially after I did *Soldier of Orange*. I got a lot of calls, even from Spielberg, who said, "I saw your movie. What are you doing in Holland? Come to the United States because it's much better here." And I doubted that in fact. I thought, "Well, I'm very happy in my country, why should I leave Holland? I can make the movies that I want to make, and I'm happy doing so, and there's a lot of talent there, especially really good actors and actresses." And it was only at the beginning of the eighties that it started to change and something very strange happened in Holland.

You have to understand the system in Holland. Films are made for 50, 60 percent with government subsidy. There are only fourteen million Dutch people, and to make a film successful, to recuperate the money you've put into the movie, there's this kind of language barrier, of course, which limits your audience pretty much to these fourteen million in Holland, and a couple million in Belgium who also speak Dutch, and perhaps some people in South Africa, but that's really limited. But altogether movies are so expensive that if you don't have this government money, it's impossible to make a movie. Now, in fact, this applies to the whole European Community. All European movies are made with government subsidy, because otherwise the European film industry would be completely dead. Now it's already pretty dead, but there's still something going on. But, without that money, it wouldn't work any more. So the situation we have to face is to get that money.

Of course you have to submit your script to a committee, and in the seventies this was a committee that was kind of right-wing, I would even say, but, being kind of right-wing, it was extremely liberal and accepted everything, more or less. If you did a good job, if you worked hard, if your films were more or less successful, you got the money for the next movie. You could go on.

And at the end of the seventies, beginning of the eighties, this committee became switched politically, I would say, to the left. And strangely enough, or perhaps not strangely, this left-wing committee, like a lot of left-wing organizations, was extremely, I would say, dictatorial or another word, would be probably close to fascistic—"dogmatic" probably is a better word, not so mean—but dogmatic in the way that they wanted a movie to be relevant. Now just entertainment was not enough, it had to be politically or sociologically or culturally relevant. And in the eyes of the committee the pictures I made in the seventies were not relevant; they were considered to be decadent and amoral, and they also thought that my pictures, especially *Spetters* made in 1980, were not presenting

Dutch society in a good way. It was cynical, negative and downbeat. And they felt that I should not get any money any more. So at the beginning of the eighties it got very difficult to finance my movies. The last one I got financed, after a lot of rejections, was *The Fourth Man,* which was also, of course, considered extremely decadent because of the homosexual items that are in the movie. And that was the moment that I started to think that probably I should not stay longer in Holland.

Then in the fall of '85, I got a script from the American studio Orion called *RoboCop* [1987], which I did not like in the first place—I thought it was a silly American movie, and I thought that the movies I had done in Holland were on a much higher level. But my wife read it and she said, "You should reconsider this because I think you can do a nice job with it, and you want anyhow to get out of Holland, so why not take this and get out?" And so she convinced me to take the project, and in the fall of '85 I came over to the United States and in '86 made *RoboCop,* and then after that *Total Recall* [1990].

I'm also preparing a movie called *Christ the Man* which is about the last couple of years of the life of Jesus.

WJ: Which of your European films do you like the least?

PV: I think that would be probably a film I made just before I came, before *Soldier of Orange,* it's called *Keetje Tippel* [1975]. This is a movie that was situated at the end of the nineteenth century in Holland and Brussels—and I felt that we never were able to solve the problems of the middle part of the movie. So dramatically it fell apart halfway. I think it's an interesting movie, with nice production design and nice parts—Rutger Hauer plays one of the parts—but basically it's the only movie that I would like to redo, because I felt that we never got to the level that we should have got to in the first place.

I still feel that the first English movie I did—in Europe, for an American company, just before *RoboCop;* was called *Flesh + Blood,* and it's a medieval movie that is very American because it has adventure and action and was kind of romantic. Of course, it was very cynical and downbeat, but I didn't realize that, so for the American audience it didn't work at all—it worked OK in France, but here it didn't work at all. I have the feeling that after that movie I would like to do another medieval movie, and try to do *Flesh + Blood* in a kind of an American way. In fact, we are just developing a project for Arnold Schwarzenegger which is a movie that is situated in the Crusades. So, it's the twelfth century, 1115 or something like that. So that's kind of a plan of mine to improve on *Flesh + Blood.* So these are the two movies, *Keetje Tippel* and *Flesh + Blood,* that I don't like.

CS: Who's the best actor you've ever worked with?

PV: The best actor would probably be Jeroen Krabbé who was the second part in *Soldier of Orange* and the lead in *The Fourth Man.* Most charismatic actor would undoubtedly be Rutger Hauer. I think Rutger has an enormous charisma and could really be a star, and, unfortunately, I think in the last couple of years he made some bad decisions in doing movies that are not worth his talent, kind of B-movies, and I think that is not improving his career very much in the United States. So, it's really a pity because I think he's a really interesting film actor. Jeroen Krabbé is the most talented real actor—he's a real actor, actor—Rutger is more a film star actor.

CS: ... When you approach a movie, how much does your view affect the project?

PV: Well, that depends of course on what stage you get the script. On a lot of the scripts I did in Europe for movies like *Soldier of Orange* and *The Fourth Man*, I worked very closely with the scriptwriter [Gerard Soeteman]. *Soldier of Orange* is based on a book, it's an autobiography by a Dutch war hero; in fact he is the main guy of the movie. When we bought the book, I worked through the book with my scriptwriter to find out what were the most interesting scenes and to put them together and structure them; so that would be something that I would do in very close collaboration with my scriptwriter. And then he would write a first draft, I would write a second one, he would write a third draft. So we would work very closely together. And on the movie he'd be the writer, I'd be the cowriter.

In the United States the two movies that I got were finished scripts. *RoboCop* was around for one or two years, and nobody wanted to make it. I mean I think they approached fifteen or twenty American directors who all thought it was too silly to do. And it was not made. I thought it was too silly to do when I got the script. And it took me a long time to realize—in fact it was my wife who put me to work on it—that I could make an interesting movie out of it. So in that case the script was more or less finished. I mean, I think I improved a little bit on it, and I colored it. It's like a black and white painting, and then you start to bring in the colors. So that's probably what I did in *RoboCop*. I pushed into the movie what I always call the "soul issue," like Murphy looking for his lost life, or I call it his "lost paradise," his wife and kids that are still there, that he cannot reach anymore. And you feel this kind of loss that is kind of an emotional issue in the movie I think a little bit. I pushed that, I pushed the flashback, I pushed also the spiritual levels of the movie, but basically all these possibilities were given in the script as a blueprint.

There's a long story to *Total Recall*. The first script was written in '79 by Ron Shusett and Dan O'Bannon, the writers of the first *Alien*, and then in the ten years that passed between the first draft and when I started to work on the movie, which was '88 or something, they wrote together with some other writers twenty-five drafts of the same screenplay. There were seven directors involved, and I think several producers and coproducers, and they started the movie several times, and it always fell apart. And so when I got the script I had twenty-five drafts to go through and to select from. Then filming you found out that first of all you have to select out what you've got for Arnold. There was never an Arnold Schwarzenegger role in the movie—it was about a very normal guy, physically, I mean. Arnold is very normal, but he has this kind of physique that is bigger than life, isn't it? But this was written for somebody who looked like Woody Allen, somebody like that, and so we had to rewrite the script completely, and alter the third act completely. I think in both movies the structure and essential elements of the script were pretty much given to me, and mostly what I did was to build the building based on the blueprints, and with the European movies I think I was more part of the blueprints.

WJ: The Dutch film industry gives filmmakers about 50 percent of the money to fund the films. One might think this is helpful because you don't have to go looking for funds, but you've conveyed a negative feeling that it may be otherwise. Why such hard feelings?

PV: Well, the problem with the system like that is that it is a precensorship situation. The censorship is not after the movie is done; the censorship starts before the movie is done. You have to give your scripts to a committee, and they judge if they want to give you the money or not. And so a certain genre of scripts is not admitted, for certain reasons, and these reasons are kind of film-political, I would say. And in my case the problem was that they felt that the scripts that I was giving to them, that I wanted to be financed, they thought were too . . . let's use the words "decadent" and "immoral," and that they were portraying that society in the wrong way. And so it got to be very difficult to convince them to give me money, and every year it got more difficult. And so, what is bad about the system is that you start to censor yourself. You think, OK, I want to do this, but I won't get that through, so let's do this. And so, it's really a bad situation, for a creative person, that you start to change your scripts even, to get them through this committee. And when I felt that I was close to starting to do that, then I thought it was better to get out and go to the United States.

I mean, I think there are a lot of advantages to a subsidy system. This is one of the big disadvantages. If the people that are in the committee—and you're always talking about two, three people—there's a committee of, probably, ten people or something, but you know as well as I do, that there are always two or three people who decide what's happening in the committee, isn't it? Always the strong people. Now if these people dislike your work, you're in problems. And that's what happened to me. In '80 or '81, the presidency of the Dutch committee was given to a film critic who had hated my work ever since I started to do short movies in I think, '62, when he was a critic for a newspaper—it was a short film of twenty minutes. He started already to write extremely negative things about me, and throughout the years he has done so. So when he became the president of the committee, it got very difficult, and instead of compromising I felt it was better to change gears and move to the United States.

WJ: What do you think can be done in this situation for other Dutch filmmakers?

PV: Well, change the committee. He will get out. I mean I think this year or next year he'll be out, and somebody else will come in, and hopefully that will be a bit more fair person. This is an unfair situation, of course. I mean, the strangest thing, of course, was that the movies that I made in Holland were all very successful. So it was not that I was spending . . . I mean, we got the money from the government, but we always paid the money back. Because that's how the system works. If your film is successful, with the money that you make from the grosses you have to pay the government back, but with an additional 20 percent interest. So, if your movie is successful, the government gets more money out of you than they have put into you—because the 20 percent is in fact higher than the normal rate [of interest]. And that's what happened to all my movies. So in fact they always got more money than they spent, and that's why I felt it was extremely unfair that they didn't consider that as an advantage, but that they judged it only on moral qualities and said, "Well, we won't give you any money unless you change moods." And so . . . it will change at a certain moment. I mean I feel that the situation in Holland . . . I mean now after so many years, when I came back with *Total Recall* this year I felt that the whole situation in Holland had really changed a lot. There were always a lot of problems with my work in Holland and a lot of controversy, but with *Total Recall* they all seemed to . . . be very positive. So *Total Recall* somehow changed the perception of my work in Holland again. Made it . . . Strange, but it happened—especially when you consider that *Total Recall* is [a] pretty violent movie—it was still strange that there was a very positive reaction from all the reviewers. When I did *Spetters* in 1980, one of the four last movies I did in Holland, it had the worst reviews, the most negative reviews as I can imagine, all over the country, in every paper, in every television, every radio program, it was really . . . I mean it was the worst. And really there was a perception that my work was perverted, decadent, and should not be subsidized anymore. This was generally in the papers, and now—this is '80—so ten years later now with *Total Recall* there was a real change, that people suddenly thought, "Oh, it's not so bad . . . it's interesting," or whatever. So . . . when I came there it was like [a] prophet coming back to his own country a little bit, or the lost son or like that. . . . It was a very positive atmosphere. So I think things are changing, but it took ten years.

WJ: What similarities do you see between the films you made in Holland and the ones you made in the U. S.?

PV: I think my movies are mostly well thought out, and I spend a lot of time in preproduction to make the movies as compressed and as fast as possible. Of course, the themes of the movies that I did in Europe are so different from the themes that I did here that it's difficult—even for a lot of people probably amazing—after seeing the American movies to go back to the Dutch ones and look at them. It's kind of amazing that the same person did them. I think there is always some things that will stay personal like some feeling for humor, if it's normal humor or a kind of black humor, and interest in people, but . . . it's very difficult for the person himself who makes these movies to see the similarities really. I mean, basically I think there's a big difference between *RoboCop* and *Total Recall* on one side and the Dutch ones on the other side. I see more dissimilarity, in the way that I think all my European work was based on reality. I mean, *Soldier of Orange* was an autobiographical book, *Keetje Tippel* was autobiographical, *Turkish Delight* was, *Spetters* was based on newspaper articles and all taken from magazines—all real things. Even *The Fourth Man*, even though it looks like a fantasy, was 80 percent an autobiographical novel. And so everything was based on reality, and when I went to the United States *RoboCop* and *Total Recall*, of course, are based on nonreality. There is nothing real there—it's all fantasy. Nobody like RoboCop ever lived and certainly the situation in saving the planet of Mars is fantasy. So I think there's a big difference in approach. I feel a little bit like . . . when I went to the United States and started to do these movies, for certain reasons, that I was going back to my childhood. I always liked special-effect movies when I was a kid. *The War of the Worlds* [1953], produced by George Pal, was one of my favorite movies when I was twelve or something like that. And I even, when I was younger, I started to make a comic book based on that. I mean I loved that stuff, but then I started to work in Europe as a film director myself and I went much more to a realistic approach. And it's like I forgot about comic books and science fiction and all these childhood dreams that I had. And, strangely enough, when I came to the United States, that came back. It was offered to me, and I jumped at the occasion because probably I had repressed it for twelve or fifteen years. I mean, I've always been working with the same scriptwriter in Holland, Gerard Soeteman, and he's an historian and an extremely realistic person. And he dislikes fantasy, he dislikes science fiction; he thinks it's all nonsense, and he doesn't want to deal with it. Now, if you work together with somebody like that, then what you do are the things that you have in common; you don't do the things that are different. So what was activated when I was working with him was my sense of reality and realism, and I think when I lost that connection with him, when I went to the United States and started to work with other people, other scriptwriters, then these other things came up. And I think at a certain moment probably I'll switch back to reality, and I think—hopefully when I can continue to work here and everything goes well—I'm sure that in the next five years I'll be more into realism, back to realism, than I'm now. I think even *Basic Instinct* [1992] is now already a much more normal movie than *Total Recall*.

WJ: Why did Orion pick you to direct *RoboCop?* What do you have over other directors?

PV: I didn't have anything over other directors. It was just that nobody else wanted to do it. It's absolutely true, and I'm not making a joke. I know there were about ten or twelve directors invited by Orion to do *RoboCop* before they asked me, and some really well-known directors like Jonathan Kaplan, who did, for example, *The Accused* [1988]. And Jonathan worked on the movie for five, six months, and then . . . by coincidence he got the script of *Project X* [1968] and he preferred that to *RoboCop*, so he dropped *RoboCop* and went into another movie. And it happened several times during one and a half, two years that they started with a director and then the director just dropped out. When I came to the movie, when they sent me the script, the project was really dead. It was just that Jon Davison, the producer, who knew my European work, thought, "Well, perhaps this Dutch director wants to do it, because we cannot find an American one." That was basically the whole idea. And it was not that I was a favorite person there, it was just the last chance, probably.

CS: How would you compare *RoboCop* and *Total Recall* to your earlier work?

PV: Deliberately, I think, these two movies are pretty far away from the work I did in Holland. They are action oriented, they're very much science fiction, there's not that much dialogue, and they're probably less personal. I realized that so many European directors have failed in the United States, they have tried for one or two years to do personal movies in the United States, and then of course when they are not so successful, they have to go back.

I felt that it would take me about five, six years to learn about the United States, to learn the language better, to learn the cultural situation, to find out what American audiences are like, not only what they prefer, but what their perception of movies really is. And so I set out to do two movies, *RoboCop* and *Total Recall*, that would not have too much dialogue. I just tried to avoid any script that was based on dialogue, because, you can guess, I mean, it was certainly not my favorite thing, dialogue. It cannot be your favorite thing when you go to a country where you know the language only partially. And so I avoided that and concentrated on films that have strong visual impact. And because I was interested in science fiction and special effects, with my background in mathematics and physics, I thought it was interesting to learn how to do special-effect movies.

And so that's what I did for the last five years, and it's only now in '90–'91 that I'm slowly starting out to go in different directions and trying to make movies that are more based on normal things than on special effects. In fact, *Basic Instinct*, with Michael Douglas, I would say is a kind of erotic thriller and is much more based on dialogue than anything I've ever done before.

CS: Why didn't you direct *RoboCop 2*?

PV: Because I thought it was boring to do a sequel. That's basically all it was about. It's very difficult to make a sequel better than the first one. If there's a concept for several sequels before you do the first one, like *Star Wars* has a concept of Numbers 4, 5, and 6, I think you can make a good sequel, but if you just base the sequel on the fact that the first one was successful, I think it's pretty bad. And anyhow I just was afraid that I would be bored when I was shooting it. So I felt that it would be more interesting to do something not completely different, but really different, like *Total Recall*, and so that's why I didn't do it.

It's very difficult to improve on a sequel; I think the best sequels are done by Lucas and Spielberg, and as you know, Spielberg, for example, is clever enough not to do one sequel after the other. After *Indiana Jones,* he did other movies in between and then he did *Indiana Jones 2.**

And when they asked me to do *RoboCop 2,* that was immediately after *RoboCop,* so it was like only one movie. I think that's killing all your creativity, isn't it? And anyway, these movies are so difficult, and you're so exhausted after you do a movie like that with all these special effects and all the action, that I think it's really bad to do one after the other. It's like selling cookies. The cookies go very well and everybody likes these cookies, so why shouldn't you go on for the next ten years selling these cookies? It makes sense economically, but artistically, from the creative point of view, it doesn't make any sense at all. So basically I would say, "No, I wouldn't do a sequel" and I have never done so. I rejected *RoboCop 2,* and the plans for *Total Recall 2,* which basically are there and I will certainly not follow up on it unless I'm in big problems probably. Sometimes it's a good way to resurge your career.

WJ: How important is the score in your movies?

PV: Very. I spend a lot of time with the composer to go through all the different cues and find the most effective music. Now of course I'm not writing the music, but you can help the composer a lot by saying, "OK, I want a rhythmic situation here, then I want to be changing the rhythm to a different mood." When you work very closely with the composer, I think you can really improve the score. And especially with movies like *RoboCop* and *Total Recall,* which are all action, I think a good score helps to make it more pleasant for the audience to look at the movie. So I think it's very important. And I like music. I like it, basically because when I read a novel or look at films or whatever I always have the feeling that I have to see if I can do something with it.

CS: What are the technical aspects of your directing style?

PV: Well, that's difficult, because that would involve probably a couple of days to tell you. But with movies like *Total Recall* and *RoboCop,* these movies are very technical, and so you have to prepare them very carefully. And every shot of a movie like that is storyboarded, and all these storyboards go to the different departments, and everybody studies them, comes up with their own solutions, comes back to me, and so basically what you are, much more I say than a painter, you're much more a general in the middle of a very complex logistics system. And of course the problem is that you could lose any real creativity, because it's more logistics sometimes than filmmaking. And the challenge always with these big movies is to be aware of all the technical problems, but not to think that they are

---

*ED: The sequence of films: *Raiders of the Lost Ark* (1981), *Indiana Jones and the Temple of Doom* (1984), and *Indiana Jones and the Last Crusade* (1989).

the most important. And I think that's basically what I tried to do in both movies, which was a little bit easier in *RoboCop*, because it was technically an easier movie than *Total Recall*.

After doing these two movies I wanted to do something with actors again. I mean, not that these aren't with actors, but there's so much more emphasis on other things than on the acting in *Total Recall* or *RoboCop* that I thought that I should go back to more normal situations, where the actors are more important than the special effects or the action. So, *Basic Instinct* at least will be a movie where the actors are important, and the plot is important, but the action is really minor, and there are no special effects.

WJ: You've done two movies, and they've had to be cut because of the ratings system in America. How do you feel about that and about your artistic expression and how that affects your use of film?

PV: Well, in both cases, especially in the case of *RoboCop*, but also with *Total Recall*, when we gave the film to the MPAA, the ratings system board, we got an X rating. And, in fact, after cutting *RoboCop* seven times, we got seven times an X rating. And it was only the eighth time that we got the R. It was easier on *Total Recall*. I think we had to go there twice to get an R rating. The committee was much more appreciative. They liked it much more than *RoboCop*. They said that they liked the movie, even that they were pleased, but that they felt it was little bit too strong, and please could I soften or tone down a couple of scenes. Then they said, "This scene, this scene, and that scene." And so we did and then we presented the changes and they said, "Oh, it's fine." It was very easy.

It's kind of disturbing, I think. I would say that every form of censorship is wrong and that people should always be able to see whatever they want, and, if the rating leads to a kind of censorship, then it's a problem. Now, there are two kinds of censorship. There is a real censorship, like they still probably have in Russia, and there's a kind of hidden censorship, like we have in the United States. If the censor board gives you an X, that is called a "rating," but in fact it's a censorship situation, because they know that with the X rating you cannot release the movie. So, in fact, they prevent you from releasing the movie by giving you an X, which is a hidden censorship situation. And I found it extremely unpleasant, when I was doing especially *RoboCop*, that I had to change it too many times and reduce the impact of the movie.

Now, I don't know about what's wrong or right there by making it so violent in the first place that I had to tone it down. I felt that the movie as I cut it the first time was *more* of a comic book, had more of the comic-book, over-the-top violence feelings than what I ended up with after all the editing. With the editing it felt more real and more violent to me than the original—which was so completely over-the-top that it was just funny. Well, I thought funny. But the rating board thought differently. Now I think adding NC-17 to the rating is probably a step forward, unless there are so many minority groups that start to protest—mostly from churches, of course—against the NC-17 that the NC-17 becomes like an X rating, and then nothing's improved, really. I think there's a clear difference between a pornographic movie and a nonpornographic movie. I don't think that *Henry & June* [1990] is a pornographic movie. It's what you would call an erotic movie, whether you like it or not. And it's very clear what a pornographic movie is. But if people start to see NC-17 as a disguised X rating, then the networks won't give you the opportunity anymore to show your spots because they will say it's a disguised X. It's moving a little bit in that direction now. The NC-17 opened it up, but now, of course, the people that make porno movies are trying to get into the NC-17. And if they get in, then NC-17 becomes the same as the original X, and then television and newspapers will say, "We won't accept the spots or the ads anymore." So that's basically what's happening now. And it will be interesting to see if NC-17 will be accepted by the majority of the media or not.

CS: How do you feel about the large amounts of violence that have been in a lot of the films lately?

PV: I like it.

CS: Do you feel that it affects the audience in a negative way . . . the children who see it?

PV: Naw.

CS: Or the youth who see it?

PV: No. No, I don't think so. I've never felt that. I mean I've seen a lot of violent movies, and I never came out of a movie thinking that I should do something violent, really. Basically I don't think that people are violent because they see a movie; I think people are violent in the first place. I think people have a violent genetic structure, and I think that if you look at the bad things that happened in the world, with or without movies, the bad things that happened, the evil things that happened in Europe in the thirties, forties, I don't think that any movie pushed Hitler to do the things he did. I don't think that bad things come out of movies. I think movies are just a reflection of what society is about.

There are two theories, of course, and what you're saying is the first theory, that violence in movies adds violence to society. The other theory is, of course, that violence in movies *reduces* violence in society, that people get enough violence in the theater that they are not violent anymore when they get out. I don't believe both theories, in fact. I think it doesn't affect society at all, I think society is violent and it always will be. But there was an interesting article in the paper a couple of weeks ago, where they did an experiment in a Miami prison where they showed for some time very extremely violent movies like *The Texas Chainsaw Massacre* [1974], and other violent movies. And what they could measure indicated that the violence among the prisoners after seeing the movie was reduced. It's a nice example in favor of saying, "Oh, the more violent the movie is, the better." But basically I would stick to what I said before—I don't believe both theories and that I think violence in movies has nothing to do with violence in society.

WJ: What was the total budget or cost on *Total Recall?*

PV: Well, we started out with a budget of $43 million, and then I went over budget, so it added up to $57 or $58 million, I think—which is an enormous amount of money, especially when you realize that then we have to add about $20 million for publicity, for spots on television and other promotional items, and there's another $5 million for prints to send to the theaters, of course, and there's probably another $8–$10 million for losing the interest during the couple of years the film is in production. Altogether the real costs are around $90 million, I would say. It's amazing, but it still works, you know. Because besides what the film will make in the United States, around the world it will earn another $120–$130 million, so altogether the grosses of the movie will be around $240–250 million. And half of that, a little bit less than that, let's say, would be coming back to the studio, which is around, say, $110–120 million.

So basically you make such small profits on the theatrical release here and overseas that, of course, it's not worth doing, because that's too small a profit, isn't it?—about $10–20 million, which is an enormous risk on a movie of $90 million. But where they really make the profits nowadays is in the video sales and on television, and that's basically why you can do a movie like that, because then there is an additional $40 million coming back to the company, immediately, after, let's say, one or two years, and then for the next ten years, there's every year $5 or $10 million dribbling in. So, although it seems to be outrageous to make a movie for $60 million, and ultimately for $90 million, from an economic point of view, it's still a healthy situation. Whether it's healthy from an artistic point of view, that's probably up to you to decide. But commercially, economically, it's "Oh—if the film works well, of course. If the film doesn't work, then . . ."

Somebody asked me how I felt about *Ghost* [1990] doing better than *Total Recall*. The grosses of *Ghost* will end up close to $290–300 million, which is about $60–$70 million more than *Total Recall*. Now when you realize that the movie *Ghost* was made probably for—say, $25–$30 million—half the price of *Total Recall*, of course it's clear that a movie like *Ghost* is to the people that make it, still talking economically, more interesting than *Total Recall*. On the other hand, nobody in Hollywood realized when *Ghost* was finished that it would do something like that. They released it in a limited number of prints—about 700 or 800—which is an indication of the belief in the movie. If you compare that with movies like *Total Recall* or others like *48 Hours 2*,* which are released in 2,300 prints, that's where you see what the industry is really expecting was going

---

*ED: *Another 48 Hours* (1990).

to happen. And then they found out that *Ghost* was doing extremely well and they added prints and then more prints. But then it's difficult to foresee a success like *Ghost* or *Pretty Woman* [1990], even. It's easier to foresee and to structure a film like *Total Recall*. And that's why we still make these movies, and if a movie does well, like *Die Hard 2* [1990] or like *Total Recall*, then it's a good investment. It's not the sensational investment that you get out of *Ghost* or *Pretty Woman*, but *Pretty Woman* and *Ghost* are really things that nobody could foresee.

CS: What's it like to work with a star like Arnold Schwarzenegger?

PV: Extremely pleasant. He's a very charming man, in fact, and he's very supportive to the director. So, for example, when I went over budget, and I had the studio then fly over (we were shooting in Mexico City), and they come over and they start to be mean to you, because they want you not to go over budget. I was already over budget probably by five or six million by then, and this was halfway into production, so they were certainly foreseeing that there would be another five million, and that's what happened, of course. And so, they wanted to eliminate scenes. If you don't fire the director, then the first thing you're going to do is to try to cut the script and take pages out that are expensive. And what happened, when they wanted me to do so? My power is not the power of Arnold Schwarzenegger—and that's not only physically. In a film-political way, Arnold's *wish* will normally be fulfilled in Los Angeles. And Arnold *wished* that the pages would not be taken out of the script. In fact he had such in his contract, and he used his influence—you could also say his power—to "convince," if you want to use that euphemism, the studio that we should do the movie as it was written. So we immediately shot the movie as it was done by the scriptwriters.

I think if Arnold really likes the director and he feels that the movie is moving in a good direction, that it's a strong movie, then he is extremely supportive, and then he's a nice fellow to have around. I'm always pretty neurotic when I'm shooting a movie—I'm normal now. In preproduction and postproduction, I'm kind of normal, but when I'm shooting a movie, I get very tense because it's so difficult. And Arnold is a very easygoing, confident man, and, when he gets to the set, it gets really very pleasant. So it was absolutely fantastic to work with Arnold and I would any time do it again.

WJ: Can you see any new concepts coming out of *Recall* that would make you want to do a sequel to that?

PV: Well, I wouldn't do it, but they are vaguely thinking about it. It will be very difficult to achieve, I think, because it's such a special theme, and I think if you copy it then it will be kind of peculiar and repetitive. Then you might be dreaming that you're dreaming that you're dreaming, or something like that, and now it's only dreaming that you're dreaming. So, I think it will be tough to do a sequel, and I hope they don't. I mean it wouldn't make sense to me to base a sequel on that. Better to do something original.

WJ: Within the past couple of years there has been a tendency in the science fiction-action-adventure genre, with movies like *Star Trek V* [1989] and *RoboCop 2*, to lose total control of the film's ending. I understand that there were a lot of problems with the third act of *Total Recall*.

PV: There were problems with the third act in all twenty-five drafts, and we tried to solve the problem as much as we could. Basically the problem of the film always was that you have a very interesting mental theme: a man finds out that he has lost his identity, that he has, let's say, the wrong memory. And there are a lot of interesting flipping-around things in the movie. The last good one in the original script is probably when this man [Edgemar], his doctor, comes into the room and tells him that he is not there, that he's still dreaming, and he's trying to prove to him that he's dreaming. And then from there on in all these drafts what always happened was that for the last forty minutes of the movie it was just one long action stuff—it was just Arnold trying to get to the nuclear reactor, or whatever it was in all these drafts, and pushing a button, and making a lot of noise. And it was very difficult to solve that problem, because basically it was difficult to find another mind-flip to add to the third act so that in the third act you at least also have the mind stuff. And what we added—it was added by scriptwriter Gary Goldman—was the situation where in the third act you find out that the person that you thought was a good guy, Hauser, who gives him all the instructions and who was his former personality, is bad, and that's the last thing that we added as a mind-flip. After that there was still another fifteen to twenty minutes to go which is then full action. If a film has a lot of good twists, then it's difficult to do without them for the last fifteen to twenty minutes and only to base yourself on action or adventure, whatever. So that was basically what I would say was the problem, and we tried to solve it as well as possible.

WJ: How does your background in math and physics help your filmmaking?

PV: Well, not really very much. I think every university study prepares you very well for anything in life but then being a taxi driver in New York would prepare you very well for a career as a director. Probably better, because you would know more about life. I think what university study does is prepare your brains; it programs your brains. It's like computing your brains to analyze problems and to solve them, and whether you do mathematics or psychology or whatever, I think that basically it's always the same. I think the only advantage I have from my math or physics, probably, because I did the mathematics of physics, . . . is that when I do special effects I can understand what a mirror image is, or something like that. But every film director without any mathematical knowledge can be an expert in visual effects if he takes the time. Spielberg or Lucas do not have a degree in mathematics at all and they are probably the best at special effects I have ever seen, better than I am, even more inventive there than I am.

I think what I did in *Total Recall* was not so much going into new ways. I think Lucas, when he did *Star Wars* [1977], invented a lot of things which were new, especially the cameras that are moved by computer. What you normally have in special effects is that the scene is shot several times: it's one shot for the background, it's one shot for the foreground, and for the middle ground, then there are the starfields that have to be brought in, some other spaceships have to be brought in, and they do that in several passes, so that every time you shoot only one element. What Lucas invented, in fact, that was the big invention, was that they did that of course before in a lot of movies, but they never did it with a moving camera. So if you look at Lucas's film you see [that] when the starships are going into the frame and things are happening, you always see the camera moving, the ships go to the side and the ships come around from the side. This is definite camera movement, and to do that if you have several passes means of course that that camera has to do that movement exactly the same every time. And the big invention that Lucas brought to filmmaking is that he established that computer system which is regulating the camera movement. So you see that there is a registration of the camera movement by the computer and then if that's in the computer, then you press the button and the computer repeats the movement always the same. And I think that's probably the only big change in special effect movies in the last twenty years. And I think I have not produced anything new like that in *Total Recall*. *Total Recall* is really using all the techniques that were available that were invented by Spielberg and Lucas and other people and using those probably in extremes, but it's still the same technique. So, I don't know, my mathematics seems to be lost.

WJ: Why did you use Dream Quest special effects instead of ILM in *Total Recall?*

PV: Money. That's what they said. What you normally do—there are four or five of these factories, production houses, that do these special effects. There are three or four in Los Angeles and one big one, the Lucas one, in San Francisco. So you give them the script and you ask them what their budget is on the special effects. And apparently the ILM budget was a couple of hundred thousand dollars more expensive than the Dream Quest one. And that's why my producers decided to go to Dream Quest. Ultimately, of course, the budget for the special effects was supposed to be $4.2 million. And Dream Quest was 4.32 and ILM was 4.5. I wanted to go to ILM, I pushed everybody to do that but I was overruled and the producers decided to go to Dream Quest. Of course when the film was finished we had to pay 8 million—so it was probably not the best decision of the world. I would have preferred to go to ILM because they are the best, they have the best people, the most experienced; also when I got there I felt very supported by them. Not that the results of Dream Quest were bad; the results were great, but the money was also great. It was very expensive.

WJ: Is *Total Recall* real or a dream?

PV: Both. To be honest, that's what I want. I made the movie in a way that it would be true on both levels, and I spent a lot of time to get that. If you want a scientific explanation, you know, of course, in quantum mechanics there is a very interesting principle, the principle of uncertainty, Heisenberg's principle. If you have a moving object and if you try to measure the place of the object and the velocity of the object at the same time, the more precisely you measure velocity the less precise place gets. So that's the principle. That means, of course, that there are different realities possible at the same moment. What I wanted to do in *Total Recall* is to do a movie where both levels are true. I mean for me, of course, the film anyhow has to do with two realities, one being the reality of going as a secret agent to Mars and discovering that there is a problem, and solving the problem, which is starting the nuclear reactor and helping the guerrillas and destroying Cohaagen. The second level of the movie, of course, is that from the moment that he goes into the Rekall chair till the end it's a dream, and I tried to make that second level work throughout the whole movie.

So there's the dream level which starts when he gets into the chair and the thing is in his neck, and that would go throughout the whole movie, so in the next scene where they say, "Oh, there's a problem, there's a big glitch here," that would be already the dream, of course. That's where the dream starts. And the next scene where they are fighting and stuff would be part of his dream, convincing him that it is real, because there is a glitch, but that would be part of the program. It would be built into the program to make him accept the fact that it's real, but it's a dream.

If you look at the movie, if you haven't seen it, or for the second time, you'll see that the whole program that's set up at the beginning when he goes to the Rekall office and he talks to this guy who sells him the program on Mars, you'll see that he gets everything that he wants: he gets the trip to Mars, he gets the girl, the exotic girl, he kills the bad guys, and he saves the entire planet. That's what he does. And that's basically the dream. Even halfway through the movie, you may remember, this other guy comes in, Dr. Edgemar, and tells him that he's in a dream, that he's still in the Rekall chair, and then Arnold says, "If I'm there, I can kill you." And he puts a gun to his head and the guy says, "Sure, no problem for me, big problem for you, because you will be psychotic from now on because the walls of reality will fall apart. One moment you will be the savior of the rebel cause, the next moment you'll be Cohaagen's bosom buddy, but in the end—you will even have these strange fantasies about alien civilizations—but at the end you will be lobotomized." And then if you see the movie, you realize that all these things happen. I mean he is lobotomized at the end. That's why at the last shot, when they are so happy and kissing each other, it slowly fades to white, which for me meant, "OK, there he goes. That's the end—that's the dream—they lobotomized him." And all the other things happened—he finds the alien civilization, he rescues the planet, he finds the good girl, he kills the bad guys—but it's a dream. Now, of course you can see it as a reality, too. So at the end of the movie, going to white means either it's a happy ending or he loses his brains, which is a probably also a happy ending, I don't know.

That was basically what I wanted: that at the end there would be two possibilities, and they would be *both* true. For me they are both true—it's not either one or the other. It's not that *either* it's a dream *or* it is a reality. It is a dream *and* it is a reality. And I think they're both there.

CS: What made you choose *Basic Instinct?*

PV: Well, first of all, I wanted to do something different. I wanted to move away from the action-science fiction genre, because you get so typecast. Everybody thinks that the only thing you can do is science fiction-action stuff. And I think I can do something different, and I did a lot of different things in Europe, but then in Los Angeles after doing *RoboCop* all the scripts I got were kind of about robots and action and all that. *Total Recall* was a little bit in the same line, but I did it because it was the best script that I could really find after reading 150 to 200 other scripts. I wanted to do something light and something normal without science fiction, without special effects. I couldn't find it. And then *Total Recall* was the best thing I could get in my hands, and so, after half a year of looking, I said, "OK, I don't want to do special effects, but in this case I like the script so much. Let's do it again." So now, after *Total Recall*, I really want to move away from science fiction-action, and *Basic Instinct* is much more a Hitchcockian thriller. It's much more about people, in a kind of a tense situation, where a couple of murders are committed, and there are two or three possible suspects—they are all women, in fact. And the story is about Michael Douglas, who is the main character, a cop, a homicide cop, and he's investigating this murder stuff, and in the meantime he falls in love with a woman who could be the murderess. So that's the story a little bit.

CS: Who are some of your favorite directors?

PV: The directors I really studied the most to learn from were Hitchcock and David Lean. I think David Lean is probably one of my favorite directors. I think movies like *Lawrence of Arabia* [1962] and even *Dr. Zhivago* [1965] or *The Bridge on the River Kwai* [1957] are some of the most interesting examples of what film *could* be, and seldom is anymore. That it is at least touching something which we called some time ago "art." And I don't think it happens very often anymore that films make you feel that film could be a form of art. I mean it has been so much reduced to entertainment alone, that it's difficult to find films of the richness and the inventivity and strengths of *Lawrence of Arabia*. David Lean I think is one of the real masters of filmmaking, like Kurosawa is, and some others.

And I think Hitchcock was extremely important for me because he is such a professional. I think every movie of Hitchcock you can study forever and you will always find new things that you can use yourself. I mean, if you know the work of Hitchcock very well, and you look at *Total Recall*, you will see that some of the, let's say, normal scenes in *Total Recall*—not the action stuff, but the scenes where Dr. Edgemar's coming into the room, where he's telling him that he is living in a dream—are shot copying more or less—well, not copying, hopefully not copying—but are at least heavily influenced by the work of Hitchcock, by the way he staged his scenes, by the way he works his cameras and that stuff. And even nowadays I'm still studying a lot of contemporary directors, mostly for technical elements. When I was preparing *RoboCop*, I studied *The Terminator* [1984] over and over again to see how Cameron was doing his shots. And when I did *Total Recall*, I studied his movie *Aliens* [1986], the second one, which has a lot of elements that are kind of identical with sucking air and all that stuff, so I studied the movie shot-pro-shot in slow motion to see what tricks he did and to copy them.

CS: When are you going to make a comedy?

PV: Well, I've been trying to find a comedy in Los Angeles. . . . One of my favorite movies of the last couple of years was A *Fish Called Wanda* [1988], and these scripts are really not very much available in the United States, and then, secondly, they wouldn't send them to me immediately. So I have typecast myself into the wrong direction, doing these two movies, *Total Recall* and *RoboCop*, because normally what I get on my table in my office are all kinds of similar movies—like action, science fiction, adventure. When they see a comedy probably it would go to Danny De Vito or John Landis. So they wouldn't send that script to me. So I think to make a comedy you have probably to develop your own material which I'm trying to do. I'm setting up kind of a black comedy about two women that are married to men who are not . . . pleasant . . . and they decide to get rid of them. So that's what I'm planning to do. But that's if it's made, because it's kind of a dangerous subject for Los Angeles, for Hollywood. It might be too dark for them, although it's kind of a comedy. So I don't know really if it will be made. It will be ready probably in a couple of months, and then it's still to be seen if you can get the financing for a movie like that, that ultimately will be much less expensive than *Total Recall*, probably will be around, say, at the maximum $20 million. But, like Spielberg said, when he wanted for years to do *E.T.* [1982], he said it's much more difficult to get money for a small movie than to get it for a big one.

CS: Are you returning to reality with your upcoming movie *Christ the Man*, and what role does the Westar Institute play in that?

PV: I became aware of Westar about four years ago. I read in the *Los Angeles Times* an article about the Westar Institute and I was intrigued. I always wanted to do a movie about Jesus; I don't know why. I mean I was always intrigued by Jesus; I was always reading about him. And then I realized that it was always so difficult, because you read in the Bible . . . you read about all these things in the Gospels, and you never can figure out on your own what you think is true and authentic or what is probably something that was invented by the early Church or even the later Church. Mark was written in 65 or something, and probably the Gospel of John, which is the last one, about 90 or 100, so that's about thirty to eighty years after the death of Jesus. A lot of things can change in thirty years, especially in seventy years. . . . And so there's a lot of things in the *Gospels* that are probably more reflection, ideas of the early Church, than things that really happened to Jesus, but they projected these events into Jesus because Jesus was the hero, of course. And so, when you want to do a picture about Jesus, I think it's essential to realize what probably happened, what things are authentic and not. The Westar Institute is preparing the Gospels in four colors, which means from red, pink, gray, and black—red being highly authentic and black being nonauthentic. That's what Robert Funk, the head of the Westar Institute, set out to do, and he brought all these scholars together—now already for five years or six years—that every half year come together. They take a part of the Gospels and they try to figure out if these things should be printed in red or pink or gray or black. And so, I think the Gospel of Mark will be soon ready, in four colors. Nothing is decisive, and this is just scholars, and it might be people might have different ideas in fifty years. The fifth Gospel, the Gospel of Thomas, was found in 45 or 50 something like that. They might find a new gospel, and there might be new things in that new gospel that might change everybody's ideas again. But for the moment this is what a majority of American scholars think is authentic and not. And I think a big part of the Markan Gospel will be printed in black, meaning that about 60, 70 percent of the Gospel by these scholars is considered to be nonauthentic. And that's what I want to know—what scholars think at this moment is authentic, and I want to make a movie that's based on the red and the pink and not on the gray and the black. That was why I went to the Westar Institute—it's my interest for realism, in fact, isn't it? I want the picture about Jesus to be realistic. It should not be a fantasy like *The Last Temptation*. It should be as authentic as possible. But, of course, nobody of our age, nobody nowadays has been there—it's all reconstruction, it's all historical stuff. But it should be trying to find the historical values, and not the theological ones.

WJ: With the reaction to The *Last Temptation of Christ* [1988], are you worried about how your film about Christ might be received?

PV: Yeah. I'm sure there will be controversy, but I don't see any sexual issues really there. I mean I strongly believe that, in the last part of his life—and that's the one that we are using in the movie, the last two, three years—I don't think that Jesus was really highly interested in sex. I think he was interested in the Kingdom of God, and he was expecting anyhow something to be happening very soon. A quite dramatic change of events he was expecting I think, and they didn't happen, of course. Nothing happened—well, he died, but I mean there was no major event, nothing, no intervention of God or something. Israel didn't change, and the people didn't change, and the Romans stayed there. And so he was expecting something radical, but it didn't happen, but I think his attention was really to the nearby and approaching Kingdom of God.

And so, if it's controversial, then it would not be because of sexual stuff. It will be controversial because people would see Jesus in a much more natural, Jewish, political environment than before. I mean, just to give you one example of what we are talking about, there is a very famous parable in the Gospels, in which Jesus compares the Kingdom of God to leaven that's put by a woman into bread. His disciples ask, "What is the Kingdom of God like?" and he says, "It's like leaven, a small piece of leaven, that was hidden by a woman in a piece of bread, and then the leaven spread out through the whole bread." Now that seems to be something neutral like, "Yeah, sure, that's an observation, isn't it? That's what leaven does, and that's why bread becomes bigger, isn't it?" But the seminar has pointed out that leaven, of course, in Judaic thinking, was extremely impure, not pure, a woman was anyhow secondary, and a woman hiding something would be triple negative. It's negative because it's leaven, which is impure, in contrast to unleavened bread, which is the pure stuff, it's a woman doing it, and it's hiding. So we have three negative elements in a row, and so it's a culmination of negative description, in fact—or strange. And then Jesus says, "But the Kingdom of God is like that." So it's pointing out to a triple negative and then saying this is the Kingdom of God, which is in a sense and was for his Jewish audience an extremely provocative way of talking, because he was not pointing at something wonderful. He was pointing out something impure, by a woman who is anyhow secondary and kind of impure, and then with the verb "hiding," which is also not a positive word, isn't it? So this is an example of what the seminar is pointing out, is working on, is trying to figure out. And I think it's really a different vision if you say, "Oh yeah, this is a metaphor for something that is small, like leaven, and it comes in bread and it goes through the whole bread, so it's like a small community becomes the whole world, isn't it?"—or whatever metaphor you want to take out of that, like a metaphor of becoming bigger and more important and spreading out like the Christian community or the Church will spread out over the whole world or whatever. But that was not what he was saying! He was saying the Kingdom of God you should compare to something like this and then gives a triple negative. So that's what we're talking about.

CS: Why all of a sudden are you making something as controversial as a film about Jesus?

PV: Well, I mean, this picture about Jesus I wanted to do for a long time, and of course we have to realize that the situation in the first century in Israel was extremely violent in the first place. It's not a movie about peace. The crucifixion was done every day or every second week, something like that. People were crucified by the thousands by the Roman governors. And Jesus' life was anyhow in constant danger. If we read the Gospels, we see he was trying to get out or he has to get out every time again because people are trying to stop him. He has to go to the hills—I mean, there's an element of constant danger in the first place. His foregoer, John the Baptist, of course, was killed by Herod Antipas because he was informed that John was preaching insurrection. And I think that you cannot see Jesus without seeing a little bit the issues that were there. In fact I think Jesus was crucified, the people that were crucified, the Jewish people who were crucified were mostly insurrectionists; in fact the charge that Jesus had to face was insurrection, being on the title on the cross, the accusation "King of the Jews," meaning a political issue, as having political power. And I think that the situation of Jesus and the way he died indicate that, at least in the eyes of the Romans, Jesus was a guerilla fighter. I don't think that's true; of course I don't believe that he was a guerilla fighter, but he was close enough to that for the Romans to perceive him like that.

So I think the film about Christ will certainly be kind of violent, not like *Total Recall*, but it will be much closer to *Soldier of Orange*, or something like that. Of course it's about characters, it's about people, and there is not violence like *Total Recall* because when you make a movie like *Total Recall* you know beforehand you are making an Arnold Schwarzenegger movie and you know that the people who are making the movie and spending $60 million expect that at least the people who like Arnold are going to see the movie. And if you aren't ready to accept that you shouldn't do a movie like that. I knew it was an Arnold Schwarzenegger movie, and that every five or ten minutes you need some violent action, so that the audience will be satisfied. Now I know that if you are making a movie about Jesus, people are not waiting for violence or action every five minutes. But then again you have to realize that when Jesus was arrested the disciples had swords, one of them was even cutting the ear off the servant of the high priest. And Jesus in the Gospel of Luke says to his disciples in the last couple of months, "Whatever I told you before now if you have some money or if you don't have money, sell whatever you have and buy a sword." So Jesus was pretty much realizing that he was in danger. And he was in my vision for half a year or something like that a disciple of John the Baptist. Jesus had a very high opinion of John the Baptist throughout the Gospels and he knew that his former master was killed, so he knew he was facing the same thing.

CS: What is your goal in making the new Jesus movie, just to present Christ as an historical figure or to give people a new point of view on him?

PV: Yes. I have the feeling . . . I'm not baptized; I'm nothing in fact. I started to be interested in Jesus when I was twenty or something like that and I felt when I was studying him, he intrigued me, he was a very interesting man. There's no doubt about that, as a hero, he's a pretty good guy, I think. There are other heroes, but he's also a good one. So, from the normal human point of view, he's worth studying, I would think. But then I felt that in the last twenty centuries, from the beginning till now, from the year that he died, which is about 30, till now that there were brought in by the Church, by the churches, so many layers of—to use a strong word—nonsense, that I thought it would be important to peel off those layers and try to go back to the original and say, "What exactly happened? What did he really want? What did he really say?" Taking away things like, of course, the Virgin Birth, Mary being a virgin and—how do you call that?—getting a child, which is, of course, mythology. Well, I say "of course," for me it is of course mythology, a lot of other people might feel differently. Not that I'm going to say anything about whether or not that Mary is a virgin, that's not the issue. What I will do, just to give an example, is to show, in the first couple of scenes of the movie, Jesus with his brothers and sisters and mother. Probably his father was dead by then, because there's not much mention of Joseph in the Gospels; anyhow, he seems not to play any important part, so probably he was dead. But in the Gospel of Mark and Matthew the names of his brothers are all mentioned—there are four brothers and a couple of sisters. So to see a Jewish family with the mother there, and four brothers and a couple of sisters sitting around the table discussing the issues of the day, problems, political issues. That will be the set-up to counter the idea that Mary was a virgin. She could still be a virgin, with Jesus, but if I don't make him the oldest brother, then she will not be a virgin anyhow. So that's basically what I want to do. Which is not provoking because I want to provoke; it's provoking because a lot of people, especially Catholic people, are not aware that Jesus had four brothers, and seeing Jesus with his brothers sitting around is kind of, "Wow! I didn't know that was happening. How do people here not know he had four brothers?" A couple of months ago I was in Spain, when I was doing promotion for *Total Recall,* and during the interview I asked all of the people who interviewed me if they knew about Jesus' brothers and none of them knew. This is a Catholic country. I had to pick up the New Testament that was in my room—you get it in your room always—I brought it down and I pointed it out and I said, "OK, read this, read this chapter," and they couldn't believe it. In the Catholic Church there is a strong resistance to accept that Jesus had four brothers. Now this is a minor item, I would say. But like the things I said before, emphasizing that he was killed by the Romans as a political insurrectionist, emphasizing that when he was arrested there was a real fight with swords—these kind of things will all be in the movie.

WJ: Any other projects?

PV: I'm preparing another movie with Arnold Schwarzenegger which is situated in the time of the Crusades.

CHAPTER ELEVEN

Stephen Frears

LESTER D. FRIEDMAN AND SCOTT STEWART

"You obviously expected a somewhat younger man," chided Stephen Frears as he gently shook my hand. "Everybody does." He was right. I suspiciously surveyed the rather scruffy middle-aged man who stood before me on the steps of the Syracuse University London Centre. Dressed in a rumpled brown corduroy jacket and a pair of baggy gray pants, his hair disheveled and waistline creeping over his belt buckle, Frears knew precisely what I was thinking: where was the fire-breathing young radical who had directed *My Beautiful Laundrette* (1986), *Prick Up Your Ears* (1987) and *Sammy and Rosie Get Laid* (1988)? "After all," he continued with an almost embarrassed smile, "I've had quite a long career, though few people outside England know anything about it." Right again. For most of us, Frears did indeed burst, seemingly out of nowhere, into prominence on the strength of the most interesting trilogy of British films made during the 1980s. These films resonated so deeply within my consciousness that I scoured video stores to find other films made during the Thatcher era. My explorations ultimately led to further research in England, where, during the summer of 1989, I taught a class called Contemporary British Cinema. Though I greatly admired the films of other British directors, I remained most affected by Frears. So, being a cheeky American, I found his number in the London directory, rang him up, and invited him over for a chat. Much to my delight, not to mention surprise, he quickly agreed, and the following interview represents a distillation of that conversation.

Frears quite correctly called my attention to the fact that he did have "quite a long career" before making his celebrated trilogy. Born in Leicester, England, in 1941, Frears, like many other British filmmakers, began his career in the theater,

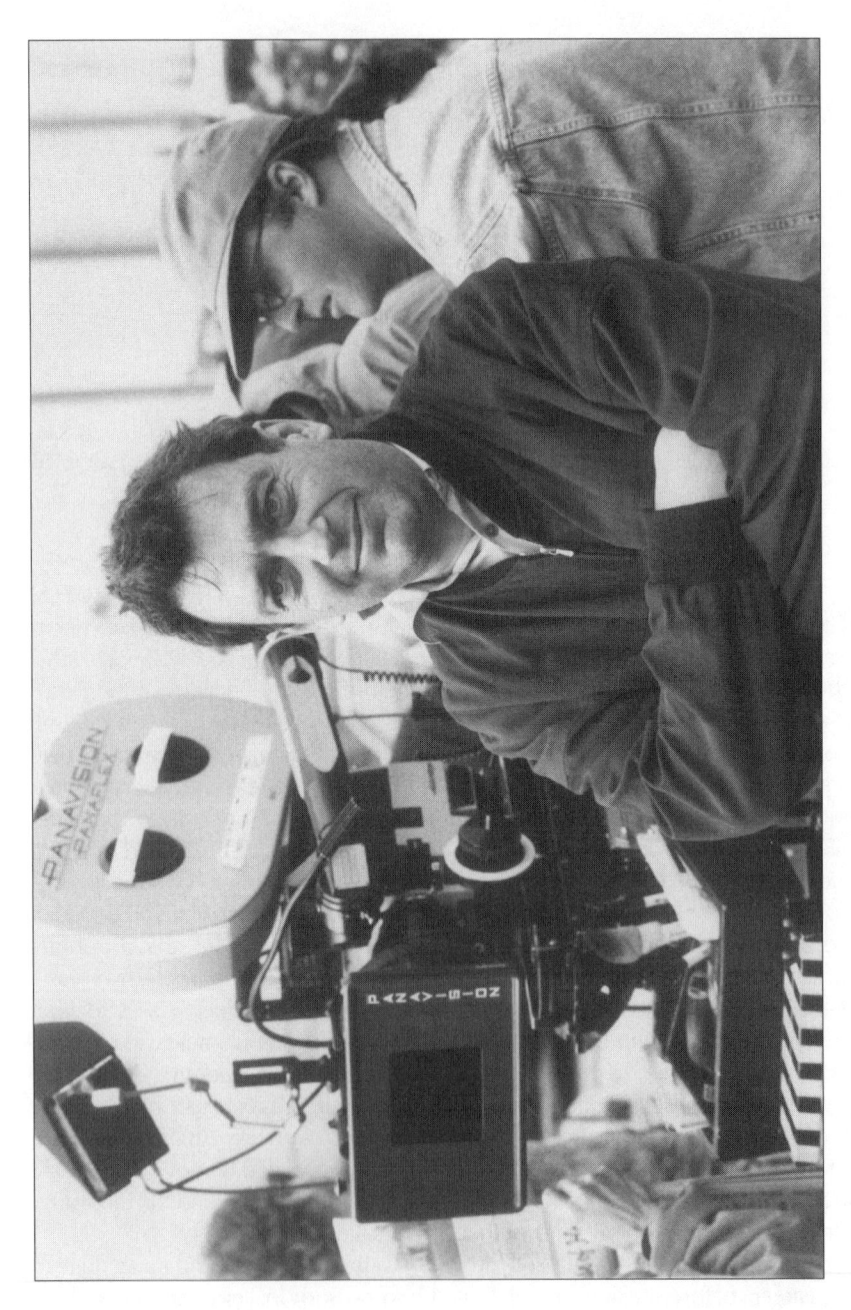

FIGURE 11. Director Stephen Frears on the set of his film *Hero* (1992). Courtesy: Jerry Ohlinger Archives.

eventually directing plays at the Royal Court (home to Joe Orton*). He also started dabbling in the cinema, working for Karel Reisz† on *Morgan* (1966) and Lindsay Anderson‡ on *If . . .* (1969). His first feature-film directing assignment was *Gumshoe* (1972), a wry detective yarn starring Albert Finney that appeared on the scene and quickly sank from view. Frears spent the next twelve years working on BBC and ITV television. While there, he joined other notable directors like Michael Apted, Mike Newell, and Ken Loach, and he collaborated with some of the finest writers of the period, including David Hare, Alan Bennett, and Christopher Hampton. He remains proud of this work, claiming that television "gave an accurate account of what it's like to live in Britain . . . something not found in many countries." In 1984, Frears completed his second theatrical feature, *The Hit*, the story of a small-time criminal (Terence Stamp) who testifies against his superiors and lives in constant fear of their retaliation. Like *Gumshoe, The Hit* was a critical success and a commercial failure.

One cannot overstate the profound impact Frears's extended internship in television had on the three films (all financed, at least in part, with television funds) he made during the 1980s, as well as on his subsequent movies. His experiences with outstanding writers gave him tremendous respect for the written word. As he says, "I start from a collaborative (with the writer) point of view." To put it another way, part of his success comes from the fact that good writers trust him "not to muck up" their work. His years in British television also inform his work habits; he quickly acquired a reputation as an efficient director who brings projects in on time and within budget—two traits which endear him to the businessmen who finance films. His television films usually dealt with "men and women who go to work and lead rather desperate lives," and his theatrical films concentrate on the gritty realism of daily existence, focusing on the position of marginalized outsiders. To this stratified cultural context, he applies the British television tradition of social criticism, a point of view that endows his pictures with a class consciousness absent in most American movies.

Frears's "invisible" style also remains indebted to the unobtrusive techniques that characterize television aesthetics; consequently, he overtly situates himself in the tradition of such "I go to work" directors as Vincente Minnelli and Billy Wilder, rather than the self-conscious artistry of more flamboyant auteurists. Unlike his flashier contemporaries (Alan Parker, Tony Scott, Adrian Lyne, and Ridley Scott) who gravitated to feature films from advertising, Frears favors story over style. As he puts it, sometimes you find that "by standing back things come out more clearly."

---

*ED: British playwright noted for his black comedies (*Entertaining Mr. Sloane, Loot,* and *What the Butler Saw*) produced in the mid-1960s.
†ED: Film director (*Morgan*, 1966; *Who'll Stop the Rain*, 1978; *The French Lieutenant's Woman*, 1981) and key figure in British Free Cinema movement of mid-1950s.
‡ED: Documentary and feature filmmaker, who, with Reisz, helped establish the Free Cinema movement.

This interview took place immediately after Frears's spectacular success with *Dangerous Liaisons* (1988) and just before he left England to make *The Grifters* (1990), for which he received an Academy Award nomination as Best Director. Yet, given the subject matter, characters, tone, social milieu, and themes of *The Grifters*, one can easily trace the connections between Frears's latest film and his 1980s trilogy.

⁂

LESTER FRIEDMAN: In a January 10 [1988] article in the *London Sunday Times* entitled "Through a Lens Darkly," Norman Stone characterized two of your films (*My Beautiful Launderette* and *Sammie and Rosie Get Laid*) and four by other directors as being "depressing," "dominated by left-wing orthodoxy," and "generally disgusting." How do you respond to this type of attack?

STEPHEN FREARS: It's the official line coming from Downing Street. That's what you'd expect someone like Stone or Jonathan Miller to say, particularly in the *Sunday Times*. One of the problems with the Thatcher government is they could never find any evidence of an economic miracle. The fact that the evidence contradicts this is rather embarrassing to them. One of the things that upset them at the time, and still upsets them, is that they could never find any novelist or painter or other artist who would actually put their finger on this triumph, except for Andrew Lloyd Weber. So, this eventually became rather embarrassing to them, particularly since the arts are rather successful in Great Britain. Also, they're a big earner—about our fifth biggest export. So, the government finds themselves connected with these people they dislike who make money for them, people who are actually quite seriously saddened by the state of the country. The Thatcher government wants someone to tell the world how wonderful they are, and the only people they can find are journalists, of whom I have no regard, and that is naturally depressing to them. They find this right-wing historian, who is this known quantity, and they set him up to it. Of course, he made a fool of himself because he didn't know what he was actually writing about. When people write or film what it's really like in England today, you have to expect that kind of response from people like Norman Stone. That is what that's all about.

LF: What would you say are the common themes that pervade your film work?

SF: Well, I suppose you start off noticing things that are going on at deeper levels. *Dangerous Liaisons*, for example, isn't clearly about the conditions in Britain, although people try to suggest it is. It may well be, however, that my interest in the material, in the novel, is due to these deeper interests. When the play came out it was a huge success. Somehow it captured the spirit of the times, when very rich people behaved very selfishly. Some people think that's the way we are now, which may be some of the reason behind its success. But we didn't make it because of that reasoning.

It seemed to me that the idea of people enjoying a story set in the 1780s was very bizarre. People were wearing funny clothes and speaking funny. To make people realize what was actually going on underneath was very interesting and enjoyable. Seeing the same ways we all behave—that was what we were really after. It was actually quite the opposite of trying to construct a portrait of the society. At the time, you start to notice certain things going on underneath the basic information, attitudes between people that are very similar, things you're more interested in than to merely reconstruct. I suppose when we make films about Britain we make them with such profound knowledge. You make films about things you know about as if you were walking across the street—an accurate photograph of the world.

LF: That doesn't seem to be the case with *Sammie and Rosie Get Laid*. There you seem to construct a rhetorical situation where you say different things to different audiences.

SF: Quite right. That film is entirely bound up in the politics of Britain—that's to say at the time, 1987. Right up to election night, Mrs. Thatcher thought she would lose the election. She actually thought she was going to lose. They broke down and started having a row in the Tory party, and somebody said the following day they had been screaming at each other all up and down Downing Street. They thought they were going to lose, and it seemed there was going to be some change. It didn't come off, of course. So *Sammie and Rosie* was made in the spirit of an account, of what it was like to live here in 1987.

Before I made *My Beautiful Launderette*, I'd made films like that in my previous ten to fifteen years working in television. It's part of the tradition of television. It has nothing to do with upper-class men running around a track as in *Chariots of Fire* [1981]. It's actually about men and women who go to work and lead rather desperate lives. That is what Mrs. Thatcher is trying to prevent us from saying. She's trying to destroy television because television embraces the concept of social criticism, not at a particularly ferocious level, but simply by giving an accurate account of what it's like to live in Britain. If you were to look at the record of British television the last twenty-five years, it would be a very, very accurate record—and quite unique.

It's something not found in many countries—people actually describing how people lived as though it were a part of the British character to record what life was really like. So we go on doing that. Then I made *My Beautiful Launderette*, which actually seemed to be another TV film, and it became very popular in America, France, Australia, and all over the world. That was a complete surprise to all of us. We had just done the same thing we had been doing for the last fifteen years. It was, therefore, quite hard to absorb why people should suddenly find my work so interesting. I still don't know the answer.

LF: You mentioned that Thatcher is trying to destroy television because it embraces the concept of social criticism. How exactly is she going about that?

SF: The government regards the BBC as a bunch of Communists. They think they're actually subversive. We, on the other hand, think that it's a rather right-wing organization and that it's our responsibility to attack the BBC. Both positions are absurd, really, because the BBC somehow walks the middle road. There are two ways she is getting at the BBC. The BBC is not funded by advertisements but by license fees which the government controls and doles out at their whim. She is trying to destroy this old system and replace it with the American system of advertisement support. Presently, the BBC is run by responsible middle-class groups which support educational shows, religious shows, and other such shows of high quality. Advertisement-supported shows, like game shows, cheapen television. This is precisely what Thatcher wants to do. She is also trying to turn it away from being so tightly regulated. She says this is part of her philosophy—not to regulate people's lives—but in fact it all becomes an ill system. In the end it has to do with process. Mrs. Thatcher claims that she is instinctively against regulation. "The market will sort it out," she tells us. Nonsense. It just means the BBC will be destroyed.

LF: What kind of effect do you feel this would have on the cinema?

SF: First, you must understand that there is no British cinema. It doesn't exist; it is gone. What happened is that we've been hiding behind television money. Using it to make films. Thatcher would like to give the money to her friends rather than to people she dislikes, people who criticize her government. She would rather give it to people who write editorials for the *Sunday Times*. *My Beautiful Launderette*, *Prick Up Your Ears*, *Sammie and Rosie Get Laid*—they all had television in there helping with the budget. That was because of a loophole that allowed some people to get a tax relief. You become rather adroit at taking advantage of things like that. You become very good at surviving in a quite tightly regulated society. People do it in all areas of life. It's like the nation has never really recovered from World War II. During the War, there was a huge black market. People were rather happy selling nylons, chewing gum and things like that. We never really recovered from that mentality. I have learned I'm very, very good at that. I can work my way through a film keeping a lot of people in the dark about what's going on. As me and my friends would say, we'll figure it out when we can get in there, and that's how you learn to do it. If you try to do it the official way, it's sort of impossible.

LF: In *My Beautiful Launderette* there were a lot of times when we see the characters through windows or glass of some sort. People come and go through glass or windows. Is that thematic?

SF: It's more technical than thematic. Think about it. If you sit in this room, a window is sort of depth, sort of like a graphic slide. In other words, if I shoot a young lady sitting against the wall, all there is, really, is her face. If, however, I shoot through the window over there, there's a window across the street, so immediately there's a depth to the shot. It's as simple as realizing the second shot is more interesting than the first. A brick wall behind a head is not very interesting. After a time, you start to play with the perspectives. You put the window there and the camera there because you can see there and there, so you can get endless perspectives, or a much longer perspective. What's interesting is everybody in relation to each other. It's always interesting seeing what's going on through the window, on the other side of the window. I've spent my life walking down streets looking through other people's windows. It's always interesting. It's sort of natural. It's there to be used. It's part of the perspective. It puts everyone in relation to one another.

In *My Beautiful Launderette*, I was always intrigued with the window shots. In one shot, for example, you see Johnny, while Omar is sitting in the car thirty to forty feet away. Then he gets out of the car and walks over to Johnny. I realized I had done similar shots through windows in the rest of the film. Here I realized someone was crossing over from alienation to being white, in a scene written by someone with a white English mother and a Pakistani father. It's about the journey from one side to another. So I realized the shot that arrived quite intuitively perfectly expressed what the film was doing, what the film was about: crossing over and integration through separation.

LF: How much do you think about theme when choosing your shots?

SF: Not at all. When I first looked at the script for *My Beautiful Launderette*, the thing that I most liked was the economics. That's right, economics. It seemed to be very funny. It seemed to be very, very good. Down the line, the idea of saying this Pakistani is a rich entrepreneur and the embodiment of Mrs. Thatcher's values seemed brilliant. Such a wonderful idea. Such a funny, outrageous idea. That's what I really liked. When I started reading it and realized it was about Asians, my heart was in my boots because I didn't want to make the movie. But then I saw how radical a film it was. The sexual anarchy came out, and the sexual was as radical as the rest of it. The jokes were funny. I was really very, very happy. So when I say I don't think about the themes, it's because films don't present themselves like that.

That tracking shot with Omar from Asians to white, the one we just discussed, is what I mean. I didn't actually think about the themes, but I actually noticed that shot perfectly expressed the theme. Again, you're trying to find out what happens when it comes to life, and you are trying to record that. Of course, you're choosing to underline certain things. By "underlining," I mean by saying we need a close-up there. Instinctively I think we need to emphasize that line, or make that line clearer. I think rather unconsciously, or not, it's saying this film is about that. It's quite practical, and it's not a very complicated thing. It's more to do with emphasis, isn't it? But out of it certain themes emerge.

You can either emphasize things or stand back. You might find by standing back things come out more clearly. What you are trying to do is make sense of it. After a while, you begin to notice that you can take the images and that they add up to something that sort of means something. You'll get people who will criticize it. You can't stop that. But when you take all this mess, and you shape it like that, it will add up to something. If you don't get the shape right, then it won't mean anything. How you do that is your affair. I can see that's what people want to know, but I don't know the answer. But that's what you learn as you get more experienced and maybe you can get better. Of course, you do it without really thinking about it because what you are really trying to do is to tell a story.

LF: In both *My Beautiful Launderette* and *Sammie and Rosie Get Laid*, there are homosexual relationships that work out better than the heterosexual relationships. Is this a comment on straight versus gay relationships?

SF: It was so right that the boys were in love with each other in *My Beautiful Launderette*. It's so poetically right. I remember when I shot it. I shot it, quite literally, like *Rebel Without a Cause*. Actually, I shot it as a parody of that film. But, of course, if you think about it, that's what the film is about: it is about taking an image, taking something people understand, and showing them it isn't like that at all. That's two boys kissing, not a boy and a girl, so the world isn't quite the way everybody thinks it is in the movies. You effortlessly create a subversive image. Most films that deal with homosexual relationships deal with them as problems. One of the things I liked about these two films is that they didn't treat homosexuality that way. Now most homosexuals I know are probably as straight forward as I am. They don't have these sort of terrible problems hanging over them. So it seemed to me to be quite lifelike and quite funny that they were the happier couple, and that all the men and women were having a terrible time.

I remember a boy in Britain saying how pleased he was, how grateful he was, that the film didn't conform to the typical film stereotypes about homosexuals. I said, "I don't know what you mean," and he said, "The two gay boys don't end up mad or dead." I said, "I'm about to make a film about Joe Orton. Do you want me to leave the death out because clearly it confirms people's worst prejudices in the film?" Yet it's nice that things could end happily for Johnny and Omar.

LF: *My Beautiful Launderette* has been criticized because the conclusion's upbeat tone doesn't match the bleak outlook of the rest of the film. Why did you feel you needed this happy ending?

SF: Because it would be too depressing without it. Like everybody else, I want the world to be happy and cheerful. It's only at the very end that there is this flicker of happiness, and there isn't much happiness at the end. Actually, it's not a completely bleak film. It seems more cheerfully defiant. I think if it had been a bleak film it wouldn't have been as well received. To the contrary, it is rather spirited—people sort of shouting back and sticking their fingers out. It was one of the reasons why it was so successful. I don't think of it as a bleak film. Any film with that sort of cheerfulness about things isn't very bleak. I think *Sammie and Rosie Get Laid* is a much bleaker film, but then times were worse.

LF: I see Omar, say ten years later, as becoming Salim. In fact, I have no problem seeing him betraying Johnny later on down the line.

SF: Yes, that's quite right.

LF: Is there anybody in the film, then, who functions as a kind of moral center?

SF: I think that Johnny, who goes to defend his mate, does. That shot of him when he's pausing—well that's like Gary Cooper isn't it? When he takes his watch off, it's like Gary Cooper when he's going to rescue someone. I think it's a very American thing that you want to have someone positive. I don't think we English quite understand this. If they're terrible, why not say they're terrible? It's really peculiar, and something I don't really understand. Some people blame it on television because the actors say, "Give me something good to do," because if they actually do something terrible or act as terrible as people in real life, people will switch them off. So I think it's sort of a rather American characteristic to look for some type of silver lining. *My Beautiful Launderette* does not avoid moral responsibility, but I don't see why the film should do the work for you. That's to say, you show it and allow the audience to form its own opinion.

I just don't think you need to tell people everything's going to be all right, largely because it generally isn't all right. It's true you get fed up making films about how ghastly everything is. But there is something wrong. The system doesn't work, and people are being penalized. Thinking about that seems to be a tremendously positive thing. It's infinitely more positive than saying everything will come out all right or that individuals can defeat the system, although some individuals can defeat the system. But still it's the system that should be changed; it's the cracks in the system that need mending. I don't necessarily mean in some revolutionary way. I simply mean if people are being penalized by it, or are suffering by it, it should be changed on that level. In fact, the people in *Sammie and Rosie Get Laid* are working out quite complicated relationships, aren't they?

LF: Because *Prick Up Your Ears* was an adaptation of a biography of somebody's life, did you feel any responsibility to do your own research?

SF: Well, they're dead aren't they? So you really can't get at the stuff you would want to. I think John Lahr* must have got it right. I knew people who knew Joe Orton, and I've also met his sister. It's quite different making films about real people. It's actually a pain in the ass to be quite honest with you because you can never actually make up your mind if it's fiction or fact. Then you get people who endlessly say, "Well he didn't always wear these kind of shoes." You say, "Well that's not very, very important." But you can never quite convince anyone.

It was really a horrible story, a really terrible story, and it seemed to have things buried in it, things I recognized as being true growing up in Britain. Joe

---

*ED: Author or editor of more than twenty-five books, including *Prick Up Your Ears: The Biography of Joe Orton* (1978). He is senior theater critic for *The New Yorker*.

was really sort of a funny fellow. I liked the idea that people who were funny and entertaining had all these other things going on underneath. Besides his dying, I remember seeing the plays while he was still alive. So in that I can identify with him. It also seemed to be very sensational. I remember that when John's book first came out people had no idea about Orton's life. People knew accounts of homosexual life, but if you had said this bloke, this famous playwright, had actually all this going on, I just don't think anybody would have believed it. So this whole story was going on that nobody knew anything about, this secret life. It intrigued me. Secrecy is very important. It's a story based around secrecy. It's a very secretive society really. We don't have a lot of openness. You seem to live in an open society compared to us, although I'm sure it's closed in many ways with many secrets. But it's definitely not in the same league with us.

LF: Is it true you were asked to direct *Scandal* [1989] and turned it down?

SF: Yes. They came and asked me if I'd make the film. The Profumo scandal was one of the two great events that happened during my life. Watergate, of course, was the best. The televising of the trials was quite wonderful. It was like a holiday. It went on for weeks. Little people like Sam Ervin just emerged from this drama that was running on. The other great event in Britain during 1963 was the Profumo scandal. But I turned it down precisely because of that. I would try to make the film the way it really happened because I was alive at the time and conscious of the events. I'd try to make it accurate and get trapped between fact and fiction. I thought it was smart of them to get someone who was barely alive when it all happened. To get someone who wasn't really aware of it when it all happened, someone who would say, "Who are these people and what was so interesting about them?" was a good notion.

LF: Do you feel that England thinks of itself as a culturally mixed society?

SF: No. But if you live down my street, well, it's like New York. It's great. It seems to me the single best thing that's happened to England. We've been brought up in a very closed society, and now we're a very mixed society. It's complicated, but it's got something that a lot of sections of British people like. Look at the British economy. When the Jews arrived before the war, they regenerated British industry and, of course, the arrival of the Asians has done the same. So, England's success in the last forty or fifty years is due largely to immigration. Then there's this whole thing with China. Mrs. Thatcher fears that if it continues all those people in Hong Kong will be coming here. Trouble in Peking and three and a half million people show up at your door with passports to live here. That's what she's worried about. What do you do with all of them? Do you say "no" to them and not make them feel welcome? It's extraordinary having a colonial past, which is what all my films are about.

LF: The role of Rosie is an extraordinarily interesting woman's role. How was it conceived?

SF: I come from a very repressed background, and it has taken a long while for women to appear in my films. For a long time, they simply didn't appear. They were just off there somewhere. I think that *Dangerous Liaisons* is about weak men and strong women. I see this as progress. Anyhow, most of Rosie was there in the script. We just went the whole way. It was terrific.

LF: What do you think of Clause 28, which limits the representation of homosexuals?

SF: I think Clause 28 was actually a mistake. It's very, very odd. As it was going through Parliament, nobody was paying any attention. Then, suddenly, the actors said, "Well, there's this law going through." Nobody really noticed until somebody said, "Do you realize what this law really means?" To be truthful, I don't think the government actually realized what it said. They hadn't really read the writing. Then suddenly it became an issue, and they don't like to be seen as backpedaling. Yet there haven't been any cases brought; there hasn't been any sort of big row. I don't think, however, I could make *Prick Up Your Ears* now. I'm not even sure if you could make *My Beautiful Launderette* now for a combination of both economic reasons and morals. But nobody's been prosecuted yet under the clause.

LF: Do you find that it leads to some form of self-censorship in many artists in one form or another?

SF: Yes, it seems to me that self-censorship is much more prevalent. The BBC comes under attack from the government and is vulnerable in the ways that I was saying. The government periodically threatens to change it all. There is legislation on the Irish subject and direct restrictions on broadcast issues. But I don't think Clause 28 was part of some deliberate conspiracy. One thing it is influencing, to some extent, is this libel law. Recently the libel cases that have come up have affected the BBC. They had something come up that was based, rather loosely, on someone's life. It ran into some problems because they actually shot some stuff around his house. They also suggested that this character wore ladies panties. They were actually rather stupid about it.

LF: The casting of *Dangerous Liaisons* seemed to get the most critical attention. What were you thinking when you cast John Malkovich in the lead role?

SF: Christopher Hampton, who wrote the play, had seen John Malkovich on Broadway. He thought John was so wonderful he went to him and asked if he would make a film of his play. John, who knew of the play, read it and said, "Yes, this is wonderful." So when I was hired, they said to me, "John Malkovich would like to do it. Do you want him?" I can remember saying to various friends of mine in New York at the time that he might do it. And, well, they were very rude about it. But anyway, I really started to think about it. I wondered if there was anyone I thought could do it better, and I couldn't think of a better American actor; I still haven't. No one has come up with a better idea.

I thought of casting an English actor, and Daniel Day Lewis came to mind; but, I didn't want to make a film of British actors behind glass. I wanted to make a film that was about emotion rather than about manners. British actors are very good about playing manners, but if you cast a lot of British actors it would be perceived to be a fashionable play, something behind glass, and it would become a piece of culture, something I didn't really want it to be. I wanted the film to be vulgar, so I gradually began to see that casting British actors would be less interesting and less irreverent, in a way more respectful to customs practiced. It would be more outrageous with a cast of American actors. So, I started to go with American actors.

Now, it's true it also had to do with economics. If you make a film that costs as much as *Liaisons* did, you have to bring in people to see it. There is no doubt that casting American actors makes it more accessible to larger audiences. Particularly, it's more appealing to American and European audiences. Even British audiences, for some unjust reason, really like American films. So one has to make some sort of economic equation, particularly if you are spending a certain amount of money. I didn't want to be caught making a film for a lot of money where the possibility of earning the money back would be less than good. All these things made it seem sensible to cast the Americans. It was both an artistic and realistic decision.

John got through because nobody could come up with anyone better. I think John is a wonderful actor. I think he's wonderful in the film. It was easy for me. When it opened, I was shocked by how many people wrote about John. A lot of critics said that casting John was appalling. Then they had the grace to say he was actually very good in the role. I noticed one thing during a preview. The audience filled in forms, and they always ranked John higher than Glenn. I had always assumed that Glenn would be the one audiences would like because she was a bigger attraction. I found that none of the audiences had a problem with John, just the critics. I then started noticing that men were more nervous about John than women were; women liked John, even though he projected an image of selfishly sexual men in life. He is now, by the way, a very good friend of mine, and a wonderful actor whom I was lucky to have in the film.

LF: For each particular picture, do you have a strong sense of your audience?

SF: It always seemed to me that *Liaisons* would be very popular. I thought that if it could actually make it to the cinema, people would enjoy the film. The story was so wonderful. If you could get people interested in the story, then they would have a wonderful time because it was so extraordinary. You know the audience is going to be filled with mostly middle-class people. You can't escape that. But within that limit, it seemed to me that audiences would really enjoy it very much. *Sammie and Rosie Get Laid*, on the other hand, was an attempt to bring Margaret Thatcher down. It clearly failed. It's actually very overt in its attempts to rally the troops. I don't think I have a sense of who the audience is other than people like me, but I think I've become much more aware of the audience, much more concerned with the audience than I used to be.

Look at *My Beautiful Launderette*. Nobody had any idea that this world existed. When Hanif* wrote it and gave it to me, I was the first person, really, to have a look at it. I thought if I could make that clear to the audience, then they would enjoy this as much as I do. The truth is, before Hanif appeared in my life, I had actually been rather gloomy. I didn't think I could make a film career. Then Hanif turned up, and the impact was overwhelming. Nobody had ever done this before. Nobody had ever written from that perspective before. It was astonishing because he got it so right. That someone could be so right, so confident about it, make the jokes, be so on the inside. So, the arrival of Hanif in my life was a tremendous event.

LF: Do you see yourself as part of a new resurgence in British films?

SF: There are enormous problems about being a British film director. It's sort of a contradiction in many respects because, in the end, people go and see American films. Just look at the financial figures here. It's particularly difficult to be a British film director because it's a very small market. It's also a small market for cars or steel or whatever, and we in film are just the same. If you make a film in America, I imagine you can get your money back by showing it to large groups of Americans. Over here, you can make a decent film and not get your money back. So I've depended on fiddling with government regulations, getting a bit here and a bit there. You also depend on becoming an export. I've become an export, like Scotch whiskey or something. I can now get my money because my films have sold in France and America. The economics are as simple as that. I can talk about money for two hours.

LF: For all your gloomy talk about this country's lack of a film industry, it does seem that British cinema is getting a lot more attention these days.

SF: It's only been in the last eighteen months or so. It's been close to death most of the rest of the time. You can chart it rather nicely. It started in 1987 and last November I remember saying to someone, "It's all over." Filmmakers are trained in where to get the money, so the number of films have dropped very dramatically recently. I think all that crop of films have come out—including *High Hopes* [1988] and *Distant Voices, Still Lives* [1988]—they've all come out and had their sort of acclaim, but they haven't generated any money.

My Beautiful Launderette came out and made money. It actually made Orion Pictures a lot of money. I think if you can guarantee four times the rate of return, they'll give you money. It's just very peculiar that at the time it came out, people like me were unlikely to have made twenty films. It's almost embarrassing when I walk into a room, and they see this middle-aged man who's been around. They

---

*ED: Hanif Kureishi, screenwriter.

didn't know about it. But it's funny. Someone will come along and make a film that will make a lot of money, and the financing will come back somehow.

LF: Why don't you go to America then?

SF: That's a very difficult question to answer because it is so logical. The Americans have an industry, and it's so much easier to make movies there. It makes sense. In Britain, everyone is caught halfway in the middle between thinking they're part of an industry and thinking they're independent. Television here in Britain is an industry, so I worked a lot in television because I could find jobs there. If you make a film in England, nobody actually needs you because they'd rather watch a film from America. So, you end up constantly fighting the system. What you have is one sort of rebel after another telling you how they fought the system. Now we could say that those who've gone to America didn't actually fight the system, but they actually wanted to make films. It comes down to what you want to make films about. If you want to make films about life in Britain, then the Americans aren't very sympathetic to it.

LF: Let's talk about your relationship to writers. You've had some of the best—Kureishi, Bennett, Hampton.

SF: Well, of course, they're enormously important. One of the reasons *Liaisons* wasn't any different than the other films was that the writer was a friend of mine. Writers were always my friends because I've grown-up with writers. I've come from a theater where the writers were regarded as what was important. There the job of the director was to realize the work of the writer. In the cinema, it's not quite like that. I start from a collaborative point of view, which is considered rather odd nowadays. I have great respect for the writers, but they do their job and I do mine.

LF: In your relationship to writers, you said, "They do their job and I do mine." What do you see as your job?

SF: In relation to the writer, I might say, "That bit's not very good" or "Why don't you do that instead of this?" I don't exclude the writer's opinions, just as I would expect the writer to have opinions on what I was doing. I can talk most about *Liaisons*. That one seems to be the clearest. I remember hiring people to do the costumes, which required very specialized knowledge. I quickly realized I should leave them alone, so I have them take the responsibility. I'd talk to them about what I wanted to see, but I couldn't really say, "That's wrong!" I can only say that in sort of a broad sense. I can only do what I'm supposed to do, which has to do with narrative, which has to do with acting, which has to do with the human values around the whole edge of the film. So, in the end, that's what I did. But, you end up taking responsibility for everything. Still, I didn't think it was my job to find new furniture or places to shoot.

LF: So you don't take a traditional auteur approach to your direction?

SF: Auteurism was only just mentioned in the sixties, so it's not all that traditional. Before auteurism there was a more traditional way where some fat producer put it all together. No, I don't think of myself as an auteurist, but I think of myself as traditional. Of course, a lot of people when they identified auteurism said that directors like Alfred Hitchcock were authors. Well, Hitchcock didn't write his films. They were actually trying to classify a lot of the American directors whose work had consistent themes in it, but who didn't write their films. These men didn't say, "I'm an artist, I'm an auteurist." They just said, "I go to work every morning." Here I mean people like [Vincent] Minnelli, who made twenty-five films for MGM. He didn't really have control over much of what he was doing, but his work was consistent with identifiable themes. Because I can find some identical themes in my films, I'm more classical than auteurist. You have to be precise.

LF: Is *Dangerous Liaisons* your transition film, the start of your move to Hollywood?

SF: No. Well, yes. But it's not that. It isn't like I'm going to move to Hollywood or anything like that. When you make a film that has the success of *Dangerous Liaisons,* you become a part of a list of directors that the studios will employ. They now think, "He's all right. We can trust him with that sort of money." So I've gone from this bloke who made these little films to someone who can handle slightly bigger films. British directors like me are very, very experienced—to the point where very few American directors in my position have done as much work as I have. It's not like in the old days. Then they'd make four or five films a year, so they'd become very experienced. They'd make B films, then they'd go on to make A films. By going to television, I choose the path to continuity and stability and regularity. I didn't actually come under contract to anybody, but I did go on and on working. I thought I could learn that way. So actually, I'm rather experienced. I'm also experienced through the sense of economy and, of course, that is quite an attractive quality to the American studios.

Now there is one certain film which I would like to make in America, which if all things go well, I'll make at the end of the year. But it doesn't seem to involve going over to live there. It also depends on what material there is at any given time. None of my friends are writing scripts right now, so I can't find anything to make here. Plus, I found the whole situation of making a film in another place, with other people, very stimulating. It's also what you read. You read about something you want to make. If it's set in America, that's that. You make it in America.

LF: So you don't see yourself, as you said in one interview, going to America and sitting around a pool in Beverly Hills?

SF: Well, I can see that sort of life. A lot of my friends did that to get work. I didn't have to do that, or I refused to do that. I didn't want to make those films. I don't want to live like that. I really don't like it there. I get rather bored. Although at the moment, I'm treated rather well there. I lived there when my filming was there, like I'm living here when my filming is here. My family is here. That's the end of it. Anyway, it's only ten hours away. Most evenings nowadays I'm on the phone trying to set up the next film.

LF: What are you working on?

SF: It's a novel by Jim Thompson. It's set in Southern California. I've actually been waiting on it for several years. He wrote it in 1963. It was the thing I most liked, the thing I most wanted to do. I don't think there's any more to it than that. Now I've found that California seems to be the place for it to get done. When I get there, the people I run across seem to be rather vigorous. It's really rather fast and productive. Here, there's no work. There might be one film going, or there's one about to start. That's it. It's really terrible here when you've got a mortgage and a family. It's a really difficult way to run your life when there's only one film being made. California will be like my office or a boarding school. It'll be like when I was eight and went away to school for six months. I'll do the film* and come back here afterwards.

LF: So are you going to make larger Hollywood movies instead of smaller British movies with British subjects?

SF: I don't think it's like that. In fact, the story I'm about to make is sort of in the middle. It isn't like a Hollywood film because it's much too dark. But it's true that I can't find anything in Britain that I'm quite interested in right now. Maybe I ran out of steam making those three films. I really don't have anything else to say about England right now. I know that must sound rather pompous, but what I mean to say is that if someone shows me something good I want to do it.

LF: Who are some of the directors whose work interests you? How about Lindsay Anderson and Karel Reisz?

SF: Those men surely don't agree with what I'm doing. What happened with Karel and Lindsay is that they changed the world. They actually rode through it. They introduced realistic films. In the 1960s, television took it over, so it just advanced way beyond what they had been doing. I was really influenced by the American cinema, mostly the classic cinema. When I made *Dangerous Liaisons* it seemed to me to be like a forties film. I watched mostly films by European filmmakers in Hollywood: Hitchcock, Wilder, lots of others. So, I think of myself in that tradition really. I know there are some British directors in Hollywood, Alan Parker and Ridley Scott for example, but I don't particularly identify with them. They come from different backgrounds. I identify with Billy Wilder, of course. He was a man who went to Hollywood and made a very, very elaborate range of films; yet, he kept his own voice. He's a man who went into a system different from his own and kept his voice. That's what I'd like to do.

---

*ED: The film is *The Grifters* (1990).

LF: What about contemporary American filmmakers like Woody Allen?

SF: Woody Allen is the most wonderful man, though I don't think he would consider himself a contemporary filmmaker. He's really the previous generation, isn't he? I don't want to speak rudely because he's absolutely wonderful. What's really good about Woody Allen is that as the years go by, he's gotten better and better. What I mean is that he made all those films, and then he made *Annie Hall* [1977]. When you make all those films over a period of time, you do get better.

LF: What is your attitude toward the direction of your actors?

SF: I think actors are very, very skillful, generous people. They do something that I couldn't. They're the ones that actually stand up and make fools of themselves. They, in a sense, get the roughest end; they get the most brutal treatment. The rest of us can sort of hide while they stand up and make fools of themselves. I take a lot of trouble when I cast people. Then again, I think I cast people rather well. But having cast them, I let them get on with it. It seems to me what we're trying to do is bring something to life. I'm just the opposite of an Alfred Hitchcock. He drew it all out before hand, and that's what he found interesting. He wasn't really interested in what was happening during the shooting and didn't care what the people were doing, since he had exercised his imagination when he did the drawing. I'm not like that. I can sort of make things up as I go along because I've solved it all at the point of casting. The actors always know far more than I know about the characters. They're full of ideas, and they do things. Then you say, "I like that," or "I don't like that," and you gradually accept their contribution. Sometimes you can add to it, and sometimes you can make it worse. Sometimes an actor will do something that is absolutely wonderful and will then get gradually worse. Often I say something because I feel like I should say something, when I probably shouldn't have said anything at all. You're actually much better off keeping your mouth shut. They're very skillful people.

LF: When you refer to handling things "as you go along," are you referring to shots, plot, and shooting at locations as well?

SF: Well, that's very complicated, isn't it? For example, say I was making a film in the street there and someone came to me and asked, "Where do we park this?" I'd say, "All right, you can park over there." What you're really saying is, "I won't shoot in that direction because there are five hundred trucks over there." So you sort of mentally say, "Let's shoot this way because the sun is coming in this direction and this and this and this." Whatever it is, the story makes sense here. So you've begun to actually exercise a director's decision because you've said, "I won't shoot that way." If you did want to shoot that way, you'd say, "Go park on another street because I want to shoot all around here." All right, so that may have been a decision that was preplanned, or I may have come and given that one limitation, or various other limitations. I would have then started to work out what I was going to do. Maybe you should come down there or maybe the camera should be over there.

LF: So there is really no preset plan or storyboard?

SF: You do have a preset plan. Some of it's preplanning whether you like it or not. Placement of the vehicle can be preplanning whether you like it or not. When we did the riot in *Sammie and Rosie Get Laid*, the fires and all, we had to do a storyboard because there was so much work to be done and we didn't have too much time. So there was no question. We had to light those fires and put a camera there. It seems to me certain things dictate themselves. For instance, in this room you'd probably want to light through the windows. Well, to light through the windows, you'd probably have to put up big rigs. You'd also put up scaffolding towers with a light on the top of it. If you put your camera there, you're going to put your lights coming in from that angle. So you see, you are endlessly making decisions on a very practical level. Whether the camera was there or there or what lens you put on was decided at the time. What you're looking for is a sort of moment of grace, aren't you? You're looking for the moment it comes to life. What I want is some sort of growth, something to flower. If you are lucky, you photograph that moment; you gradually strip things away to get at that moment.

LF: You've worked a lot with both the professional and nonprofessional performers. Frances Barber, from *Sammie and Rosie Get Laid*, said she had a hard time working with nonprofessionals in that film. I was wondering what you prefer?

SF: I don't quite know what Frances means. If you make a film with a lot of black or Asian actors, generally speaking they've had few opportunities to act. So there aren't many good English-speaking Asian actors. To find the boy who plays Sammie, well there really wasn't much of a choice. So you end up with someone quite inexperienced. If I had been casting a white person, there probably would've been a choice of ten. So that's what happens when you make films about groups of people who haven't been in films with other people. That's just part of the deal. There's nothing you can do about it unless you change the names or paint people's faces. It's as simple as that. The working conditions don't change, except some people are more experienced than others. You make films about minorities, at least partially, to advance that situation.

LF: You said that with *Sammie and Rosie*, you did the riot in one take. In *My Beautiful Launderette*, the fight between Johnny and his friends didn't look very staged at all. Was it also done in one take?

SF: It wasn't one take. It was a lot of takes. But, then again, we sort of made it up. What happens is you have this thing called "stunt arrangers." Since they're usually in James Bond films, they think everybody has got to be John Wayne and slug it out. It's choreographed as if everything looks like a western. If you've seen a street fight, it's not like that at all. It's messy. So, gradually, you take what people offer and you subvert it. You turn it to your own purposes. Fights are quite interesting because they're like set pieces.

When I made *Gumshoe*, it had a very, very good killing in a tunnel, an awful sadistic killing. But it was a gangster film. Eventually, I began to realize if you make a gangster film, you may have to do these killings. They're sort of like a big number in a musical. They have to satisfy people because that's what they're there for. These stunt arrangers would come and say, "Well, how do you want to kill 'em?" I thought that was beyond discretion. But then I began to realize that was the whole point of it. So I had to ask myself, what kind of film do I want to make? Eventually, I worked out one that I was actually very, very proud of. It was very, very good. You realized that that was part of it. In *Liaisons,* the duel was the same thing. The fight was messy and awkward and grubby.

So that's what happens, and it's strange how it happens. It takes some kind of identifying. By the end of *Liaisons,* the bits I really liked were every time there would be a horse and carriage; it seemed to be very authentic. If you're making a film about the eighteenth century, you have to have scenes with a horse and carriage. I started thinking that we didn't have to shoot anything with a horse and carriage. It's kind of ridiculous. But by the end, I came to realize it's part of the language of it. I just loved it when those people in the coach would come around. You become very attached to those little details which you don't think you care about. You realize the film is made up of things like that.

LF: What does British realism mean to you?

SF: That sometimes you can create material that contains some accurate aspects of life. It's hard. I'm increasingly sort of confused by it. When you are making films about England, you are making films about a way of life that is easily identified. In America, it seems different because there isn't a consistent way of life, because life on the East Coast is so different than life on the West Coast. So it's hard to say this is what life in America is like. Directors like Hitchcock, Lean, and [Carol] Reed* worked a lot from the written word and were able to extract a lot out of it. A lot of arguing goes on in Britain about television and cinema—which is more visual? It's a whole issue I find very uninteresting. As you can see, I find it very difficult to answer your question.

When I made *Dangerous Liaisons,* I felt like making it in the studio. All my life I've been trying to get back to the studio. It's funny. At the same time people like Lindsay and Karel have been trying to get back on the streets, I've spent my whole life on the streets and want to get to the back lot of MGM. I'd love to do car scenes with back projection. Once I made a documentary when I was younger, and I thought it would be easier if I had actors who could say what they want to say. These real people are getting in the way. You're just trying to take diverse elements and make them coherent. I think that I do prefer it when the film process all starts with a basis in something believable. I think *Dangerous Liaisons* is a wonderful story about living in Paris, but the truth is that I would have rather made *Dangerous Liaisons* in Paris, Paramount than in Paris, France.

---

*ED: Best known for *Odd Man Out* (1947), *The Fallen Idol* (1948), and *The Third Man* (1949).

CHAPTER TWELVE

Atom Egoyan

PETER HARCOURT

When talking about the differences between the classic English Canadian and Québécois cinemas in the 1960s, I often talk in technical terms. The English Canadian cinema prefers the telephoto lens, isolating individuals from their environments and allowing anglophone filmmakers to keep their distance from their subjects. The Québecois cinema, on the other hand, prefers the wide-angle lens, relating individuals to their environment and implicating as well the francophone filmmakers in the action. The most consistent examples can be found respectively in documentaries like Don Owen's *Runner* (1962) and Michel Brault and Gilles Groulx's *Les Raquetteurs* (1958), but these technical preferences also inform the two features that so securely announced our cinema in 1964, *Nobody Waved Goodbye* and *Le Chat dans le sac*.*

What I have always found amazing in *Next of Kin* (1984), Atom Egoyan's first feature, is that when refusing the Angloceltic values of his posh West Coast suburban home to adopt the values of the Armenian world in downtown Toronto, the protagonist moves from a telephoto world to a wide-angle one. Furthermore, like the disgruntled central character in Owen's *Nobody Waved Goodbye*, Egoyan's character is named Peter; and like the equally disgruntled character in Groulx's *Le Chat dans le sac*, he introduces himself to us.

---

*See Peter Harcourt, "1964: The Beginning of a Beginning," in *Self-Portrait*, ed. Piers Handling (Ottawa: Canadian Film Institute,1980): 64–76.

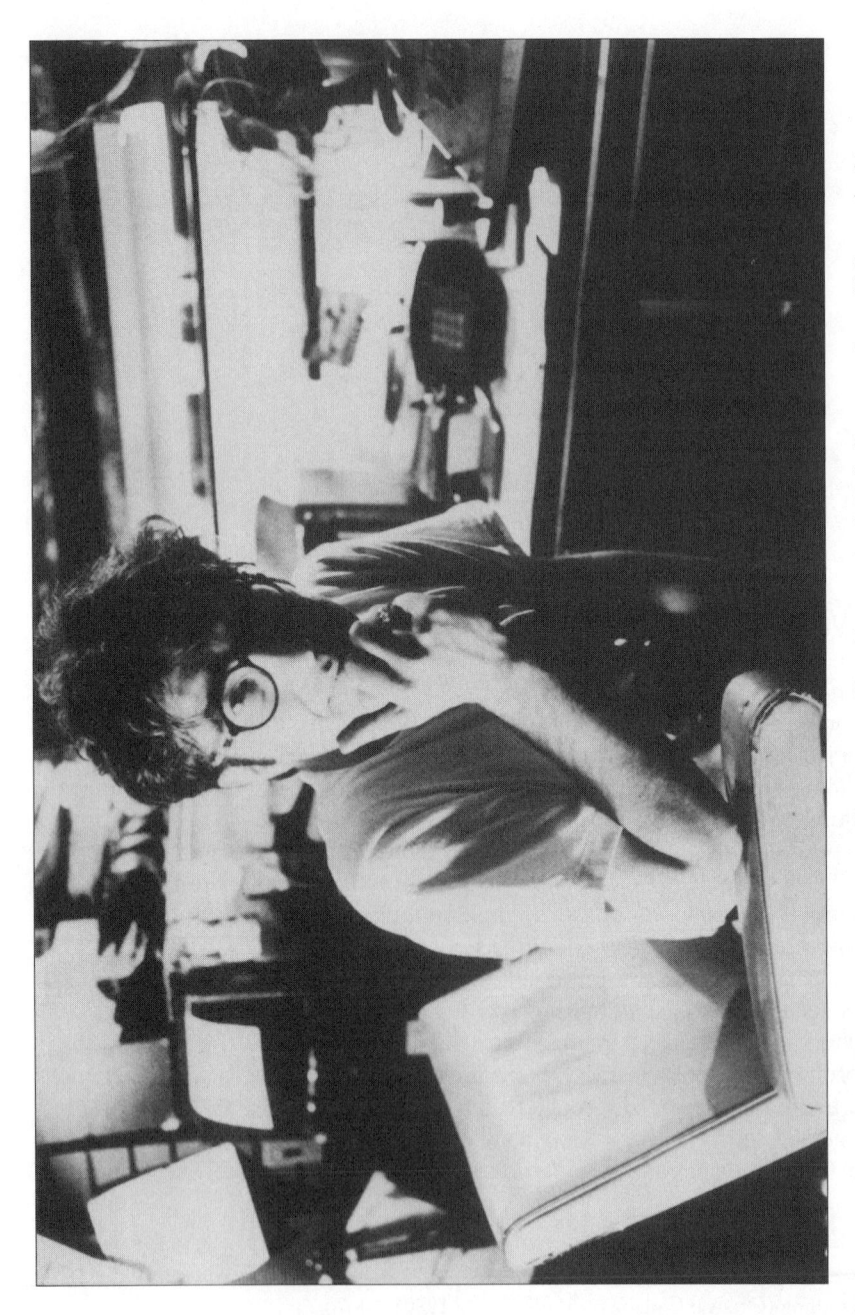

FIGURE 12. Atom Egoyan in a pensive mood on the set of his film *Exotica* (1994). Courtesy: Jerry Ohlinger Archives.

While working on an article on his films for *Film Quarterly** last year, I visited Atom Egoyan in his offices on Niagara Street off Queen Street in downtown Toronto. The visit took place in March 1994, just as *Exotica* was being invited to Cannes. I asked him if he was consciously referring to the technical strategies and situations of these two seminal films from the 1960s.

⁙

ATOM EGOYAN: *Nobody Waved Goodbye* was one of the first feature films I saw. There was an NFB† office in Victoria, B.C.; and I remember when I first got involved in film, I just loved this idea of being able to project films in my own basement. I used to be able to go there and rent a 16mm projector, and most of the films were, like, McLaren‡ shorts or documentaries, but they had one feature film there and that was *Nobody Waved Goodbye*. So I saw that when I was really young.

The reference is subconscious. But it was a very important experience for me, watching that in my basement. It was one of the first feature films I saw which I could imagine how it was made, as opposed to most Hollywood films, which at that point in my life were completely mystifying.

Perhaps to give himself more control, perhaps to mark his own work off from the Canadian documentary tradition, Egoyan has always built most of the sets for his films. In fact, quite comically, he tells the story that at Cannes he got as many inquiries about the actualities of the strip club in *Exotica* as he did inquiries concerning the rights for the film. It was, of course, a set; but even for *Family Viewing* [1987] the old people's home was constructed.

PETER HARCOURT: Where was the set constructed?

AE: That was built, here, in Toronto. We built that at the Factory Theatre Lab,§ in the back space there. We just took over that space and transformed it into this home. And the women's hostel at the end was the same location. We just, as you have to do, changed the angle.

PH: Are the photographs on the tombstones at the opening of *Speaking Parts* [1989] an invention of yours?

AE: Yes. But I had seen that. If you go to any Italian cemetery you will see photographs, and certainly in an Armenian cemetery as well: you do find these

---

*"Imaginary Images: The Films of Atom Egoyan." *Film Quarterly* 48.3 (spring 1995): 2–14.
†ED: National Film Board.
‡ED: Norman McLaren, animator, early member of the National Film Board, and recipient of an Oscar for *Neighbors* (1952).
§A well-known theater site in Toronto.

photographs in glass. When we were in Armenia, it was quite amazing, the reproductions that were carved—and they became almost photographic—into granite. This notion of having to preserve an image of the dead is something that I heightened in that scene; but you do find them in cemeteries.

In Hong Kong, when I was traveling there, there are special mausoleums constructed entirely out of photographs that are kept quite apart from where the bodies are kept, which are meant to be a place of memory and preservation.

PH: I think you said once that you had actually seen something like your film mausoleum.

AE: No. Someone else told me that they were in Japan and that something like that was being developed. That was a few years ago, and I haven't heard about it again since. But to me, it's entirely conceivable.

The thing is that when you're dealing with technology, you have to question whether or not you're using a device which is contrived or a bit stretched; and I never felt that with the mausoleum. I remember that as I was inventing it, it just seemed to me to be emotionally very resonant and true.

While the mausoleum makes use of video technology, there is one moment when the grieving Clara enters the shot with his now dead brother. She is filming him, but with an 8mm camera. I asked Egoyan why he employed this device.

AE: Well I was thinking about this the other day. I am fascinated obviously about the process of creativity. I think that within the films themselves there are all these people who are finding a creative means of making images or making scenarios which somehow satisfy these neurotic compulsions. So I think I place a lot of perverse faith in the actual process of creativity. But I think it gets skewed very often, where people lose sight of what it is or why it is that they're trying to do what they do.

PH: And they're all little producers.

AE: Exactly. And I think if you look at the film, you can divide the world in the film into people who are active producers or would-be producers, who would like to be producers but who are not quite getting it.

While Egoyan constructs his main sets, there is a strange conglomeration of ancient-looking buildings that form the backdrop for the televisual interviews with the producer in *Speaking Parts*. I asked him about those structures.

AE: At that time, I was doing these gigs as a director and I was directing a "Twilight Zone." We were shooting at the Kleinberg studios,* and as we were shooting

---

*Quite substantial film studios, located a few miles north of Toronto.

there in this field, there was this deserted set that was for a feature film called *Burning Love*, meant to be about the Salem witch burning. The film never got out. It was an aborted project, but this medieval village was there and deteriorating. And I thought, what an incredible backdrop. And so we used that, for free, this location.

I just love the idea of you looking at this and having no idea what type of a film this might be. As the producer says, "I'm shooting three of these suckers right now but this one is very special to me." And so it just is one of these projects, with all these people running around.

PH: It's yet another displacement of the real.

AE: Of course. And in this case, it's so surreal, with the interfacing of this modern technology with this very old communal type of environment.

PH: Another bit of luck occurred with the central location in *The Adjuster* [1991]. They managed to find an actual model home stuck away in the middle of a field.

AE: That was one of those things. It was in the script and I thought at a certain point, we'll never find the place and we don't have the budget to build it and I thought I was going to have to change it. But one day I got this call from the location manager saying, "I've found it!" It was in *Woodbridge** and that was the story: they'd built this model home and the developer had actually just left it in a state of suspension. It was phenomenal. And we arrived there one morning and we were shooting these scenes with this wonderful light and this light mist. It worked out beautifully.

Knowing how Antonioni loved to paint his natural sets and noticing an intricate colour coordination in *The Adjuster* between the motel itself and the cars in the parking lot, I asked him whether that had been planned.

AE: Yes, sure. Actually, it's probably the most carefully color-coordinated film I've done. You probably wouldn't see it on the print but there's great work within the motel rooms as well—this flesh color and the flame had a very heightened sense of color. And you know, 'scope lenses have a wonderful way of saturating colour.

On the other hand, about the mythological references in *The Adjuster* that the French critics especially take entirely seriously, he is not too sure.

AE: It's funny because, as you can tell with that book,† the French take it very seriously. It becomes a bit scary. The notion of things having references beyond the obvious and alluding to other structures or narrative or storytelling is something which I had a lot of fun with. But that's not to say that you can't interpret

---

*An area just west of Toronto, a part of what is now called Mississauga.
†See Carole Desbarats, Danièle Rivière, Jacinto Lageira, and Paul Virilio, *Atom Egoyan*, trans. Brian Holmes (Paris: Éditions Dis Voir, 1993).

these things at a literal level. To me that becomes so heavy handed. Noah, the ark, the notion of salvation: to me those are things that become quite funny. So I'm not quite sure what the exercise of taking it seriously provides other than rather an intimidating text for me to have to go through. Because, for instance, Hera is also an Armenian name. I've always loved that name and it is the wife of Zeus but I thought, well isn't that funny? It is the wife of someone who is a god, a king, and yet obviously he's someone who is so completely dysfunctional at a certain level. But I never really took it much further than that.

But with the image of the archer—I mean people do construct mythologies around their own lives. And when you're dealing with notions of pornography and this notion of her creating this very private mythology which she brings back to her sister and exchanges stories and how convoluted that becomes in the film—you know, people's processes of exchanging stories, exchanging histories, exchanging mythologies, creating mythologies, deconstructing mythologies. The notion of having references to classical mythology was irresistible. But I think ultimately it's irresistible to me just because it's so ironic. I'm not someone who would have a lot of patience, I think, with my basing the story on a very direct mythological reference. I don't know what the point of that would be.

PH: The film so much has to do with touch and with being out of touch.

AE: Right. One of my favorite moments is when he leaves the room where he's just had the encounter with the gay man and as he's walking towards his own room, he has this fantasy of stroking his son. I find that moment really strong. As he's walking, he starts stroking an unseen figure beside him and he finds great comfort in that.

PH: The closing shot in *Exotica* is disturbing in the extreme. That cut back in time to Chrissy when she was just a young girl and was baby-sitting for Francis's daughter who was still alive seems to give the film a serial dimension where the actions of loss and of grief will repeat themselves over and over again. The ending of *The Adjuster* is somewhat the same, though not many critics picked up on this rhetorical device.

AE: That really dismayed me and I still don't know how I could have made it clearer. I think the people who didn't pick it up tend to be the most analytical viewers, because they're reading too much into that moment. They're seeing it as a projection, or fantasy he's having of saving his own family in front of the fire or something like that. And of course I never use flashbacks and the first one I use misfires somehow. And maybe it's because of my own tentativeness.

But it is a flashback. It's how he met the family. What I've always done before is that the actual mechanism of the flashback becomes part of the narrative. In *Family Viewing*, the reason I got so excited about that film when it came about is that these flashbacks in the script could be a mechanical device that he actually shows us, and of course that works in *Speaking Parts* as well. There was no such way out of that in both *Exotica* and *The Adjuster*.

Of course, in *Calendar*, I go back to that same technique of the mechanical process creating a blurry distinction between what is a flashback and what is being viewed at the moment. And those shifts and movements in time are fascinating in *Calendar* [1993], where you have this idea where it takes place over the course of a year and it also takes place over the course of the two weeks that we are in Armenia and it also takes place perhaps over the course of one evening where he's watching these tapes. But it's never really made clear. That whole notion of time being fluid as opposed to the timelessness of these monuments was something that I found very appealing.

And yet, as a writer, there are times when you have to use a flashback. It rears its ugly head and what do you do about it? In *Exotica* I think it's more explicit. However, I have had one informed viewer tell me that he didn't get it— he didn't get that it was the younger Christine that was being driven home. He thought that it was a different actress.

I asked Egoyan about Bubba's mask at the end of *The Adjuster*, about whether it was devised for the film.

AE: It's a Balinese mask. It's the monkey and it has associations of evil in Balinese culture. But it was a found object. Like the talking teddy bear—speaking Armenian, actually. It's a sort of Armenian nursery rhyme. It's just a children's rhyme. It doesn't mean anything in particular.

But this idea of other objects becoming allusive, of having the weight to signify something else. I mean, if you look at what he's done to that room at the end, Bubba, it's quite phenomenal, the mask being just one thing. All the props that we've seen scattered about the film have been brought to this location. But he knows exactly what is going to happen. He knows from the moment he sees that house, I think, that this will be the sacrificial site of his own demise.

And why? Why is this house the place he chooses? I think because it is emblematic; it's an icon. It's the idea of a house, with no neighbourhood. And somehow he finds it the perfect metaphor for his state of mind—his crazed state of mind. So he decides that this is the place where this will happen, where the one fantasy that got out of hand will take place. We don't know what went on; but what happened with those boys is probably a fantasy that went too far for him.

PH: But is it really a flashback at the end of *The Adjuster*? Is that the right word for these final moments that call into question everything we have seen?

AE: What I find exciting are movements in time which are not signaled by devices that would lead the viewer to believe we are entering into the subconscious or the memory of the character. Like Resnais,* who is phenomenal. What

---

*ED: French director whose films, such as *Night and Fog* (1955), *Hiroshima, Mon Amour* (1959), and *Last Year at Marienbad* (1961), are often reflections on memory, time, and history.

he does with movements in time are not signaled by the classical close-up or the classical music cue. So the viewer has to make this conceptual leap. And it's a huge leap. It completely jars your senses.

I asked Egoyan about the business of sexual intimacy in his films and about the relationship between Van and Sandra in *Family Viewing*.

AE: I think she's very unhappy in that place and I think she's in love with Van. And I think that they have had intimacy. You know, people talk about why can't there just be normal sex in the films and for me it's very clear that the situations are so unusual and people use sexuality to reflect what is going on inside of them. So if they are dysfunctional, I think their sexuality becomes dysfunctional. Someday when I choose to make a film about people who are completely balanced and who do not have any problems, then their sexuality will be different.

PH: You get that in *Calendar* in a way.

AE: Of course, which a lot of people find very erotic. You don't see much, but I think that that is a healthy relationship.

PH: But there's the whole sense of incest in *Exotica*.

AE: I'm going to have a bit of trouble there. I think what has happened is that, I don't think that he had an incestuous relationship with the daughter. I think that the moment that became suggested during the interrogation that in his mind he is wracked with feelings about whether or not that was what he was feeling for his daughter. That's my take on it. I mean, one day Francis walks into this club and he sees Christina wearing this uniform and it starts this grotesque process.

Again, it's very much like the other films. In order to preserve the memory of someone, you go to this very artificial means. In this case it's not a video or a photographic reproduction, it is a theatrical one. In that sense it's a departure but it's as dangerous as the others, if not more so, because it's a live element.

For all of Egoyan's films, Mychael Danna has composed the music. I asked Egoyan how he would describe it.

AE: He describes it best. He calls it "emotional minimalism." *Exotica* is his best score, and it's going to come out as a separate release. There's also a very heavy use of foreign sounds and foreign instrumentations.

PH: Does he do that all the time? Or is that something that he does for you? The Arabic bit at the end of *The Adjuster*?

AE: No, I think those are things that he's developed for these films. The notion of the exotic. And *The Adjuster* is specifically Armenian. That's an Armenian instrument—a duduk. It's like a flute and it has a particular sound. In *Exotica*, he wanted the sound of a specific Indian instrument called the shehnai and he couldn't find it anywhere in North America. So he ended up going to Bombay and recording it, and bringing it back. That's how obsessive he gets.

PH: And the way those octaves work at the end of *Family Viewing*.

AE: That's a breathtaking score. And you know what I find with his music too is that with *Family Viewing*, if you look at that film without music, it's just too distant. His music is very emotional, and it's music that if it was used in other films, it might be over the top; but because of the emotional place of these films, it just sits well.

Finally, I asked Egoyan about the role that the creative imagination plays in his films, and to what extent it can be destructive.

AE: I think this goes down to the very roots of why we make art. We make art to provide order and purpose in a world in which we feel deprived of that in some way. Edward Bond, the English playwright, said that the reason he wrote his plays was to address his frustration in not being able to see the world in an ordered way. He can create order through chaos. Even when his plays are about the most destructive elements in the human mind, someone has written it, someone has actually organized these elements—organized and disciplined his time.

I'm very attracted and always have been attracted to the creative effort. As a child—and you think about these things when you have a child*—I wasn't told a lot of stories, I wasn't told a lot of fairy tales by my parents; but both my parents were painters. It's not that they ended up doing much with this but my father has always painted. And even as a very young child I was always very impressed with this notion of the process of doing that.

So, on the one hand, I'm very attracted to the process; and yet, it's an isolating process. It's something that you do by yourself and it only really makes sense if you're able to share it. But so often, the means of distribution, where you are able to share it, are withheld. For any number of reasons.

So what fascinates me are characters who are very creative but don't know who their audiences are or who have become so aware of the isolating qualities of the creative act that they go a bit mad. And yet, the desire to create is completely comprehensible given what their situations are. Given the traumas in their lives that they've had to deal with, given the things that are left hanging, it's the only thing they can do.

There are people who make films about criminals and I guess I make films about artists, but none of them are artists professionally or in a socially sanctioned way. The one person who tries to be, Clara, let's say, in *Speaking Parts*, is so marginalized, maybe because of the fact that she can't really write a good script. I think from the small peeps we get into the script she's writing through

---

*Egoyan's wife, Arsinée Khanjian, had just given birth to their baby son, Arshile.

the auditions with Lance, it's not very good. And then the producer is probably able to realize that, to realize it is a great story she has but she just doesn't have the particular talent it takes to pull it off.

I think there is some sort of strange attraction I feel towards the artist, let us say, towards the creative person who has a tremendous source of inspiration but is not able to articulate it properly. And that could be a metaphor perhaps for the whole immigrant experience as well—for a person who, you know, never finds that language, never finds the complete control of his new environment.

Whatever the distressed state of his characters, Atom Egoyan is someone who step by confident step has seized control of his chosen environment of cinema. With such a distinguished track record behind him at the age of only thirty-five, it will indeed be exciting to watch his progress hopefully for the next thirty-five years.

CHAPTER THIRTEEN

Louis Malle

RICHARD A. MACKSEY

The following comments by director Louis Malle (*My Dinner with André*, 1981, *Atlantic City*, 1981) were made in Baltimore, Maryland, on March 20, 1982, after a screening of *Pretty Baby* (1978) and *Lacombe, Lucien* (1973). The exchange was moderated by Richard A. Macksey of Johns Hopkins University.

AUDIENCE: How did you first become interested in films?

LOUIS MALLE: I was taken out of school when I was twelve. I had a heart murmur, so I worked at home for two years. That is when I started going to a lot of film societies and seeing lots of films. For some reason, I got interested in films at a very early age. It's almost a cliché example of an early vocation. I was sort of a whiz kid. I passed my baccalaureate—the French equivalent of high school—when I was fifteen, just because I was working faster at home. I went to see my mother when I was thirteen and I said, "I have something to tell you: I want to be a film director." She was so surprised and so shocked that she slapped me, which was great. It was great because it decided my vocation for good.

I suppose that's why I'm very much against permissive education. I think you really need to be hit on the head sometimes. I must say my parents are wonderful people. I started using an 8mm camera.

I don't think it was even super 8. It was just straight eight. Then, through a succession of compromises, I convinced them to let me go to the French state

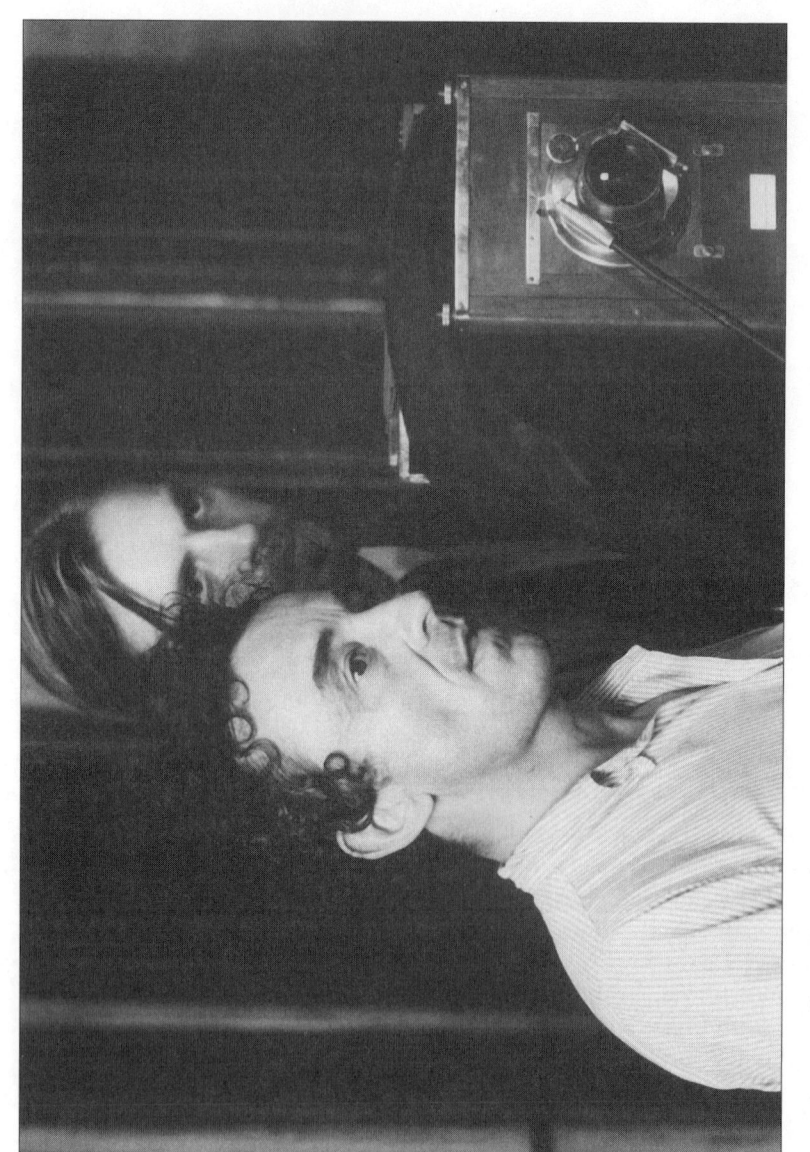

FIGURE 13. Louis Malle (with Keith Carradine, background) on the set of *Pretty Baby* (1978). Courtesy: Jerry Ohlinger Archives.

film school, provided I passed the entrance examinations, which were very difficult. Three hundred people would show up and the school would take ten. But by a miracle I got in, and then I started studying films.

Of course, the language of film or the practice of filmmaking is certainly not something that you can learn in school. When young people ask me what they should do to get into filmmaking, I always tell them, first, don't go to film school. That's the ABC's. Of course, it's difficult to find other ways to enter the film industry. What I used to do instead of attending courses was see a lot of films with friends. We would just leave the school and go and see films.

Then at some point I was very lucky because Jacques Cousteau came to the director of the school and asked if one of the students would like to join his crew on the Calypso, Cousteau's oceanographic ship. The only requirement was that the student had to be a good swimmer and I was an excellent swimmer. I got the job and was supposed to stay three months, and I stayed four years. I never went back to that school. Of course, I was not supposed to get a diploma, but when I became a full-time director a few years later, they sort of forced me to take it because it was good for the prestige of the school to put me down as an ex-student. They gave me my diploma which I certainly didn't deserve. I started working with Cousteau when I was nineteen. I worked for four years with him and it was a complete one-man show. I remember, for instance, that in the Persian Gulf I had to do a short documentary about what Cousteau was doing at the time with his divers, which was a very boring thing like taking geological samples at the bottom of the Persian Gulf. I filmed under the water and above the water. I directed myself doing it. I took the sound myself. Then I went back to Paris, and I had to cut it. This was a film which was entirely shot by one person, completely a one-man operation. That was a great education because in a matter of a few years I learned everything about the technique, which is something that of course has helped me tremendously because I can discuss microphones with the sound man or I can discuss lighting. I've really done all of that. Especially editing.

A lot of the editing that I did for Cousteau was very helpful. Then we ended up with a feature documentary which was called *The Silent World*. I was twenty-three and Cousteau was really a gentlemen: since I had worked so hard on it, he gave me credit as codirecting with him. It was a "film de Jacques Cousteau et Louis Malle" which was wonderful for him to do. This documentary was extraordinarily successful. It won the Golden Palm at the Cannes Festival—a real surprise. It went on to win the Oscar as best documentary. I wanted to keep working with Cousteau, but I broke my two eardrums diving, and it's the kind of thing you don't want to happen twice because it's dangerous. I decided I should stop diving, so I came back to solid earth Paris.

One year later I directed my first feature film, which was called in this country *Ascent to the Scaffold* [1958].* Then, a few months later I did *The Lovers*

---

*ED: Also known as *Frantic*.

[1959], which was also very successful and that was the beginning of the New Wave in France. That was it. Then I kept making films once in a while, not very many over the last twenty-five years.

AUDIENCE: Would you say something about your most recent film?

LM: *My Dinner with André* is a very special experience. The one thing I'm really pleased with is that 90 percent of the spectators believe that it's been shot in one afternoon with two cameras and the two actors improvising their lines. Actually, it took them two years to write the screenplay. We rehearsed for months. There's not one dot that's not been discussed. For instance, it took André Gregory six months to learn his lines because this is easily the longest part in the history of movies. There's never been and there will never be as many lines said by the same actor. I hope not. It was a very elaborate process. For instance, for weird reasons, we ended up shooting it in Richmond, Virginia, in the ballroom of this great Victorian hotel called the Jefferson Hotel which had just closed down, so we took it over. It was a perfect sound stage, and we put up our little pillars and mirrors and panels and made that set, that restaurant. Then we started rehearsing, then shooting; we were there for three weeks. The first week we just rehearsed, and I tried to figure out how to film it. I realized very quickly that the one thing that I was not allowed to do was to fool around with the camera, which, of course, was a natural temptation because when you're stuck with two people seated at the table without even moving for an hour and forty-five minutes, you would like to have a crane and dance around them. I realized very quickly that that exactly was the wrong approach because the moment that the spectator felt the camera, then the spell would be broken. A lot of people have told me, "I felt like the third person at the table," which is exactly what I had hoped. Also, you never feel the camera so that you completely forget that it's even a film. I think a lot of people don't even look at it as a film. They look at it as something weird between theater and I don't know what.

For every moment, for every segment of this picture, I had the choice between fifteen possibilities. I shot a lot. For instance, we shot the first week. Then the next Sunday I started at six o'clock in the morning and I ran all my rushes, just myself at the editing machine. I realized that I didn't like what we had shot. I didn't feel that it was right, but I realized that some of the angles and some moments really worked, so I came on the set the next day, the next Monday, and I said, "Well, we are going to start all over again." We reshot the entire piece in the next five days, the last five days. The editing was very difficult and pretty long because again that conversation was meant to seem like an uninterrupted flow. You should not feel the camera, but actually, when you think of it, there are a lot of cuts. Of course, there's a little manipulation of the audience in the way I've used, for instance, Wally Shawn's reaction shots, because one of my points was to make audiences aware that they were not absolutely required to take seriously what was being said. I wanted actually to make clear that they were perfectly allowed to make fun of André Gregory, for instance, because he says a lot of funny stuff. It ended up being a lot funnier, and it's one of my great rewards that when I drop in to the theater in New York, two blocks from where I live, the theater that's been showing it for now I think twenty-three weeks or something like that, I can hear people laugh and participate and really react.

Usually I originate my own stuff. I receive ten scripts a week, but it never happens that you find a script and you decide: this is it, I want to do it. Well, it happened to me with *My Dinner with André*. They came to me with a great script. Also, I felt I was very much on the same wavelength with them. The two of them were friends of mine anyway, so I felt very close to what was going on. I thought I should do it, but of course we had a tough time raising the money which was almost nothing compared to *Reds*. It took like $400,000 to make it, but raising that $400,000 was more difficult probably than raising the $55 million of *Reds* [1981]. People would read it and say, "Are you going to make a film about that? This is not a film." And the only thing I could say was, "If I film it, it is a film. What is your definition of a film?" Films in the past have had similar long dialogue scenes, but of course there has never been a film like this. People would ask me, for instance, "Are you going to use flashbacks?" and I said, "Of course not, I'm not going to use flashbacks. It's for every spectator to make his own flashbacks. It's a very visual conversation; there are a lot of great images evoked in that script, and if it works people should fly away to the Sahara Desert with André Gregory." The thing I'm proud of is I think I made it work—which was not so probable. I must say I was fighting the odds. But I was always confident. My only obsession was to get the two actors to be as good as possible. Wally Shawn is actually a very experienced actor, but André Gregory had never acted before. I mean a little stage acting, but he's never been on the screen; so when I worked with them I would use a videotape machine, and I would keep filming them and showing them, just like a football coach.

AUDIENCE: How biographical is the relationship between the actors and the characters they portray?

LM: The film is meant to be like a slice of life, right? It's meant to be about these two guys getting together and talking a lot. It's actually a little more fictional. But there is more to it than that. You have the two originals, Wally Shawn and André Gregory; they turn elements of their lives into a screenplay in which they become characters. Then actors play these characters, but the actors happen to be Wally Shawn and André Gregory! It was very incestuous and difficult, and I really encouraged them to look at it as actors doing a job and not as this very difficult thing of playing themselves.

What happened at the beginning is that they used to be very close friends, Wally and André, and it is true André staged Wally's first play. Then André dropped out and went to all these places; actually he spent most of his time in Long Island. Wally went his way and he started having plays staged; all of them since have been staged at Joe Papp's Public Theater. They got together again a little more than two years ago—now it's almost three years—and they wanted to do something again together.

They started discussing, and André is such an irrepressible raconteur that I had heard most of those stories just having dinner with him. You know, he would never stop. So they decided to tape those conversations, and they ended up with something like 7,000 pages of transcripts. That's what Wally did by himself, which I think was remarkable. He disappeared for one year and came back with a script which was 180 pages.

Then we started working on it when I said, "Yes, I'll work, I'll do it with you, I would love to do it with you." We started rehearsing every day, and we trimmed it down to about 130 pages, in the process of which I encouraged them to go more and more into fictionalization because I felt it would be easier.

Of course, obviously there are some very intimate moments when, for instance, André Gregory talks about his mother; all of this is true. Everything that's told is true, but it's dramatized in the sense that lots of other things were dropped, and Wally has made his character into this little playwright trying to make a living, when actually he is a very adventurous person. He's spent years in India. He's traveled a lot. In the film he pretends that he never leaves the cigar store in this neighborhood, but it's not quite true. He pretends to be the Cartesian one, the rational one, but about halfway through the film you realize that he's even crazier than André.

Essentially, the film's something that they decided to do. I know for some time they considered having it take place not in a restaurant, but in a train, going, let's say, from Paris to Zagreb or something like that. But that was not a very good idea. That was too fancy.

AUDIENCE: Has the script of *My Dinner with André* been published?

LM: People keep asking me about it. It's been published by Grove Press, but it doesn't seem to be anywhere in bookstores, and I really don't know why because the picture is doing very well. I even get letters asking me can we have a transcript of the screenplay, and I have a ready-made answer per Xerox, telling people to ask their bookstore and order it. It was published last October.

AUDIENCE: After coming right off a play after a sequence of films, do you want to say anything about the experience of directing?

LM: I'm always reluctant to direct a play because I'm a little spoiled as a film director. It's generally accepted now that films are the director's medium. God knows I've worked very closely, for instance, with [screenwriter] John Guare on *Atlantic City* and a lot of what people like about *Atlantic City* he must get the credit for. His brilliance and imagination have done, for me, wonders for that script. But I still very much think of a film of mine as a film of mine; I always take complete responsibility, and I'm the one who makes the final decisions, so it's my show. Now things are quite different when you direct a play, unless you're an egomaniac director—and of course there are quite a few of those—but I'm not one. I just believe that when you are directing a play, your job is to serve the play and the playwright as well as possible. I did convince John to change a few things (in *Lydie Breeze*, 1982), especially dealing with the visual aspects and setting and the rhythm and to make some cuts. The casting was very interesting, and I think one of the best qualities of this production was that we had a remarkable ensemble of actors. Still, I would always feel that this was John Guare's play. Also, there's something very frustrating for a film director because we started previewing, and at the beginning it didn't work too well, but I kept working with them every afternoon and little by little it got better and at some point scene by scene they seemed to come exactly right. My instinct was always to say, "Print, print, and put it in the can. This one we've got. Let's get to the next one." And of course the next night it would be a little different. I must say this is also the very powerful pleasure and the danger and the excitement of the theater that anything can happen any time. It's always a working process and by definition it is live, alive. It was for me quite odd. I had not worked on stage for more than fifteen years, and I must say I found it such an interesting experience that I might possibly do it again. I'm considering doing it again one of these days.

AUDIENCE: What are you working on currently?

LM: A while ago we came up with what we thought was a funny idea, starting from the ABSCAM affair and the FBI arresting a crook, a swindler, and convincing him to work for them and to help them frame politicians with the help of a fake Arab sheik. We started from that, but we moved very quickly to something else. What it ended up being was sort of a political farce. It has a lot to do with the FBI. It's a very funny script. I was very interested in working with Danny Akroyd and John Belushi, so actually the script was written for them. Now we're a little bit in the middle of nowhere. We're going to recast it, but in recasting it we're probably going to also have to re-write it because Belushi was supposed to play this fairly ugly crook and a very wild character.* I very much admired Belushi for his invention and his craziness and the fact that he would really push situations to the extreme. I liked him a lot, and I must say it has put us in a weird situation now; so we're probably going to proceed with it, but now we've almost to start from scratch.

RICHARD A. MACKSEY: Would you care to say a few words about the films we have seen today?

LM: I'm very happy that you've seen these two pictures of mine, *Lacombe, Lucien* and *Pretty Baby*. I had not seen *Petty Baby* literally since it opened. It was a very weird experience. It is always a weird experience to see your old movies.

---

*ED: Malle subsequently made *Crackers* (1984), a comedy with Donald Sutherland, Jack Warden, Sean Penn, and Wally Shawn.

You usually would like to remake them completely, but I must say that some of it I liked. I remember it differently because for a director it's a huge step to direct in another language. It's not so much to work in a different country—I've worked in Mexico, in Italy, a few other European countries, and in India. Film crews, film technicians and their habits, and their techniques are pretty much the same all over the world. When I was in India, one of the things I did in Madras was go to one of the huge studios where they shoot those five-hour epics, those extraordinary extravaganzas. It didn't look very much different from a studio in Paris or in Los Angeles, except that there was a little altar in the corner of the soundstage where the crew would go and make an offering. And there were flowers on the cameras, but outside of that I felt it was pretty much the same. But what is really difficult and takes adjusting is to switch to another language, and that's where actually a lot of European directors had trouble when they came and worked here. . . . I've spoken English most of my life, but dealing with actors in a different language, for instance, was a problem. And obviously I was less in control than I usually am. That's one of the things that I think I do in my work. I'm very, very much in control.

In *Pretty Baby* I had some problems. I had problems with the script. I had problems with some members of the cast, so I had to adjust constantly and to improvise on the set, which I don't especially care to do. And we had to do a certain amount of cuts and changes in the cutting room. I had this funny impression that I was seeing a film that was actually a little different from what I remembered because I remember some of the cuts. And for some reason there were a couple of cuts that I thought were still in the movie, so it was weird.

We had a problem with the plot line obviously and it's certainly the weakness of *Pretty Baby*. It's a very impressionist film. It's about moods and ambiance, and I must say in that sense I think it succeeds pretty well because it gives a feeling of the heat and the squalor and the sort of endless afternoons in this house. You know one of the challenges of *Pretty Baby* is that for the first hour and ten minutes or something like that you stay in that house. You don't see anything of New Orleans; New Orleans is only evoked in the sound track, and that works pretty well, so that when we come out it's at first a great relief. Also, it gives this impression of people in sort of a very luxurious jail.

AUDIENCE: You mentioned the way the sound track works in this film, and I was struck that you came back to music this time. Some of your very first films move through Miles Davis and of course the Brahms sextet and the Satie pieces and so on. Then it seems that you moved away from music for a bit, and here at the end you have that homage to Mr. Jellyroll and I guess Tony Jackson too. How do you work with music? Was this a production where you had a tight musical soundtrack?

LM: Music plays a large part in my films because it plays a very important part in my life. For instance, when I was in adolescence, from the age of twelve I was totally addicted to jazz. I dropped out of Beethoven and Chopin and started with Louis Armstrong and then New Orleans musicians and Jellyroll Morton. We used a lot of his music in *Pretty Baby*. I ended up with Charlie Parker, which I used in *Murmur of the Heart*. At the beginning of *Murmur of the Heart* [1971] the young boy goes to a record store and steals a Charlie Parker record, so I kept using Charlie Parker's music, but not very much. I never use too much music. I'm pretty much against score music. I like to use source music, music that has to do with the scene or comes from something and relates to something that's actually happening. I don't really like to have the kind of music that's very much used in movies and which is basically there to tell you how you should feel and how you should react to the scene. It's a little bit of the Pavlov's dog syndrome, and sometimes it's used with such a lack of finesse that it really becomes, for me, very much in the way.

I remember, for instance, in *Atlantic City*, I always wanted to work with Michel Legrand, who is a wonderful musician, and I had very precise needs. There were moments where we needed music, and so I started working with him and he said, "Louis, you know there are other places where I would like to add things." So essentially, for me, we had to redo Bellini's *Norma* for the lemon scene, you know the famous lemon scene. We had to rerecord that. For some reason we couldn't get rights to existing music, so I ended up in London with ninety-seven musicians from the London Symphony, and that was, for me, the most important thing. Then Michel wanted to add some more, so there was a lot of score music, and I told Michel, "You know, I don't promise to keep it." As a matter of fact, when we got into the mixing room, when we started putting together all the soundtracks, little by little I took away every one of his scores. I was a little embarrassed about it, but it's because each time I felt it was superfluous, a pleonasm; it didn't help the scene too much. People sometimes rescore a picture when it is in trouble. There's a famous example recently of a picture called *Neighbors* [1981], which was completely rescored after the previews. They came up with the kind of a score where the music laughs for you. I've never been really very much into that.

For *Lacombe, Lucien* I used the music of Django Reinhardt, but it was the music that actually comes from those years, from the German occupation years. There's something about the music of Django Reinhardt* in the years 1941–1942 that evokes exactly the mood of that time: gloomy, crepuscular, a sort of tiredness and a sense of nostalgic melancholy that I thought would be perfect. Of course, maybe it seemed a little refined for those idiot hoodlums of the French Gestapo to play Django Reinhardt. That was a form of stylization, if you want, but I felt that kind of music would fit so well the mood and ambiance of the time and of that bar where the Gestapo were hanging around and drinking.

---

*ED: Guitar legend, inducted into Big Band and Jazz Hall of Fame in 1984. Documentary about his life (1910–1953) written by Jean Cocteau and Chris Marker was released in 1959 as *Django Reinhardt*.

Pretty Baby was a different thing. Actually, one of the reasons why I was so interested in making a film that would deal with Storyville and the end of the red-light district in New Orleans had to do with my old passion for jazz and the fact that I knew this period and I knew Storyville better, almost, than anyone in this country because I had become almost a scholar of that moment when jazz was born. In the sixties I worked on a project that was actually the life of Jellyroll Morton, but nobody would touch it. They would say in the mid-sixties, "You want to make a film about a black musician? Are you kidding?" Now, of course, they've made a film about Billie Holliday;[*] it was very successful. Recently they've come back to me and asked me if I want to do a film about Charlie Parker, which I don't want to do; but Jellyroll Morton nobody wanted. He had an extraordinary life, but of course the pianist that's shown in *Pretty Baby* was not Jellyroll Morton; he was actually a pianist called Tony Jackson, who wrote "Pretty Baby" and was a very extravagant, very brilliant, and quite an extraordinary character.

The jazz musicians all took off for Chicago when the red-light district was closed in 1917. Louis Armstrong had left a couple of years before. What really made jazz famous was they played in the black district of Chicago and started recording in the early twenties. That's how jazz spread, because in New Orleans it was still very little known. I was always interested in this, and some of the writing of the picture was centered around the musical evocation of this period. And we also used some wonderful material from ragtime, from Scott Joplin, Louis Chauvin, and a few other of the great ragtime musicians. So *Pretty Baby* is an example of a film that had a lot to do with music. I mean, music was absolutely essential to it.

AUDIENCE: How do you sense that an actor will develop the character that you want?

LM: That's a good question because you never know. I've always said that casting is half of directing. Once you've cast somebody wrong, you're in big trouble. Sometimes through experience and a lot of work and a little manipulation in the cutting room, you can save a performance or sometimes even make it work, but basically you're always trying to save it, which is wrong. For me, one of the most important parts of my work is the casting process. I usually spend a lot of time on this.

I'll give you a good example. I said I had some problems with the casting of *Pretty Baby*. I don't want to talk about Brooke Shields because she's a phenomenon by herself, and actually I thought she was pretty good in *Pretty Baby*. She just had some limitations, but at the same time nobody else could have done it better in the sense that this was a very unusual and almost impossible part to cast, to find a girl who could have almost experienced what the character had

---

[*]ED: *Lady Sings the Blues* (1972), with Diana Ross, Billy Dee Williams, and Richard Pryor, and directed by Sidney J. Furie.

experienced. It just happened that Brooke had started modeling when she was one year old; so when we dealt with her, she had already had eleven years of selling her beauty. There was no way that she could be traumatized or shocked or would not understand. She was so much on top of the part that that was already completely unique. I just knew by casting her, because I made lots of tests with her before, that there were certain things that she would have problems with. At the same time, what she came up with was this toughness which was essential to the part.

Pretty Baby is entirely based on a true story; half of the scenes in *Pretty Baby* are actually reenacted scenes. For instance, when they sell her virginity, that was almost traditional in those plush whore houses in New Orleans. There are a lot of such scenes, so she had to be really, really tough. But there was a dimension that I missed, for instance, when she deals with Bellocq. There were a few scenes that I didn't even shoot, and some of them I cut in the cutting room. I must say retrospectively she makes me look very good as a director for the work she's done since. She makes me look terrific.

I want to give you another more interesting example: Frances Faye who plays the Madame, who is an extraordinary comedian, singer, and a wonderful woman. She is a little more retired now, but at the time she was still very active. How old she is I won't tell you, but she was still playing in clubs, and I saw her in Los Angeles when we were finishing writing the picture. I was so impressed by her that I thought she would be wonderful as Madame Nell. It was all fine, and she was wonderful, she was perfect, she's got this extraordinary sort of impressionist face; and when she snorts cocaine, she's just fabulous, except that she just could not memorize anything. We would have to do twelve takes for her to say, "Shut the door." She just couldn't remember anything. I had a lot of problems with her. I had to cut some scenes. She had a very strange rhythm sometimes. She was a mixed blessing. If I were to do it again, I'm not sure I would cast her because she really gave us a lot of problems and forced me to make some changes in the shooting that I regret because it was a wonderful part. Better actually than it is. Seeing it again today, I must say I felt good about her because she's great; she's just a wonderful character.

Let me talk about casting Keith Carradine as Bellocq in *Pretty Baby*. First, we've done a lot of research on Bellocq, and the very romantic notion that he was a dwarf with a hydrocephalic head is not true. It's like the Toulouse-Lautrec Syndrome. I think there's a lot of fabrication about Bellocq to the point that I've a friend who works at the photography department of the Bibliothèque Nationale in Paris who keeps affirming that Bellocq never existed and that these photographs are fakes by this modern photographer called Freelander. I don't think it's true or else Freelander is a genius. We know there was a Bellocq who was a photographer. We don't have the proof that these photographs that were found eventually about ten or fifteen years ago in an attic in New Orleans are Bellocq's. But little by little, especially in the book of Bellocq's photographs that was published by the Museum of Modern Art in New York, they came up with this version of the New Orleans Toulouse-Lautrec hanging around in brothels, a photographer instead of a painter, but very much the same romantic view of the deformed artist who photographs beautiful women; and we have no proof that it was so. I thought it was a cliché. I don't know if you watch television, but in a program called *Fantasy Island* there's this little French character. He came to me and he said, "You're not giving me the part of Bellocq?" And he was very aggressive. "Me, a compatriot of yours?" And I said, "Surely not, and get out of here." I thought, my God!

AUDIENCE: I am curious about your choice of Pierre Blaise in *Lacombe, Lucien*. He had no acting experience at all?

LM: Oh no, not only had he no acting experience, but he was from a farming family from that part of France, from the southwest, which is where I live actually. He lived in a tiny little village in a family of eleven brothers and sisters. And not only had he never seen a camera, but he'd never seen a movie. That part of the country was so remote that his only experience with images was television. He was from a very poor family, and he started working on his own when he was fourteen years old climbing and cutting trees, cutting branches, a very dangerous job. I saw, again, that I needed somebody totally fresh. I couldn't even think of using an actor.

The same thing happened to me in *Murmur of the Heart*. I started seeing professional children actors. Most of them are just little monsters. They take the worst habits usually; they're just impossible. So I ended up twice with an unknown, and in the case of *Lacombe, Lucien* I didn't even try to look for actors because it had to be somebody also with the knowledge and experience and background of the character. Actually this boy, Pierre Blaise, could have been *Lacombe, Lucien*. Really, he was very violent. He was very extreme. He was wonderful, wonderful. I really loved him, and we stayed very friendly until he was killed in a stupid car accident with two of his friends. The three of them were twenty years old. It was a real shame.

I had my headquarters in Toulouse, the capital of the southwest of France, and with my assistants, we must have seen some two thousand boys. He eventually showed up, but he didn't really want to come too much. He'd been sent by his mother because she'd seen a piece in the local paper in which I was trying to describe the character, and she said, "Pierre, you must go because it is you." He went sort of reluctantly. As soon as saw him, I was terribly interested in him doing it. I ended up with five boys and I started working very closely with them, then I ended up with two, and finally I ended up with Pierre. He was such a natural.

The technique of film acting is very precise. You have to take a position, then move to another position, and you must put your weight on the right foot because if not, the camera is just behind you and you cover the shot—you know it's a matter of inches many times—and he did that like an old pro in a matter of days. He was very, very gifted except that at the end of the first week, he said, "Well, I don't like doing this. I don't like acting, and I'm going home." And he went to his hotel and he packed. I remember we spent the night trying to tell him, "You can't do this to us." Then he got interested. He was quite an exception. He was actually extraordinarily gifted and so close to the character. It was very bizarre sometimes.

AUDIENCE: Do you see any trends in the film industry today?

LM: What's very dangerous is definitely the trend in the film industry now, not only in America but also in Europe. I saw on an interview program on CBS Cable, this program called *Signature,* the chairman of Universal Pictures. He was very arrogant, and he said, "Oh, don't worry. We're going to make less and less pictures but they're going to be better and better." What does that mean? I suppose "better and better" means costing more and more money, of course. It seems to be such an absurd gamble and so much against the odds that even from their own point of view, I think it's stupid. This is what they try to do.

If they have $100 million they would probably rather make three pictures, very expensive, and try to put everything in them so that they will please everybody, which is always a dangerous approach because it's reaching for the lowest common denominator. They usually fail, and fortunately they've been failing a lot lately because (a) they're not very smart, and (b) if somebody could predict what's going to be successful with audiences, everybody would be a billionaire. It would be very simple. I've always made that very optimistic gamble that if I'm really interested in something, then other people will also be interested so I'll find an audience, but if you keep saying to yourself, "Oh, I'm going to do that because they're going to love it," you don't know. Audiences sometimes are surprising. Sometimes you're really stunned to see a real piece of crap becoming a blockbuster. Also, you're sometimes very pleased to see that some little film or something interesting, something with a difference, something with invention, finally comes across.

In the old days in Hollywood a studio like Paramount, for instance, would come out with more than a hundred pictures a year. So the great Hollywood movies actually were the B movies. Today there are no more B movies. Even when I worked on *Pretty Baby*—I spent almost a year in Los Angeles—they were still making some of these. For instance, *Pretty Baby* was one of them. It cost three million dollars, and they don't make these anymore. So they make very few pictures, and that's a very unhealthy trend. I believe a lot in diversity. I believe in luck. I believe in taking chances. I was in Los Angeles last week, and these days there are very few movies being made except sequels and remakes. It's really bizarre. Fortunately, I think they are losing a lot of money these days, so there might be a couple of changes in management. I think the studios, Hollywood studios, have had the worst management in their history in the last three or four years. These people should have been all thrown out and should go into television.

PART IV

Behind—and in—the Scenes

CHAPTER FOURTEEN

James Woods

RIC GENTRY

James Woods has become what he initially aspired to be, "a great actor." It's not that he's won countless awards—Emmys, Golden Globes, Academy Award nominations—but that he invariably creates riveting, complex, idiosyncratic, wholly credible characters with fathomless emotional depth: the disenfranchised journalist in *Salvador* (1986); the aging Southern gentleman assassin in *Ghosts of Mississippi* (1996); the bitter, pugnacious attorney in *Citizen Cohn* (1992); the troubled, wayward founder of Alcoholics Anonymous in *My Name is Bill W.* (1989); the remorseless, defiant former drifter in *Killer: A Journal of Murder* (1996); the tough-minded, tenacious crusader in *Indictment: The McMartin Trial* (1995); and the hopeless schizophrenic in *Promise* (1986).

Usually remembered for his edgy, incendiary, antiheroic misfits, Woods's range as an actor is often overlooked. Critic Pauline Kael wrote of his cunning killer in *The Onion Field* (1979) that Woods was "the most hostile actor in America." But after *The Summer of Ben Tyler* (1996), in which Woods plays a prominent, politically ambitious attorney who adopts a black teenager in the deep South during World War II, Pulitzer Prize-winning TV pundit Howard Rosenberg of the *LA Times* wrote that "James Woods is rapidly becoming television's contemporary version of Jimmy Stewart—always the perfect choice for a story about an ordinary man facing an extraordinary moral dilemma."*

In the sixteen months before this interview, Woods worked on six films in succession: John Carpenter's *Vampires* [1997], which at over $19 million was the

---

*Quoted from notes provided by Woods's publicist.

FIGURE 14. Actor James Woods. Courtesy: Jerry Ohlinger Archives.

largest grossing film to debut on Halloween weekend and for which the late critic Gene Siskel averred that Woods should receive at least another Academy Award nomination; *Another Day in Paradise* [1998], a much underappreciated and overlooked film that Woods also produced; *True Crime* [1999], directed by and costarring Clint Eastwood; *The General's Daughter* [1999], written by William Goldman; *The Virgin Suicides* [1999], written for the screen and directed by Sofia Coppola; and *On Any Given Sunday* [1999], written and directed by Oliver Stone.

Woods's deep passion for his art and his insistence on excellence makes him difficult to work with and often misunderstood. It's true, however, that he barely avoided fisticuffs with several of his directors and once hammered Robert Downey Jr. between takes for "doggin'" his performance on the set of *True Believer* (1989). At the same time, very few film industry personalities summon such prompt, unsolicited affection from their peers. "I love the guy," says Jodie Foster of Woods. "I love Jimmy," says Natasha Gregson Wagner. "I adore him," remarks Jim Belushi. "I love him," says John Savage. "I love him deeply," comments Oliver Stone. "Jimmy was one of the few Hollywood people I invited to my wedding," says Sharon Stone. "He is simply a wonderful man."[*]

In a personal interview with this author, John Carpenter said that "Jimmy could be tough on an inexperienced director. I mean, the man is a force of nature. When you cast James Woods, you are going beyond ordinary casting. He brings something to the screen that very, very few actors can bring. He gives you much more than what you're looking for, moments of unexpected genius.

"When Jimmy got his star on *The (Hollywood) Walk of Fame*" (last November), Carpenter continues, "Melanie Griffith said that whatever you plan for a scene with Jimmy goes right out the window, that she was confident about how she was going to do it and all of a sudden she was in a crisis. I think a lot of actors feel what Melanie does when they work with Jimmy. He just turns it on when a scene starts. But she also said that she would never hesitate to work with him again because he brings the most out of you, that Jimmy requires that an actor give an optimal performance."[†]

In effect, James Woods makes every movie a better one—more compelling, more trenchant, more real, more powerful.

But something almost preternatural is driving James Woods, something so ferocious that mere achievement is not enough. Where does that come from? And as a mathematic-scientifically inclined, bona fide genius with a tested IQ of 184, why did he become an actor?

This interview took place over three encounters. The first was during December 1998 at a hotel suite in West Hollywood, then on January 1, and finally later in the month at his 1936 Frank Lloyd Wright-style Taliesin home in Beverly Hills,

---

[*]Quotes from personal interviews, respectively: January 8, 1999; January 29, 1999; January 16, 1999; January 11, 1999; December 16, 1998; December 20, 1998.
[†]Personal interview, December 17, 1998.

a glory of mahogany, copper and straight lines that overlooks the entire city of Los Angeles, clear to the inland, snowcapped San Gabriel mountains.

When Woods gets going, you can almost see the synapses firing through his system. The language rushes out in torrents, words never quite keeping up with the speed of thought. His blue eyes dart like the jostle of tachometer needles pushed to register the RPMs of an engine accelerated to the floor. Woods is kinetic energy personified.

RIC GENTRY: With more than sixty films for theatrical release or television, you're easily one of the most prolific actors working today. I'm wondering what it is that drives you. Many of your characters seem equally driven.

JAMES WOODS: Sometimes there's no simple answer. Basically I've always worked. I love doing what I do. I can't get enough of it.

Part of it though is that I went through a period where I wasn't getting enough work, really. I was with CAA (Creative Artists Agency) for seventeen years and my experience with them was that they get you to a certain point and then they want to farm you out to these glossy, packaged films for a lot of money to get the commission. They had a policy of never telling you what you were up for, of not reading scripts that were submitted to you and basically treating you like a retarded infant.

I did a couple of movies like that, *Immediate Family* [1989], *Straight Talk* [1992]. They were nice experiences with great people but I didn't think they were going to get me hired by someone like Martin Scorsese, who, with Oliver [Stone], is the greatest director in the world. He hires people because they're great, not because they're in a hit film necessarily. So this tug of war went on; I was trying to get more pictures that were Academy Award oriented rather than box office oriented. Meanwhile, I saw two scripts in a year.

The turning point came when Quentin Tarentino asked me why I turned down *Reservoir Dogs* [1992]. I said to him, "I hope you're fucking kidding," because I never heard a word about it and at that point I hadn't worked (on a theatrical feature) in a year. But he said, "Your agent said you wouldn't think of working for fifty thousand dollars" or whatever it was they paid the actors for that. I said, "Man, I would have made that movie for free."

So I walked into CAA and said, "This is just not going to work." And I went over to ICM (International Creative Management) and I said to the new agents, "I feel like I'm just out of the business at this point." People didn't really notice because *Citizen Cohn* had come out and had fourteen Emmy nominations and so on. And I said to them, probably in a more polite way, "I want to read every script that's out there. And I'm going to be real adamant about this, so you understand. If I ever hear of a script that you haven't already sent me, you're fired. I won't even bother to call you. Just know you're fuckin' fired. I never want anyone making my decisions again but me."

That was some years ago now and they've been great about it. Now I get an average of ten to fifteen scripts per week. [The agents at ICM] have tremendous insight and advice, really care about doing good material and never bring up the issue of money per se.

It was all part of a campaign that I launched to get back into the zone I wanted to be in, which was to work with the best directors in the world on good material with other good actors. I didn't give a shit about the size of the part, the salary or anything else. It was one of the best decisions I ever made.

Because there's one absolute, unequivocal equation for success in this business so you can last: just do good work, every time you act. When they do my contracts, I don't even ask what my billing is. I say, "Do the best you can but I want to do this picture." I was in a big lull because I wasn't doing what was true to myself as a man and as an actor.

I remember my agent saying, "There's absolutely no part for you in *Casino* [1995]. All the lead parts are cast." I said, "But it's Marty Scorsese. I'll do anything for Marty Scorsese." So I read the script and found this beautiful little part.

I called [Scorsese]. Left him a message: "This is James Woods. I know you're doing a movie and I have eight words for you: any part, any where, any time, any price." He called me back and said, "Are you serious?" I said, "Yeah." He said, "Well, then I have this great little part." I said, "I'll do it and I'll do it for free," or for scale, whatever that is to conform to the union rules.

It was a two-day part. We improvised a lot. I worked with Marty and Sharon [Stone] and it became a wonderful little cameo. It actually got me a lot of attention.

You know, I was walking out of the sequel to *The Fugitive* [1993] when someone from CAA asked me how I would commit the perfect crime. I said, "I'd go into Macy's on New Year's Day, blow somebody away with a revolver, then sign with CAA and never be heard from again and get away with it." You know, they'd just fuckin' let you disappear.

RG: Of your recent films, you were the producer on *Another Day in Paradise*. It's also extremely un-Hollywood.

JW: That's one thing I love about it. It's not the kind of movie you see very often. It's always the off-beat movies that I love. Just from an acting and producing point of view, it's so rewarding to be involved with something where you're surprised every day by the kind of work you're doing. You're going to places rarely approached in the usual Hollywood film, which are usually so predetermined in how they're going to look and how they're going to be shot. You might do great work (as an actor) but it's kind of trapped in the predictability of the coverage, a kind of feral thing neutralized by the same old camera angles. I know every shot a director's going to make in a big commercial film. I'm usually way ahead of him.

But here, with *Another Day in Paradise*, with a free-wheeling documentary kind of feel, you're just jammin', covering it in different ways. We were shooting angles that you can't precisely repeat because so much was interdependent on the movement of the actors and the movement of the camera according to the impulses of the moment. A lot of the dialogue was improvised. Everything was very alive, like grabbing lightning for a bottle. I think the whole thing just crackles.

RG: How did you become involved with the project?

JW: The script was brought to me by Nikki Pfeffer at ICM, who called to tell me that "This is your next picture. I guarantee it." And she was right. But there was an immediate time pressure because the bank financing the film insisted that the film start shooting at a certain date. So I called [writer-director] Larry Clark [*Kids*, 1995] and [writer] Steven Chin in New York at 2 A.M. and said, "I love your script. I'd love to do it." Larry said, "I never thought I'd get someone like you. We don't have the money." I said, "Don't worry about that. But I do want to produce it. I'm here but we'll work something out."

Then I said, "We've got to get Melanie Griffith to play Sid." And Larry said, "I love that idea but we can't afford her either." Now the way they hired me as an actor is they paid me with ownership in the film. And I said, "I'll tell you what. I'll give Melanie half my salary and half my ownership in the film so that she feels she's being treated fairly."

They said, "We can't get the script to her in time before the bank date." And if we sent it to her agent, who is the same agent at CAA I used to know, I knew how that was going to turn out: "Oh no, we're not going to have Melanie play some junkie in a movie for no money." I knew what their response was going to be. And she was doing movies I didn't think was up to her talent. You know, *Milk Money* [1994], typical CAA.

So Larry and Steven couldn't call Melanie up directly. They'd have to go through the agency and that would be the end of it. So I called Melanie up. I said, "I've known you since you were sixteen years old. You're one of my best friends. I've never asked you a business favor. You must read this script and you must give me an answer before noon tomorrow. There's not a lot of money but I'll give you half of whatever I've got in the film." And she read the script and said, "I love it. I'm in."

I wanted someone who was sexy, vivacious, sensual with that sweet voice of hers and everything else and had taken a turn around the hardest curve in a woman's life, turning forty years old. And now she's faced with a beautiful young girl, Rosie, the Natasha Gregson Wagner character, who's pregnant. Melanie's character doesn't have a kid. She's living with a junkie, my character Mel. She's a junkie. They're thieves. Her time is passed. She's kind of holding on to that hope. Her maternal instincts have been thwarted throughout her life because of the kind of life she lives and now it's all rekindled by the presence of Rosie. And then there's the sadness of knowing she's going to bring these kids Rosie and her boyfriend Bobby into their kind of life, the ambivalence she'll feel and so on.

So there was a lot for an actress to tear into if she has the courage to do it. You have this sex kitten playing a sex kitten passé. Yet she had to have the acting chops to go into real dark places. "You're going to be lifting your skirt and sticking a needle in your groin on camera. You're going to be doing some hard stuff here. You can't say you're going to do it and then get on the set and say, 'Well, I don't know if I can do that. I'm a star.' None of that." And everything that was expected of her she did and she went right to the edge of the envelope every time. And I knew she'd do it because she's a real actor.

It was a great part for her. For all of us really. I think in this case it completely validated her courage as an actress, an artist, as a woman, as a professional. The Bible says you cast your bread upon the water and it comes back seventy times seven. In the process of seeing her come to fruition with this part, I gave what for me is maybe the best performance of my life I think.

I've been in some of this territory before but I've never had the charm of this character. The slightly out of focus quality he has, being a longtime heroin user. I'm not as in control for some of it. I'm a little out of control and then back in control. Those edges really work for me. He's slightly like a drunk guy trying to walk a straight line. You think he's in control but you then realize he's not.

RG: Is there a standard approach you take to preparing for a part?

JW: You won't believe this but I usually read the script once and never look at it again until we get to the set and then I kind of scan it and then go do it. Because I'm such an analytical person by nature, I can get a little stiff if I prepare too much. The only time I do preparation is if I have to do an accent or a physical thing, where the guy has a tick or something. Or playing a schizophrenic where you have to know the background of the character, or you have to know stuff like handling weapons or a hypodermic needle as in *Paradise*. When it comes to the actual scenes I prefer never to rehearse, never do anything, just kind of go in there and do it by instinct. I'll rehearse if anyone wants to but I prefer not to. If you're too prepared it sounds like a play.

With *Paradise* you just have to get in the frame of mind to do those scenes. It's hard because you have to focus on those scenes and then be out of focus. As soon as you start thinking about what's going on, you lose something. That's the hardest thing, where you look like you're under the influence of something. It's very hard. And that's why it's one of my favorite performances, because I had it the way a chronic user would, just a tone of belligerence, a tone of being smacked out. And it just has to permeate the performance. It's very hard to do that. You just have to get in that frame of mind.

What I loved about *Paradise* is that we improvised so much, whole scenes. For example, after the shootout and I'm in the car talking. That was originally scripted with Melanie laughing hysterically, not saying anything and she just didn't feel that it worked. So we're sitting in the car and Larry said, "OK, just fuckin' jam with something." I just started talking. That whole speech was just made up.

But as I mentioned, I tried to just barely learn the lines so that I talked the way someone who's been a junkie a long time would talk. Larry kind of stutters a little bit, stammers. You know, he's a chronic drug user by his own admission in print so I'm not putting him down, and he kind of stumbles over things a little bit. And I loved that Mel, as voluble as he is, he kind of stumbles over things, like his mind is a little bent or something.

Another character though, like *The General's Daughter*, I learned word for word perfect because the guy's a very clever, accomplished warfare expert who's engaging in a game of psychological chess with a man who is interrogating him for murder, so I really, really wanted to be on top of it. So it just depends on the part.

RG: What's interesting is that *Another Day in Paradise* was written for the screen and directed by a man who's lived that life. The author of the novel the film is based on is Eddie Little, who apparently also lived it.

JW: Larry's in pretty serious rehab now. There were stories that he tried to shoot himself. Eddie Little was arrested because I heard he pulled a knife on a cop who stopped him at traffic light or something like that. I don't know the details.

It's a great source of inspiration when you're making the movie, but at the same time you're working with people who are a little difficult to deal with to say the least. You know, the experience on this picture is crazier than a bag of rocks. It was all very tough in the making. But when all is said and done, and the warfare was engaged and met, we made a great picture and that's all that counts.

I think it comes down to the fact that two incredibly strong egos, like Larry and myself, both had a real passion for the film. I won't deny Larry's passion and he won't deny mine. We both put a hell of a lot of blood, sweat, and tears into it, as a special one-of-a-kind document of a way of life that he knows intimately.

But Larry's very unrealistic about the business of film which I tried to protect him on. I've made fifty, sixty-some pictures and he's made two. On *Paradise*, for instance, there are thirty-eight days to shoot. There's no thirty-ninth. There are thirty-eight days. That's it. We can't go an hour over. If we go an hour over then the bank or the completion bond company is going to take over the film. It will no longer be "A Larry Clark Film." We'll have a bean counter making the film and the film will be destroyed.

We made our schedule but we lost some time with some nonsense that as an absolute, unabashed professional I was infuriated by. My rule is, "You're on time, you know your lines, you're straight, and you're prepared to go to work." I don't care if it's about heroin and wild and crazy and everything else. You've got to have the ABCs down before you can speak the language. There's no excuse for anything otherwise.

RG: Was there tension between you and Larry, since you're the producer and he's working for you, really?

JW: Well, you know, I can't watch myself when I'm working. I'd say to Larry, "What do you think of this?" Sometimes I'd just try something. There were times when I would just go his way, give him what he wanted and see what happened. Then maybe we'd try my way. Whatever worked. I'd rather be 100 percent wrong and make a good film than vice versa any time.

But there was tremendous contention on the set. Larry fired his DP [Director of Photography] at one point, though it's still beautifully shot. And Larry kind of focused in an inordinate way on the boy [Vincent Kartheiser] in the film. I didn't know what the deal was. I couldn't put my finger on it. But people were showing up late, there were reports of drug use and there was a subtle rebellion by the crew on the set kind of against Larry and his friendship with the kid. I went to [cowriter and coproducer] Steven Chin once and said, "Show me the boy's birth certificate." He said, "He's eighteen years old." I said, "I want to see that documented." Because I'm the producer on the picture and I'm liable if any strange stuff is happening here.

RG: What were you suspecting, that there may have been drug influence or a homosexual influence or even an introduction into theft?

JW: All I can say is that I felt civilly and criminally much more comfortable to know that as an official producer of record on the film that the boy was eighteen years old. That's all I can say to you.

RG: You won't dismiss anything I just mentioned?

JW: Let me just say that in this universe anything is possible. I just don't have any knowledge per se except that there was a lot of discomfort on the set about a lot of stuff. There was lateness and reports of things. You get a feeling from a crew. And they were really uncomfortable, you know, wondering, "Where are they?" "Well, they're in the trailer." "Go get 'em." And they'd want to send a girl over, maybe a twenty-year-old production assistant, and she'd say, "I'm not gonna go knock on that door." I mean, maybe they're over there talking about the script, which it could very well have been because Vinnie gave a brilliant performance. I'd like to think that's what it was.

Vinnie's young and you can forgive a lot with youth, though other kids his age were dying on Omaha beach fifty years ago. He's going to see his way in life and he has the raw talent, but I've watched them come and go all my life. It's a necessary condition to have raw talent to be a long-term success as an actor, but it's also a necessary and imperative condition to be professional. It's not enough to be talented.

RG: What about postproduction?

JW: Toward the end, I don't know all the facts, but there were apparently serious problems with heroin, alcohol, amphetamines, you name it. Larry wasn't always available to finish the cut. I don't like to go in the editing room as an actor because I can't be objective and don't want to influence the performances. During the production I didn't see any evidence of it in the way I did in postproduction. He was not the same man that I thought he was when we started working and seemed pretty clear.

His original cut was some two hours long. It's now a completely different movie than the first cut. He had final cut and signed off on his cut. You know: "Here it is." But there was a better movie in that cut, a great motion picture if you could sever twenty minutes of it. We had to wrestle with him for months. "Fuck you, it's my picture." We said, "Let us show you what we mean on the Avid."* He belted Steven because he didn't want the picture further edited without his consent. Even his agent tried to persuade him. Larry wanted to show the picture to the studio but if we did that and it wasn't the cut they were satisfied with either, it would be a very tough, impossible sell to do a second time. The studio would say, "Well, we saw that picture." Finally he gave in but it was a nightmare.

But let me say the positive part of it. Anyone that passionate—and I'm one of those people—they're going to make some mistakes along the way but they're going to be a special kind of artist. And I'll take a guy that stubborn, that annoying, that aggravating, that frustrating, that absolutely time consuming, who's interested in making this kind of movie every day over a cooperative bore. OK? And I admire him for his pigheaded stubbornness, to put it negatively, but admire him for his sense of passion and determination, to put it positively. Larry and I had to be separated once from having a fistfight on the set but I can't wait for this love/hate relationship on our next picture together. I'm proud that I gave more to this picture than an actor usually gives. It was a fucking bloodbath, but what's important is that after a big war, a big Armageddon, that somehow you wring out the blood from the cloth, hold it up and you have the Holy Shroud.

RG: What was the budget on *Another Day in Paradise?*

JW: $4.5 million. That was everything. That's not even what they pay some movie star and the fifteen assistants in his entourage. There were no salaries to speak of. To be honest with you, you don't even make that much money on your points, foreign sales and all. Any money we make will probably go back into promoting the picture and video.

But how much fuckin' money do you need? I mean, I don't need money. I have a beautiful home. A nice car. I can take care of my family and myself and my dog. I'm fine. I don't need $20 million a picture. I'll do *Another Day in Paradise* any time over a billion dollars to be in *Godzilla* [2000]. I want a secure life but I'm paid well enough.

I put my heart and soul in that picture. I've been working as a producer every single day since October or November (of '97). There hasn't been a day when I haven't been on the phone with someone—the actors, the director, the press, Trimark (the studio) with negotiations, with the publicists, whoever, dealing with this picture to make sure it gets across the finish line because there are too many great pictures where at the last minute someone just screws up and destroys the fuckin' picture.

---

*A digital editing system that could provide an alternative cut on video.

RG: Are you thinking of any film in particular?

JW: *Once Upon a Time in America* [1984], one of the greatest pictures ever made. Three weeks before they released it they decided to cut an hour out of it and ruined the picture. I just sat there, stunned. It was like someone cutting the arms off your infant child. And I vowed that that would never happen to me again, never in my lifetime.

Sergio [Leone] had this great operatic vision. He said to me, "You and Bobby [De Niro] want to change things and I find myself amending the scene because of what the actors are giving me. I've never worked like this before." It was his last picture. I loved the man. I feel like crying, just talking about it. I never really saw him again after the movie and didn't know whether to call him or not when it was such a disaster. I was too young and insecure to call him and say, "We made a great picture together and I can't tell you how sorry I am." It's a shame. He was a great visual master, one of the greatest.

His last three films are a twelve-hour cinematic triptych of the creation of America via a Marxist perspective. It goes through the construction of the railroad, the Mexican-American War to the rise of organized crime and its influence on corporate America. There's no cinematic triptych as profound as that, except maybe *The Godfather*.

But I want to add that despite the work I did on *Another Day in Paradise*, Melanie and the kids, Lou Diamond Phillips working virtually for free in a great cameo, Larry's tremendously impassioned vision of how this film should look and feel and the areas to where it should go, and whatever dynamic, brutal or not, that electrified us to get there, it's a collaboration which made it possible for us as a group and as relative individuals to achieve that. Like I was saying, I look forward to the next chapter of this love/hate relationship with Larry, which I'm sure is how he feels about me. I must be crazy but we made a great film, so something's right and whatever it is I'm going for it.

RG: It must have been very different working with Clint Eastwood on *True Crime*.

JW: Oh, Clint. Clint is the exception that proves the rule. The old story with Clint is that everyone in the film business should spend a day on one of his sets to see how a film should be really made. All the effort goes into putting it on screen. None of it's about the nonsense that seems to affect so many movies.

He's everything you hope and pray he's going to be—brilliant, funny, a man's man, a great cool guy who loves his wife and is good to his friends. You want to be around him all the time. He's one of the few icons who's everything he promises to be. Working with him was an absolute, unequivocal joy. I didn't want it to end. Great material, having fun. No blood on the walls this time. It was as delightful an experience as I ever had making a film.

And Clint's a terrific actor. He's known as an icon and a great director and producer but people forget why he's a star, which is because he's a great actor. And as a director he's a dream. He doesn't make a big deal about it. He'll say,

"Why don't we roll the camera and see what we're doing here." You're doing the rehearsal and all of a sudden you're shooting the scene. And he said, "I like it real and people make mistakes and I want to see human behavior as it is. You do twenty takes to get it perfect and it's antiseptic."

I had a six-page scene with him of nonstop dialogue. He plays a newspaper reporter who's a kind of burned-out, philandering, reformed drunk trying to prove that someone about to be executed was wrongfully accused, a kind of racist mistake. I play his boss at the paper, who likes and respects him and tries to tell him, "Don't be a washed-up jerk." The scene is very witty, full of wisecracks, fast and furious in a kind of Ben Hecht style. Clint said, "I don't want a split moment of silence in this scene. I want it to go like a machine gun. I want it like those old Spencer Tracy-Katharine Hepburn or *His Girl Friday** [1940] whippet-quick performance repartees." I said, "How are you going to do this in your laconic Clint Eastwood way?" He said, "Don't worry. I'll keep up."

People told me I should be prepared when I went in. So I had it nailed when I came in there. And so did he. We did a take right off the bat. No rehearsal, nothing, man. It was like, "Let's roll and see what happens." And when we finished he looked up in that Dirty Harry way and smiled, as if to say, "Well, good. Looks like you made the cut, kid."

RG: One take?

JW: One take. And I said, "That's it?" He goes, "You were terrific and I felt good. Camera got it? OK. What do we want to do another take for?" I said, "For safety?" He said, "What does that mean? That doesn't mean anything. If it's all great, why fix it?" And that's how he works.

Sometimes a big Hollywood movie can be well done and artful. With *True Crime* we did great work in a very commercial entertainment. There's the crisp, fast dialogue, terrific performances, and a gut-wrenching drama.

RG: You've been rehearsing with Oliver Stone's for his next film, *On Any Given Sunday*.

JW: It's a film about professional football, but let me tell you, it's not just an entertainment about football. It's a powerful story about men at war in a sport that uses people up as fodder while big corporations are making millions and millions of dollars. It's a drama but some of it is very funny and very moving, because under the heart of corporate greed, exploitation, and so on is the very moving story of a great game that really inspires people. But you've got to cut through all the shit that corporate America has imposed on this very pure exercise in manhood.

Oliver is a great writer and a great director. A great man and one of my best friends in the world. He's been a mainstay in my artistic life since *Salvador*

---

*With Cary Grant and Rosalind Russell, directed by Howard Hawks.

[1986]. We've done five pictures together with this one, two that he produced and there were others that I wasn't available for.

He doesn't let his ego get in the way. He brings the actors in and reworks the script according to their lines and improvs and points of view about the characters. He knows what works and doesn't work. Oliver has a very secure ego in the making of a film. He's open to any idea. He's a great leader. He knows when to delegate. He really does his research. He just works his ass off. He's a very hard working man. He's an inspiration, really. Oliver works harder than anyone I've ever seen.

You know, after *JFK*—

RG: He took a lot of heat for that film. He was a real media darling before *JFK* but that changed a bit then. The press just got hysterical, which I never understood. Roger Ebert wrote something rather extensive about that. All they had to do was some fundamental research. Oliver's courage in making that film was profound, the death threats and everything. But should *JFK* be required viewing for all Americans?

JW: Yeah, and *Nixon* [1995] as well.

RG: Is *Nixon* a masterpiece?

JW: A masterpiece, definitely. And people say, "Maybe we should make another movie about monsters walking through New York and stomping on taxi cabs." And here's this guy who can make any movie he wants and he chooses to make a movie about Richard Nixon. I mean, Hello? This guy's a national treasure. That's what pisses me off about people who criticize Oliver. Even if his films were flawed, and I don't think they are, his intent alone is A triple plus.

RG: And stylistically and visually he's been so innovative. I was speaking with Stan Brakhage* once and he fully agreed. He couldn't praise Oliver enough.

JW: Yeah, and that's the other thing about Oliver. People are so busy talking about his politics that they forget that he's been as inventive in the grammar of cinema as any director in the history of film. He's introduced ways of expressing ideas visually no one's seen before. I also thought *Natural Born Killers* [1994] was another landmark up there with *Citizen Kane* [1941].

RG: Can we expect *On Any Sunday* to be as visually interesting as Oliver's films usually are?

JW: Oh yeah. Absolutely. You won't be disappointed.

RG: And then there's *Virgin Suicides*.

JW: Yeah, I'm very proud of that. It's directed by Sofia Coppola, who adapted the novel by Geoffrey Eugenides. It's a black comedy. I'm the dad who has five

---

*Renowned experimental filmmaker, former film professor at the University of Colorado in Boulder, who passed away March 9, 2003.

daughters and they all commit suicide. My agent said, "You want to do another low-budget picture?" And I said, "I just have a feeling about this one. And about Sofia." I love her. And it's just going to shock everyone to see how good this picture is, how talented she is.

From a personal point of view, I was trashed by the press because of the crazy behavior of my (second) ex-wife and a lot of her shenanigans and I suffered a lot for something I never did. And Sofia went through a similar thing with *Godfather III* [1990]. She was a teenager and she was helping out her dad and got crucified. I'm really glad to see that she's going to be exonerated when they see how talented an artist she really is.* A lovely woman, kind, sweet, decisive, talented as you could ever imagine. It was a great experience. The last year has been great. I love working. I don't plan to stop, either.

RG: I'm intrigued by a remark Alec Baldwin once made. He referred to you as "the actor as terrorist." You could interpret that several ways.

JW: *[Laughs.]* I think he was saying that tongue-in-cheek. I took that as a compliment and it was meant as a compliment. When I go into a scene I push it to the limit but that makes for electricity on screen. You know, you just have to put yourself on that artistic gang plank, where you're trying things, often in the very moment of doing it, and maybe you've got to work everything up to a fever pitch and it might involve a little contention with the director or someone with which way you're going, but that's part of the process to get there. And yeah, it gets a little rough sometimes. It's not for the faint of heart. My argument is never about a better trailer or where my name is on the back of my chair or any of that bullshit. It's only about, "How do we make this scene better?"

I make a movie as if it were life and death. If the stakes are that high for you personally, it's like lead, follow or get out of the way. I just take it all extremely seriously. And for that I will never apologize to anyone ever on the face of the earth.

Someone once asked me when I started out, when I was about nineteen or twenty, "You want to be rich? You want to be a movie star?" I said, "I don't give a shit about being a movie star. I just want to be the greatest actor in the world." The only thing I wanted anyone to say about me—and whatever else they say I don't care—is "This guy's a great actor."

If I'm so difficult to work with, why have I worked with Oliver on five films? With [director] Harold Becker on three films? With James Garner on two films? With Sharon Stone on two films? Why do people work with me again and again and again? They understand that sometimes you've got to make a little noise to make a great scene.

When I was younger I was sometimes a little bit of an asshole, always trying to ratchet things up, seeing how we could make a scene a little more explosive. "Let's make it rough," you know. I mean, I put my edge of craziness into mak-

---

*ED: She is the writer and director of the critically acclaimed *Lost in Translation* (2003).

ing it work better, rather than something like, "Let's do smack and hang out at the Viper Room." I never did any of that stuff. I just wanted to perform. I mean, some people rebel by doing drugs and everything. My rebellion was channeled through work by exploring dark characters. It was interesting to explore the rebellious side of life but do it through my art.

But there's no room to consider other characters' feelings when you're acting. I'm speaking of characters now, not the actors personally. I'm very respectful of other actors. *On Any Sunday*, for example, I play the team doctor with Matthew Modine (an assistant team doctor), a great actor I've always wanted to work with. But as we rehearsed the scene I'm jumping all over his lines. I'm running roughshod over him. As a character I'm sort of chopping away at him. I said, "Matthew, I kind of did that to show you what I would do. You've got to find a way to force your way through," which he's very able to do of course. "If I wait for you to say each line, the ruthlessness of my character toward your character's innocence isn't as interesting as it is if I really push you and you completely stand up to me," which as a brilliant doctor he's very much capable of doing. But I don't want to give him 30 percent less from me to make his job easier. I want to make his job harder, so he can demonstrate a higher degree of difficulty and achievement.

Drama, which I do more than comedy, is about shocking the audience and electrifying them through real confrontation. And that means you push the other actor as hard as you can and they come back to you as hard as they can. No one wants to watch a fixed fight.

RG: I'm still wondering where that drive and intensity and relentless energy come from. In your estimation, how much do you personally resemble some of your more volatile characters on screen? You know, the "actor as terrorist" also means jolting the viewer emotionally. There must be a catharsis or some gratification in that.

JW: A lot of the best stuff I've done is based on true stories. *The Onion Field*, for example, *Salvador, The Boost, Another Day in Paradise, Ghosts of Mississippi, Citizen Cohn, My Name is Bill W.* You have a lot of rich resources when you try to understand who these people are. But I can play someone like Bill W. and do a real complex, dark, disturbed man who ends up being a great hero to millions of people. It's an edgy performance but it's not the same as another substance abuser like Mel in *Paradise*, who in fact is a sociopath. I just like playing enormously complicated, volatile, passionate characters because they're a greater acting challenge. It's not that big a challenge to play a customary leading man. I'd be bored doing that.

RG: But you play incendiary, antiheroic, defiant characters with such conviction. *Killer: A Journal of Murder* [1995] is another exceptional performance.

JW: My mom always said, "God, I wish people understood that you're the opposite of a lot of characters you portray, that you're really sensitive and, in a weird kind of way, shy." I don't know why I'm telling you that because people are going to read this and go, "Oh, yeah. James Woods is sensitive?" But in fact I think I'm kind of hypersensitive.

One reason I'm so intrigued by violent, evil, and repellent people is that I don't understand them. When people ask, "What are you most proud about yourself?" I always say how kind I am. Believe it or not, I'm a kind person compared to a lot of the roles I play. I want to explore that part of human nature that I don't understand and I'm frightened by. I'm frightened by those characters. I don't understand serial killers and that kind of evil because I come from people who were so truly and fundamentally good.

I have principles that I think give me the courage to be absolutely ruthless. If someone were to threaten my loved ones I would have zero conscience in destroying that person. I mean, destroying that person. I'd sleep like a baby. But I'd have to find that corner of myself in order to do it. It's there. But it's not natural to me.

You know, I'm really interested in people. I love the idea of creating characters who are so believable and are such a window into the human soul. I remember when we met those three guys who helped us with *Promise* who were schizophrenic. They said, "Everyone makes fun of us." And I said, "I will give you the most dignified [depiction]. I will truly tell your story with my heart and soul." I was so moved by those guys that my emotional, heartfelt response to them was as genuine as anything I ever felt in my life and it filtered into every day of my work. Every day I thought, "I'm doing this for Lance, Bill, and Sam." I still remember their names, thirteen years later. "I'm doing this for them."

RG: Your performance in *Promise* alone is enough to make you immortal.

JW: Well, thanks. I think it's my best performance. There's not a single frame I would change. Sometimes I would marvel at what I would do instinctively with that character. Sometimes a character just takes you over.

I'm emotionally moved by the goodness and sweetness in people. And I'm really intimidated by the violence and evil in people. The second woman I was married to was a truly dangerous and evil human being. The most dangerous woman I ever met in my life. We were married for three and a half weeks and she had me in court for four and a half years. We were two ships passing in the night, only I didn't realize she was the Exxon Valdez.

I think the biggest adjustment in my life was—and I do this as ruthlessly as anybody could in his existence—that if anybody ever says anything untrue about me, malicious to me, humiliating to or about me, I remove that person from my life forever and I never speak to that person again and never engage with them again and do everything I can to just assume that they're dead.

I'd never speak to my second ex-wife again. If she was on fire in the street I'd walk by her and never look at her. As far as I'm concerned, she died a long time ago and God rest her soul and she doesn't exist for me. After dealing with someone that pathological I just completely redefined my life. The pattern of self-destruction I had was in trusting people too much.

RG: I'm still wondering what it is that drives you, where all that fire and energy and passion comes from.

JW: Maybe it's something in my childhood.

RG: From what I understand, your father was a decorated U.S. Army intelligence officer and your mother was a preschool teacher. And it was a rather itinerant life, with residences in Illinois, Virginia, and Guam but most of it in Rhode Island.

JW: I can say unequivocally, without any peradventure of a doubt, that I was raised by parents with the kind of love that most people can only dream about. My mother and father loved me and my brother like we love the air we breathe, out of necessity. It was a necessity for them to love us in some deep inner genetic calling in their hearts and minds and souls.

They also tremendously encouraged me to be successful, but never made me feel bad if I failed at anything. So the only paradigm I knew was, "Success is fabulous, but don't worry, even if you fail we're going to love you." So I've got nothing to lose and everything to gain by being successful.

And my parents were smart and took a great deal of interest in educating us. My mother used to read adult-level novels to me when I was literally three and four months old because she heard somewhere that if you speak to a child like an adult, instead of a lot of baby talk, and you read to a child every day, even when the child doesn't understand, that you can increase the kid's intelligence and literary capability and now, recently, in the last year there was a test that bore that out. I don't know how they test for that but she always felt that. And my father used to read Shakespeare to me when I was five and six years old, which he knew by heart after memorizing it in the war.

And I was a very inquisitive kid, just insatiably curious. I've always had a tremendous amount of intellectual curiosity. Why this? Why that? Why this? Why that? I drove my mother crazy but she always, always took my questions seriously and she would always give me an intelligent answer. You had to be a college professor to be my mother but she never dodged it.

I passed some standardized tests in the third grade and I had the highest score in the history of my school system. And when my brother took the tests years later, he had the same scores that I did. We had the two highest scores in the history of the school system, so my parents must have been doing something right.

RG: And then there were some sudden tragedies.

JW: My best friend was killed by a passing car as he rode across the street on his bicycle, right in front of me. My father died a couple of years later (after surgery on lingering war injuries). He died the day of my seventh grade awards dinner.

He'd written a letter to me from the hospital saying how important it was for me to go to the dinner. Everyone there knew he died that morning but me. I always cherished that letter.

I don't think I was very content when I was younger. I was a little angry. I just took some of the bad luck very hard. I did a lot of soul searching.

RG: And you contracted polio when you were you a kid.

JW: I was eight, yeah. It left me with chronic back problems. It inhibits my golf swing so I can't hit the ball very far. But no one wants to play me at my handicap because when I play in a tournament I dig down psychologically; I'm almost unbeatable. Everyone asks, "Why is it that you play so much better in a tournament?" Because everyone is watching and there's a first prize. Within my handicap I'm like the best eighteen out there. Trust me. When the stakes are right, I'm unbeatable.

My attitude in everything I do is, I'm looking for the words "And the winner is." That's how you succeed. They don't have the Nobel prize runner-ups in the history books. No one remembers who lost the Super Bowl. If you want to be great in life, you've got to hear in your mind every day, "And the winner is." And you've got to see your name there.

Name five good films you saw last year. You'd agree that it's hard to come up with ten or fifteen good ones. Let's do the math. They made maybe a thousand films last year and there are how many thousands of actors in the Screen Actors Guild? In five or ten good films there's maybe two or three where you're right for the part or you really want to do it. How many thousands want that part? So guess what? I've got to be the best there is every time out. Thousands want two or three parts. Hello?

And let me tell you something. I'm not that good looking of a guy. I think I'm talented. Not the most talented actor in the world, necessarily. But—when I play golf, people say I've got the swing of an eighteen (handicap) and the heart of a four. That's how I am as an actor.

In other words, if you've been blessed with an intelligence and you've been blessed with parents who gave you ambition and you've been blessed with a God-given talent and you work really hard to put all those elements together and milk every drop of whatever you can of everything you've got, chances are, you're going to be ahead of the people who are lucky but not smart, smart but not lucky, good looking but not talented, have a little bit of it all, etc. You've just got a better chance than the other guy.

And I can tell you, we're promoting *Another Day in Paradise* with virtually no budget for a little studio; they're very supportive but they don't have any budget. We have no chance at it, you know. But Steven [Chin] my partner and I are working every single minute—it's New Year's Day and I'm talking to you for hours. I'm enjoying this but nonetheless, I'm trying to get this out there because we don't have the budget for the advertising and it's really important. I want people to see this film. I'm very proud of it. I'm putting a lot of effort into this. You put enough effort into something—you ever watch an ant with a grain of sand? Those guys are astounding. You can't believe what you can do with determination, free will, and passion in unlimited quantities. I mean, I love watching those guys, those ants at work. They can fucking build the pyramids.

RG: How old were you when you learned what your IQ was?

JW: I think I took the IQ test at the same time that I took the army scholarship test to MIT. I got an army scholarship because my dad died in the service and I'd been nominated for the Air Force Academy but got disqualified when I ran through a glass door and severed everything in my right arm to the bone. It's a long story but I was at UCLA studying linear math on a National Science Foundation grant between my junior and senior year in high school and I was fooling around with a friend and ran through a glass door. I was in and out of the hospital for ten months having operations, reconstructing my arm, but I was disqualified from the Air Force Academy. I don't have full sensation or mobility in my right hand but the doctor did a very good job.

RG: That also dashed your aspirations at the time of becoming an ophthalmologist, but were you startled by the results of the IQ test?*

JW: No, to tell you the truth, because I was always good at taking tests. Now I don't know what I'd get. But I can also give credit to our school system in Warwick, RI. We had a thing called the "academically talented program," smart kids in the same group all the way through school. And we had just the best teachers and the most advanced texts and stuff like that and we were really pushed hard. Most of the kids in that class went on to major universities like Harvard and Brandeis and Penn and the University of Chicago on full scholarships. It's like my theory about acting. We were really talented kids pushed to our limits. And guess what? You get results.

RG: How did you become interested in acting?

JW: In my senior year I was asked to perform in a high school production of *Little Foxes*. My arm was (in a cast) since I was still recovering from more surgery. But I won the New England Drama Award for Best Actor, and I just thought, "This is a really cool thing to do."

RG: And you had no training and no previous acting experience before then?

JW: There was just something waiting to get out I think.

RG: Then you went to MIT as a political science major on a full scholarship, but you also continued auditioning and performing?

---

*Woods also scored 1575 of a possible 1600 on the SAT, with a perfect 800 on the verbal part of the exam.

JW: Right. All over. At MIT, the University of Rhode Island, the Loeb Theatre at Harvard, the Provincetown Playhouse, the Agassiz Summer Theatre. Then I would shuttle off to New York in those days on Eastern Airlines for $13 per commute to see plays and audition there and then go back and show up (for class) and take my tests and everything.

I had a great advantage over other young people when I got to New York. Other kids were going to acting classes and doing a scene from Shakespeare and I had already done thirty-six full theatrical productions. I was twenty-one years old. You need an accent? I can do it. You need an old guy? I can do it. I mean, I'd done it all.

Someone saw me at the New Theatre (in New York) and signed me as a client, an agent named Judy Parrish. I appeared in *Saved* off Broadway [1970] and won an Obie Award and the Clarence Derwent Award (for Most Promising Actor) and the *Variety* Critics Poll. Then I was cast in *Borstal Boy* on Broadway [1970]. I had a little more than a semester left at MIT and thought, "Fuck it. I'm staying here."

RG: Then you were cast in *The Visitors* (1972) directed by Elia Kazan. That was your first film.

JW: When I first met Kazan I didn't have an impact on him for some reason. About a week and a half later he called me up and said, "Casting director Allan Shayne says you're the most promising young actor in New York and I should meet you." I said, "You already met me." He said, "I don't remember." So I went in again and I read (from the script) for him. Once I got a chance to read, I got the part.

It was an important lesson because to this day when a director doesn't think I'm right for something I say, "Why don't I read for you?" They say, "I can't have you do that. You're a big movie star." Well, that's nonsense. I don't have any hubris, that I'm "too big" to read. My attitude is that if I can give a director some insight into how I can play the character that he can't easily envision, then it's worth doing. I say, "If I don't read for you, you're going to cast someone else." With *Ghosts of Mississippi*, Rob Reiner didn't see me for the part so I read for him. The same thing happened with the part of Haldeman in *Nixon* for Oliver. He said, "You're very energetic and charismatic and Haldeman is this buttoned-up, contained guy, black and white with square edges." I said, "It'll be a challenge for me. I can do it." I went and got a crew cut and read for him. I had no ego problem reading for a guy who I worked with ten years earlier and got an AA nomination with.

RG: How were you cast as Richard Boyle in *Salvador*?

JW: I went in for the Jim Belushi part (of Dr. Rock). And Oliver didn't think I was right for it. And you know, I was still a struggling actor. So I thought right then and there, I better take a stab at the lead. And I said to Oliver, "I should play the Boyle character." And he said, "I've already got Marty Sheen. I saw you as more the sidekick." I said, "Marty Sheen's a great actor but, you know, think about it." Then Oliver said, "Well, he's a very religious guy and he's not real comfortable with the violence and the language in the film, the cursing and all that." And I said, "You've got to have that. You want a guy like me."

Oliver's then-wife Elizabeth was there and she said, "He's right, Oliver. You need a guy who wants to go for it." I said, "Yeah, Richard Boyle* would go for it." You know, I just hustled it.

So Oliver called Marty the next day and asked, "How do you feel about this?" And Marty was very good. He said, "If you have someone more suited for it, that's cool, because I'm not comfortable with the nature of some of the material." So I ended up getting it.

RG: That's remarkable, because that's not only a definitive, quintessential James Woods performance but obviously completely redefined the movie.

JW: I tried to stamp my personality on that character. The drinking and drugs I didn't relate to but this guy had such heart and soul in an epochal sense buried under the bullshit. I like to think I have that but it's not buried. I like to think it's right there. The tone of the character is like me, in the way he talked, moved, hustled.

RG: He's the moral center of the film, though in the beginning you don't think he has any morals. It's a great adventure that's also about this man's redemption.

JW: Exactly. That's one reason it's called *Salvador*. And it was a very tough, rugged shoot. Oliver and I were at each other's throats the whole time, like a couple of Tasmanian devils wrestling under a blanket. He'd really put his ass on the line, mortgaging his house and everything to make the film, giving up his salary so that he could shoot a battle scene that he otherwise didn't have the money for. But there was a struggle of wills going on between us and the whole shoot was a nightmare. But show me a film as richly passionate and raw-edged as *Salvador*. Part of what made that a great film was the volatility it took to create it.

RG: Getting back to *The Visitors*, you had some confrontations with Kazan.

JW: We were secluded in this farmhouse (in Connecticut), where we were shooting. Kazan liked to use these method acting techniques. He was famous for that, where he would use every vulnerability an actor had to get a performance from him. He drove Andy Griffith to a nervous breakdown on *A Face in the Crowd* [1957]. He sent a telegram to the actress on the set of *A Tree Grows in Brooklyn* [1945] that said her mother had died to get her to cry on screen.

And with me, because I play this isolated character, he didn't want any of the other actors or anyone else to talk to me. You know, we were having dinner and they'd all ignore me. Finally, I said to Kazan, "You know, this is fuckin' bullshit. I know how to act. I don't have to sit here after a day's work and have everyone

---

*The journalist of the same name on whom the character was based.

ostracize me." I refused to put up with it. I didn't care if he directed *On the Waterfront* [1954] and *East of Eden* [1954] and these other famous films. I didn't give a shit who he was. All that shit may have worked with these other wimps but it's not going to work with me.

RG: And then, since your character (in *The Visitors*) implicates two of his friends for war atrocities in Vietnam, you asked Kazan to tell you what it was like to reveal the names of alleged communist sympathizers before the House Un-American Activities Committee.*

JW: Yeah, I asked, "What was that like?" And believe me, that didn't go over very well. He simply wouldn't talk about it. But I said, "You want to steal from me for your art, why shouldn't I steal from you?" I didn't care if he was Elia Kazan and I was nobody. I didn't care if he could've given me a bad rap and made it difficult for me to work again, someone of his stature in the business. But I'd rather not work than live a lie. I'll go work in a bookstore.

But you know, I was a theater actor and I never remotely thought I'd ever be in movies or on TV. I never thought I had the matinee idol looks for that. In the theater, no one ever cared how you looked. No one gets a role off Broadway because they're good looking. It was the merit system: if you're a great actor you get the part. With movies it was different. Being handsome or pretty was more important.

And then all of a sudden I'm in movies and I thought, "What the fuck am I doing? I don't look like a movie star." All of a sudden I was made to look at an area of my life I'd always felt uncomfortable about. I've come to feel, because other people say it, that I have an interesting look. But looks weren't going to do it for me in movies. I had to have something more.

RG: What was it like when you first came to L.A.?

JW: It was very different when I first got out here about twenty years ago. No traffic. Very relaxing. But L.A.'s not like any other place. It's so suburban. People don't realize that. I had an apartment at the corner of Crescent Heights and Fountain (in Hollywood). They were called the Tennis Court Apartments. Then I bought a house in Laurel Canyon. But most of the time you live in your car. I liked it though, coming out here.

RG: I've noticed that as the day progresses here that the light through the windows seems to illuminate hidden nooks and corners and that the shifting shadows seem to throw a new slant on what is basically the geometric architecture.

JW: I love that about this place. It's like the Grand Canyon, where the relationship between space and light is never the same at any time of day.

RG: And your library is fabulous. There must be ten thousand books in there or more. Do you still read a lot?

---

*In the 1950s, resulting in a blacklist of Hollywood filmmakers.

JW: I love to read, but lately it's mostly been scripts. It's a bit of a curse but it's the only way to do it. I haven't read anything right for me in awhile.

RG: Who are some of your favorite authors?

JW: I love Dostoevsky, especially *The Brothers Karamazov.* I love Shakespeare. Conrad. Hemingway. My favorite is Joyce. I identified with the Irish writers a lot. That scene in *Portrait [of the Artist as a Young Man],* where the father says, "My dead king Parnell" and the kid is sitting there shocked. That is the greatest dinner scene in the history of literature. *Ulysses* is fantastic. And Samuel Beckett. His plays are great but I love his novels. Read *Murphy.* It's the funniest book I ever read in my life. You will howl.

And I love Camus and Sartre, the existential writers. I hate to say it, but most of what people feel in life is essentially a manic denial of the existential truth that you're going to live awhile and you're going to die and that's all there is. You're put in a hole in the ground and that's it. As a Catholic I'd like to believe otherwise. But as a scientist I'm pretty sure, sadly, that this is it. And there's not much meaning to a life that ends forever and you just disappear and you never exist again. So you've got to make the most of everything you do.

And I guess that's the answer to your question, finally. We finally got there. What with all the drive, what makes me tick. It's like an analytic session. If everything is finally and fundamentally absurd because of the inevitability of death, then the best a man can do is create meaning out of the whole cloth of chaos and do it with every bit of passion he's got.

There's a French philosopher named Marleau-Ponty. And basically his philosophy is that essentially everything is chaos. And once in a while there's a kind of contingency event that'll make it seem that there's an order to the universe but it's really an illusion. So all we can do is impose order on chaos by the sheer force of our free will. And that's how we make meaning. We make meaning out of nothing.

And I think that's what an artist does. People always think of artists as entertainers or something, as people who are kind of frivolous. And the irony is, the only things that are remembered from any civilization, ever, is the art. And statues to some warriors long forgotten who deserve to be honored but even then, they're remembered through a form of art, the sculpture. But the bottom line is, what do we remember from Egypt? The art. What do we ever remember from the Renaissance? The art. We don't remember anything else.

I have the most important job in the world. Now, most people would laugh at that. Most people think it's a frivolous job. I think it's one of the most important and noble professions in the world if you bother to respect it as such. As an artist, you know.

I mean, I take what I do incredibly seriously. And that's why, when frivolous sorts of people in the business say, "Oh, you know, Woods is difficult," my answer to that is, "Because you don't give a shit about what you do and you're willing to settle and I'm not. And I'll stack my accomplishments up against yours any day. I'm fighting for immortality here, babe. You're just fighting for a fancier car or a prettier girl. I couldn't give a shit about those things."

RG: The only word that readily comes to mind for that kind of commitment and dedication is "sacerdotal."

JW: Sacerdotal, yeah. It means "holy orders."

Now, by the way, I want to make sure that I don't sound like I'm a little too much on my high horse, talking about, you know, this great existential scheme. I'm the guy who danced with Dolly Parton in *Straight Talk* [1992]. But let's just say, by and large, when all is said and done, at my best, I aspire to be the person I'm talking about. I don't always succeed to say the least. I've made some really glaring and notable errors in my life. But I can tell you that no one bats 1,000. And yes, if someone asks me, "Who are you as a man?" I'm the guy who has those passions and those beliefs and those aspirations, at least by design if not finally by execution.

CHAPTER FIFTEEN

Dede Allen

RIC GENTRY

Outside of the industry itself, very few motion picture editors experience much recognition. Of these, Dede Allen is by far the best known. She credits much of this to her association with the great directors she's worked with, many of whom were lionized as "auteurs" in the United States in the 1960s and 1970s; for her contributions to an industry almost entirely dominated by men at the time; and because for most of her career she was situated in New York, beyond the Hollywood mainstream and closer to the more influential bastions of serious cinematic study.

But Allen is modest and perhaps somewhat unfair to herself. While what she says of the attention she's received is true, she is nevertheless probably our greatest contemporary film editor. Her distinctive sense of visual rhythm is all but unmistakable. Her bold, innovative use of pace and transitions have long since become common features of movie syntax. Her sensitivity and empathy for character and her use of image and sound in counterpoint continually embellish as they enlarge the poetic context of the drama. If she had cut nothing else but *Bonnie and Clyde,* her place in cinema history would be virtually assured. Allen's roster of credits includes *Odds Against Tomorrow* (1959), *The Hustler* (1961), *America, America* (1963), *Bonnie and Clyde* (1967), *Rachel, Rachel* (1968), *Alice's Restaurant* (1969), *Little Big Man* (1970), *Slaughterhouse Five* (1972), *Serpico* (1973), *Dog Day Afternoon* (1975, Academy Award nomination), *Night Moves* (1975), *The Missouri Breaks* (1976), *Slap Shot* (1977), *Reds* (1981, Academy Award nomination), *Mike's Murder* (1984), *The Breakfast Club* (1985), *The Milagro Beanfield War* (1988), *Henry and June* (1990), *The Addams Family* (1991), *Wonder Boys* (2000), and *John Q* (2002).

FIGURE 15. Dede Allen. Courtesy: Dede Allen.

But Allen did not become an editor or a success overnight. She started out as a messenger at Columbia Studios in 1943 and didn't cut her first major feature film until sixteen years later at the age of thirty-four. Her very gradual progress can be ascribed to the film industry's initial resistance to women in her field and to the fact that, in accordance with the times, she nearly jettisoned her career to become a mother and a housewife in the early 1950s. Eventually, however, Allen anticipated many of the tenets of latter-day feminism, enjoying a family while flourishing professionally.

Allen's best collaborations have been with talented, original, very independent directors who were also secure enough to allow her to fully contribute to their films, such as Robert Wise, Robert Rossen, Elia Kazan, Arthur Penn (six times), George Roy Hill, Warren Beatty, Sidney Lumet, Paul Newman, Philip Kaufman, and Curtis Hanson. As many of these directors have noted, especially Penn, Allen's unyielding diligence, grasp of the medium and pursuit of excellence have inspired them to the fullest, most refined articulation of their visions. Allen is nothing if not a director's editor.

Usually credited with establishing the New York School of Editing, Allen served as mentor to a number of now prominent editors: Jerry Greenberg, Barry Malkin, Richard Marks, Steven Rotter, Evan Lottman, and Jim Miller.

In 1992, Allen made a major if not rather unexpected career move. Recruited vigorously by Warner Brothers, Allen accepted the position of vice-president and, later senior vice-president of Creative Development at the studio. She remained there for seven years and lent her vast experience and expertise to countless projects. While Allen enjoyed her tenure, she also observed the increasing corporatization of the studio, as Warner Brothers was assimilated with Time-Life and then with America Online. "More and more decisions were made by committee," she remarks, and there was "greater interference" by the studio with productions at nearly all stages.

Always a champion of the idiosyncratic visions of the artist, a people's rights advocate (Allen was a shop steward at Columbia when the studio was unionized in the late 1940s) and a skeptic of the establishment's official line, it is easy to see how Allen, "a fox in the chicken coop" from the outset, became discontented if not somewhat disillusioned by the changes at Warner Brothers. While readily acknowledging that quality films were made, she also objected to ones that too often placated or pandered to demographics rather than challenged or enlightened viewers. "People are not encouraged to have a grasp of history," Allen comments. "They are barely equipped with the basic skills to read and write." Movies, in effect, were too often a part of the problem than part of the solution. "We are deluged with media that is controlled by vested interests," she adds.

While she enjoyed her years as an executive at Warner Brothers, Allen was likewise pleased to return to the editing room to work with Curtis Hanson for *Wonder Boys*, a character-driven film with a provocative subtext and entrenched social realism that brooked no studio interference. Equally significant perhaps, Allen adapted herself to a radically new method of editing this film. After working for decades on an upright Moviola, a mechanical editing device that she preferred for its precision over the latter-day Kem, a lateral, electronic method, Allen became fluent for *Wonder Boys* with the very complicated, nonlinear Avid digital editing system, which is now state of the art but a huge leap from the Moviola and a sheer inspiration for anyone daunted by new and unfamiliar technology.

At seventy-six, Allen is obviously, as she maintains, still learning. "That's what it's all about," she says. "If I stop learning, then I stop giving. If you lose that I think you lose everything." A passionate, captivating speaker, Allen is gracious, thoughtful, candid, and wholly unpretentious and laughs easily. Our conversation was completed in two sessions, the last of which was while she was preparing to leave for Toronto to work on *John Q* with director Nick Cassavetes, featuring Denzel Washington, the story of a family hampered by the engineered deprivations of a corporate HMO, a project that would seem to suit Allen ideally.

RICK GENTRY: How did your tenure at Warner Brothers come about?"

DEDE ALLEN: I accepted it on the basis that I would get involved with pictures but I wouldn't physically cut. The guy who had the position before me would always push everyone to the side, come in with his own crew and finish pictures by cutting them himself. He was a nice guy, British, would work eighteen hours a day and just had the attitude that, "Oh, my dear, I do it so much better than anyone else." He's a director now and I wasn't going to replace him with that approach. If I was going to do it, I wanted to be there through the entire development of a project, really participate from beginning to end, from the scripts through the marketing, really learn how the whole business worked from the executive side.

RG: How were you approached for the position?

DA: I received a call from Bruce Berman, who I knew well and had been the executive at Universal on *The Breakfast Club* [1985] and was then at Warner Brothers. I was dubious at first but he said, "Don't say 'no.'" I said, "I'm no good at sitting with executives. I work with directors." But he urged me to come in and talk about it. Meanwhile, Billy Weber, an editor I dearly love, called and said, "You're not going to take that, are you? That's not for you." So I was a little in the middle about it for awhile.

Then Richard Donner, who does the *Lethal Weapon* films, whom I know from New York, called me and said, "Please take the job. We need you." I said I wasn't going to accept it and do it like the guy before me did. Richard said, "You don't have to do it that way. Tell them what you want out of it, but we really need you here." So then I had a meeting with [then Warner chairman] Bob Daly and [then president] Terry Semel and told them what I wanted to do, that I was very interested in seeing how the whole business worked, all the way through marketing, even with previews and those nightmare [evaluation] cards [by the test audience] and all that stuff.

RG: Both Bob Daly and Terry Semel (now departed from WB) were so well respected.

DA: Oh, fantastic. They were both great guys, very intelligent, extremely good at what they did. It was still very paternalistic while they were there, in the sense that it was more of a family then. This was before Warner Brothers merged with Turner. But Bob and Terry were very agreeable when I met with them. We worked it out and I took the position.

RG: What did that entail?

DA: It was never the same, really. I didn't work with the writers but I would look at every stage of the script, and I'd watch the scripts go through these myriad of writers and I would express my opinion at the meetings. The rewrites would come in every week. I may have stepped on a few toes but a lot of them loved me for being so honest because usually there's all this bullshit that goes on and everyone being political and so forth. I got to be known as the truth person, which doesn't always go over well with the executives in the creative department. At one point we had a table with fifteen or sixteen people. Not every studio does it that way but Warners has its own style. Then we'd have a look at the finished films and sometimes I'd go out of town to the location during production.

RG: Were there particular films you were involved with or that were made under your stewardship, in a sense?

DA: I was involved in almost every film that was made there, whether good, bad or indifferent, unless it was a "pick up" [outside acquisition]. But in terms of being involved, almost all of them had something to work with, a problem of some kind. Obviously there are directors who didn't need me around. I only tried to be helpful at the meetings when I could be or they wanted me to be or with troubled films that needed attention.

RG: That's a lot of movies.

DA: A lot of movies—a lot of scripts, a lot of previews, a lot of test screenings, a lot of marketing screenings. I enjoyed it and I learned a great deal about the other side of the business. Richard DelBelso was there at the time as chairman of publicity and marketing, who I knew very well much earlier at Universal. He was very important at WB and I had a lot of friends who were very generous. But as the years went on it became more and more frustrating because you had less and less effect on the projects. It took so long to green light something. Films were made by committee and by numbers. After a while you get a sense for what the business is about, what big business itself is really about.

They were also beginning to make more of what are considered "franchise" pictures, those surefire formula things, like *Lethal Weapon* [1987] and *Mission Impossible* [1996]. I would work through that and it wasn't always that stimulating or challenging. But the more corporate it became the more indecisive and the more unstable and the more impersonal, really. It's not necessarily the way you make good movies. Although some do get made. Someone with a lot of power, a very proven track record. Michael Mann kind of does his own thing. *The Insider* [1999] was outstanding.

Oliver Stone has done great work. I'm a great admirer of Oliver's films. I loved *Any Given Sunday* [1999]. You really felt that you were in there with the players during the [football] game. And it had one of the greatest soundtracks I've ever heard. Oliver has great energy and I just love the way he makes movies. Steven Spielberg or Clint Eastwood, they never have to have their pictures approved. *Unforgiven* [1992] had its initial screening the first month I was there, which was January of 1992. If you'd have done a test screening of that, in one of these malls, it would have done ludicrously. It was long and dark, something that would just not have tested well with a teenage focus group out there, but of course it was a great movie and very successful.

But Clint Eastwood has made so much money and so many great pictures that he doesn't have to submit to the usual studio process and has his own independent situation. He's also a very responsible producer, great on meeting budgets and schedules, and he's extremely respected for that. But who knows what will happen now that AOL has come in?

RG: They might tinker with his situation at Malpaso?*

DA: I didn't say they would tinker with it, but you just never know what's going to develop. It's true of every business in this country. No business is exempt. What it did was give me a very good economic and social vision, that as far as I'm concerned Karl Marx wasn't all wrong. We live in a period of great greed and tremendous privilege for the rich and of a middle class who neglects to remember that they came from the working class. They're all stockholders now. But as I was saying, it was fascinating to watch. I enjoyed my time there and they were very generous to me. When I left, they gave me a whole year's perks. In fact, I had my car insurance for a year and a half. I understand why executives do so well.

So it was interesting how a studio, where everyone felt secure as long as they'd been there, suddenly began looking over their shoulders, people who had been there for fifteen years or more and whose life was at Warner Brothers began getting nervous and sure enough a lot of them are gone now. But that's happening in every business.

RG: What were the circumstances for you there to make *Wonder Boys?*

---

*Eastwood's Production company.

DA: As I mentioned, things were changing at Warner Brothers. Bruce Berman moved on to do a different thing. Lorenzo Bonaventura came in a little less than a year before I left; [he's] very, very bright and obviously someone with a future. He shared the presidency with Billy Gerber, but that didn't work out for either of them or the studio. They're both good guys. They just weren't a good pair. It was kind of like no one knew who to answer to. Billy got moved into a production deal, which I think is what he really wanted, and Lorenzo took the reins. He and I didn't always totally agree but I have tremendous respect for him.

Anyway, after my time as an executive, I wanted to get back to cutting. I still had six months left on my contract when I got a call from Scott Rudin, who was my producer on *The Addams Family* as you remember. He was making *Wonder Boys*. He does many of his pictures at Paramount with Michelle Manning, who's in charge [of production] there and who I know very well. I'm sure it was Scott's idea or his and Curtis [Hanson's] together to get in touch with me, though Michelle also knew I wasn't totally happy. So I got together with Curtis, whom I'd met many years ago when he was doing an article on *Little Big Man* [1970], and he offered me the job.

So I went back to Lorenzo and he said he thought it was a very exciting opportunity. I had a feeling they weren't going to renew me for an eighth year anyway because the whole company had changed. I mean, except for the production people, there's almost no one left who was there when I started. They had a very good editor, Frank Urioste, and I think they wanted to bring in someone like him to physically take over the film features, something as I was saying I wouldn't do and never did. Frank's very good and a terrific guy. But that's how I began to work on *Wonder Boys*.

RG: How have films changed, in your estimation?

DA: You mean technically?

RG: That's a multileveled question. You mentioned some of the factors being economical.

DA: Well, the bottom line. You have bean counters telling you how to make movies now and frequently making decisions. When you had good, strong people like Bob Daly, whom you might not always agree with in their taste in movies, you still have someone with integrity running the studio. I don't mean that the people running it now don't have personal integrity in terms of their home and families, but it's greedy—very, very greedy now. There's no such thing as profits being enough anymore. Whatever the profits are they want more.

RG: Is there any love for cinema, as such?

DA: Oh, yeah. There's always the romance of cinema, of the theater, of writing. But a lot of times, I mean, who are they making films for these days? The kids at the mall haven't got an attention span from here to here. They can't sit through something that they have to follow very well. *Wonder Boys* is a good example. It's about ideas and people talking. They're not used to watching people talk, certainly not people older than they are.

That doesn't mean there isn't a market for films like *Wonder Boys*, which got tremendous reviews, but there was a challenge in marketing nonetheless. It's going to be rereleased this fall some time. But it's so expensive to market them. It's very hard. There are more independents now and they've been responsible for some very good films but they had to struggle to get there, though the Academy has begun to acknowledge them, even though some of them have been pretty eccentric, but partly in reaction to the less interesting mainstream stuff.

RG: Would you find resistance to your suggestions?

DA: No, not most of the time. Occasionally. It's always exciting. You always learn something. I always enjoyed it. There were a couple of times in the beginning when a couple of editors who didn't know me would seem to think, "What is she going to do? Come in and take over?" Only one was rather unpleasant because the editor was rigid and the director was rigid and they didn't want anyone helping them. But that was rare, really.

But, again, I didn't come in while they were cutting. I didn't see it until they presented it. I had a director come and ask for help. We worked on a couple of pictures for a long time before we showed them to the studio. I would always tell [Bruce Berman] and he would always endorse it and never ask me about it again until we were ready. That didn't happen much toward the end because the people who got involved right away were the head people. You know it's more of a procedure now and they come in and think, "Oh, you cut here and here and here," but they don't understand the dialectics of it. There's also not enough time to think it through when that happens. One of the biggest problems I think is that you don't screen enough.

RG: You must think that editing technique has changed a lot.

DA: You have people who come in who don't know anything about story or character and who think quick, flashy cutting is the answer to everything. They don't know any better. They cut it the way they would cut something else. Usually when you got called in for something like that, they were grateful for what you could show them. But a lot of it comes from the fact that they've never cut that kind of film before.

RG: Their history had been commercials or music videos then?

DA: Sometimes. In the days at Columbia when I was just starting there under Harry Cohn, a director from the theater who knew how to work with actors would be surrounded with support from creative people who'd worked in films for years. They might even have editors on the set. And even today, with a director who hasn't done many mainstream pictures, an intelligent studio head should try to match him up with someone experienced. There are a lot of fine editors with experience who are available for that.

RG: That was why you were put together with Barry Sonnenfeld for *The Addams Family* as I recall. He was a cinematographer making his first film as a director.

DA: That's right. He was new and I wasn't. *[Laughs.]*

RG: And you were involved in *The Addams Family* while there were still preliminary discussions.

DA: The script was still being worked on so I partook in a lot of that discussion. I always do when I come onto a film because it's the last chance one has to clarify story. If you leave it for the editing, which unfortunately is done too often, it's much harder. It's like making an omelet and then trying to add ingredients later.

RG: Not every editor gets involved with the scripting of a film.

DA: Well, it depends on whether you're invited to partake or not. I always speak my mind when something doesn't work. Whether they listen or not is up to them. It's the kind of situation where, if you've worked enough years and you have enough background in trying to work out story problems, you can make some kind of contribution.

RG: Would that be in terms of structure?

DA: Right, but not just that. It's mostly character. It's how I'm going to work on the characters. You have to know who the characters are, what they're going to do, how they're going to react. The director of course guides you in this and with how he shoots it, at least much of the time. In *The Addams Family* the director was very specific in how he shot it. Other films I've worked on there will often be a whole lot more improvisation. Then characters develop. It just depends completely on the story and the manner in which the director works with the actors and the camera and what the actors bring to the characters. I like to get involved in anything to do with rehearsals or story because it helps me know where I'm going with the characters, particularly in a story like this where the characters are so unusual.

RG: Was it difficult to acclimate yourself to editing such characters?

DA: Yes, it was kind of strange at first, but then you get totally involved in it, just the way actors get into a role. You have to take the characters very seriously. They have to become very real people to you. They're not, really, but they're totally in character.

I found the script very interesting, fun, energetic, and full of whimsy. I wouldn't have become involved had I not liked the characters. I liked the casting particularly, too. I thought it was beautifully cast. That's always important to an editor, I think. Good actors give much more life to characters, rather than actors who are really just good "indicators," who indicate emotion, who indicate anger or fear or joy. That's the difference between good actors and limited actors. Good actors create whole characters.

RG: And certainly you've had some great actors to work with over the years.

DA: Oh, yes. I've been very lucky. Very lucky.

RG: There were challenges on *The Addams Family*.

DA: I've never worked on a picture that was sold to another studio right in the middle. That was one thing. Right after principle photography was completed, the production was sold to Paramount. It was a long shoot. Then we physically moved over to Paramount right after we were in first cut. It was kind of traumatic for everyone.

It wasn't the move that was so traumatic. I've moved on many pictures. Hell, I moved from England to New York for one picture, from Florida to California for another one. This was just from one place in Hollywood to another. The move was not a big thing. It was that this was not a planned interruption in the schedule.

RG: Do you usually work on location with the production?

DA: It depends on the circumstances and on the director. I'm not always on location at all. I worked for years in New York when Arthur Penn was out on location. I was in New York while Kazan was in Greece shooting *America, America*. The film went from Greece to California for processing and then to me in New York.

RG: Those directors obviously trusted you to begin working with the footage on your own.

DA: There has to be trust. That's exactly what editing is all about. It's a relationship with the director. If they don't trust you, they shouldn't be working with you because that's a terribly important relationship.

RG: And no two editors would cut a film in the same way.

DA: How characters behave, I believe, is interpreted differently by everyone who is there to interpret them. I think the editor makes a difference on every picture. And I've never worked on a picture that was shot in the camera. I get the hard ones. *[Laughs.]*

But the question is, always: Are you going to do the characters justice? Are you going to do the story justice? Are you going to make it the best it can be in terms of what it's trying to say? That's the challenge of every film.

RG: It was also a challenge to work with a director making his first film?

DA: Always. But Barry [Sonnenfeld] is very talented and a very quick study. He was a cinematographer before. He shot *Blood Simple* [1985] and *Raising Arizona* [1987] for the Coen brothers, for example. He's extremely bright and has a great sense of humor.

The important thing though is that you have to establish the same relationship as you would with any other director, whether it's Bob Wise or Elia Kazan or a first-time director. You have to have the same kind of openness to whatever they're going to do and whatever their ways are. People are very interesting that way. You can learn from everyone. I learn from everyone I work with.

RG: Off the top of your head, can you mention what you've learned from certain directors?

DA: I learned a lot about story from Robert Rossen. I learned a lot about performance from Arthur Penn, with whom I did six pictures. I learned a lot about everything including psychology from Kazan. From Newman I learned a great deal about acting. From Warren Beatty you learn a lot about everything, including how to be smarter in life. Warren's one of the best producers I've ever had. He was our producer on *Bonnie and Clyde*. He was thirty years old then. He's a very, very brilliant guy. You learn and he learns from you because he lets you teach. He works with people very well, much like Kazan does.

RG: What makes Warren Beatty a great producer?

DA: A persistence such as you've never seen. Also a persistence for detail. Sometimes it takes him a long time before he gets going but when he does he's a very single minded guy. A good producer is very important. I've seen a good director working under a bad producer and not do his best work. On *Bonnie and Clyde*, Warren put the right person with the right picture and fought all the right fights to see that picture through. I didn't do *Dick Tracy* [1990], which was one of the reasons I wanted to do *[The Addams Family]*. I thought this might be my last chance to do this kind of film.

But learning is what it's all about. If I stop learning then I might as well quit, because if I stop learning then I stop giving. It's all part of the same thing. Every time it's a challenge and every time you really don't know if you're going to be good enough for it.

RG: Do you really wonder about that?

DA: I'm nervous before every movie. I'm always nervous. Will I be good enough for it? I think everyone's that way. You can't lose that sense of challenge. Particularly these days. Well, all days. I mean, movies are very expensive and they're hard to bring to life. They're very hard being born.

Getting something made from the original concept, through the process of writing, casting, and everything that it takes and getting someone willing to back you financially is so hard. Everyone involved has such a big responsibility. If we didn't take it all very seriously we would not be professional or we would be very foolish. By "seriously," I mean you can't ever say, "Oh, hell, I've done this before. I know this as well as the back of my hand." The minute you do that you might as well quit as far as I'm concerned. I'm kind of an intense person.

RG: You also have a reputation for being meticulous.

DA: Details, yeah. Editors are detail people. You shouldn't be an editor if you don't like details, countless details, and you have to be very flexible. You have to use your knowledge very flexibly.

For instance, with Barry, he had very strong ideas for how he wanted *The Addams Family* to look. If I questioned some of that or discussed something with any skepticism, I tried not to be too forward or too rigid. Very often he knew exactly what he wanted but sometimes you have to encourage them to find their way to it because not having directed a picture before, they might not know how to get to it.

Someone might say, "I see this scene in three shots. It's this, this, and this." And you answer, "Yeah, but what if you want to do that too?" And they say, "No, this is the way I want to do it." But later they might find that the story needs something else, or that the scene needs something else, but there's nothing to work with because nothing else was shot. You may have anticipated the problem editorially but you can only nudge them in the shooting so far. It may work out beautifully, but sometimes it doesn't.

With Paul Newman on his first film, *Rachel, Rachel,* the first thing he said was, "Rachel has to be in every shot." Now Paul is a very gracious man, very intelligent but very modest and he was very concerned about protecting his actors. But I said, "Paul, she can't be in every shot. You have to have cutaways." He said, "I don't want cutaways. I want this to center on her. It's all about her experience." Later we were in a restaurant in Connecticut and we were discussing and diagramming how you cover scenes. After a while he said, about one of the shots, "This is great for the long complicated move, but here's a part of this that I like better." And I said, "OK, this is what I meant before. If I don't have anything to cutaway to, how am I going to get between this take and that take?" Then he understood.

From the editor's side, too, you have to allow people to do things [their way]. You can't become rigid and presume there's a right and a wrong way and you always know what that is. You can't learn anything if you approach it like that.

RG: Have you always cut concurrently to the film as it's shot?

DA: Usually. On *Slaughterhouse Five* I didn't start until they finished the Dresden scenes, which were actually shot in Prague, and came back to work in the U.S., which was about two months into the shooting. When I started to cut it was all in story continuity, which is the way I like to work best, particularly when I'm working on something as fragile as the story point of view in *Slaughterhouse Five*.

RG: The time element in that film was very important and the way the transitions were depicted was very interesting.

DA: George Hill had planned every transition very carefully but not all of the transitions worked in telling the story. Eventually we began to consider transitions in a different way. They seemed to work better if we compressed them and played them off the Billy Pilgrim character. I had to get rid of some really beautiful shots. There were also some others that we discovered in the material. For each transition to work it had to be right for the scene, the time, the place, the story and move you along. But even then, with all of the changes we made, all of that worked as well as it did because of the meticulous planning George had done. He provided what was needed to tell the story that way and to give it that kind of visualization.

But I've started editing at different times with different directors. I never started cutting until Kazan came back from Greece. I came on to *Slap Shot* late because I was finishing another picture and so I was able to start at the beginning (of the story). I like to do that because the story evolves, characters evolve. But you can't always do that. On *The Addams Family* I worked totally out of [story] continuity. I worked in the continuity that we shot in. Directors like to work as much in sequence as they can, but that's not the way budgets work. I mean, you have to finish a set. You have to finish an actor. That's the reality of every film.

RG: Is there any particular way that you like to organize yourself before you start to cut?

DA: I memorize everything. I work until I memorize every frame of it. Then I feel totally free. I never feel terrified of the scene again because it will always be there in my head. I'm getting older but my memory still works very well.

I work on the memorization right from the start. For instance, I don't ever mind seeing dailies several times. I don't care how often I see them. I'll run them as often as anyone wants to, within a sensible time frame of course, and I never get bored looking at them. I'm always seeing or finding something else in them.

An editor has to remember every frame. It's like a chess game. You have to be able to think ahead and think back. You have to know where the scene is going to go and how that character is going to evolve. About the most dangerous thing I can do is work in a hurry and cut the scene glibly, before I really know the material.

RG: So you usually have a very clear idea of what takes or portions of takes you're going to use to assemble the scene?

DA: Pretty much so. I never sit and rough it out. I know that a lot of people do that with a scene. I think the timing and the tempo of my cuts are different than the way someone else might do it just for that reason. I don't do an Eisenstein kind of board, with all the cuts laid out, which is what I call "talking a good cut," you know, intellectualizing. I feel my way through the characters. You just viscerally, emotionally feel the way the characters feel. You basically become so involved in a scene that you become moved or stimulated or amused. Actors say they have to become the part. Well, the editor has to become part of the part. You live in the world that the story is.

That's one reason I ask directors a lot of questions. I want to know what they have in mind. Sometimes I get a little rambunctious in trying to find out. Sometimes I get pretty forward in getting them to think about something they may not have thought through and it's not always something that they want to do. That can make things a little uncomfortable, though most directors I've worked with don't feel threatened. They're usually very confident about themselves and in what they're doing and welcome suggestions. But I spend a lot of time with directors trying to get a total feeling about how they feel about the characters and the story.

My first cuts usually play very smoothly but sometimes rather dully because they're too long. One thing I've learned is not to leave anything out at that point. Even if a scene doesn't work, a director always wants to see what it was. You may be a step or many steps ahead of the director before he sees the first cut, but that's because you've been living with it in the editing room for much longer. But it doesn't make any difference. You have to go through that period where there's too much footage. A first cut can be a nightmare of overabundance, with all of it playing and very tight within itself. It won't be loose, without attention to story and performance and character. It'll have all that and run smoothly. It'll be a very carefully constructed first cut. But it'll just be too long and cumbersome and sort of unwieldy.

Then I'm not afraid to cut into it, to make it move faster. Coeditors sometimes get very upset with the way I work. I'm not afraid of rough edges, for example. If I'm in charge of a picture and I step in and change a scene because it's to the point where it has to begin to move and I'm cutting "deeper," they might say, "Oh, you're going to ruin the cut." But I'll say, "No, it energizes it."

But you have to know what you're looking for in a scene. You don't just chop. I'm a great believer that you have to know the rules to break the rules.

RG: Before the Avid,[*] you used to cut on the Moviola.

DA: I used two Moviolas to cut. I made changes on flatbeds and I screen on flatbeds, but I always cut on two Moviolas, side by side. Basically I worked on the Moviola to my left and the one on my right to compare takes and line readings. When people are working on an eight-plate Kem, they're in effect working with two Moviolas but they don't get their hands on the bits and pieces of film. With the Moviola you're very close to it. I found that when you stop on a Kem it doesn't stop right on the frame. You can't sneak it forward and back. It stops and then it chatters on for a frame or two, which is very imprecise for me.

The rhythm with which you cut on a Moviola is just much easier I think. You're more likely to get tired on a Moviola than on a Kem but you deal with it. After years of standing over a Moviola I had to retrain myself to cut sitting down. It made a difference. But all of that started with the two Moviolas on *America, America*, when Kazan went away and left me alone drowning in footage. There wasn't anything in the budget for an assistant to work overtime and I had to find a way to get through it all; so I used a second Moviola with a silent head that someone had given me. I paid for the second Moviola myself on several films because I couldn't get the budget for two. I just began renting another one out of my own pocket. You do what you have to do to make it work.

---

[*] A nonlinear digital editing system.

RG: In terms of memorizing the dailies and deciding what you're going to use for a given scene, how do you manage that with an actor like Dustin Hoffman who, as I understand it, might give you ten, twelve, or fourteen takes per scene, all very different and very interesting?

DA: Ten, twelve, or fourteen, huh? More like that many per angle. And with Warren, more like forty or fifty per angle. Yes, it's hard to memorize all that because it is an overwhelming amount of footage, but if you just organize yourself mentally and know that you're going to memorize it, you can.

The thing that's overwhelming usually, particularly these days, is everything having to go faster, faster; you have to get it out faster. The studios these days are run by people who don't know the process like they used to. They think you just put on more bodies and it all comes out. When I was working in what I call "the good old days," you made a film in a kind of orderly process without what I call a "gang bang," which is what happens when they put ten editors on a film and which is evidently happening more and more. It's more of a factory process, but the reality of the industry is that pictures are so expensive and interest rates are so high that there's a real urgency to get it out faster.

I feel very fortunate to have worked at a time and in a way and with the kind of people I did that very few have the opportunity to experience today. I'm sure Marty Scorsese still works that way with Thelma [Schoonmacher] but it's much harder when you get on these huge-budget pictures where so much rides on it. As I was saying, there are also all these previews where the audience decides what to cut. They take the picture, which isn't even finished, with temp music and temp optical shots and other temp stuff, to a mall audience and let them decide what should be cut. I find it a very difficult thing to deal with.

RG: Do you find that the heads of studios are not really that film literate anymore?

DA: Well, again, studios are run much more by bottom-line people now, money people. Very often you'll meet someone in charge of your picture who hasn't the faintest idea of how pictures are really made. And depending on the person and what their priorities are, some of them don't give a damn, either. They just want to push the thing through.

Sometimes it's agents who become heads of studios who aren't really filmmakers and don't really know what that's about and don't look at films as a filmmaker does. On the other hand, many agents are very creative people who've dealt with story and artists for a long time and have picked up all the lingo and know what they're doing. If they've been an agent it doesn't mean they're going to be any worse than anyone else.

But after all, my first studio was Columbia and the head of Columbia then was Harry Cohn. I worked there four years. It was a very different era then.

RG: Let's talk about that. How did you get started?

DA: I started when I was eighteen in 1943 at Columbia Pictures. I was in Scripps College out here [in Claremont, about fifteen miles east of L.A.] when I got a summer job as a messenger between my sophomore and junior years. They were taking in what they called "girls" for the first time. It was during the Second World War and there was a shortage of available male personnel. I never went back to college after that.

RG: So you're from California originally.

DA: No, I was born in Ohio but I never lived there much. I lived in Switzerland for much of my childhood because my sister had TB and my mother brought her to the Magic Mountain and I went along for the ride. I was three when we went over and my first language became French. I came out here when I was about twelve, first to San Francisco and San Rafael and then Pasadena. I went back to Ohio for the last few years of high school.

I was interested in films ever since I was a kid. My mother was a great movie buff and there was nothing we didn't go see. We sometimes went to the movies four times a week. I saw a lot of theatre too because my mother had been an actress and my grandfather was very interested in the theater. He was a surgeon in Cincinnati but his whole life really revolved around the theater. When I came out here my grandfather wrote a letter for me to Elliot Nugent Jr.,* who you might find in the history books. He was (a Broadway writer and director) doing his first picture with Danny Kaye about that time, called *Up in Arms* [1944]. Elliot Nugent saw me and said, "Young lady, if you want to become a director, you should get into the cutting room." That was his advice. I never became a director but I became an editor.

But it took a long, long time. It took a long time to become a messenger, which I was for ten months. Then I got into the sound effects department at Columbia, where I was for three years and became an assistant in sound. At the end of the war I had gained seniority and was able to stay while a lot of others got bounced out. I became a sound effects editor but could never get into picture editing at Columbia. Few women of my generation got into picture editing in Hollywood until they were somewhere in midlife.

RG: How was it that you began working in New York?

DA: I got married and my husband and I decided to move [in 1950]. Steve [Fleischman] had started as a screenwriter but didn't like the life in Hollywood so we went to New York. I was script clerk for awhile (and helped organize a script clerk's union) and then got a job cutting pictures at Film Graphics for commercials and industrials. I was having my children and Steve was a freelance writer† and we thought one of us should have a staff position. I went to work at Film Graphics for the next four years.

---

*Broadway writer and director.
†He later became a network television news and documentary producer.

RG: Did you feel that you were perhaps taking a professional step sideways or backwards, leaving Columbia for a different life on the other side of the country?

DA: I wasn't looking at it quite like that. I thought I would have children and just retire and never work again. But it didn't happen that way. About eight weeks after my son was born, they called me and said, "Are you ready to come back to work?"

RG: Did you consider your experience in commercials and industrials as especially valuable?

DA: Oh, definitely. I became much more fluid with all the technical stuff. We always had to lay out our own opticals, for example. I used to have to do the sheets because they were always too busy for us. In desperation to make your dates you just did it yourself. Whatever you became proficient at became a new tool. All of it is helpful. What seems like a dead end can be a very valuable learning experience if you get through it. There's nothing you can't learn from.

I still very much believe that if people want to do something, they can't sit home with their nose in the air. I know a lot of people who say, "I don't want to work in television." Then they sit unemployed. That's stupid. You work where you can. You can learn from everything if you have the proper attitude. It all interrelates, particularly if you're going to become an editor. To learn something that has technical facets makes it much easier to be creative as you go along. I'm not afraid of anything technical.

RG: It was also very unusual for a woman to be a professional at the time.

DA: Yeah, it was. There were women who had professions but everyone didn't work and have children the way they do now. It was unusual to work in film.

RG: You were about thirty years head of your time.

DA: That's what they say. But there were people in my mother's generation who did it, too. During the Depression there were women who worked because they had to. I came out of the generation right after that and the feeling then was that you shouldn't take a job because it took it away from a man. When I grew up that's what you were always taught. You had to take care of yourself and be independent because of the experience during the Depression, but you must never take a job away from a man who has to support a family. It was that kind of ethic.

I had a cousin who wanted to be a teacher. She was very bright. She graduated from Bryn Mawr with all kinds of honors. She came from a well-to-do part of the family. She had a nervous breakdown. She wanted to go into teaching and I remember my aunt always saying that it was improper for her to take a teaching job. It was just very hard for her to accept that. This was in the thirties. But all kinds of lives have gone on since then with different mores.

RG: Was it particularly difficult for a woman working in the film industry?

DA: You had to put up with a lot of bullshit. You have to learn more than anyone should have to know to be taken seriously, especially with the labs, which is why you get as good as you are at what you do. If you learn it and become good, then they respect you. But you just have to work a lot harder and you have to know a lot more. I got very tired of it after awhile. Each time you started with a new lab you had to go through the same battle all over again. But once you had their respect, you had it eternally.

But I like labs. I like the people who work in labs. They can do wonderful things for you, which is often the case with people if you treat them with respect. Technical people are very often kind of shoved aside as noncreative but the truth is that they're all part of the creative process. The look of a picture, the sound of a picture, all of that is terribly important.

RG: As an editor, to what extent were you involved with the lab?

DA: From the very beginning I was involved with the film until the follow-through. Everything involving the prints and the timing and all of that.

RG: Usually the cinematographer does that.

DA: I was a New York editor and the cameraman was seldom around. Barry Sonnenfeld, who is also a cameraman, couldn't believe that in all the years that I've done pictures, I had only three where the cameraman came in on the timing. He said, "You mean you always used to go in to do that?" I said, "Yes, always." You used to have to do it because the cameraman was almost always away. On *Bonnie and Clyde*, [cinematographer] Bernie Guffey couldn't come to the lab, and the timing on that was very involved.

In fact, *Bonnie and Clyde* was the first one where I became heavily involved in the color timing because Arthur [Penn] hated what they had done with the picture the first time he saw it. The color was saturated and very heavy. He wanted more of a Japanese look and discovered that none of those guys had seen anything like that.

RG: He wanted the color to be more pastel.

DA: Yeah. A more washed look. Arthur was very intrigued with that. We were finishing at Warner Brothers. He had to go East so I stayed for eleven days and worked with Technicolor. At that time they had the matrix process, the three [color] separations. Films could be beautifully preserved, forever. *Gone with the Wind* was done that way and that's why it's still perfect. But it got too expensive for this country and it was sold to the Chinese, but it was the way Technicolor became Technicolor. It was a wonderful process.

RG: Were there timing difficulties with *The Addams Family?*

DA: Where we had a problem was with the [Eastman Kodak] 5384 print stock. It was the same number we were familiar with but it didn't perform the same and Kodak claimed that it did. At first we thought it was a problem at Technicolor [producing the release prints] and so we went back to Deluxe where the dailies were processed and ran a roll [of the 84] at the same [timing] lights, which were still in their computer from the original dailies and the same thing happened. The color was flat; it had a lot less snap. The blacks weren't rich.

So then we called a representative at Kodak and showed him the original next to the print stock. He said, "Oh, it doesn't look different to me." And Barry said, "Well, if it doesn't look different to you, there's something very wrong. But let's assume that you're just saying that it doesn't look any different. Then you've either changed the stock or your controls are off, and if your controls are off you're really in trouble." But Kodak denied it. They denied everything.

Only with a lot of trial and error and diligent assistance from Technicolor did we get what we wanted. We did it by changing the "aims."* But the whole reason this happened is that there's now a new interpositive-internegative system.

See, after the old Technicolor process we had something called CRIs (color reversal internegative) that was really awful. They degenerated. You remember the big fight Scorsese and all these people had to save films that were fading? That was the CRI process. It faded and it looked like hell and everyone was pushing Kodak to develop something that was at least salvageable. With the internegative-interpositive process you'll get a print off the original negative that will be beautiful and exact. But when you go to an internegative and a (duplicate print), it suddenly goes very contrasty and saturated. That's where we are today and every director and cameraman is screaming that it looks terrible.

Our theory is that instead of trying to solve the problem in the internegative-interpositive stage so that you can match the original on the dupe, Kodak was simply making a less contrasty print stock. It's definitely less contrasty but that's not the solution and they're not telling you what they've done.

RG: When I spoke to [*Addams Family* cinematographer] Owen [Roizman], he was very critical of Kodak. He was very unhappy about their lack of candor. He had lots to say about being misled and not being informed about changes in their stocks.

DA: Everyone says that they keep things too much under their hats. My only involvement with something like this before was the nightmare problems editors were having in the 1960s with a positive stock that you cut on. When you made a splice but later took the tape apart it would lift a layer of color off [the stock] so at the splice it always showed up bright green. This went on for about three or four years and every editor was complaining. The whole advantage of cutting with tape [relatively new at the time] was kind of disappearing because every time you removed a splice and changed it, it would show.

Finally, John Kowalek at Movielad [lab in New York] called me one day and he said, "I discovered what it was." He'd made some tests and discovered that Kodak wasn't finishing the color layers in the same way they had before, so that when you pulled off the tape you also pulled off one of the colors and ended up

---

*The arc of the interpositive to produce greater piquancy in the print.

with what we called a "greenie." It was a money-saving thing. Finally Eastman changed it but it was John who caught them out on it and it disappeared one day as fast as it came. But Kodak knew what they were doing. They just weren't honest about it. They had a monopoly.

RG: How did you get to cut your first feature film?

DA: After Film Graphics I went to work as an editor with Carl Lerner, who was in charge of a couple of TV series. I'd first met Carl in Hollywood. He had come out of the theater and he and his wife went to Hollywood when all the theater people were moving from New York and getting into film. Later he became an apprentice in the picture department at Columbia while I was in the sound department. He was one of my closest friends for many years. Later he moved back to New York. He was an excellent editor who went on to establish quite a reputation. Through him I got to cut *Terror from the Year 5000* [1958], one of those AIP horror films, as I was saying before, with a wonderful actress named Salome Jens who hopes no one ever remembers it. Then when Carl was doing *Middle of the Night* [1959], he recommended me to Bob Wise for *Odds Against Tomorrow* (1958) with Robert Ryan, Shelley Winters, and Harry Belafonte, which was my first major feature. I was thirty-four by then. I'd been in the business for about sixteen years.

RG: What was it like going to work with Robert Wise? He'd been an editor himself and, most notably, had cut *Citizen Kane*.*

DA: I was terrified. I thought, "Shit, I won't last a minute." But it turned out that he was just the greatest thing that ever happened to me because he imbued me with such confidence. He's a very gentle but firm, knowledgeable professional with great grace.

There was a Saturday when I was to show him my first scene. This was so far back that we were still using foot splicers, great big machines where you hot splice the footage to seal the splices together. If you made a change you lost a frame and you had to put in black slugs instead. They still use the foot splicers in the labs to cut negative. When I went to show him what I'd cut, the scene was filled with black slugs because I'd changed my mind so many times. The first thing he said was, "Gee, you played with that a lot. I like that. Don't ever let that frighten you." That was a tremendous gift of support, especially if you're editing for a guy like Bob Wise and terrified you're going to fall on your face. In other words, he made me feel comfortable. I was never afraid to put slugs in after that, whereas some editors might be embarrassed to have it show that they were struggling with the scene.

There were maybe ten people up for that job with Bob and many with a lot more experience than I had but he went with me because of my training and my

---

*Wise also went on to direct *West Side Story* (1961) and *The Sound of Music* (1965).

background in sound. He had been in music editing at RKO and knew the head of the sound department at Columbia, John Liverdary, for whom I'd worked as a sound editor.

RG: That's interesting, because you've always used sound very imaginatively in your work.

DA: Sound is as important to me as picture. I think the whole question of rhythm in a scene is often related to sound. It's probably an advantage that editors with experience in sound effects have. You hear and see.

I often cut silent when I'm in a rush. That was more by happenstance the first couple of times. I was in a terrible rush to get a scene done and the only way I could do it was to just drop the sound and not work with the synchronizer and just do it silent and then put the track on it later. I found that my timing was such that I could do that and almost not have to change a frame of it and I think that was due to my background in sound. In other words, after I had memorized the dailies I could still hear the sounds in my head. It never goes away.

RG: Do you remember the first time you tried it that way?

DA: I think it was *America, America,* because everyone had heavy accents and the main character, a boy named Stavros, couldn't speak English very well. After awhile I just began lip reading.

I remember a scene very well from *Bonnie and Clyde.* Jerry Greenberg was my assistant. He had been a music editor so he was very good at sound. We were rushing for a screening and I had this scene—it was right after the first killing—and they go and hide out in this movie theater and on screen they're playing "We're in the Money" and C. W. is sitting in front of Clyde and Bonnie. We only had an hour to make this screening and I knew the lines. I just took the film and instead of trying to run it with a track I just did it completely silent. I handed it to Jerry and he put the lines in. I could time what was being said over a character's back to another character's face. Jerry tracked it and it worked.

RG: Was that scene ever recut at all?

DA: No, that scene was never recut. I discovered you could really do it, though I only do it if I'm in a rush or it's a montage or a battle scene or something like that.

But I also like to add sound to the images. It's exciting and it invigorates the scene. Without it, one of your dimensions is missing. It looks like it's just sitting there. You have no sense for what it is. It's very hard for anyone, even a good director, to envision the sound if it's not there. You have to have something and what it is enriches the scene incredibly.

Though silence is also sound. In other words, you use silence in the same way, as an effect or for punctuation. Silence will do something emotionally that's very interesting to a scene.

In *Little Big Man,* at the death of Sunshine, Jack Crabb's wife during the massacre of the Washita in the snow, it suddenly goes silent there and that's the way I always had it. The scene got so intense that I just cut it without sound. I showed it to Arthur and we never tried it another way. When Sunshine dies it goes totally silent, totally dead.

RG: It's a beautifully shot scene, too.

DA: It is. It's wonderfully shot. I was very moved by it. And when I started to track it, I couldn't track that part of the scene. It seemed right to stop it at that point. It was the kind of scene I had to cut silently. It was an intuitive thing. But I like working with sound. I'm kind of oriented that way from having worked as a sound editor first.

RG: The scene in *Bonnie and Clyde*, just before they're ambushed: it's all very quiet. You hear the sound of their car idling and then the flutter of wings from a flock of birds suddenly taking flight from behind the brush. Clyde looks away and then realizes what's about to happen and he turns to Bonnie and there's this volley of images between their faces as they look at each other for the last time. There's this sense of helpless panic and impossible yearning over a very understated level of sound until the machine guns erupt moments later. I always thought that was a beautiful use of sound for dramatic effect.

DA: Jerry Greenberg cut that scene. With great delicacy. I only polished it. He was my assistant on that picture and that was one of the scenes I gave him to cut. That was beautifully done and, yes, the sound is wonderful.

RG: There were some interesting uses of sound in *Odds Against Tomorrow*.

DA: One of the things I did was bounce sound forward and backward to help propel scenes. Bob Wise really liked that. He said, "No one in Hollywood would ever do that. I love when people try things."

I also added temp music to a scene. It was shot up in Hudson, New York, with all these beautiful shots of churches. The idea was to develop the town where they're going to pull this bank robbery. I went out and got some music, a record. I don't remember where I got it from. I didn't want to present the scene without sound and I like to have something [to cut to] rhythmically. Bob was very delighted with that, too. He liked the initiative. I tend to cut slightly off the rhythm of the music. I don't know why. I don't do it consciously. It seems to be the way it works. But it's amazing the way images and sound kind of find each other.

Working with Bob was a very exciting experience. He was fascinated that as a woman I saw things differently, everything from the way you approach material to the way you would play a romantic encounter. But the whole thing was exciting. He's not the kind of man who sits around and spouts Talmudic scholar talk. He's just a very practical filmmaker. He's very visual. He plans his stuff very well. You'd have to be an idiot not to learn a mountain from him. He was always so encouraging. He pushed you to excel. You'd kill yourself for a man like that.

And to this day I still get excited when I edit a scene that works. You always get excited about it. It's a very visceral thing.

RG: Given your experience with Wise, did you begin to find that there were also advantages to being a woman in the business or as an editor?

DA: Yeah, there were advantages. You could be less inhibited than a man. You can be more emotional. You can cry if you get mad. In other words, you don't have to conform to the same standards. I also think a woman can have a unique perspective.

RG: Your next film was *The Hustler*.

DA: Well, there was a year between the two. I went back to cutting industrials. There weren't that many movies made in New York. I had to give one up because it was summer and my kids needed me and I felt like I'd never get another opportunity. Finally I got *The Hustler* through Wise. He recommended me to [writer and director Robert] Rossen.

RG: Rossen made some interesting films.

DA: Rossen was the kind of guy who spoke like this [out of the side of his mouth], "You better be good, kid." He was a terrific writer and he loved to experiment with film. We switched sequences around all the time. He was constantly trying to improve the structure. We'd make a change and then he'd run the whole picture all over again just to see how the change would play.

And it's very interesting what kinds of things come out of a story, particularly in terms of characters, when you start rearranging things a little. Even a very little thing usually affects everything else. If you switch a scene around, it can have reverberations on story, on rhythm, on emotion, on understanding. This is true of any cut. Who is it that makes the first move in a romantic situation? This can change everything in how you view the characters.

For someone new and inexperienced a lot of rearranging could be calamitous. But with someone like Rossen, who was also a writer, you could do it and the reason for doing it was story. He was just great on that. I learned story from Rossen.

We ended up cutting a scene from *The Hustler* that Paul Newman always claimed cost him an Academy Award. It was one of the scenes in the pool hall and Newman gives an impassioned speech, an absolutely brilliant performance. The problem was that it was very similar to another speech that couldn't be cut because that scene was connected to plot on both sides. We waited as long as we could before we threw out the other scene. It was very painful but it didn't move the story.

But in the way that Rossen would switch sequences, he was in a sense writing the picture after he'd shot it. But you always do that in some way. Writing goes right on until the end, down to what you put in the loop lines.

RG: Are there other films you worked on where that was particularly the case or very important?

---

*Including *All the King's Men* (1949), *Body and Soul* (1947), and *Lilith* (1964).

DA: On *Bonnie and Clyde* we did a lot of writing. Bob Towne did a lot of our writing for our loops.

RG: Do you remember any of the specific scenes Towne did in that way?

DA: The whole big shootout, where Buck is shot and wounded.

RG: The scene where Buck says—he's kind of delusional just before he dies—and he says, "I think the dog's got my shoes, Clyde." Robert Towne wrote that scene?

DA: Those lines were shot on camera if I recall. I think they were in the original script (by Robert Benton and David Newman). It was a very well-written screenplay. It's hard to remember exactly who did what because Bob worked on it too but was not officially credited, which often happens.

Bob was a young writer and he worked with Arthur a lot. But he also came in later when we sat for about three days working on loop lines for those big shootout sequences, all the extraneous stuff, all the stuff with the terrible kind of circus atmosphere, like that one morning when they're surrounded for the kill. All those lines were written by Bob. They were all loop lines.

RG: That was a very powerful scene. The whole sequence is exhausting.

DA: Yes, and it was a very exhausting looping job and a very important one because it added a lot to the tension of the picture. It also helped to explain what the scenes were about.

On *Slaughterhouse Five* we did a lot of writing with the loops, with the Tralfamadorians. Remember them? A lot of directors I've worked with use that very well. Sidney Lumet is a good example.

RG: You introduced a new kind of transition to film with *The Hustler*.

DA: I didn't use the dissolves that were indicated in the script. I just used cuts instead. It gave it a different style. I think it surprised Rossen, but he left it. Once he saw something that worked he never fiddled around. He used to say, "It works. It plays. Leave it. Don't improve it into a disaster."

RG: Let's talk about *Bonnie and Clyde*. That was a very important film and revolutionary in a number of ways.

DA: It turned out to be revolutionary. I didn't really know it at the time, though Arthur always had a gut feeling about that. He sort of knew.

RG: The editing was extremely different for the time.

DA: We used a kind of shorthand in *Bonnie and Clyde* because of the nature of the story, and the kind of coverage and performances it had. We were able to go in with angles and close-ups and only pull back when we wanted to show what Arthur called the "tapestry." Arthur really wanted to give it all this energy. He kept saying, "Look at the film again. Make it go faster." I did that two or three times and as I did it got more interesting. I broke many of my hard and fast rules about story, character, and how a scene plays.

I think a lot of people at the time thought it wasn't good editing. The first time Jack Warner saw a cut, he couldn't believe that we were going to fade out at the end of a scene and then cut in with the next, or vice versa. He thought it was crazy. The way that started was when I tried a fade on one side and the other side wasn't ready yet. We looked at it that way and Arthur liked it and we began using it. It moved faster. It whooshed you in to the next scene, which Arthur thought was so important. A full fade has that black in the middle which stops.

Later *Bonnie and Clyde* acquired this mystique which was pretty widely imitated. Even the way commercials are cut, with all that acceleration, was something *Bonnie and Clyde* helped to start. But it was all Arthur. It was his rhythm.

RG: Another thing about *Bonnie and Clyde* that was very different, unprecedented I think, was the way it juxtaposes comedy with tragedy and comedy with violence.

DA: The thing that Jack Warner so hated about the picture was, as he said, "You can't tell the good guys from the bad guys." Of course, that was the whole point. The good guys had bad things in them and the bad guys had good things in them. This was not the kind of filmmaking Jack Warner was used to. To him, good guys were good guys and bad guys were bad guys and it was very clear. To the day he died he never understood why that picture was a success. He was very honest about it. That scene [when Clyde shoots the banker through the car window] was a turning point in the film, too. They quite literally go around a corner and they can never turn back. It was a very important scene.

RG: It goes to the scene you were talking about before, in the movie theater where on screen they're singing "We're in the money."

DA: That's right.

RG: I think *Bonnie and Clyde* is also one of the first American films to make reference to other films and movie culture in much the same way as the French New Wave.* That scene in the movie theater is the first obvious instance but there are a number of others. It's a very interesting and even integral dimension to the film.

DA: Yes, and some of that was in the writing. But Arthur's best films always had a compelling quality about them, a real sense of conviction and often something to do with America. A lot of it had to do with Kennedy's death.

RG: In what way?

DA: For him, the whole last scene of *Bonnie and Clyde* [where the protagonists are ambushed and riddled with bullets] has to do with the Kennedy assassination. The whole manner in which it was [photographed]. A fragment of Clyde's head is blown off. It has to do with the fact that we are a very violent nation. Arthur felt that this was a very violent country, that we're very violent people. And we are. It's strange how America takes this sacrosanct attitude toward weapons.

---

*The script was first offered to Godard and Truffaut, respectively.

Little Big Man furthered some of Arthur's preoccupation with a lot of this, with a look at our history. His best pictures were ones that he had a passionate interest in. *Night Moves* was a very layered picture. It may not have been a totally successful picture or screenplay, but it had a lot of very interesting layers.

RG: Wasn't there an allusion to Kennedy in that film as well?

DA: A lot more than we ended up with. In fact, the most interesting scene in the picture dealt with that and it was cut out. It was a love scene between the girl [Jennifer Warren] and Hackman, where she's going through this whole trauma talking about Kennedy. At first he's trying to offer comfort but then he goes down on her. She kept this up about Kennedy and it went through this whole big pathos, explaining much of her character and how it related to the day Kennedy was shot. It was really a powerful scene, just heartbreaking. It was the kind of scene that made Arthur's pictures special, that offbeat kind of stuff.

Arthur's friends in New York who came to see the film all thought it was a wonderful scene. But when we screened it out in Hollywood, the men didn't like it. They all thought she was manipulating the man or something. We ended up losing that scene and I was very, very pissed off about it. Arthur said, "Well, you just have to get used to that. Sometimes things just get cut out." But I was very upset.

RG: Were you excited by [the footage] that was coming in?

DA: Oh, yeah. It was a wonderful movie. Like I said, it was very long at first, the first cut. Arthur directs everything in full, in terms of performance. The performance he'll shoot will be so interesting that you'll over expand it.

RG: I understand that Penn is a director who really likes to cover his scenes.

DA: He does. The scene in *Little Big Man*, when Custer says to Jack Crabb, "You go down there." Custer moved to various places and Jack Crabb was sitting on a rock. It looks like a very simple scene but I had Jack Crabb on the rock in every conceivable way. I had coverage of Dustin Hoffman's every look. A lot of directors wouldn't do it that way. They would just shoot a close-up of Jack Crabb generally looking in Custer's direction. But Arthur won't allow one close-up to serve for various eyelines. He wants the eyeline to correspond more precisely than that. What this does is give the angle the nuances and eye contact that allows the character's performance to be played more specifically.

But as for *Bonnie and Clyde*, I had a good feeling about it the very first day I was on it, that somehow it was all going to work. I loved that picture. I loved *The Hustler* in the same way. Sometimes you have this feeling that it will all come together and it doesn't, but "sometimes magic works." It's what Old Lodge Skins says in *Little Big Man:* "Sometimes magic works."

RG: Let's talk about *Reds*, on which you were also Executive Producer.

DA: *Reds* took ten years of my life—in two and a half years. It was two and a half years with no days off. But I wouldn't have missed it for anything. In the beginning, Warren didn't have an office. My living room in New York was our office. Finally my husband Steve kicked us out. We had to establish an office and we got one on 57th Street. Over the years Warren had gotten in touch with people we would interview (and who would become The Witnesses, an intermittent documentary part of the film) and the list kept growing. We finally organized a shooting schedule but there wasn't a studio yet affiliated with the picture. Warren paid for the interviews with the old people himself. We went around the country and did all the interviews in a three-week period. We shot around 250,000 feet of film. The Henry Miller interview was eleven reels, because Henry Miller loved to talk and Warren loved that interview. We shot all the witnesses with money filtered through my own bank account. Fortunately I had the sense to get different colored checks but it drove my accountant crazy.

RG: Given all the takes Warren Beatty tends to shoot, it must have been challenging to edit.

DA: There was a tremendous amount of footage. We shot continuously from August (of 1979) until nearly the end of December. We were editing in England. During a three- to four-week hiatus at Christmas I set up a video system that Warren badgered me into doing. It was something [Stanley] Kubrick had devised, this early kind of system with Sony Betas. It was basically a way of recording, with a Moviola on its side.

It was a very simple system, really. The British give every scene its own code number, and the code number matches the scene number. In other words, what you do is set up a system where on the screen you can see not only the scene and take but also the exact footage that matches your code number. You can immediately pick the line reading you want, go to the roll, and the coding matches the footage.

On that film we had to develop very careful notes because so much of it was improvised. We had take after take after take without slates in between. Basically they took off on a scene and did it a hundred different ways, improvising. I had to get a lot of the footage transcribed because no two takes were alike. They didn't have the same dialogue. For the whole Eugene O'Neill area of the film, there were innumerable takes. Jack Nicholson, who was just wonderful in that film, would say different things in each one.

I couldn't tell you how much footage we shot on that picture. I never keep track. Officially, what was it Warren said? "We shot 700,000 feet! Not a foot more!" But the negative cutter tells me that we actually shot more than *Apocalypse Now* [1979] and *Apocalypse* held the record until then.

But it was a wonderful movie. *Reds* and *Bonnie and Clyde* are two of the few pictures that didn't have many things that didn't work. It's so exciting to work on a whole picture where you could look at it over and over again and it plays. You get lifted each time.

When I think of some of the films that have been made in the last ten years, and even some of the films I've worked on, it makes me so sad. It's hard to feel the same kind of enthusiasm. The scripts aren't the same. They're not daring anymore.

RG: It seems that there's really been a seminal change in that respect.

DA: As I was saying, a lot of the movies being made then would never have passed the marketing screenings they have now. You get an audience from a mall, these kids, fifteen to twenty or eighteen to twenty-five, and they're given a questionnaire. It's very interesting how they load the questions. And then the film is adjusted according to what the responses are to the questionnaires. They tell you at Paramount: "We don't have final cut. The audience has final cut."

It's all part of marketing, making movies with census takers. That's the way movies are now. If you had to put *Dog Day Afternoon* or *Bonnie and Clyde* or any of the other films I consider the most interesting I've worked on, they never would have made it in one of these screenings with a test audience. The kids from the mall wouldn't know what they were about. They never would have opened well. It's very frightening.

And it's because movies cost so much and prints and advertising are so expensive. You might order 1500 to 2000 prints, splash the country with them, and if they don't make it in the first two weeks, the movie's dead. All that started right after *Reds* and it's been that way ever since. It's very depressing. It used to be that if you opened in seven or eight cities that was a lot and it gave a picture a chance to grow. Things are just so different now.

RG: Do you have any advice for a young editor in learning his or her craft?

DA: I used to tell people who started out, "Go to the theater. Work in the theater. Start learning what makes a scene play. Start learning about performance." I think that's of key importance.

Often when I was working with people who were just starting out, I would find that they had wonderful instincts but they had no knowledge of what makes a scene work. I'd suggest to them, "Go to the theater. Find out what scenes are about." I think theater training for an editor is very important.

I had it out here while I was still working at Columbia. I spent every night and weekend working at the Actor's Lab. I learned a lot about theater then, a lot about lighting, sound, props, performance. I also took acting and directing classes and stage managed a lot. The Actors Lab was made up mostly of the old Group Theatre in New York who came out here. One of them, Joe Papp, died in 1993, though when I first knew him he was Joe Papparowsky. The Lab was located behind Schwab's on Sunset Boulevard and then it was kind of put out of business as a left-wing organization. People like Roman Bohnen, J. Edward Bromberg, Morris Carnovsky, and Lee J. Cobb were all there. That was before some of them became rats! Some of them turned in people.

RG: Were you something of a leftist yourself early on?

DA: Oh, yeah.

RG: How far left?

DA: Well, I was named a few times [in the HUAC hearings]. I worked with people who handled strong points of view. That's true. I also worked with people who ratted. Robert Rossen named fifty-seven people, among them a lot of people I knew. But I never got involved with him politically. Kazan named a lot of people. I never knew him politically. I just knew him dramatically.

RG: You were never summoned to testify before or during the McCarthy purges or anything like that were you?

DA: No. A couple of times, I'm told, I was in the transcripts, but I was never called to testify or blacklisted or driven out of a job.

RG: Did you go to meetings or organize, anything like that?

DA: No. I was involved with the Hollywood Strike but not in a political sense.

RG: Why did you move to New York?

DA: I went to New York because my husband didn't want to be a screenwriter.* His sister was a screenwriter and his brother-in-law was a screenwriter. He really didn't like the life out here. He wanted to go to New York. It had nothing to do with anything political.

RG: But so many of the directors and films you worked on had emphatic social if not also political points of view. There was Kazan, Rossen, and all those films with Penn. *Reds* is very political, steeped in social criticism and evaluation and a kind of idealism even if in the end it's a failed idealism. But that kind of thing seems to inform your work.

DA: It does. I don't think I would have done it any differently even though I know a lot of it doesn't work very well, nor would I ever deny anything like that in my past. I think that's one of the richest parts of my past.

RG: How would you define your politics now, Dede?

DA: Oh, I've always been left of center. My mother got very upset because she was always a liberal. She came from a totally Republican family and she was a Democrat and she lived in Europe a lot. She lived in Paris and anything left of her was radical and I got left of her! *[Laughs.]* I guess had my father lived I might have become a nice reactionary Republican. But I was kind of a black sheep.

RG: Does that mean that you basically endorsed Socialism?

DA: I would say that I was a pretty good Socialist. Now I don't quite know what a Socialist would be. I'm not cynical but I'm more cynical than I used to be. I

---

*Allen has been married to Steve Fleischman, a highly successful newsman, for over fifty years.

worry about human nature. I always thought there were things people could overcome but now I'm not so sure. The world is a small place and it's very overpopulated and there are so many problems.

RG: I sense that your grasp of drama and human interactions in films must have some relationship to your sense of politics.

DA: I guess it does. It does activate my emotions in a different way. I feel strongly, one way or the other. But I think that people feeling just as strongly the other way might be just as passionate in their work. I was always a bleeding heart. I was a shop steward when I was at Columbia, when we went from a guild to a union. It wasn't a big deal, really. All you did was make sure everyone was paid and treated right. We had meetings once in awhile, before the union meetings. I got involved in things like that.

RG: Getting back to *Wonder Boys*, it must have been a radical change to begin working on a new editing system.

DA: Well, I started on the Avid before that, actually. There was a job I was put on while still at the studio that was a mess and needed attention and there was an assistant there, Stacey Clipp, with whom I became familiar. Later, Nora Ephron and Richard Marks gave me this long scene to cut from original material for *You've Got Mail* [1998], and to work on that I hired Stacey, who said she'd love to train me on the Avid. She and Rolf Fleischman (no relation) stuck close by me in the beginning, because I didn't know how to type. I never took typing because I was afraid I would end up a secretary, which was stupid really, because I should've learned that. But anyway, now I have a G4/OS9 computer which I'm getting better at. I actually wrote something on it the other day for the first time.

But it was an adjustment. There's something about digital numbers that don't look like real film to me. I have the big-screen Avid so I can see it all clearly. I've been treated very well and I'm demanding about getting what I need. And good sound. What was difficult for me in the beginning was that I could do it so fast the old way and you just have to be patient with the Avid while you're still learning in order to do what you want to do because once you learn it the Avid is much faster. It's really amazing what the machine does.

RG: Do you miss having your hands on the film?

DA: I guess I did miss the tactile part in the beginning, yeah. But I still take the same notes. I'll sit with the director and put "CH" for Curtis Hanson or "DA" if it's my note. Stacey worked out a wonderful system where we can put the notes on the left side of the screen and I don't always have to go back to the papers, so when I'm working I have it there and I can memorize it the way I used to when I screened dailies. It's the same procedure as before. I've just adapted it to the Avid.

RG: I remember speaking with one of the editors on *JFK,* and he told me that if they hadn't used the particular editing equipment that they did, the movie would've looked different. In other words, the technology influences the style. Do you find that to be true?

DA: It could be. It influences the director in certain ways. But I think I have the same basic rhythm for a scene. I was very comfortable with it toward the end, especially with sound. It drove Curtis crazy sometimes because I'd always insist on tracking something and he didn't pay much attention to sound. Of course, when we got to the mix, Curtis has one of the greatest ears of all time. It wasn't that sound wasn't important. He was just looking for something else, more visual, and tracking the sound properly took more time.

RG: Where was most of the film shot?

DA: One stage was built but otherwise in locations all over Pittsburgh. There was a lot of night shooting. We were in a building downtown. We had double shifts and weird hours because sometimes the dailies were viewed at three or four in the morning.

RG: Other than the fact that you were ready to do something different than you were doing at Warner Brothers for those seven years, is there anything in particular that attracted you to *Wonder Boys*?

DA: It was a wonderful script. It was about teaching and about maturing. It was dramatic and it was humorous and very tender and about ideas. Curtis is also a great director and this was very different than *LA Confidential* [1997]. The actors were terrific, too. Robert Downey Jr. is wonderful. And so is Frances McDormand, who always is.

RG: You must have enjoyed stepping back in as an editor again.

DA: Oh, I loved it. I love cutting. I wanted to get back to who I was.

CHAPTER SIXTEEN

Vittorio Storaro

RIC GENTRY

British cinematographer and Oscar winner John Alcott recently remarked to me that Vittorio Storaro's *Reds* (1981) was "the most beautifully textured film ever made." Haskell Wexler, a multi-Academy Award winner for cinematography, said to me that Storaro's *Agatha* (1979) was "a beautifully lit film. The pinnacle of what can be done in our profession with light."

Light is of the essence in Storaro's work. He prefers the term "photography" for what he does, "which originally meant 'writing with light.'" For him it is an implicit search for the components of his own soul. Lush, lyric, sensuous, exquisitely illumined, each of his films is the outcome of deep aesthetic premeditation and a mastery of film technology.

Starting out as the youngest first assistant cameraman and camera operator in the Italian film industry, then a black and white cinematographer, Storaro's career took a dramatic turn when he met the young Bernardo Bertolucci. Their subsequent films together remain among the most important and influential of our time: *Spider's Strategem* (1969), *The Conformist* (1970), *Last Tango in Paris* (1972), *1900* (1975), and *Luna* (1979). In each film, Storaro's imagery perfectly and richly complements the text, illustrating a panoply of thematic underpinnings with light and color. Bertolucci has said that "not even my marriage was as close as my relationship with Vittorio."

Storaro is a passionate, serious speaker, and one is immediately entranced by the mellifluous tone of his voice. The winner of Academy Awards for *Apocalypse Now* (1979) and *Reds* (1981), Vittorio Storaro was interviewed at his home

FIGURE 16. Cinematographer Vittorio Storaro. Courtesy: Jerry Ohlinger Archives.

on the Via Divino Amore near Rome in the autumn of 1983 as he was preparing to depart for a project in England. Our conversation was in English.

RIC GENTRY: I understand that it was your father who originally inspired you to work as a cinematographer.

VITTORIO STORARO: My father was a projectionist with a major Italian company. He encouraged me into a school that taught photography. I was about fourteen years old, so I really didn't have a very good idea of what this was about. It was something my father thought he might do but he never did, so he influenced one of his sons into photography as a continuation of his own ambitions. Much later, however, I discovered that photography allowed me to express myself. I can say today, very truly, that I don't see myself doing anything but trying to express myself through light.

"Photography" originally meant "writing with light," and it is the term I prefer for what I do. It's writing with light in the sense that I am trying to express something within me: my sensibility, my cultural heritage, my formation of being. All along I've been trying to express what I really am through light. When I work on a film, I am trying to have a parallel story to the actual story so that through the light and color you can feel and understand, consciously or unconsciously, much more clearly what the story is about.

RG: This "parallel story" that you speak of complements the director's vision?

VS: Of course. I believe that making a film can be compared to conducting an opera. Whether the director is the author [of the screenplay] or not, he is still similar to the conductor. The orientation, the language, the style that we are going to seek for the story originates with him. What is really very important for me is the relationship between the main author, the director, and the coauthors: the composer of music, the art direction, the costume design, the photography, and so on. As the photographer, I listen to what his feelings are, how he thinks about the material that is before us, what his concepts are. Then I read the script with all of that in mind, trying to visualize his concepts in terms of a style. Essentially I am trying to continue our dialogue. Then I suggest to him what can be done to augment his concepts in the photographic area, how the story can be represented in an emotional, symbolic, psychological, and physical way. If we reach an agreement, if we really know in which direction we are going, I go back to the script and, scene by scene, apply to it, in a specific way, the general concept that we have established, the principle that guides me in lighting any single shot. Of course, step by step, day by day, I can make changes, always trying to come closer to what the visual concept is. It will take you through the picture as it is made, as it evolves. Because you can see something along the way that is more attractive, more beautiful, but that is not right for the picture you've set out to make.

You should always be very strong in resisting these distractions. You must select only the right kind of light, the right kind of tonality, the right kind of feeling, the right kind of color for the story. This is my approach, and the work I do with the script has helped me a lot, usually. Also, from the moment I begin a picture, I also try to find stimulations, corroborations through external sources, such as images, museums, films, music, people, locations, costumes, that add to my feelings about the material. I am always trying to come closer to my original impressions of what is photographically needed.

The first few days of any new picture are very difficult, very frightening, because you are taking a step forward. You are starting over, and until you know what you want to do, there is incredible pain and suffering. Yes, it is like being born. I remember every first screening of every picture I've ever done. There is an incredible emotion as you sit and wait for the screen to be lit by an image. Then it is magic, when you see an image moving. It almost doesn't matter at this moment what kind of image it is. That you can see it and it is there is something very powerful, magical. Until then, it is all very painful. Until the light beaming through the positive stock breaks the obscurity of the room and you can see an image. After that, you can analyze what you think of it, whether it is good or bad, but that moment in the screening room is an incredible moment. Sometimes I think you live for that moment.

RG: Let's discuss some of your conversations with Bernardo Bertolucci, and how you developed the look of those films.

VS: To do that, we should start at the beginning. *Spider's Strategem* was our first film together. When we were trying to get an idea about the style of the picture, he talked to me about the paintings of Rene Magritte. In a Magritte painting there is an open perspective; that is, the picture, the depth, does not end at a specific place. It is always through something, through a window, through a wall, through a tree, through a body. It's how you see something or somebody else, other information, other things to observe through something, through a medium or a barrier.

On top of that, in talking with Bernardo, my idea was to bring the naive, the primitive painting into the style of the movie. The story [was] about a young man living in a town who was going to visit for the first time the town where his father once lived. The idea was to show this little isolated place in the country as an enormous stage. The kind of color we decided to use was very strong, very pure. But in the town he came from, whether it was Rome or Milan or another, there are things which interfere with the true color of things, the smoke and the fog that filter them out. You don't really see the basic things, the red of the sunset, the green of the grass. So it was an incredible and moving experience to see the pure color of nature in the clear air. It was also impressive to hear without the noise of cars, refrigerators, televisions, machines, everything that is the big town. But when you remove this camouflage of noise, you suddenly hear the leaves move, the wind blow, subtle things with new clarity. This kind of experience had to do with the whole style of the film.

So, in other words, the big town, the city, was always very monochromatic, but leaving the town for the country was a discovery, a kind of new emotion about to be experienced. This is what I proposed to Bernardo, and he went along with it.

During *The Conformist*, he did research by looking at films of that era in Italy [the late thirties and forties], and so eventually he was to construct a style for the film that we saw historically, that we saw through the history of the Italian film industry. That's where we started, but I was also developing the concept that the Fascist period in Italy was very closed, very claustrophobic, without any communication between shadow and light. The line in pictorialization was very hard, but it never reached a conclusion. The line was hard, but broken. It was also a time when things were not completely real. It was the time of Mussolini, a dictatorship. The promises in that historical period were very great but their impact on reality was very small. One of the things we did was to shoot interiors on location, but outside the window there would always be something artificial, never the reality of the setting. It would be a painted background, something unreal. We wanted to show the conflict between the reality that was stated and the reality that existed.

RG: The train sequence is a good example of that.

VS: Yes, we did the train sequence with rear screen projection. Once more, I applied the idea that the light was not reaching the shadows. They were not communicating and they were very separate. *The Conformist* is almost a black and white picture in the beginning. I was trying to get a very high contrast between light and shadow in the first part of the picture. But then, step by step, when the characters moved out of Italy on the train to France, the style changes. I wanted to express a sense of freedom by letting the light go into the shadows, very gradually, and to have colors that were not in the film before. In Paris, you see the world very differently. The colors come up more and more and more. The idea of being caged, the claustrophobia of the light is relaxed.

For *Spider's Strategem*, the blue color of the little town was suggested by the script itself. The story itself was not something that really happened. The killing of the father of the protagonist was accepted and believed to be true, but it was not true. So the idea was to show the little town as a stage, as the setting for a fiction. The way we did the night was very close to a Magritte painting, in the sense that there was always light in the sky. I once again took this idea of night and used it for *The Conformist*. I was using blue as the place of the intellectual, as a display of intellectual freedom, as the color that returned to us in Paris or after the fall of Fascism. Also, whenever the character, the protagonist, is going to speak of the admission, about the killing of the young teacher when he was a boy, the light is changing. It becomes like the claustrophobic light in the beginning.

When we did *Last Tango in Paris*, one of the first impressions I had was how interesting that town was lit in the wintertime. The sun in the sky was very low. So each shop, each apartment, everything was lit with artificial energy. The conflict between the natural energy and the artificial energy was very distinct, very important, very dramatic. In that situation, the high wavelength of the artificial energy was approaching the yellow-orange and red of the color spectrum. It told me what grade of Kelvin to use and the colors to approximate this tension between energies. Orange became the prominent color, a color of passion. The apartment where the two characters meet was to be orange. We incorporated the winter sun, which, again was very low, into our photography in the daytime. The sunlight gave us warm tones, and the color of the artificial light beside the daylight hinted at the color orange.

I was always trying to show these specific colors as part of the story, as a kind of vibration, a kind of conflict between male and female, between natural and artificial energy, between night and day, between positive and negative, between light and shadow. It was as if the two different worlds were fighting to exist in one place together.

Also about *Last Tango*. Bernardo and I discovered that there was an exhibition of the works of [painter] Francis Bacon in Paris while we were there. We went to see it. By this time we had already talked about the concept of the picture, the idea of pictorialization, and the style. And what we saw when we arrived at the exhibition amazed us, because there were so many ideas in Bacon's paintings that were similar to what I had already discussed with Bernardo. From then on, we kept Bacon in our minds. What Bacon had to add to our point of view was that you often seemed to view [his work] through a sort of translucent material, that would split the image and blur the form. Often he used a kind of glass to do this, the glass of a kind of shower door or dull eyeglasses, anything that was breaking up the clarity of the line in the image.

RG: Several scenes from *Tango* come to mind. One is where Marlon Brando is listening to the account a woman is giving to him of the questions the police came by to ask about him and his wife's suicide. She is cleaning the blood from the bathtub, and he is viewed through a frosted glass, very much like a shower door. I remember thinking how much it looked like a modern, almost abstract painting, like dabs of ruffled color that indicated but withheld a face. Another thing was that the Brando character would retreat into shadows, to the point where he is listening to Jeanne in the dark and she discovers him there by turning on a light. The apartment was also very compartmentalized, where they speak on other sides of the wall, and once in the same apartment over a telephone. There are many examples of this, which I guess comes partly from Bacon.

VS: It is his work that you see over the beginning titles. That too is split.

RG: What about *1900* [1977]?

VS: *1900* was like the realization of everything [Bertolucci] and I had done together until then, a culmination of the three films we'd made. But on top of what went before, we added one specific concept: the four seasons. The four seasons reflect the development of the human being, from a child, to an adolescent, to a man, to old age. To that, Bertolucci plotted the history of this century for Italy. For childhood was summer, adolescence was autumn, when the rise of Fascism was approaching. Winter was the Fascist reign, the adult, the man. And spring was the old man when, after Fascism, the world as we knew it was ruined. We were trying to demarcate these four aspects of the human destiny according to this century's Italian history and the story we had. At the same time [Bertolucci and I] were revisiting our own past, together, our work up to that moment.

RG: You seem to return to this conflict between opposing visual ideas quite often. With *Apocalypse Now*, I think you once said that there was a conflict of artificial and natural energies there as well.

VS: Yes, what you say is true. The primary conflict of Joseph Conrad's *Heart of Darkness* was between modern technology and natural technology, the artificial against the natural, a new world on top of an old one, one culture on top of another culture. I visualized *Apocalypse Now* as a fight between artificial energy and natural energy, imposing one against the other, so they would clash. In my opinion though, these energies should combine, assimilate, find a balance. It is the thing we all must do. It is what I must do.

But in that place and time, they were separated, which is what I wanted to illustrate in the party sequence, in the jungle at night with the girls from *Playboy*. Or during the surfing sequence, that something was unnatural, askew, out of context about this going on there. They were in a place where they didn't belong, where people live and feel and think in another way, a more primitive way. They were bringing their culture with them, which was also their mentality, so they didn't understand the people who they were surrounded by, and fighting, and didn't like. If they understood this culture, they would think differently about the war being fought in this land. This was the tragedy of the story.

The conflict between natural and artificial energy is something that goes back to my earliest work. It is part of my evolution, the dialectic between opposing forces. Day opposed to night, white opposed to black, technology opposed to nature, male opposed to female. When I began my first color film it became even more evident. Always two things in collision. And when they are brought together, into harmony, there will be a balance, which is the level all things seek. It is a very beautiful moment, but it is very hard to attain.

RG: Were you always consciously aware of this dialectic? For example, the conflict between artificial and natural, male and female, in *Last Tango*.

VS: Ironically, at that time, I was quite unaware. It was intuitive, a kind of feeling. It was just something I did. Now I am much more conscious of it. I really think my work up to now is not only a professional story, it is my own story. I am trying to reach a balance. I am trying to reach equilibrium with my life, and I am trying to represent that through elements I have [to work with]. The two elements that are usually separated are man and woman, artificial and natural, moon and sun, light and darkness, energy and matter. Before I was doing it without knowing specifically why. It was an instinct. Now it is very clear that this is what I am. It is a search for balance, a search for equilibrium. The opposites are distant, but they should combine together. In the future, there is plenty of light.

RG: When did you realize all this?

VS: I can't really say. It is something that came step by step, dream by dream, moment by moment, and only recently did I realize it. Within the last five years I think.

But you will see in *Spider's Stratagem*, *The Conformist*, and *Last Tango in Paris* that the shape of the lights I used in those pictures was often round, a globe. It is the image of two halves put together. The circle is my symbol. Even then, however, it was not conscious.

RG: When you began to become conscious of this theme, did it have any immediate bearing on your work?

VS: With *Apocalypse Now*, I believe. I believe that *Apocalypse Now* was the sum of my work up to that time. It was everything I did in the moment of my past, and everything I could do in the moment of my present. After that, I was so exhausted, terribly exhausted; the world was so empty because I'd given everything I could up to that time. It was very difficult to begin again. There was nothing to give me an idea, or inspire me, or replenish my own energy. I refused several pictures because I felt that I had nothing to offer them. My battery needed to be recharged again.

So as I did once before, when I was very young and the Italian film industry came to a halt, I retreated into my books and all the knowledge I gained before when I was in school. I became a student all over again. I went through all the books I have at home, and books in the libraries, and in particular I researched the meaning of color, the philosophies of color. And as I went along, I began to evaluate my films and, step by step, I became more conscious of why one story was this color or that color, why I did *The Conformist* in blue, why I did *Last Tango* in orange, why *1900* is the way that you saw. And progressively, everything became clear to me. It was a kind of visitation into myself—who I was, who I am, who I will be.

RG: It must have been a very gratifying experience.

VS: Yes, it was a very important time for me. I wrote a paper on what this research meant. *Luna* was the first film I did with this new understanding, with a more conscious idea of the meaning, the symbolism of color. *Luna* was very clearly a movie designed around psychoanalysis. In psychoanalysis, luna, the moon, is the symbol of the mother. I tried to make the mother a symbol in colors that would identify her with that. Also, with the light, I tried to give the characters depth, volume, by encircling them in light. I wanted strong presence in all of the characters. I tried to give them all a dense, strong physical presence.

RG: As with sculpture, say?

VS: In a sense, yes, but not so that they were stonelike. Only that they were massive in this presence. But mainly I wanted to work with the symbolism of color in *Luna*, to arrange the emotions in colors. Everything represents something specific in an emotional sense, according to color in psychoanalysis. When you dream, something is dramatized by the colors, something related but additional or separate to what is happening in the dream. In *Luna* I used this idea of what colors symbolize to correspond with the emotions of the characters.

In *One From the Heart* [1982], I went to the physiology of color, in the sense that I wanted to show the kind of reaction the body itself has in the presence of one color instead of another color. Part of the human development, through the centuries, has been the way we respond, physically, to color. It is not something new. Scientists have known this for a very long time. But when the body is exposed to light, you are likely to be active, and you want to be active. When the body is exposed to darkness, the body tends to want to relax or rest. Working conditions are often improved when the color of the walls, the environment, is conducive to the work. People could not work very well if the walls were black, especially if it is daylight outside. The contrast is too great. It is hard to work if the walls are red, because red excites and distracts from the work. Scientists have determined that a red environment can make your heart beat faster, your pulse go up.

When Francis Coppola and I went to Las Vegas to prepare *One From the Heart*, which takes place in that town, I was amazed at the incredible amount of light that pulses in the casinos and the hotels. It is all artificial light. You cannot see outside. The windows are tinted blue to keep the sun out. You are not sure whether it is early or late. The casinos are always open, and all the light inside stimulates you, regenerates you, surrounds you with energy. The purpose is to make you want to stay and gamble. The principle of light and the principle of color are used in the casinos to have a specific unconscious stimulation on the body and the people there.

For characters in a story which takes place in Las Vegas, I wanted to use this physiology of color to create an atmosphere. *One From the Heart* was about emotion, about the feelings between people in such a place.

RG: Let's talk about *Reds*.

VS: The title of the movie is a color. It's also a political color. At first, the film was titled *The John Reed and Louise Bryant Story*. It was not called *Reds*. That came later. So my approach to the film was not through the title, but through the story. It was the story of a relationship that was very modern, yet relationships are always the same—between man and woman, between husband and wife. That is to say, timeless. As I was telling you before, there is always the same kind of polarity, male and female. It is as if there are two halves or two souls in the human being.

RG: In a way, you're describing the principle of Tao, the yin and yang, the struggle between those forces which gives each of them definition as they try to assimilate.

VS: Yes, I think that is accurate. Only when opposites complete each other is there a balance.

With *Reds*, I started out from a monochromatic tonality of color, from brown. Brown is the color of the earth, the color of the roots. Brown is the one major color that does not exist in the rainbow. A pure brown light is outside the possibilities of the Nature that we know. It is an earth color. That's why the story starts from the apartment, the floor, the hearth. The hearth which keeps alive the flame of tradition, the past. It is the essence of "home," I think.

The tradition was the fifty-five people telling the story to us, the witnesses. My interpretation of the story was sort of in the configuration of a tree, coming out of the earth through the roots. And the roots for me were the old people, the testimony, so that the story was very alive.

The roots generated the trunk, which was the politics and the imperative to write for John Reed, which was really his body. I saw a relationship between his need to complete himself with a relationship with a woman or with politics, which were the same thing, coming from the same impulse, to find completion. The balance of the world and the balance of himself were the same.

So the roots were coming up in him. The old people, too, wanted this balance. He was like them. He represented their impulse, which is universal but which made them seekers. In John Reed's relationship with Louise Bryant, I started with something totally monochromatic that was coming through a brown tonality, but which then opened into all the colors of the spectrum, all the emotions between a man and a woman.

RG: You've described, throughout your films, ways that you consciously or unconsciously used color or light for different themes and effects. Yet, one consistency is a lush, sensual texture that tends to be a little diffused, lighting that is a little soft. I'm especially thinking of *1900* and *Reds*. Also *Agatha*, the film you did with Michael Apted, which was one of the most pristinely lit and piquantly spectral films I've ever seen. But my question is, do you use much filtration, technically, especially diffusion or fog filters?

VS: No. Originally, many years ago, I think with *The Conformist*, I tried to amplify the high contrast of the film with net filters. I stopped soon after that. I don't use filters any longer.

I made experiments when I was younger to see what these things would do. Along the way, after a year working in the theater with Luca Ronconi, I saw that light was the essential beginning. The camera, the lens, the negative or positive film stock—each of these things contributes and affects the final positive image. I learned through these how the light, the energy is registered. When I say "light," of course each beam of light can be split off from pure light into a color, a beam of light or ray of light.

It is difficult to transmit your feelings into pure energy. You have to translate the energy. When I realized that, I began to really understand what cinematography was about. Light is energy. The energy is stopped by an object or a person and received on film through a little piece of glass and then processed in the laboratory and printed. It's like the paper and pen for a writer, or a canvas for a painter. These things must not get in the way of my expression and what I want to say. It's the pen, the brush. To answer your question, you use only what you need, and you must know what to use.

I seldom do two pictures with the same technique at the lab. The pictures are always different. At the same time, there are some basic things I do, which is part of myself, part of my expression that you will see from movie to movie. And that's because of the person I am, the things which appeal to me, like any other person trying to express himself through something.

Sometimes it is very difficult working with the labs in the United States. There were sometime very, very difficult meetings with the Technicolor lab and Kodak in order to find the right combination to produce a negative that would create the prints as I wanted them, especially for *One From the Heart*. In Italy it is a little bit different. About seven years ago, we got the cinematographers, the film labs, and film manufacturers together, and we worked out what we wanted from the film, and how we were going to get it. The result has been a great improvement in the quality of the image we get from our labs, a kind of standardization. Something like that would be good, very useful in the United States, I believe.

It is one thing to let yourself make discoveries as you go along with a picture, to get closer to the original concept, but technical functions and procedures must be predictable. You must be able to rely on what they will do. It is important that the lab meet the requests and expectations of the cinematographer. If you have no control, then you have no way of exerting your personality over the processing of the film, and without that you are lost. You must have an instrument tuned to play it uniquely.

RG: Of the different directors you've worked with, Bertolucci is the one who evolves most during the making of a film. Is that right?

VS: Yes.

RG: And do you find that you actually get closer to the heart of the movie when you work with him, than maybe another director who is a little more careful and restrained?

VS: Bernardo is a very free director, and he is always moving, as you say, to the heart of the picture. Once the shooting begins, he has the script committed to his memory, and does not consult the script anymore, not even for the dialogue. Because he knows completely what he's trying to get from the script, and he tries to rewrite it when he's shooting with the camera. So the script is like a start for him, too. He does not like to illustrate something that is literary, but something which exists, which is happening in reality. He wants it to be like an improvisation, a *cinéma vérité*. I never know from one day to another what Bertolucci is going to do, in one sense. I know the basic idea, the basic concept. That is very clear. But I don't know up to the last moment which shot, which angle it's going to be. There is never a storyboard, never. But I retain my specific photographic orientation, the visual style, and because of that I can move, I can adapt myself in any situation.

RG: Do you make any specific suggestions about the composition? Is that implicit in your visual design? Or is that the director's responsibility?

VS: Generally I think it is the director's responsibility. But there is no doubt that watching his composition, what Bernardo is doing with his camera, is really his way of telling the story. It is something that is very important for him. I mean, it is very definitely the language, the style of his narration, just as for me it is the lighting. There is no question that watching him frame his shots and watching him move the camera gives me ideas. Similarly, the way that I combine light with darkness and one color with another color gives him ideas for composition. And these things should be complementary, composition and light, because you find one in the other.

RG: In *The Conformist*, there was a great deal of dreamlike or surrealistic imagery. A man walks across a stage with a huge bronze eagle. Or another man, old and decrepit, with a lantern, I think, crosses through a corridor. And there's no reason in the scene for these things to be happening. I spoke with [Bertolucci] once, but I never asked him if these instances were generated by his preparation, or something decided spontaneously on a given day. Thematically they work impeccably because they add to the "unreality" that you were talking about before.

VS: Those things are coming from him. Those are his ideas. They happen very suddenly. He is always trying to make the movie happen in the moment, and to find the image, even the detail that will correspond best with what he wants to say. There is a kind of water in him which is never quiet, never calm, never like a lake. It's like a river, always like a river, water and energy that are constantly in motion. And that is the most beautiful thing in working with Bernardo, that the energy is never still, but always moving, dynamic, always searching. With him, we are never satisfied. We always struggle and search for the best way to articulate a scene, and even if we find the way we keep trying to improve it. Even the next day we'll look for something better.

RG: His shots are rarely static. They have a kind of baroque choreography to them. Would you say that, because of this inner dynamism that he has, his camera is always moving?

VS: No, I couldn't say that. No. I would say that his energy is always moving, but that is not necessarily why his camera is moving. You can compare it to the writing of William Faulkner perhaps. Often in Faulkner's writing he puts the comma after thirty pages. That is his style, his *kama sutra* with the material. For Bernardo it may be the same, only with images, moving through a thought that is in flux, that goes everywhere before it is finished, with or without the actors, all coordinated before it comes to a stop, a period. The period may come as a surprise, because after a while you stop expecting it. You want more of this beautiful thing which is in motion.

RG: Do you share Bernardo's political views? Are you a member of the Italian Communist Party?

VS: No, I am not a member of the Italian Communist Party and, no, I don't completely share Bertolucci's point of view in political thought.

RG: Wouldn't you say that, for him, politics is always viewed through the prism of psychology where, for example, innocence betrayed leads to some kind of political awakening, and the deep psychology of his characters absorbs and reflects the social inequities that surround them?

VS: That's for sure. That's quite right. For Bernardo, the organization of the family is often the miniature, the microcosm of the entire society, which is a circle within a circle within another circle. But the circle is imperfect. His characters struggle, many times, with leaving the circle and the security of keeping within it, of perpetuating it. Sometimes it is because it is all they know. They want to be free, and sometimes they find madness at the end of freedom. Or they flee from the fear of madness back into the safety of the circle, the circle which is also a noose, sometimes.

There is a relationship in his films, many times, between the confusion over values and the ambiguous nature of perception, especially when images, art, film, literature, the mass images, take over and dominate the reality. Then you have no starting point. You are rolling away from a point which is X. This is to start with something very unstable, psychologically, and very disturbing, politically, because you have no way to make a judgment, to process and apply what you learn. Whatever is your political thought, you are overwhelmed. You are just carried along. I think this is many times where his characters find themselves.

I think Bernardo uses basic psychological conflicts as the structures for his dramas, many times, and builds them up into their political implications, so that they touch each other and they are difficult to separate. That he uses the immediate, the moment, to make a *cinéma vérité* out of a fiction is to him a political idea because he is resisting predictability, resisting set patterns of image making, resisting the authority of the script or the illusory power of the camera. He wants the reality, the immediate to intrude onto the screen, to make you notice.

Also, he wants to be free and the flashes from himself to be allowed to manifest themselves, to show freedom at work, and to show how spontaneity can translate ideas into drama. You see how this is psychological and political for him.

RG: There's been a lot of theoretical discussion regarding the nature of the screen experience, as to whether it is more real or dreamlike. Do you have a view on that?

VS: There is no doubt that each movie, each sequence, each shot, each frame is subjective, someone's point of view of reality. Whenever you take a photograph, or you position the camera, you are selecting only a part of reality to represent. You use only as much as you want to show. You sometimes manipulate the reality to make it conform to your vision. That's why you use this lens instead of that lens, why you move your camera to the right or to the left, why you superimpose light over shadows, why you choose a profile of the actor instead of a frontal view. Even if you are trying to be as realistic as possible, even if you are making a documentary, this is your interpretation of reality. There is no objective reality.

RG: You worked extensively with video for Francis Coppola's *One From the Heart*. How different was that from your ordinary working methods?

VS: That's a confusing story. Francis originally preferred that I shoot *One From the Heart* through a system of electronic imaging. However, I was not able to achieve the final image electronically, because we would have to transfer to film to show it to an audience. At that time, the technology was not really ready, either to do this on a large scale for audiences or to achieve high quality in the transfer from an electronic signal to an optical image. My suggestion to Francis was to use all the electronic facilities and equipment in the preparation, in the preproduction, in the visual screenplay, but to shoot the principal photography on film. Also to use the electronic system for editing, but leave the final image on the negative, because film is still superior in registering an image.

RG: How did Coppola use video in the preproduction then?

VS: We applied it to several levels for the picture. The script was programmed into a word processor, enabling everyone to easily look at the script in its original form and, instantly, in its revised form. Second was a kind of electronic storyboard, where Coppola and Dean Tavoularis and myself discussed the overall plan of the film, the design. Something like two thousand sketches went onto video disc. Then there was a kind of radio play where the lines of the actors for the entire movie were recorded. The sketches were combined in the computer with the lines of the actors, so the film was entirely planned before time. During this time I was visualizing the lighting for all the sets. Then we taped the actors on a rehearsal stage, for about fifteen days, just to get an idea of how everything was working, for the actors. Then, after the sets were built, and conceptual difficulties were resolved, we shot the cinema version, the one that appeared in theaters. Francis used the electronic system to edit the film. That is, all the film was recorded simultaneously on the electronic system, and then edited on the electronic system. When the footage is assembled electronically, the final cut is made, the original film is then cut in a pattern parallel to the final video version. It is much faster that way.

RG: What are your feelings about the video image? Do you think that it will eventually be the equal of or superior to film?

VS: I don't think you can say equal. Nothing is equal to something else. But there is no doubt that video will be our future. I did a test in Venice with the high definition video system from Sony which achieved 1,125 lines, thirty images a second in a screen ratio of three to five in stereophonic sound which, without any doubt, will be the television of the future. It may even be the cinema of the future. In other words, the high definition as part of the video image may be the marriage of cinema and television. It will create an electronic cinema, maybe. Cinema and television as we now know it could become one and the same.

RG: So, you see the possibility of films being made entirely with video?

VS: Sure. The only problem really lies in the mass application. The technology is just not quite ready. There are only a few prototypes with high definition. And there is a long study to be delivered about the screen itself. What we need to do is reach a standard, a worldwide standard for this technology, so that everybody can work together and make developments that are going in the same direction. And whether we want it or not, I think the world television industry will eventually disappear, and the world cinema will disappear. It will be another medium, another world in which they join together.

RG: Looking at movies, there is a certain texture, a certain grain that is produced chemically that gives us a quality that may be called a "past tense." We watch and seem to accept what we see as something that has already happened. Whereas with video—

VS: I understand your question, but don't forget that the way to communicate with people, a very long time ago, was to make a scratch on the wall. After that, someone was painting on huge frescoes, and then there was the change to easel painting, a much smaller dimension for the painter, a canvas instead of a wall. Then we went through a history of printing techniques, and photography and cinema and now television. And each period was wonderful. We can't live within the confines of a period, however. I think that man, the human being, needs an evolution. The chemistry of the optical image is a wonderful, incredible medium for people to communicate with one another, to allow artists to translate their ideas in film to a very large audience. Cinema will remain as literature or painting or music remains. But the dominant mode of expression will change. Whether we use cinema or tape or something in between, I don't think makes much difference. It is just a new way, an evolution of how people communicate with one another.

RG: And you approve of this progress?

VS: Absolutely. Even if the new medium is not as effective as the one that is just ending. Because when you reach a conclusion with one thing, it is always at its best before it becomes obsolete. When we start on something new, we start from the beginning. It may be primitive now, but it will be extraordinary later. But we have to pay for everything.

RG: Is the influx of video going to be accelerated because it is cheaper and faster?

VS: It is definitely faster. Cheaper . . . well, *One From the Heart* was a prototype, a new method of work. It was a way to see what the making of movies will be like in ten years. For that reason it was not really cheaper. But the first automobile was comparatively more expensive than the ones available after the automobile had become commonplace.

Francis paid the price of experimenting. But in the future, other directors, producers, cinematographers, and so on will learn from our pictures, just as they learn from any new picture, from any new way of trying to express ourselves through images. In my opinion, the human being will be honored by this progress. They should pay tribute to Francis in the future each time they are going to use something that was part of *One From the Heart*.

RG: We have a society that is now very image oriented. In most cases, it is not used to the best advantage. People like yourself have very high, profound, and pure aspirations for their use of the media. But when we are exposed to television we are exposed to some of the worst, most hideous uses of mass communication. Many times this is in the name of free enterprise, with irony placed on the word "free," because much of this, the commercials want to subjugate us, manipulate us, invoke neurosis, create needs where there aren't any. Do you agree with that, and if so, how can we protect ourselves from this kind of control of information and the psychological manipulation of the imagery?

VS: I do agree with you. We are unquestionably living in the century of the image. Images have even become a form of entertainment for children. My children are playing video games. And images are the simplest way to communicate with people, and we are surrounded by images, deluged.

But things are different here than they are in the United States, at least as far as TV goes. Each year we pay a rent to the government for our television reception, so there are no commercials, no interruptions through the middle of the program, any program. It can be the news, a football game, a concert, you can have a commercial at the beginning or at the end, but never as an interruption. I think this is very, very important, because it shows respect for what other people are doing. When a play, a concert, any kind of program is interrupted by a soap commercial, you are saying two things. One is that the program is not any more important than the soap commercial, that whatever the program is, it is as banal as soap. Because of this, your values can get flattened out, you lose the ability, however subtle it is, to discriminate what's valuable about our lives. Everything and everyone is cheapened by this. Second, the commercial is saying that it is okay to violate your attention. You are not important either, and the viewer is reduced, brought down to the value of soap. I think this is very bad, a great violence, a great disrespect. I don't think the company that thrusts such a commercial at you is doing much of a service to their own product. Whether I see this in America or whether I see it in Italy, because it is beginning a bit in Italy, too, I get very upset and I stop the picture. Usually I cannot watch TV in America.

It is better to introduce the sponsor at the beginning or the end of a program, because you remember it more positively than when there is a violence between programs. This violence is very bad, a very different kind of violence than physical violence. It's a psychological violence, especially bad for the way a country is raising its children, who are subject to this.

RG: Do you think that commercials use color and editing techniques and special effects to impose an impression upon us, and do you think they do that immorally, as opposed to the way that you use color to evoke a feeling, or a painter might use color?

VS: Color is a very simple language that everybody can understand. Don't forget that for the children the most simple language is the cartoon, a symbol, a caricature of a man, a woman, or whatever it is. And when you add color to this caricature, you make a statement that can be grasped very quickly. You understand it unconsciously, because as I was saying, your body reacts to this, to the presence of green or red, of each color in a completely different way. So yes, the answer is yes. When they are making a commercial, they are aware that they are going to make you react whether you want to or not. That's why Las Vegas is an industry. Las Vegas is the most voluminous commercial ever built.

RG: Is there a way for an individual to protect himself or herself from this psychological violence that is all around us?

VS: We need to know what the choices are in the marketplace so that we can make purchases that apply to our specific needs. This should be done with the best, most tasteful presentation of the product as possible. But this is not the mentality of the advertisers. With color, energy, sound, everything, even if you know what they are doing, they are still having an effect, because your body is stimulated by these things, unconsciously. You may not know what it is doing to you, you may not be thinking about it, but there is an effect. I mean, you can't do anything. The only thing is not to watch, or to change channels or go away. But even that is a violence. You may be sitting somewhere else, much later, concentrating on something else when something as banal as the commercial that you hated comes back to you.

RG: What distinction would you make between intuition, the unconscious, and reason?

VS: That's a very difficult question. What we call the conscious is what we know, what we are aware of. There is also the unconscious, which we are not always aware of, but we develop each of these things simultaneously. Intuition is like our overconscious. It's like the outcome of a flash, an idea. Intuition is like the elevation of ourselves into a point of supreme understanding that would be impossible for us to maintain all the time, because it would mean something completely new, a new kind of awareness, and the human being today is not new yet. If it is going to be at all, it would be something only that the individual could achieve. We all have the chance to touch this level once in a while. Intuition is a kind of knowledge about which we are certain, and which incorporates and represents all that we know, without the need for logic, which is a more mathematical process. Logic can always be argued against. We cannot argue with intuition.

RG: It reminds me of Bergson, the French philosopher, a little bit, perhaps. But what about the unconscious? Is that somewhat more biological?

VS: No. I think you may be confusing the unconscious with the id. They are not the same thing. The unconscious is our safety valve in the sense that we put into it whatever it is we are not ready to deal with in the present, at the moment. So the unconscious is a kind of protection. I mean, if I pose a particular question to you, or a problem that you are not ready to answer, you may let it settle until maybe the following day, or following week or month, when you can better answer this question. Everything that you experience, that I experience, innumerable things go into the unconscious, even if we don't put them there consciously, with a kind of consent. The problem is when you are overloaded with this stuff.

RG: Then what happens?

VS: You break down.

RG: Because you are trying to process or deal with more than you are able?

VS: In a way, yes. But it is more like the mind turns over, it capsizes. There is too much that is unresolved, that is forced down, that you are not or won't deal with. It happens when you are in a difficult period in life. Sometimes one thing that disturbs you very much makes you push everything else aside, into the unconscious, until it is too much.

RG: When you work, would you say that you use any of these mental facilities more than any other intuition, reason, or the unconscious?

VS: I think you use yourself, and into yourself there is everything. I mean, you can't separate one from the other. Sometimes you don't ask yourself why you are doing something. But you know that is what you want, that this is what you feel, and this is right. Sometime later you may discover why. I really didn't know why I did Paris in blue tones for *The Conformist*, and then, not long after, two years later I did Paris in orange for *Last Tango*. At the original moment, it was the feeling I received through these wavelengths and these colors. About eight years later, I discovered what these colors mean, what they symbolize, what they represent. Originally, it was something I felt, something emotional.

It is easy to talk about that now. When you are working, when you are in the creative moment, it is very difficult to talk about it. If you already have it completely understood, that you know what you are going to say, then you are already done. Only if you have a sense for the potential of what can be achieved, and a feeling for what is the right way to do something, then, step by step, each day, then you can start; you can do it. Later you can try to talk about it, to comprehend what you did more intuitively in the beginning. In the beginning you really don't know if it will work or not. You know, as a professional, that you have a good chance, but there is no certainty, no guarantee. I can say this: if you create an image and you want to do it over again exactly as you did the first time, it is not possible, because it will never be a moment that you can duplicate; it will never come back again in the same way.

RG: You cannot cross the same river twice.

VS: Exactly. You can try, you may even think that you are doing it, but you cannot. Nothing is ever the same in two moments. Consider the technology. The standard of the lab is changing each day, for example. The tolerance changes, the compounds for the emulsions change. The screening changes according to what theater you are in. The bulb in the projection booth is changing, at every instant that it is radiating energy, because it is being depleted by time. Each day then, actually each moment, you have a different image, even if the same film goes through the projector. I am of the opinion that the feelings of the people who are at work creatively in the making of an image will affect the image. The film is sensitive, and it can be impressed with the emotions of the people who are there. You can see a movie and you can sense the emotions of the people who made it, whether they were happy or angry or passionate or indifferent. If there is a different grip, anyone on the crew who is different from one day to another, the emotion of the group working on the film will be different. Everyone has a responsibility that has an effect, a feeling, a value that is registered indelibly on the image which is the result of the work. The dolly can move faster one day to the next, and that changes the movie. You can hang your lights a little differently each day, just a little, just a millimeter enough to make a difference, and that changes the movie. These are little, simple things. But a picture is the interaction of many human beings putting it together. It is a community of people who in varying ways have an influence on the result of your effort.

RG: On another note, Vittorio, do you yourself dream vividly and frequently?

VS: Yes. Not every time and with the same power. I can't always remember my dreams as well as I would like. It is very important to dream, because it is a kind of survey of your unconscious, what is really happening there.

RG: While you're working on a film, do you dream more often?

VS: That's an interesting question. I don't know, really. I mean, I never noticed if I dream more when I'm working. I'll try to be aware of that more next time.

RG: Do you think that when the mental system is overloaded that it dreams more often? That seems to be my experience.

VS: I think so. I think when too many things are stored in the unconscious it becomes like a cauldron, that bubbles and steams and won't settle down. It's like the light or energy rising up from the unconscious of the dreamer, reporting to you something that is unresolved.

RG: And you call it the light or energy of the unconscious?

VS: Yes, the images.

RG: Would you say that there's almost a spiritual quality about light, a mystical quality?

VS: Light is energy, and I think we not only derive from energy, that we originate from this energy, it is also our reality. Energy is everything. I mean, the essence of light has this spiritual quality whether we know it or not. Even if we don't understand, even if we don't believe, even if we refuse, even if we don't know, it has to be.

RG: Do you think, in the world today, we have enlarged our sensory field, our imaginations, and our chance for survival with the use of mass images, or have we become so overloaded that we are not as sensitive as we once were and have lessened our chances to adapt to the future?

VS: I don't think we can be overloaded by literature or music. They are by nature a more patient mode of expression, of communication. They exist, really, from another time, another era, when man's rhythm was slower. When you refer to images, you are primarily talking about pictures. I think we may be overloaded with bad pictures. But pictures, images, are the way that we communicate and express ourselves today. We are watching more than we are reading. My children, unfortunately, are watching and receiving more images than they are reading. Then again, they may be experiencing what is proper for this time, what is necessary for them to prepare for the future. It is not clear right now how well or how poorly we are receiving these pictures.

But the destiny of mankind, of the human being, is not ending right now. I mean, we can go up and down, up and down, in our evolution. This is the moment of the image. In another generation, everyone will be so acquainted with the image, it will be so natural to them perhaps, that they will use it more carefully, in a better way, in a more balanced way, as we have learned to use other things. I don't know for sure.

After all, this is the place of man now. The eleventh century, the fifteenth century, the nineteenth century, were all so totally different. In two more centuries we will think what we are doing today is utterly primitive, utterly backward. But we have to accept where we are. We have to try to make the best of our lives, to make them more positive, more correct. I don't mean ourselves, meaning you, but ourselves, together, as one human being.

CHAPTER SEVENTEEN

Horton Foote

GERALD C. WOOD

Previous interviews and articles, though often mistaken in details, have established the general patterns of Horton Foote's career. They have emphasized, for example, his childhood in Gulf Coast Texas, his use of Texas landscape and history, and his work as an actor (in California and New York) throughout the 1930s. Later in that decade, as he has explained, Foote began writing as an exercise for Mary Hunter Wolf, and with the support of Agnes De Mille, at the American Actors Company. During the war years he quickly established a reputation as a promising young writer for New York theater. But feeling the need to experiment with his new craft, to develop a personal style, he moved to Washington, D.C., where he taught and wrote, directed and produced plays during the last half of the 1940s. By 1950 he was ready to return to New York, first to the theater and then to television. During this especially fertile period, Foote worked with the visionary producer Fred Coe, with talented directors like Vincent Donehue, Arthur Penn, and Delbert Mann, and with many gifted actors, among them, Kim Stanley, James Broderick, Lillian Gish, Joanne Woodward, and Geraldine Page. *The Chase, The Trip to Bountiful,* and *The Traveling Lady* all were first produced between 1952 and 1954.

He also wrote occasionally for film in the 1940s and 1950s, gaining screen credit for *Storm Fear* in 1956. Little came of this work, however, until 1962, when his adaptation of *To Kill a Mockingbird* won the Academy Award. Subsequently he became active in film, working on *Baby, the Rain Must Fall* (1964), *Hurry Sundown* and *The Chase* (both 1966), *The Stalking Moon* (1969), and *Tomorrow* (1972), though only the first and last of these were uncompromised, satisfying

317

FIGURE 17. Horton Foote, (right, in trenchcoat) on location during the filming of *1918* (1985). Courtesy: Jerry Ohlinger Archives.

projects. Then, in the mid-1970s, he became deeply absorbed in a much more personal series, *The Orphans' Home,* a cycle of nine plays based on his father's childhood and the marriage of his parents. Since this cycle, and his second Academy Award (for the original screenplay *Tender Mercies,* 1983), Foote's work has once again appeared regularly on both stage and screen. In the last ten years more than fifteen of his new plays have been produced, and he has completed three screenplays, in addition to writing and producing *The Orphans' Home* for film. Three of the stories from that cycle—*1918* (1985), *On Valentine's Day* (1986), and *Courtship* (1987)—were released as features and then reedited as the PBS series *The Story of a Marriage* (1987). As he describes below, Horton Foote is today very active in theater, though filming *The Orphans' Home* saga is his highest priority as an independent writer, director, and producer.

This interview in many ways complements one Terry Barr and I published in *Literature/Film Quarterly* in 1986, focusing on Foote's writing methods, film interest, difficulties with Hollywood, themes, and works-in-progress. It is transcribed from a phone conversation of March 18, 1990, placed from Samford University, Birmingham, Alabama, to Horton Foote's Greenwich Village apartment. I want to thank Maria Dorman and Pat Brown for their work in the preparation of this document.

GERALD WOOD: Writing has always begun for you as listening, hasn't it? Getting characters who speak a familiar language is essential.

HORTON FOOTE: Well, that was instinctive with me; I think I was a born listener. But I was thinking this morning that I do work on language. I mean, I don't just record it without any sense of editing; I think you have to be very selective about it.

GW: You really make a kind of poetry out of the language.

HF: Oh, absolutely. I'm not a tape recorder.

GW: You write concrete details and specific images.

HF: Yes. I do.

GW: But I think a lot of people misunderstand that as a kind of literalism.

HF: . . . a kind of reporting. It's not that at all.

GW: In one of your recent interviews, you use the word "textured" to describe your writing. Do you mean your details actually follow patterns?

HF: Let me see if I can think of a good example of something that would be very specifically important to me as far as texture is concerned. . . . Well, let me come back to that.

GW: Would you say your work as an actor would be valuable experience for writers, especially writers for theater?

HF: Well, yes, at least be involved in the theater. I mean, acting, directing, you know. . . . Now, everybody, can't take off a period of their life and become an actor, particularly if they don't have the urge (which I have very strongly) to be an actor. It's not something you can make up. But I think it's very valuable for playwrights, if they can, to study acting.

GW: Because of your background, do you give the actor a little bit more room to interpret?

HF: Well, I don't know that's anymore than a composer gives a conductor or the instrumentalist. . . . I mean, things are filtered through the human personality. And it's a collaborative art, and I trust actors and don't put in a lot of nervous scribblings like "smile" and "frown" and "angrily." And I think that the situation inherently tells you what you should do. I mean, if you've written it correctly, I think an actor must know from what you've written what to do.

GW: I'm interested that you use that comparison with a composer. In the beginning of the film *Day for Night* [1973], Truffaut compares the making of a movie to composing for a symphony.

HF: Yes.

GW: Adaptation isn't your favorite kind of writing. You have said that it's more structured and that it relies more on the conscious processes.

HF: There are exceptions. Now one of the exceptions is *Tomorrow*, which, as you know, I invented and redid. And there's a whole half of *Tomorrow* which doesn't exist in the short story, which is the relationship between the man and the woman. When you're adapting, you're always searching for a way to kind of get into the material so that it becomes more organic for you. And I think I've told you this before, but I got interested in *Tomorrow* when I began to think about this black-haired, this black-complected woman, I think [Faulkner] describes her. . . . She's unnamed, and I think she only has two little paragraphs. And I just began thinking about her a lot and really began to write about her and that's how I got into the adaptation of it. And I gave her a name and I gave her a history and I gave her almost half the screenplay.

GW: How does this change when you're working with adapting your own work? Is it harder to make the adjustment from one of your own plays, rather than somebody else's work—

HF: No, no.

GW: —to film?

HF: It's much easier on your own. It's easier because you're in touch with all those kind of subconscious feelings that gave it birth in the first place. Or you find a way to reawaken those feelings.

GW: That even helps when you're converting to a visual medium, like film.

HF: Oh, absolutely . . . to me it does.

GW: So if you had to modify a scene or what a character says, it would actually be easier if it was your own work?

HF: It is for me because I don't feel the same sense of responsibility.

GW: You once described adapting as getting inside somebody's skin, and I wondered what it's like when the skin is yours.

HF: Well, I'm already there somehow, you know. I never left it.

GW: How do you choose material to adapt? Does that always come from the outside?

HF: Sometimes it's offered to me from the outside and I turn it down . . . mainly because I don't think I could serve the project. I mean, I don't think you can just adapt. I think you have to feel it is interesting and important; you have to be very careful. I've been very fortunate, I think, in the things that I have adapted. There've been one or two mistakes, but I did those for very external reasons. I did them because at the time I needed to get some money in a hurry.

GW: Would you say that's worked out best when it's literature that you're real familiar with?

HF: Not necessarily familiar with, but certainly authors' works that I feel sympathy for.

GW: So you feel that connection that you've talked about before, that you can easily get inside their skin.

HF: Yes.

GW: You recently did *Spring Moon*,* which is quite different because it doesn't have your Texas place. How has that worked out?

HF: Well, actually it was different because I had to do a lot of exploring, and of course I had no real emotional connection with it, I mean in the sense that I have with the American South. But I was sympathetic to the material, and I got fascinated by the culture of China and learned a lot, and I think it turned out pretty well. When we'll do it, God knows, because the logistics are horrendous. But, anyway, my work is just about done, and I felt very, very comfortable with it.

GW: Alan Pakula, who obviously understands your work real well, had chosen something that he thought you could move into.

---

*A novel by Bette Bao Lord. Foote was commissioned by Alan Pakula and Jake Ebertz to write a screenplay from the novel. He drafted that work between 1985 and 1987, but the film was never produced.

HF: Actually, I would never have chosen it for me; I mean, I would never have thought of me. But he did, curiously enough, after he saw *Trip to Bountiful*. He'd been wanting to do it himself and thought he wouldn't be able to do it because of his time schedule.

GW: Do you feel that you'll do something like that again?

HF: I'm at the stage in life now where I have to be very cautious about my time. And I have so many things of my own that I want to do that I'm just saying "no" to everything.

GW: So you can focus right in on your own work now?

HF: Yes.

GW: I think that you're one of those writers who wouldn't want to overemphasize the differences between the media. You've said that your work in television in the early fifties wasn't all that much different from writing in theater. But I wonder if in an experience like *Tender Mercies* you could see some subtle differences between working in film.

HF: Well, it's so funny, because I'm really basically a storyteller, I guess. The medium is the material, you might say. And I just take whatever's at hand and try to tell my story technically as well as I can. It was interesting—I just saw *Grapes of Wrath* [the play] yesterday afternoon and it just might be a film. I mean, all the techniques are film techniques . . . practically. And it's interesting how close the two have gotten. Now, mind you, as far as theater's concerned, there's great joy. That's why I sometimes like to do one-act plays, because the restrictions are so classical. The unities are still there to be observed. And that's wonderful exercise and wonderful discipline. But you have to take advantage of all the technical things. I mean, my God, look at Shakespeare. Look how he jumped around all over the map. He really wrote screenplays in some ways, didn't he? I mean, in spite of heightened language, he'd just go from a palace to a battle ground.

GW: So it's really the storytelling that's the focus?

HF: Yes. As a matter of fact, I've heard that Griffith based all of his early film techniques on a study of Shakespeare's plays. Now, I can't authenticate that, but I've heard it.

GW: There are references to his close allegiance with Dickens, for example, that the Russian filmmakers write about.

HF: I think it gave him the freedom to jump, to break the unities as we know them in Shakespeare. In that sense, there's no unity of place or time.

GW: I want to ask you once again about your troubles with Hollywood and the Hollywood system. Apparently a key factor is your loss of creative control when you become a writer for hire.

HF: Well, that's true, but at the risk of sounding precious or an elitist, which I certainly hope I'm not, I was thinking the other day that my quarrel with Hollywood is even much deeper than that. It's simply, again, texture. It's just that their product seems to me overblown; it seems to me pretentious in the wrong way, and too loud, too overemphasized and vulgar. There are, of course, a million exceptions, but I almost dread going to films because the minute you go in they begin to manipulate you. There was a wonderful piece in the *New York Times* business section, of all places, by a guy who's writing a book about this. He said that more and more Hollywood films are almost like adjunctive advertising. And incorporating in their films, you know, products. I understand Disney's sending letters out saying that for $20,000 (I'm not sure of these figures) you can see the product displayed. For another $10,000 you'll see the character use it.

When I go back again to *The Dead* [1987], which is a great favorite of mine, you see the loveliness of that, the purity. In Hollywood ad executives are in charge. But, you know, I'm no great fan of the forties or fifties either. Now a film like *Dodsworth* [1936] to me is indestructible, and that certainly came out of that period. But, the ones I chance upon, and the ones I remember, were romantic in the wrong way and hokey.

GW: You said on another occasion that you don't write for audiences, that you write out of personal need and satisfaction. But it's also clear . . . that you give audiences a lot of freedom to judge, that basically you assume that they're intelligent, sensitive people. What would you wish that they would take home from their experience of your writing?

HF: Oh, gee, I have no concept of that, Jerry. That's something I've never . . . I just hope they would be involved and moved. I guess I never know what I would want them to take home; that's manipulative.

GW: But it's very moving to you that people do have a reaction—that they have a strong emotional reaction.

HF: Oh, I'm delighted, I'm delighted . . . and I'm always curious about what their reaction is. I have no way of knowing what that reaction's going to be. I never even think about it.

GW: Would you say something about your viewing habits? I take it that you're familiar with personal filmmakers like Francois Truffaut and the Italian neorealists. But you were just talking about the *Grapes of Wrath* [1940].

HF: Well, you know, I have very peculiar tastes in films, I think. I'm not a film buff; I just can't sit down and watch a lot of films. And I'm not a student of this man's lighting, this man's editing. I have to see a little something more. For instance, there are certain films that stick with me. Now there's an Agnes Varda film called *Vagabond* [1985]. I've seen this film twice, and I've never forgotten it. And I can't wait to see it again. There's a film of Harold Pinter's called *Accident* [1967], which has meant a lot to me over the years.

GW: And you already mentioned *Dodsworth*.

HF: Oh, *Dodsworth*, I just think is a masterpiece. And the *The Dead* I guess I've seen as many times as I can get hold of it. And *Jean de Florette* [1986] *is* another one that I like a lot. And *Manon of the Spring* [1986]. Oh, there are a lot of films that I like a lot. Certain Bergman films mean a great deal to me. I had never seen, until lately, way after everybody in the world had seen it, that wonderful one about the old man, you know . . .

GW: *Wild Strawberries* [1957]?

HF: It just knocked me out. And I thought, that's exactly what I'd like to do.

GW: Do you see lot of Truffaut films?

HF: I have, and I go back and forth about them. I have to be very honest. I find *Jules and Jim* [1961] very manipulative. When I first saw it, I thought it was just remarkable. One of his I just absolutely worship; "worship," that's the wrong word, but I'm very deeply moved by it. *[The Story of] Adele H.* [1975]. Oh, that just kills me. I've seen that a number of times, and *400 Blows* [1959] is of course very moving to me.

GW: Have you seen *Stolen Kisses* [1968]?

HF: No, I haven't, no—a lot of his I haven't seen, and I really have to get to it. I know when I first saw the one about . . . the earlier one than *Jules and Jim* . . . the one, I think, that has a piano player in it . . .

GW: *Shoot the Piano Player* [1960].

HF: Now I loved that when I first saw it, but again, when I saw it again, it seemed, again, tricky. I guess *Adele H* would be my favorite that I've seen.

GW: You find things that are personally very responsive; you come to films with your own deep convictions and emotions. When they resonate with what you have, you will like a film. But you're not going to be a person who goes to films to go to films.

HF: I'm not, in that sense, a student of films.

GW: In a recent review of your work, Fred Chappell says there's a connection of your characters with the past that gives them a sense of strength and a sense of peace. He says the "characteristic point" in your writing is that "by renewing a relationship with the past, one can aid a determination to live more amply and effectively in the present."*

HF: I wish I could say that I was as fancy as he is. I'm very flattered by that. But I don't consciously think that, Jerry. I can't lie to you.

GW: Yes, but that doesn't make it any less real for me, and I'm sure for Fred Chappell. A lot of people look at your work and say, "He's really nostalgic, he

---

*"Understand Me Completely," *Chronicles*. 13 (November 1989): 35.

really likes the old ways." They see a sweetness . . . and try to turn you into a Frank Capra. Fred makes a brilliant point: your people need to be connected, like Horace [Robedaux, in *The Orphans' Home*], for example. His strength comes from his being better connected with his past than a lot of his relatives. But he uses that connection to live better in the world with the problems that he has rather than just sort of return there and sentimentalize about that.

HF: I don't feel sentimental about the past at all.

GW: So you agree with him, that people get strength from their connection to the past and it does help them.

HF: I would think so.

GW: Another reviewer was angry at the apparent passivity of your characters. The writer said that the women were often victims. The issue isn't passivity at all; it's more like control and mystery. It seems to me that the characters, especially the women, learn a lot about what they can't control in life, and when they do that, they achieve a kind of strange freedom. And especially the religious women get a peace and strength because they're able to assert that life is essentially a mystery. The two examples that come to mind are Rosa Lee in *Tender Mercies*, who seems to just have this quality, and even Carrie Watts who grows in *The Trip to Bountiful* when she gives up some of her stubbornness and her resentfulness. She becomes more flexible.

HF: Yes.

GW: After she's returned to Bountiful it seems to me that she's ready to let go of some things. I wondered what you thought about this idea of life as a mystery.

HF: Well, I think, my God, how can you say it's not a mystery? You never know what the next day is going to bring and you just sit and wait and you do the best you can with what's there. Of course I don't see my characters as passive at all. I feel that they are involved and kicking and screaming every minute, in some ways, you know. I think it is essentially naive to think that you can really control life, because you can't. You may work to better certain aspects of life in a social sense. But you don't know, for example, when your child is born what capabilities your child is going to have, and you may help that child, but there's certain givens that you just have to accept, I think. But I believe in thrashing around a little. I really don't want to just float through life. I'm, you know, a worker in that sense. . . . Listen, I don't pretend to have any answers, Jerry, and whatever I put in these plays are things that I've observed modestly and humbly and try to give back as clearly as I can. And if a person perceives this as passivity, that's their right. It's all so subjective, you know.

GW: Well, the other reason people like me keep bothering you is we feel that you, despite your humility, have a genuine and valuable vision that needs to be understood and shared.

HF: If I have a vision, I don't sit down and plan it. If I have a vision, it's unconscious.... I mean, something asserts itself out of my own sense of living. But I'm delighted when people tell me certain things. Sometimes I'm pleasantly surprised and in awe.

GW: As I study *Tender* Mercies in more detail, it is becoming clearer to me how you see film as a genuinely collaborative medium. You want to keep control over the script, but you seem willing to rewrite and develop as the project is in process. You have to keep yourself flexible to a certain point.

HF: In the theater you do the same thing; you rework because you see how to do it better. I really want to get the most effective thing I can get, either on the stage or on the screen, and sometimes there are sound circumstances for change. I mean, for instance, when you're suddenly in a location, you are a fool to ignore it and not to try to use it in certain ways to stimulate imagination. And the same in *Tender Mercies* with the music. The minute we decided to use that music, in the way that we do in the film, you'd be foolish not to take full advantage.

GW: Could you expand this a little bit? I know your relationship to film has been evolving and changing over the last ten years. Could you talk about what you think your best role is in the filmmaking process, what things you find yourself valuably involved in?

HF: Well, I think I'm valuable from beginning to end because, in spite of the Hollywood custom of believing that anybody can edit, or cut, or rearrange a film, I think the architect is essentially the writer, and he's the one who can make the best decisions. And that's why I like to be in the editing room and to sometimes do things that the director doesn't want to do. I feel that if the writer really understood the process, they really wouldn't be enemies. There would be a real collaboration because they both must want the same thing, which is to make a film that has meaning.

GW: I know at one point you thought it was going to be necessary for you to train yourself for directing, but you feel confident now that you can work well enough with directors?

HF: Listen, I have to always get the right director. But I've been fortunate so far, and I think I'll be fortunate again. We just have a rapport. For example, Pete Masterson* and I, you know, we just have no disagreements.

GW: Speaking of directing reminded me that at one time you were thinking about Barbara Loden directing *Tender Mercies*.

---

*ED: Actor on Broadway in 1960s, worked in movies, and then became director (*Trip to Bountiful, Convicts, Lily Dale, Mermaid,* and others).

HF: Yes I was. I wanted her very badly to do it. I'm, of course, very admiring of a film of hers called *Wanda* [1971]. And she also was supposed to direct, when she first became ill, *Barn Burning* [1980], which I adapted for the American Short Story series.

GW: Had negotiations about Barbara Loden working with *Tender Mercies* gone along pretty far?

HF: No. No negotiations because we hadn't a producer by that time. Just that Bob wanted her badly, and she and I had had many talks about it. . . . Well, we did have a producer as a matter fact at that time, and he was very sympathetic to Barbara and he handles her *Wanda* right now. He was very close to her.

GW: *Tender Mercies* at one point was going to have a woman as a director.

HF: Yes.

GW: What's about to appear and what do you hope to do in the near future, say the next six months to a year?

HF: Well, of course, *Convicts* is coming out.

GW: This summer?

HF: No . . . we'd never release that in the summer; it will be in the fall.* Then *Talking Pictures* is being done at the Asolo [in Sarasota, Florida]. And then another production of *Dividing the Estate* is being done at the Great Lakes Theater in Cleveland. That will go into rehearsal in September, and I think they rehearse for six weeks, so probably, October, or thereabouts. And there's a production of *Traveling Lady* in Dallas right now at one of their professional theaters. I think it runs for six weeks.

GW: And the films, how are they coming along?

HF: Well, on *Widow Claire*† I'm just waiting. We still don't have that money in the bank, but I'm waiting every moment to—

GW: But it's just about ready?

HF: It's just about ready to start, yes.

GW: And what's the latest on *Roots in the Parched Ground*?

HF: Well, there's nothing. It crops up and then it all dissipates.

GW: And what are you working on right now?

HF: Three plays, which is my way of doing it; I kind of skip around from one to the other.

---

*ED: *Convicts* was released in 1991.
†ED: *Widow Claire* and *Roots in the Parched Ground* are two of the plays in Horton Foote's *The Orphans' Home Cycle.*

GW: Could you say anything about the titles or subjects of those plays?

HF: Well, they're all contemporary, if that means anything.

GW: They're all contemporary east Texas?

HF: Well, southeast Texas.

GW: You never know how long they're going to take?

HF: No, because there are too many demands on me now to do things. I'm working all the time, but you can't say it'll be ten hours a day for the next six months until these films get done.

GW: Are there other strong, pressing interests that you'd like to move to next?

HF: Well, of course, I want to get all of the films done.

GW: That's really your biggest priority—to get those plays filmed?

HF: Right now, yes. Well, I'll tell you one other project that I want to get done sometime in the summer. I'm very anxious to do another production of *The Roads to Home*. And we've been asked by a theater in Los Angeles to do it. They're going to finance the production, and I'll direct it. As a matter of fact, the Spring Dance section has just been done in Chicago and it's gotten fantastic notices. That same section was done by a college in Florida, and they just sent me a tape of it. It was very moving.

GW: *Roads to Home* might stop some of this silliness about sentimentality. Plus it has a poetic quality that more people need to be exposed to. Plus the trilogy fits together so well. . . . But we never got this thing of texture figured out.

HF: Well, I think texture is revealed in the specifics. For instance, in *Bountiful*—not in the play but in the screenplay—when they're waiting on the bus to Corpus Christi and someone says, "Do you know what that means in Spanish? The body of Christ." Well, they'd never heard of that. And suddenly Mrs. Watts is intrigued with that, and she asks the Black woman if she knew that, and the Black woman says no, she did not know that. They ask a Spanish man, who can't even understand English, so he doesn't even know what the question is. I mean, that, to me, is texture. It has nothing to do with the forward action of the thing, but it has to do with what enriches it. Does that make any sense?

GW: Yes. Yes, it does.

CONTRIBUTORS

LEO BRAUDY is University Professor and Bing Professor of English at the University of Southern California, where he teaches seventeenth- and eighteenth-century English literature, film history and criticism, and American culture. He has previously taught at Yale, Columbia, and The Johns Hopkins University. In addition to numerous articles and reviews published in newspapers, magazines, and academic journals, he is the author of six books: *Narrative Form in History and Fiction: Hume, Fielding, and Gibbon* (Princeton University Press, 1970); *Jean Renoir: The World of his Films* (Doubleday, 1972); *The World in a Frame: What We See in Films* (Doubleday, 1976); *The Frenzy of Renown: Fame and its History* (Oxford University Press, 1986); *Native Informant: Essays on Film, Fiction and Popular Culture* (Oxford University Press, 1992), and *From Chivalry to Terrorism: War and the Changing Nature of Masculinity* (Knopf, 2003).

WHEELER WINSTON DIXON is the James Ryan Professor of Film Studies, professor of English at the University of Nebraska, Lincoln, and co-editor in chief of the *Quarterly Review of Film and Video*. On April 11–12, 2003, he was honored with a retrospective of his films at the Museum of Modern Art in New York, and his films were acquired for the permanent collection of the museum, in both print and original format. Dixon is the author or editor of numerous books, including, most recently, *Film and Television After 9/11* (Southern Illinois University Press, 2004); *Visions of the Apocalypse: Spectacles of Destruction in American Cinema* (Wallflower Press, 2003); *Straight: Constructions of Heterosexuality in the Cinema* (State University of New York Press, 2003); and co-editor with Gwendolyn Foster of *Experimental Cinema: The Film Reader* (Routledge, 2002).

GERALD DUCHOVNAY is the general editor of *Post Script: Essays in Film and the Humanities*, and professor of English at Texas A&M University-Commerce. The author of *Humphrey Bogart: A Bio-Bibliography* (Greenwood, 1999), he has published articles on literature, educational pedagogy, and film studies. For fourteen years (1990–2004), he served as head of the Department of Literature and Languages at Texas A&M University-Commerce.

GWENDOLYN AUDREY FOSTER is an associate professor in the Department of English, University of Nebraska, Lincoln, and co-editor-in-chief of *Quarterly Review of Film and Video*. Her most recent books include *Captive Bodies: Postcolonial Subjectivity in Cinema* (State University of New York Press, 1999); *Troping the Body: Etiquette, Conduct and Dialogic Performance* (Southern Illinois University Press, 2000); *Performing Whiteness: Postmodern Re/Constructions in Moving Images* (State University of New York Press, 2003); and *Experimental Cinema: The Film Reader* (Routledge, 2002), coedited with Wheeler Winston Dixon.

LESTER D. FRIEDMAN has a dual senior appointment in the Radio/TV/Film Department and Program in Ethics and Humanities at Northwestern University. He has written on American Jewish cinema, post–World War II Hollywood films, British cinema of the 1980s and multiculturalism in film. His latest book is *Cultural Sutures: Medicine and Media* (Duke University Press, 2004). Currently he is completing a book on Steven Spielberg and is series coeditor of *American Film/American Culture*.

RIC GENTRY is a Los Angeles writer and filmmaker. His articles and interviews have appeared in the *Los Angeles Times, Rolling Stone, Film Quarterly, American Cinematographer*, and other publications.

PETER HARCOURT has taught in Great Britain, the United States, and Canada. He is now retired from Carleton University in Ottawa, where he was a professor of film and Canadian studies. He has written for *Sight & Sound, Film Quarterly, Film Comment, The Canadian Forum,* and *CineAction!* He is the author of *Six European Directors* (Viking Penguin, 1974), *Movies & Mythologies* (Canadian Broadcasting Commission, 1977), *Jean Pierre Lefèbvre* (Canadian Film Institute, 1981), *A Canadian Journey: Conversations with Time* (Oberon, 1994), and editor of *Jean Pierre Lefèbvre: Vidéaste* (Toronto International Film, 2001).

WADE JENNINGS is Professor Emeritus of English at Ball State University. He has published articles on Judy Garland in Jay Telotte's *The Cult Film Experience* (University of Texas Press, 1991) and in *Handbook of American Film Genres* (Greenwood, 1988), edited by Wes Gehring, and is coeditor (with Joseph Trimmer and Annette Patterson) of *eFictions*, 5th edition (Harcourt, 2002).

ROBERT P. KOLKER is Professor Emeritus at the University of Maryland. He is the author of *A Cinema of Loneliness: Penn, Stone, Kubrick, Scorsese, and Altman,* 3rd ed.

(Oxford University Press, 2000); *Film, Form, and Culture* (McGraw Hill, 1998), an introductory text and CD-ROM; *Alfred Hitchcock's Psycho: A Casebook* (Oxford University Press, 2004); and numerous other articles and books on film studies.

RICHARD A. MACKSEY is an award-winning teacher and cofounder of The Humanities Center at Johns Hopkins University. He has held a joint appointment in the Humanities Center and in the Writing Seminars, and has written and edited numerous translations, poetry, fiction, essays, monographs, and books, including *The Structuralist Controversy* (Johns Hopkins University Press, 1972) and *Velocities of Change: Critical Essays from MLN* (John Hopkins University Press, 1974).

MARK CRISPIN MILLER is professor of media ecology at New York University, where he also codirects the Project on Media Ownership (PROMO). His writings and commentaries on the media have been published worldwide. He is also the editor of the American Icon series, which Yale University Press will start to publish annually in 2004.

CHRIS SHEA is professor of classics at Ball State University in Muncie, Indiana. She has published on Homer, Vergil, the Roman elegiac poet Propertius, and other classical authors. In the world of film, she focuses on film as myth making and has published on John Boorman's *Excalibur* as well as on the works of Paul Verhoeven. A Fellow with the Jesus Seminar, she has collaborated on the publication of *The Five Gospels* (Macmillan, 1993), *The Acts of Jesus* (Harper, 1998), and other texts, and has been a member of the board of directors of the Westar Institute.

SCOTT STEWART at the time he assisted in transcribing and editing the Peter Frears's interview was completing his master's degree at Wesleyan University, and was involved in freelance film and video productions.

GERALD C. WOOD is chair of the English Department at Carson-Newman College in Jefferson City, Tennessee. He has written articles on various topics in literature and film, including Lord Byron and satire, the horror film, and movie versions of American history. Wood edited *Selected One Act Plays of Horton Foote* (Southern Methodist University Press, 1989) and authored *Horton Foote: A Casebook* (Garland Press, 1998). His critical study *Horton Foote and the Theater of Intimacy* (Louisiana State University Press, 1999) was nominated for both the George Jean Nathan and the C. Hugh Holman awards. His most recent book is *Conor McPherson: Imagining Mischief* (Liffey Press, 2003), on the contemporary Irish playwright and filmmaker.

INDEX

Abel, Alan, 133
Abelove, Henry, 115n
Absence of Malice, 57
Absolute Power, 4, 67, 69, 72, 74, 76, 78, 82
Academy Awards, 61, 73, 111, 241, 243–244, 265, 287, 297, 317, 319
Accident, 323
Accused, The, 179
Actors and filmmaking process, 2–3, 6, 9–14, 23–24, 51–55, 97, 100, 174, 211–212, 232, 236–237, 273–274, 320
Actor's Lab, 292
Adams, Ansel, 66
Addams Family, The, 8, 265, 271, 273–277, 282–283
Adjuster, The, 219–222
Adventures of Helen and Mary, The (radio), 43n
Adventures of Sebastian Cole, The, 157
Advocate, The (magazine), 161
African Queen, The, 86n
Agassiz Summer Theatre, 260
Agatha, 297, 306
Age of Innocence, The, 6, 156
Akerman, Chantel, 125
Akroyd, Dan, 231
Alcott, John, 297
Alice's Restaurant, 265
Alien, 176
Aliens, 190
Allen, Dede, 7–9, 12, 14, 265–295

Allen, Woody, 177, 211
All the King's Men, 287n
Altman, Robert, 1–3, 8–9, 14, 17–32
Aluminum, Our Shiny Friend, 139
Amblin Entertainment, 72
America, 139
America, America, 8, 274, 278, 285
American Actors Company, 317
American Film Institute, 151
American Graffiti, 48
American Tail, An, 7
Anastasia (1997), 7
Anchea, Juan Ruiz, 104
Anders, Luana, 137
Anderson, Laurie, 113
Anderson, Lindsay, 197, 210, 213
Anderson, Paul Thomas, 141
Anger, Kenneth, 136
Animation, 6–7, 143–152; difference from cartoons, 150–151; European, 151
Annie Hall, 211
Another Day in Paradise, 10, 243, 245–251, 255, 258
Another 48 Hours, 184
Antonio, James, 135, 137
Antonioni, Michelangelo, 219
Any Given Sunday, 270
Apocalypse Now, 2, 8–9, 37, 39, 50, 291, 297, 303–304
Apted, Michael, 197, 306
Araki, Gregg, 159
Arau, Alonso, 8

333

334   INDEX

Arbus, Alan, 135–136, 140
Armstrong, Louis, 233–234
Arzner, Dorothy, 121
Ascent to the Scaffold (aka *Frantic*), 227
Ashby, Hal, 140
Ashes and Diamonds, 48
Ashley, Elizabeth, 51
Asolo Theatre, 327
Atkinson, T. Grace, 116
Atlantic City, 14, 225, 230, 233

Babbit, Jamie, 5–6, 153–162
Babo, 133
Baby, the Rain Must Fall, 317
Bacall, Lauren, 31
Bacon, Francis (artist), 9, 302
Bakshi, Ralph, 147
Baldwin, Alec, 9
Balls Bluff, 132–133
Ball State University, 11, 169
Bancroft, Anne, 51
Banjo, the Woodpile Cat, 146–147
Barale, Ava, 115n
Barber, Frances, 212
Barn Burning, 327
Barr, Terry, 319
Barris, Chuck, 138, 140
Barthes, Roland, 111, 115
Basic Instinct, 12, 169, 179–180, 182, 189
Basil, Toni, 137
Battle of San Pietro, The, 87
Beatty, Warren, 8, 26, 267, 275, 291
Becker, Harold, 254
Beeson, Coni, 126
Beggs, Richard, 50
Behrendt, John, 67, 69
Being There, 140n
Belafonte, Harry, 284
Belushi, Jim, 243, 260
Belushi, John, 231
Belzer, Richard, 139
Bennett, Alan, 197, 208
Benning, Sadie, 124n, 124–125
Benton, Robert, 288
Bergman, Ingmar, 324
Bergson, Henri, 314
Berman, Bruce, 268, 271–272

Berman, Shelley, 139
Bertolucci, Bernardo, 8–9, 297, 300–303, 307–309
Bird, 69, 85–86, 90
Blache, Alice Guy, 125–126
Black and White, 142
Blaise, Pierre, 14, 236–237
Blind-bidding, 31–32
Blood Simple, 274
Blue, 157
Bluth, Don, 5, 143–152
Body and Soul (1947), 287n
Bogart, Humphrey, 30
Bohner, Roman, 292
Bonaventura, Lorenzo, 271
Bond, Edward, 223
Bond, James, 212
Bonnie and Clyde, 8, 265, 275, 282, 285–286, 288–292
Boogie Nights, 5, 141
Boone Gallery, Mary, 126
Boorman, John, 169
Boost, The, 255
Booth, Howard, 24
Born on the Fourth of July, 2, 94–95
Bornstein, Kate, 113
Borstal Boy, 260
Boucher, Sandy, 119
Boyle, Richard, 98, 260–261
Boys Don't Cry, 6, 162
Brackett, Charles, 111
Brakhage, Stan, 253
Brando, Marlon, 86, 302
Braudy, Leo, 17–32, 51–62
Brault, Michel, 215
Breakfast Club, The, 265, 268
Brennan, Eileen, 139
Brewster McCloud, 1, 30, 160
Bridge on the River Kwai, 189
Bridges of Madison County, 4, 70, 72–75
British Free Cinema, 197n
Broderick, James, 317
Bromberg, J. Edward, 292
Bronco Billy, 69, 82, 86
Brown, Pat, 319
Bryant, Louise, 305–306
Bumstead, Henry, 71

Burbank Studio, 66
Burke, Florrie, 112
Burke, James, 169
Burnett, Carol, 30–31
Burning Love, 219
Burns, Michael, 159
Burton, Tim, 165
Bush, George, 84
But I'm a Cheerleader, 6, 153–156, 159–164

CAA (Creative Artists Agency), 244–246
Caine Mutiny Court-Martial, The (1988, television), 36
Calendar, 221–222
Callahan, Harry, 82–83
Cameron, James, 190
Canadian Film Board, 22
Canby, Vincent, 31
Cannes Film Festival, 28, 61, 217, 227
Capra, Frank, 325
"Captain EO" (video), 47
Caravaggio, 163
Carmel, California, 65–66, 84
Carnovsky, Morris, 292
Carpenter, John, 241, 243
Carradine, Keith, 235
Carter, Jimmy, 24
Case, Sue-Ellen, 111
Casino, 9, 244
Cassavetes, Nick, 268
Casting, 1, 3, 14, 23, 77, 159–160
Castle, Terry, 121
Castle Keep, 53n, 56–57
Castle Rock Entertainment, 74, 79
Cather, Willa, 6, 117–119, 121–122
Cavett, Dick, 21
Censorship, 11–12, 177, 182–183, 205
Chablis, Lady, 69, 71
Chafed Elbows, 5, 133, 136
Chalfont, Kathleen, 122
Chandler, Raymond, 30
Chaplin, Charlie, 86, 111
Chappell, Fred, 324–325
Chariots of Fire, 199
Charles, RuPaul, 153, 159, 164
Chase, The, 317

Chat dans le sac, Le, 215
Chauvin, Louis, 234
Chin, Steven, 10, 246, 249–250, 258
Chinatown, 86
Cholodenko, Lisa, 159
Christie, Julie, 25, 29
Christ the Man, 175, 190–194
Chronic, 127
Cibrian, Eddie, 153, 161
Cimino, Michael, 24
Citizen Cohn, 241, 244, 255
Citizen Kane, 98, 253, 284
Cixous, Hélène, 111, 115
Clark, Larry, 10–11, 246, 248–251
Clause, 28, 12, 205
Clément, René, 142
Clipp, Stacey, 294
Cloninger, Sally, 112
Close, Glenn, 206
Cobb, Lee J., 292
Cocteau, Jean, 233n
Coe, Fred, 317
Cohen, Leonard, 155
Cohn, Harry, 272, 279
Coleman, Dabney, 59
Color in films, 282–283, 303–306, 313–314
Columbia Studio, 17, 267, 272, 279–281, 284–285, 292, 294
Coming Home, 140n
Conformist, The, 9, 297, 301, 304, 306, 308, 314
Conjugating Niki, 155
Conrad, Joseph, 303
Conversation, The, 2
Convicts, 326n, 327
Cooper, Gary, 203
Coppola, Francis Ford, 2, 8, 33–50
Coppola, Sofia, 9, 243, 253–254
Corinne, Tee, 116, 120
Cort, Bud, 155, 159–160, 163
Cosper, Skip, 157
Cotton Club, The, 44
Cotts, Gerald, 134
Courtship, 319
Cousteau, Jacques, 13, 227
Cox, Joel, 77

Crackers, 231n
Crimson Tide, 106
Cross Creek, 25n
Croupier, 141
Crowther, Bosley, 133
Cruise, Tom, 95
Curtin, William, 117
Cusack, John, 69–70

Daly, Bob, 268–269, 271
Dangerous Liaisons, 13, 198, 205–206, 208–209, 213
Dangler, Wolf, 139
Danna, Mychael, 222
Danner, Blythe, 141
Davis, Miles, 85, 232
Davison, Joe, 180
Day for Night, 320
Days of Heaven, 157
Dead, The, 7, 323–324
Death of a Salesman, 93
Deerfield, Bobby, 62
DelBelso, Richard, 269
DeMille, Agnes, 317
Demme, Jonathan, 129
Dempsey, Patrick, 140
De Niro, Robert, 251
Deren, Maya, 125–126
Desert Blue, 159
DeVito, Danny, 190
Dickens, Charles, 322
Dick Tracy, 275
Die Hard 2, 185
Dietrich, Marlene, 95
Director's influence, 3, 9–10, 208–209, 230–231, 248–253
Discharge, 156
Disney, Walt, 145, 150
Disney Studios, 6–7, 143, 145–146, 149–150, 158, 323
Distant Voices, Still Lives, 207
Dividing the Estate, 327
Dixon, Wheeler Winston, 6, 129–142, 153–165
Doctor Zhivago, 189
Dodsworth, 7, 323–324
Dog Day Afternoon, 8, 265, 292

Dole, Robert (senator), 99
Donehue, Vincent, 317
Donner, Richard, 268
Dooley, Paul, 31
Doom Generation, The, 159, 162
Doors, The, 94, 98
Dorman, Maria, 319
Doughty, Frances, 122
Douglas, Michael, 6, 158, 180, 189
Downey, Elsie, 133, 137
Downey, Robert, Jr., 129, 133, 136, 139–140, 142, 243, 295
Downey, Robert Sr., 5, 129–142
Dream Quest, 187
Driggers, Luther, 68, 76
Dr. Strangelove, 48
Duchovnay, Gerald, 143–152
Duff, Howard, 140
Duigan, John, 6, 157
Durning, Charles, 59
DuVall, Clea, 153, 159–161
Duvall, Shelley, 2, 28, 33, 43
Dyke Tactics, 125–126

East of Eden, 262
East of the Sun, West of the Moon, 152
Eastwood, Clint, 3–4, 10, 14, 63–91, 243, 251–252, 270
Ebert, Roger, 253
Ebertz, Jake, 321n
Economics and filmmaking, 1, 3–4, 6, 8, 11–12, 14, 22, 28, 31–32, 42, 150–151, 159, 174–175, 184, 200, 207, 228–229, 237
Ed (television), 155
Editing, 46–47, 49–50, 75–76, 115, 265–295
Egoyan, Atom, 13, 215–224
Eisenstein, Sergei, 37, 46–48, 95, 277
Electric Horseman, The, 55, 58
Elephant Man, The, 32
Eliot, T. S., 56
El Norte, 104
Emmy Awards, 241, 244
Endangered, 127
Entertaining Mr. Sloane, 197n
Ephron, Nora, 294

Ernst, Laura, 140
Ervin, Sam, 204
Escape from Alcatraz, 69
E. T., 190
Eugenides, Geoffrey, 253
Exotica, 217, 220–222
Experimental Cinema, 111–112

Face in the Crowd, A, 261
Factory Theatre Lab, 217
Faderman, Lillian, 121
Fahey, Jeff, 87
Fairie Tale Theatre, 2, 33–36, 42–49
Fallen Idol, The, 213n
Fall of the Roman Empire, The, 94
Fame Whore, 159
Family Man, The, 5, 141
Family Viewing, 217, 220, 222–223
Farewell to Arms, A, 63
Farnsworth, Philo, 38
Faulkner, William, 309
Faye, Francis, 235
Fellini, Federico, 5, 20, 30–31, 48, 132, 136
Fellini's Casanova, 20–21
Fellini's Satyricon, 136
Fight Club, 158
Filmation, 147
Film Graphics, 280, 284
Film Quarterly, 217
Fincher, David, 6, 158
Finding Nemo, 7
Finney, Albert, 197
Firefox, 82
Fish Called Wanda, A, 190
Fistful of Dollars, A, 79–81
Flamenco, 8
Fleischman, Rolf, 294
Fleischman, Steve, 280, 291, 293n
Flesh + Blood, 175
Flower Thief, The, 114
Fonda, Jane, 57
Foote, Horton, 7–8, 317–328
Forest Hills Bob, 5, 129, 141
Foster, Gwendolyn Audrey, 6, 109–127
Foster, Jodie, 243
Foucault, Michel, 124

400 Blows, 324
Four Quartets (T. S. Eliot), 56
Fourth Man, The, 11, 174–176
Fox and the Hound, The, 146, 151
Frankenheimer, John, 49
Frantic (aka *Ascent to the Scaffold*), 227n
Frasca, Marilyn, 112
Frears, Stephen, 12–13, 195–213
French Connection, The, 48
French Lieutenant's Woman, The, 197n
French New Wave, 228, 289
Freud, Sigmund, 114
Friday the 13th, 32
Friedkin, William, 48
Friedman, Lester D., 195–213
Friedrich, Su, 124, 157
Ford, John, 103n
Frog Crossing, 153, 156, 159–160
Frost, David, 101
Fugitive, The (1993), 245
Fuller, Millard, 169
Funk, Robert, 191
Furie, Sidney J., 234n

Game, The, 6, 158
Gandhi, 98
Gardens of Stone, 33
Garner, James, 31, 254
Garr, Terri, 59
Gate Theatre, 133
Gauntlet, The, 82
Gelbert, Larry, 61
General's Daughter, The, 9–10, 243, 248
Gentry, Ric, 2, 8, 10, 14, 33–50, 63–106, 241–316
Gerber, Billy, 271
Ghost, 184–185
Ghosts of Mississippi, 241, 255, 260
Gilmore, Leigh, 115
Gilmore Girls, 155
Girlfight, 157
Gish, Lillian, 317
Glennon, John, 104
Godard, Jean Luc, 106, 141, 289n
Godfather, The, 2, 39, 251
Godfather II, The, 2, 39
Godfather III, The, 2, 254

338 INDEX

Godzilla, 250
Go Fish, 6, 162
Gold, Ari, 156
Golden Globes, 241
Goldman, Gary (animator), 143, 146
Goldman, Gary (screenwriter), 186
Goldman, William, 243
Gone with the Wind, 282
Gong Show Movie, The, 138
Gosford Park, 1
Gottlieb, Stan, 134
Gould, Elliot, 30
Goya in Bordeaux, 8
Grant, Cary, 252n
Grapes of Wrath, The (movie), 323
Grapes of Wrath, The (play), 322
Greaser's Palace, 5, 131, 135–138
Great Lakes Theater, 327
Green, Jack, 70
Greenberg, Jerry, 267, 285–286
Greene, Laura, 134
Gregory, André, 228–230
Griffith, Andy, 261
Griffith, D. W., 91, 111, 322
Griffith, Melanie, 10, 243, 246–247
Grifters, The, 198, 210n
Grimes, Tammy, 139
Grooms, Red, 162
Groulx, Gilles, 215
Group Theatre, 292
Guare, John, 230–231
Guffey, Bernard, 282
Gumshoe, 197, 212

Hackman, Gene, 89, 290
Hair, 132
Halperin, David, 115n
Hamamoto, Darrell Y., 112n
Hammer, Barbara, 5–6, 13, 109–127
Hampton, Christopher, 197, 205, 208
Hancock, John, 4, 67
Hanna-Barbera, 147
Hanson, Bill, 71, 76
Hanson, Curtis, 7, 8, 267, 271, 294–295
Harcourt, Peter, 13, 215–224
Hard Day's Night, A, 47
Hare, David, 197

Harold and Maude, 140n, 160
Hauer, Rutger, 175–176
Hawks, Howard, 252n
Hayslip, Lely, 98
Health, 1–2, 17, 19–21, 24–26, 30–31
Heartbreak Ridge, 76, 82
Heart of Darkness, 87, 303
Heartwomen, 119n
Heaven and Earth, 2, 4, 98, 100–101
Heaven's Gate, 24
Heavy Metal, 147
Hecht, Ben, 252
Heflin, Marta, 31
Helen of Troy, 94
Hemdale Films, 104
Hemingway, Ernest, 63, 65
Henry & June, 183, 265
Hepburn, Katharine, 252
Hermine, Pepi, 135
Hermine, Ruth, 135
Hide and Seek, 157
High Art, 159
High Hopes, 207
High Plains Drifter, 69, 80–82
Hill, George Roy, 7, 267, 276–277
Hiroshima, Mon Amour, 221n
His Girl Friday, 252
History of Sexuality, The, 124n
Hit, The, 197
Hitchcock, Alfred, 96, 105, 189–190, 209–211, 213
Hodges, Mike, 141
Hoffman, Dustin, 53–54, 57, 61, 279, 290
Hoffman, Philip Seymour, 5, 129, 141–142
Hofstra College, 37
Holliday, Billie, 234
Hong, James, 140
Hope and Glory, 169
Hopkins, Anthony, 97, 103
Houwer, Rob, 11, 173
HUAC (House Committee on Un-American Activities), 11, 262, 293
Hugo Pool, 129, 140, 142
Hunter, Holly, 161
Hurry Sundown, 317
Hustler, The, 265, 287–288
Huston, John, 86–87

ICM (International Creative Management), 9, 244–246
Idle, Eric, 140
Idziak, Slavomir, 157
If..., 197
If These Walls Could Talk, 157
ILM (Industrial Light and Magic), 91, 187
Images, 1, 25, 29
Immediate Family, 244
Improvisation, 3, 13, 23
Incredibly True Adventure of Two Girls in Love, The, 162
Indiana Jones and the Last Crusade, 181n
Indiana Jones and the Temple of Doom, 181n
Indictment: The McMartin Trial, 241
Insider, The, 270
Institute for Cinematographic Studies (Paris), 173
In the Line of Fire, 74, 82, 85
ITVS (Independent Television Service), 126
I Vitellone, 48
Ixtlan Productions, 94

Jackson, Glenda, 31
Jackson, Michael, 47n
Jackson, Tony, 232
Jaffe, Sheila, 160
Jarman, Derek, 163
Jean de Florette, 324
Jeffers, Robinson, 66
Jenkins, Tamara, 160
Jennings, Wade, 169–194
Jens, Salome, 284
Jeremiah Johnson, 61
Jewel, Richard, 83
JFK, 2, 97, 101–102, 253, 294
Jive, 138
Joe Kidd, 82
John Q., 265, 268
Johnson, Arnold, 134
John the Baptist, 193
Jones, Chuck, 148
Joplin, Scott, 234
Jourdan, Louis, 60

Journey of August King, The, 6, 157
Jules and Jim, 324

Kabuki Theater, 43–44
Kael, Pauline, 28, 241
Kaplan, Jonathan, 179
Kartheiser, Vincent, 249
Kaufman, Philip, 267
Kaufmann, Bob, 61
Kaye, Danny, 280
Kazan, Elia, 7–8, 11, 260–262, 267, 274–278, 293
Keetje Tippel, 175, 179
Keller, Marthe, 28
Kennedy, John F., 102, 132, 289–290
Kennedy, Joseph, 102
Khanjian, Arsinée, 223
Kids, 10, 246
Kieslowski, Krzysztof, 157
Killer: A Journal of Murder, 241, 255
King, Rodney, 89
Kissinger, Henry, 93
Kolker, Robert, 17–32
Kosovic, Jasmine, 157
Kovic, Ron, 95
Kowalek, John, 283–284
Krabbé, Jeroen, 175–176
Kruger, Barbara, 126, 162
Kubrick, Stanley, 48, 291
Kureishi, Hanif, 207–208
Kurosawa, Akira, 48, 189
Kusama, Karen, 157

LaBarthe, Jules, 160
Lacombe, Lucien, 13–14, 225, 231, 233, 236–237
L. A. Confidential, 295
Ladd, Alan, Jr., 29
La Gravenese, Richard, 72–73
Lahr, John, 203–204
Laird, Murdo, 50
Lamb, Derek, 22n
Lancaster, Burt, 53
Land Before Time, 7
Landis, John, 190
Lange, Jessica, 59
Last Detail, The, 140n

Last Resort, 141
Last Tango in Paris, 9, 297, 302–304, 314
Last Temptation of Christ, The, 191
Last Year at Marienbad, 221n
Lawrence, D. H., 2
Lawrence of Arabia, 48, 94, 189
Lean, David, 189, 213
Legrand, Michel, 14, 233
Leone, Sergio, 10, 75–76, 79, 94, 251
Lerner, Carl, 284
Lesbian and Gay Studies Reader, The, 115
Lesbian Cyberspace Biography, 119
Lethal Weapon, 268, 270
Let's Pretend (television), 43
Levinson, Barry, 61, 63
Lewis, Daniel Day, 157, 206
Lewis, Michael, 140
Lilith, 287n
Lily Dale, 326n
Lion's Gate Films, 2, 19, 159
Little, Eddie, 248
Little Big Man, 8, 265, 271, 285, 290
Little Foxes, 259
Liv, Sandra, 112n
Liverdary, John, 285
Living Out Loud, 161
Loach, Ken, 197
Lockhart, June, 139
Loden, Barbara, 326–327
Loeb Theatre, 260
Lola Montez, 30
London, Jack, 66
Lone Star (unmade Altman film), 24
Long Goodbye, The, 1–2, 30
Loot, 197n
Lord, Bette Bao, 169, 321n
Lost in Translation, 254n
Lot in Sodom, 123
Lottman, Evan, 267
Love and Other Catastrophes, 159
Lovers, The, 227
Lucas, George, 47n, 48, 60, 181, 186–187
Lumet, Sidney, 7, 267, 288
Luna, 297, 304
Lupino, Ida, 121
Lydie Breeze, 231

Lyne, Adrian, 197
Lyonne, Natasha, 153, 159–160

Macchio, Ralph, 140
Mack, Nina, 43n
MacKendrick, Alexander, 132
Macksey, Richard A., 225–237
Madden, Joe, 135
Madsen, Axel, 121
Magnolia, 5, 141
Magnuson, Ann, 140
Magritte, René, 300–301
Mailer, Norman, 63, 65
Malcolm in the Middle (television), 155
Malkin, Barry, 267
Malkovich, John, 205–206
Malle, Louis, 8, 13–14, 225–237
Mann, Delbert, 317
Mann, Michael, 270
Mann, Wesley, 163
Manning, Michelle, 271
Manon of the Spring, 324
Marciano, Rocky, 72
Marker, Chris, 233n
Marks, Richard, 267, 294
Marlowe, Philip, 30
Marschallin, The, 124
Martin, Andrea, 140
Martin, Biddy, 115
Marx, Karl, 270
Maryland Committee for the Humanities, 17
Maryland Film Guild, 17
*M*A*S*H*, 1, 31
Masterson, Peter, 326
May, Elaine, 61
McCabe and Mrs. Miller, 1–2, 19–21, 25, 27, 29, 31
McDormand, Frances, 295
McDowell, Malcolm, 24–25, 140
McGuire, Don, 61
McLaren, Norman, 217, 217n
McLuhan, Marshall, 80
Mead, Taylor, 132
Mean Streets, 48
Mekas, Jonas, 125
Menken, Marie, 125

Mermaid, 326n
Meshes in the Afternoon, 125
MGM/UA Entertainment, 29n, 143, 209, 213
Middle of the Night, 284
Midnight Express, 98
Midnight in the Garden of Good and Evil, 3–4, 63, 66–68, 75–78
Mike's Murder, 265
Milagro Beanfield War, The, 265
Milano, Alyssa, 140
Milk Money, 246
Miller, Henry, 291
Miller, Jim, 267
Miller, Jonathan, 198
Miller, Mark Crispin, 51–62
Minerva, 67, 71
Minghella, Anthony, 142
Minh-ha, Trinh T., 111–112, 124–126
Mink Stole, 159–160
Minnelli, Vincente, 197, 209
Mission Impossible, 270
Missouri Breaks, The, 265
Mitchell, Radha, 159
Modine, Matthew, 255
Moll, Richard, 159, 163
Morgan, 197, 197n
Morgan, George, 133
Moriarity, Cathy, 140, 153, 159–160, 164
Morrison, Jim, 98
Morton, Jellyroll, 232–234
Movielad, 283
Motion Picture Production Code, 123–124
MPAA (Motion Picture Association of America), 99, 182
Mrs. Brisby and the Rats of NIMH, 148
MTV, 153, 160
Mull, Martin, 139
Murmur of the Heart, 233, 236
Murray, Bill, 59
Music, 3, 26–28, 85, 222–223, 232–234
My Beautiful Laundrette, 12, 195, 198–203, 205, 207, 212
My Dinner with André, 13–14, 225, 228–230
My Name is Bill W., 241, 255
Mystic River, 4

Nashville, 1, 24, 26–27, 31
National Enquirer, 30
Natural Born Killers, 2, 93–94, 96–99, 101, 105, 253
Nealy, Ronald, 135, 137
Neighbors (1952), 217n
Neighbors (1981), 233
Nelson, Gunvor, 125
Newell, Mike, 197
Newman, David, 288
Newman, Paul, 57, 267, 275–276, 287
New School of Animation, 152
New Theatre, 260
New York School of Editing, 267
Next of Kin, 215
NFB (National Film Board of Canada), 217
Nicholson, Jack, 291
Night and Fog, 221n
Night Court (television), 163
Night Moves, 265, 290
Nilsson, Harry, 27
1918, 319
1900, 9, 297, 302–304, 306
Nitrate Kisses, 5–6, 109, 117–120, 122, 127
Nixon, 2, 91, 93–94, 97–98, 101–104, 106, 253, 260
Nixon, Richard, 93, 98–101
Nobody Waved Goodbye, 13, 215, 217
No More Excuses, 133
Norma (opera), 233
Norman, Zack, 139
Nothing Could be Worse Than Two Dykes in Menopause, 122, 127
Nowhere, 159
Nugent, Eliot, Jr., 280

O'Bannon, Dan, 176
O'Brien, Sharon, 117
Odachi, Tom, 134
Odd Man Out, 213n
Odds Against Tomorrow, 8, 265, 284, 286
O'Horgan, Tom, 132
Olivier, Lawrence, 86
On Any Given Sunday, 243, 252–253, 255

Once Upon a Time in America, 10, 251
One from the Heart, 40, 43–44, 305, 307, 310, 312
O'Neill, Eugene, 37, 291
Onion Field, The, 241, 255
On the Waterfront, 45, 262
On Valentine's Day, 319
Ophuls, Max, 30
Optic Nerve, 127
Ordinary People, 32
Orion Pictures, 175, 179, 207
Orphans Home, The, 319, 325
Orton, Joe, 197, 202–204
Other Side of the World, The, 86n
Outlaw Josey Wales, The, 80, 86
Owen, Don, 215

Pabst, G. W., 47
Pacific Intermountain Express, 83
Pacino, Al, 100
Page, Geraldine, 317
Paget, Debra, 60
Pakula, Alan, 321, 321n
Pal, George, 179
Papp, Joe, 136, 138, 230, 292
Paramount, 69, 158, 213, 237, 271, 274
Parker, Alan, 197, 210
Parker, Chan, 85–86
Parker, Charlie, 85–86, 233–234
Parrish, Judy, 260
Parton, Dolly, 264
Party's Over, The, 5
Patton, 98
Pavlikovsky, Paul, 141
Pee Wee's Playhouse (television), 163
Peggy Sue Got Married, 33
Penn, Arthur, 7, 267, 274–275, 282, 288–290, 293, 317
Penn, Sean, 140, 158, 231n
Peoples, David Webb, 88
Perfect Couple, A, 1, 27–28, 31
Perfect World, A, 4, 67
Perlman, Janet, 22n
Person, Ethel S., 114n
Peter Pan, 145
Peterson, Floyd, 136
Peterson, Wayne, 159

Pete's Dragon, 143
Pfeffer, Nikki, 246
Phillips, Lou Diamond, 251
Picking Up the Pieces, 8
Pinter, Harold, 323
Player, The, 1
Playhouse 90 (television), 49n
Play Misty for Me, 76–77, 86
Poitier, Sidney, 51
Politics and filmmaking, 40, 56–58, 83–85, 174–175, 198–200, 292–294, 309
Pollack, Sydney, 3, 14, 51–62
Pollard, Michael J., 139
Pomeroy, John, 143, 146
Popeye, 1–2, 17, 19–21, 23–25, 27, 29, 31
Popular (television), 6, 153, 160
Postman Always Rings Twice, The (1946), 30
Pound, 129, 136
Pretty Baby, 13–14, 225, 231–235, 237
Pretty Woman, 185
Prick Up Your Ears, 195, 200, 203, 205
Private Lives (play), 44
Project X, 179
Promise, 241, 256
Provincetown Playhouse, 260
Pryor, Richard, 234n
Purple Noon, 142
Pusser, Bufford, 27
Putney Swope, 5, 129–131, 134–136, 142

Queer Edward II, 163
Quintet, 1, 28, 31

Rabe, David, 5, 136, 138
Rachel, Rachel, 8, 265, 276
Raging Bull, 32
Raiders of the Lost Ark, 181n
Rainer, Yvonne, 125
Raising Arizona, 274
Raquetteurs, Les, 215
Ratner, Brett, 141
Rawhide (television), 79n
Rawlings, Marjorie Kinnan, 25
Reassemblage, 126
Rebel Without a Cause, 202

Redford, Robert, 53, 55
Reds, 8, 229, 265, 290–291, 293, 297, 305–306
Reed, Carol, 213
Reed, John, 305–306
Reeves, Jennifer, 127
Reiner, Rob, 260
Reinhardt, Django, 233
Reisz, Karel, 197, 210, 213
Remember My Name, 17
Rented Lips, 139
Rescuers, The, 143, 151
Reservoir Dogs, 9, 244
Resnais, Alain, 221
Return of the Secaucus Seven, The, 157
Reubens, Paul, 163
Revele, Steve, 97
Rice, Ron, 114
Rich, Adrienne, 117, 121
Richardson, Bob, 94, 102–104
Riesenberger, George, 48
Riggs, Marlon, 125
"Rip Van Winkle" (television), 2, 36, 43–49
Roads to Home, The, 328
Robe, The, 94
Robin Hood (1973), 143
RoboCop, 11–12, 175–182, 189–190
RoboCop 2, 180–181, 186
"Rocking Horse Winner," 2
Roizman, Owen, 282
Ronconi, Luca, 306
Roots in the Parched Ground, 327
Rosenberg, Howard, 241
Rosenkavalier, Der, 124
Ross, Diana, 234n
Rossen, Robert, 267, 275, 287–288, 293
Rotter, Steven, 267
Rubin, Cyma, 136
Rudin, Scott, 271
Rudolf, Alan, 17
Rugoff, Donald, 134–135
Rumblefish, 36
Runner, 215
Russell, Rosalind, 252n
Ryan, Robert, 284

Sackett, Barnard L., 133
Salvador, 2, 9, 98, 104, 241, 252, 255, 260–261
Sammy and Rosie Get Laid, 12, 195, 198–200, 202–203, 206, 212
Sanctus, 127
Saura, Carlos, 8
Savage, John, 243
Savannah, Georgia (city), 66–69, 72
Saved, 260
Savoca, Nancy, 157
Sayles, John, 6, 157
Scalphunters, The, 53n
Scandal, 204
Scarface, 98
Scent of a Woman (1992), 100
Schisgal, Murray, 61
Schoonmacher, Thelma, 279
Schwarzenegger, Arnold, 175–176, 185, 188, 193–194
Scorpio Rising, 136
Scorsese, Martin, 6, 9, 48, 156–157, 244–245, 279, 283
Scott, Ridley, 197, 210
Scott, Tony, 197
Screen Actors Guild, 258
Secret of NIMH, The, 6–7, 143, 146–147, 149–152
Secret of Roan Inish, The, 6, 157
Seilor, Sonny, 76
Semel, Terry, 67, 269
Serial Mom, 165
Serpico, 265
Seven, 158
Sewing Circle: Hollywood's Greatest Secret, 121
Shakespeare, William, 322
Shampoo, 140n
Shawn, Dick, 139
Shawn, Wally, 14, 228–230, 231n
Shayne, Allan, 260
Shea, Chris, 169–194
Sheen, Martin, 260–261
Sherman, Cindy, 162
Shields, Brooke, 234
Shoot the Piano Player, 324
Shusett, Ron, 176

344 INDEX

Siegel, Don, 75
Silent World, The, 227
Siskel, Gene, 243
Slap Shot, 265
Slaughterhouse Five, 8, 265, 276, 288
Sleeping Beauties, 6, 153, 158–160
Sleeping Beauty (fairy tale), 158
Sleeping Beauty (1959), 145
Slums of Beverly Hills, 160
Small One, The, 146
Smith, Barbara, 111, 113, 125
Smith County Widow, The, 25
Soeteman, Gerard, 11, 173, 176, 179
Soldier of Orange, 11, 172–176, 179, 193
Some Like It Hot, 55
Sonbert, Warren, 124
Sonnefeld, Barry, 273–274, 276, 282
Sopranos, The (television), 160
Sound of Music, The, 284n
Spacek, Sissy, 28, 158
Spacey, Kevin, 69
Spain, Doug, 160
Speaking Parts, 217–218, 220, 223
Sperling, Andrea, 157, 159, 162
Spetters, 174, 178–179
Spider's Stratagem, 297, 300–301, 304
Spielberg, Steven, 7, 48, 86, 72–73, 156, 174, 181, 186–187, 190, 270
Spring Moon, 321
Stalking Moon, The, 317
Stamp, Terence, 197
Stanley, Kim, 317
Stanton, Harry Dean, 49
Star Maps, 160
Star Trek V, 186
Star Wars, 60, 151, 180, 186
Steenburgen, Mary, 24–25
Sterling, George, 66
Sticks and Bones (play), 5, 136, 138
Stolen Kisses, 324
Stone, Norman, 198
Stone, Oliver, 2–3, 9, 11, 14, 91–106, 243–244, 252–254, 260–261, 270
Stone, Sharon, 243, 245, 254
Storaro, Vittorio, 8–9, 40, 47n, 297–316
Storm Fear, 317
Story of Adele H, The, 324

Story of a Marriage, The, 319
Straight Talk, 244, 264
Strauss, Richard, 124
Streep, Meryl, 4, 10, 70, 73
Stuck, 155
Sturges, Preston, 5, 129
Sullivan, Michael, 137
Summer of Ben Tyler, The, 241
Sundance Film Festival, 159–160
Sutherland, Donald, 231n
Sweet Smell of Sex, 133
Sweet Smell of Success, The, 132

Talented Mr. Ripley, The, 142
Talking Pictures, 327
Tango, 8
Tarantino, Quentin, 9, 244
Tavoularis, Dean, 310
Technology, 1–2, 22–23, 33–36, 40–42, 310–312, 315
Temple, Shirley, 111
Ten Days That Shook the World, 37
Tender Fictions, 5–6, 109, 112–119, 127
Tender Mercies, 319, 322, 325–327
Terminator, The, 190
Terror from the Year 5000, 284
Terry, Jennifer, 121
Texas Chainsaw Massacre, The (1974), 183
Thatcher, Margaret, 12, 198–201, 204, 206
That Cold Day in the Park, 1, 29
They Shoot Horses, Don't They?, 51, 55–57
Third Man, The, 213n
This Property is Condemned, 51, 53
Thompson, Jim, 210
Three Days of the Condor, 53, 55–56, 58, 60
Three Women, 1, 21, 23–25, 28–29
THX 1138, 48
Tightrope, 82
Tilly, Jennifer, 139
Tin Men, 63
Titan A. E., 7
Toback, James, 142
To Kill a Mockingbird, 317
To Live and Die in L. A., 5, 141
Tomorrow, 317, 320

INDEX   345

Too Much Sun, 139
Tootsie, 4, 51, 53–55, 57–62
Totally F***ed Up, 159, 162
Total Recall, 12, 169, 175–182, 184–190, 193–194
Total Recall 2, 181
Towne, Robert, 288
Townsend, Clayton, 103
Toy Story, 7
Tracy, Spencer, 252
Traveling Lady, The, 317, 327
Treasure of the Sierra Madre, The, 86
Tree Grows in Brooklyn, A, 261
Trip to Bountiful, The, 317, 322, 325, 326n, 328
True Believer, 243
True Crime, 10, 243, 251–252
Truffaut, Francois, 289n, 320, 323–324
Turkish Delight, 11, 174, 179
Twentieth-Century Fox, 17, 29n
Twilight Zone (television), 139, 218
Tyson, Mike, 142

UCLA Film School, 38
Understanding Media (McLuhan), 80
Undressed (television), 6, 153, 160
Unforgiven, 69, 74, 86, 88, 90, 270
United Artists, 24, 30
Universal Pictures, 237, 268–269
Up the Academy, 139
Urban Cowboy, 24
Urioste, Frank, 271

Vagabond, 323
Vampires, 241
Varda, Agnes, 28, 323
Verhoeven, Paul, 11–12, 169–194
Viertel, Peter, 86–87
Vinterberg, Thomas, 142
Violence in movies, 11–12
Virgin Suicides, The, 243, 253
Visitors, The, 260–262
Von Braun, Werner, 171
von Sternberg, Joseph, 95

Waering, William, 132
Wagner, Natasha Gregson, 243, 246

Wag the Dog, 63
Waite, Terry, 169
Waits, Tom, 155
Walking Tall, 27
Wanda, 327
Warden, Jack, 231n
Warner Bros., 8, 66–67, 99, 148, 153, 160, 267–271, 282, 295
Warner, Jack, 289
War of the Worlds, The, 179
Warren, Jennifer, 290
Washington, Denzel, 268
Watermelon Woman, The, 162
Waters, John, 164–165
Wayne, John, 82, 86, 212
Way We Were, The, 57
Weaver, Dennis, 169
Weaver, Sigourney, 24
Weber, Andrew Lloyd, 198
Weber, Billy, 268
Wedding, A, 1, 26
Welles, Orson, 86, 103n
Westar Institute, 190–191
Weston, Edward, 66
West Side Story, 284n
Wharton, Edith, 122
What Else is There, 132
What the Butler Saw, 197n
White, Dan, 84
White Hunter, Black Heart, 86–87
Who'll Stop the Rain, 197n
Why Me?, 22
Widow Claire, 327
Wilder, Billy, 187, 210
Wild Strawberries, 324
Wilkinson, Chris, 97
Williams, Billy Dee, 234n
Williams, Jim, 68, 71–72, 76
Williams, Robin, 23–24
Winnie the Pooh and Tigger Too, 143
Winters, Shelly, 284
Wise, Robert, 7–8, 94, 267, 274, 284, 286–287
Wonder Boys, 8, 265, 267–268, 270–272, 294–295
Wood, Gerald C., 7, 317–328
Wood, Natalie, 51

Woodress, James, 117
Woods, James, 9–11, 241–264
Woodward, Joanne, 317
Writers, importance of, 1, 4, 7, 58–60, 72–73, 208, 230, 319–320
Writing with Light: Vittorio Storaro, 8
Wyler, William, 103n

You Are There (television), 49
Young, Gig, 55
You've Got Mail, 294

Zapata, 8
Zoetrope Studios, 50
Zworkin, Vladimir K., 38